TRIALS and TRIUMPHS

A History of the Church of the United Brethren in Christ

TRIALS and TRIUMPHS

A History of the Church of the United Brethren in Christ

Edited By
Paul R. Fetters

Church of the United Brethren in Christ
Department of Church Services
Huntington, Indiana
1984

Acknowledgments

Quotations on pages 37, 39 and 40 from "This Freedom Whence?" are reprinted by permission of the American Tract Society, Garland, Texas.

Numerous quotations throughout the book are reprinted from History of the Church of the United Brethren in Christ, by A. W. Drury, published in 1924 by Otterbein Press, Dayton, Ohio.

Library of Congress Catalog Card No. 84-71211

Printed in U.S.A.

AUTHORS

Part I	1752-1800
The Beginnings	Paul A. Graham
Part II	1800-1841
The Church Takes A Name	Raymond Waldfogel
Part III	1841-1889
The Best and The Worst of Times	Mary Lou Funk
Part IV	1889-1929
The Trials and Triumphs	Harold R. Cherry
Part V	1929-1981
The Challenges	Melvin I. Burkholder

A Tribute

to

Dr. J. Ralph Pfister
1902-1978

For half a century, Dr. J. Ralph Pfister was a steady spiritual scholar, writer, pastor, and historian in the Church of the United Brethren in Christ. The last thirty years of Dr. Pfister's life were spent in his beloved educational scholar's niche at Huntington College. Here he taught Church History, Doctrinal Theology, and Christian Education in the Huntington College Theological Seminary until his retirement in 1970. Huntington College awarded John Ralph Pfister a well-deserved honorary Doctor of Divinity degree in 1957. Even after that, continued growth in further studies led him to gain a Master of Theology degree at the Winona Lake School of Theology in 1964. He was honored in 1972 by being named Associate Professor Emeritus at Huntington College.

Considered by the entire denomination as a most able Church historian, the General Board of Administration commissioned him to write a United Brethren in Christ history. Although he, aided by the Reverend William Bias, collected voluminous materials for this project, illness and death prevented the performance of the task. However, a portion of his time and great historical knowledge was used in compiling a history of the first three-quarters century of Huntington College, entitled *75 Years—Where Character and Culture Blend.*

He will be remembered for his meditative little cough, as he gained a moment to collect his thoughts in a seminary course or in teaching a Sunday School lesson to the College Park Golden Rule class. He will be remembered by the College Park Church as the originator and mentor of the White Gift program at Christmas. He will be remembered by his seminarians for his dry humor, designed to enliven otherwise deep class discussions.

Dr. J. Ralph Pfister, by his life of scholarly witness, quietly portrayed James 3:17: "But the wisdom that is from above is first pure, then peaceable, gentle, and easy to be intreated, full of mercy and good fruits, without partiality, and without hypocrisy."

E. DeWitt Baker
President Emeritus
Huntington College

Table of Contents

Foreword

The Church of the United Brethren in Christ has the distinction of being the first American born denomination. Its history has both *Trials and Triumphs*.

The roots of the United Brethren reach back into German pietism which was preached in America by Philip William Otterbein. This pietism of a "here and now" assurance of salvation and the insistence on personal piety preached in the churches and protracted evangelistic meetings met opposition in colonial times (1726-1800). The emerging church struggled with selecting a name, drafting a Confession of Faith, writing a Discipline, and adopting a Constitution (1800-1841). Reflecting the national crises of wars within and without, the church found some of the social and moral discords of temperance, slavery, and secrecy insurmountable (1841-1889). Division leaves one with mixed emotions especially when men feel satisfied that their consciences have led them to this end of heavy hearts and awesome burdens. In its unsettled state the church was blessed to have a preserver with the temperament of Milton Wright (1889-1929). Change in context and culture spell conflict for a church—the more rapid the change the more serious the challenge and possible collision. Ecclesiastical developments have no spectators whether it be the modernist-fundamentalist controversy; the merger of main line denominations; the multiplication of parachurch structure outside the walls of the church; or a challenge to the existence of the church within the four walls (1929-1981).

The writing and publication of a United Brethren history has had its own trials since it was first authorized in 1894. One is surprised that so many individuals have been assigned the task of writing a United Brethren Church history. Reports to the general conferences and boards indicated that each of the writers had done a yeoman's task in research, and that each writer was about to submit a manuscript to the publishers. However, the general editor of this volume and the writers found no drafts written by previous writers and have relied on original research and writing.

9

Milton Wright—1894

In June 1894, five years after the division in York, Pennsylvania the Publishing Board "requested and fully authorized Bishop Milton Wright to gather material and prepare the manuscript for the extension of the history of the church." Wright intended that the church would have a history in two volumes: the first would be the church history by John Lawrence covering the church through 1865; the second would be by Wright beginning with 1865 to 1894 or until published.

The General Conferences of 1905, 1909, and 1913 continued urging Wright and/or the Publishing Board to publish a history in such tones as:

> Whereas the church is without a printed history which records the facts of our church life up to the present time, and the needs of the same is becoming more imperative each year, we recommend that this conference [1913] elect a special committee which shall take immediate steps to publish a handbook of United Brethren history; . . .

Wright died without preparing a history for publication.

Fermin L. Hoskins—1917

The General Conference of 1917 recommended:

> That immediate steps be taken . . . to furnish an up-to-date United Brethren history. By selecting a man . . . to prepare . . . a history . . . . Bishop F. L. Hoskins was selected.

The General Conferences of 1921 and 1925 kept continual pressure on F. L. Hoskins and the Publishing Board just as they had with Wright, but upon the death of F. L. Hoskins, the church continued without a history. The General Conferences of 1929 and 1933 continued recommending that ". . . the Publishing Board make provisions for gathering of material and for publishing of a church history."

W. E. Musgrave—1945

After eight years of silence in the general conference sessions of 1937 and 1941, the call for a church history again was heard in the General

10

Conference of 1945. Bishop W. E. Musgrave was chosen to prepare the manuscript for a new United Brethren church history, with the assistance, counsel, and approval of the General Board of Administration, in making such ". . . revisions and additions to Lawrence's *United Brethren Church History* that would bring it up-to-date." The General Conference of 1949 pressed for the history, but Musgrave died before the completion of such a work.

Clarence A. Mummart—1954

The General Board of Administration on May 17, 1954, commissioned Bishop C. A. Mummart to write a history of the Church of the United Brethren in Christ. He wrote several articles in the *United Brethren* magazine about a *history of the history* but died before a history was completed.

J. Ralph Pfister—1971

In May 1971, action was taken by the General Board of Administration to commission J. Ralph Pfister to write a history of the Church of the United Brethren in Christ. Again in 1978, Bishop C. Ray Miller informed Pfister of the ". . . commission to write and the need for a history since 1889." Pfister died in the summer of 1978, and with him were gone his vast mental resources of a subject he had studied and taught at Huntington College and Theological Seminary for at least three decades.

Paul R. Fetters—1979

In March 1979, the Executive Committee of the General Board of Administration informed Paul R. Fetters that $3000 was added to the budget and would be perpetuated annually for a church history until it was completed. In June 1979, Bishop Miller informed Fetters that the General Board of Administration had approved the writing of a United Brethren Church history, had named him as the general editor, that he should ". . . feel free to name other writers, and that funds were available as needed."

It is the opinion of the general editor that too many years have passed for one individual to write the History of the Church of the

United Brethren in Christ. The editor carefully selected writers for the five divisions of history because of their particular aptitudes.

Division One: Paul A. Graham is the philosophical one who is willing to look into the origins. Need I say more?

Division Two: Raymond Waldfogel is the ponderous one with a temperament needed to labor through the labyrinth of critical issues involved in the organization and constitutional period of our history.

Division Three: Mary Lou Funk is the thorough one. She has for many years had a personal interest in Milton Wright and his family. Her popular style unfolds the drama preceding the division and characterizes the personality of the man upon whose shoulders the preservation of the church fell.

Division Four: Harold R. Cherry is the analytical one. His style is forthright, objective, and critical—necessary for the period on litigation after the division of 1889.

Division Five: M. I. Burkholder is the charitable one. Finesse in writing in a discrete style is needed when the developers of history and/or their offspring are still living. He has lived this period of time, has helped form the history with his peers, and has remained non-judgmental of his colleagues and church.

William W. Bias, our researcher, is the determined one who for years with J. Ralph Pfister and alone has covered the miles from Alaska, to North Carolina, and from Pennsylvania and Maryland to California and Oregon ferreting out bits and pieces of our United Brethren heritage.

I also desire to express my appreciation to Jane Mason, archivist, for her aid in collecting information, compiling lists, and verifying facts. To my wife, Barbara, who has lovingly adjusted her personal and family schedule to assist me in editing *Trials and Triumphs,* hugs and kisses.

As I submit the manuscript to the publisher my sentiments are expressed by St. Augustine after having written *City of God* the first great Christian philosophy of history: "Let those who think that I have said too little, and those who think that I have said too much, forgive me, and let those who think that I said just enough, give thanks to God with me. Amen."

Paul R. Fetters

Graduate School of Christian Ministries
Huntington College
March 1984

Part One

THE BEGINNINGS

1752-1800

The Rev. Paul A. Graham

BIOGRAPHICAL DATA

Paul A. Graham was born and grew up near Grand Rapids, Michigan. His parents were Carl and Jessie Graham. He made his commitment to God when he was nine years old. A call to full-time Christian service was experienced and strengthened during his high school years in Grand Rapids and Caledonia.

His undergraduate work was taken at Huntington College in Huntington, Indiana. A Bachelor of Divinity was earned at Huntington Seminary and further work was taken at the University of Michigan extension in Detroit.

Paul and his wife, Hazel, have three children. Darlene of Huntington, Paul David of Westland, Michigan, and Kaylinn of Chico, California. He has pastored 29 years in Ohio, Indiana, and Michigan. He also has served the National Association of Evangelicals as a field director and at Huntington College in development services.

PERSPECTIVE

The style of writing for this history is in harmony with 1984. This influences the format, the priority of interests, and even the very nature of history. The average pastor and laymen have been kept in mind while preparing this story of the United Brethren Church.

Materials covered include items of general interest and significant events. These chapters serve as an introduction to the life and ministry of the church in 1752 to 1800.

Paul A. Graham

1

THE YOUNG MISSIONARIES ARRIVE IN AMERICA:
SHEEP IN THE MIDST OF WOLVES

Six young men from Germany stepped from their sailing vessel to the wharf in New York harbor on July 28, 1752, a warm humid day. They had sailed from the Hague in Holland and had arrived in a leading city of the colonies, a small town of less than 10,000 inhabitants. The streets were dusty, dirty, and pockmarked with deep holes. The homes were mainly frame structures with clapboard sidings, store buildings, a few small industries, and several inns. They stayed that night in New York City, a gateway to the new world.

The sponsor of these six missionaries, Michael Schlatter, (1716-1790), guided them through the city. During their brief visit in New York they met an old friend of Reverend Schlatter, the Reverend Henry Melchoir Muhlenberg, (1711-1787), supervisor and administrator of the Lutheran churches in the colonies. Before parting he gave this blessing to the young men, "Behold, I send you forth as sheep in the midst of wolves: be ye therefore wise as serpents and as harmless as doves."[1]

One of these young missionaries, Philip William Otterbein (1726-1813), was to become a leader of the Reformed Church in Pennsylvania and Maryland, a renowned preacher, and one of the founders of the Church of the United Brethren in Christ. Otterbein would become a link connecting the German colonists with their spiritual heritage in Europe. He brought with him the legacy of a devout family and a profound Christian faith steeped in the Calvinistic teachings of the Reformed Church. His whole life was tempered by a warm German Pietism. Otterbein's talents were sharpened to a fine edge by his education in the schools at Frohnhausen and Herborn.

The roots of the Church of the United Brethren in Christ lie deep in the seedbed of the Christian church in Europe. The background reaches like the tentacles of a vine, back beyond the Reformation to the Waldensians,[2] and John Huss. The Christian church was *reformed* under the guidance of Martin Luther, Philip Melancthon, Ulrich Zwingli, John Calvin, Conrad Grebel, and Menno Simons. The Lutheran, Reformed, and Mennonite churches owe their legacy to generations following them.

A spiritual decline developed following the noble days of the Protestant Reformation when in the 1600s the spirit of Scholasticism and (dead orthodoxy)[3] gripped the church with the strong arms of tradition and temporal power. Then a new life movement came into the church with blessing, and power. Known as Pietism[4] in Germany, it spread through the Great Awakening[5] in Great Britain, and reached the English speaking colonies in America.

The social, spiritual, moral, and economic conditions in the colonies during the seventeenth and eighteenth centuries produced rebellion, revolutions, and a revival. These pages tell the story of that revival among the German immigrants who settled in Pennsylvania, Maryland, and Virginia, and one of the results of that revival, the establishment of the Church of the United Brethren in Christ.

FOOTNOTES

[1]Augustus W. Drury, *History of the Church of the United Brethren in Christ* (Dayton, OH: The Otterbein Press, 1924), p. 50.

[2]The Waldensians were followers of Waldo, (d. 1217) a rich merchant of Lyons, France, who was converted to a life of sacrificial devotion to God. They were not anti-church, as were the Albigenses. They revered the Scriptures, lived simply, heard confessions, observed the Lord's Supper, and ordained individuals to the ministry. They were excommunicated by the Catholic Church in 1184 but have continued to the present time. Their influence upon the reformers was profound.

[3]Scholasticism was a system of logic, philosophy, and theology that was influential in Europe from the tenth through the fifteenth centuries. The university scholars or schoolmen, who were followers of this movement, based their teachings upon Aristotelian logic and the writings of the early Christian fathers. It reached throughout all church structures with a special emphasis upon traditional doctrines and methods. Christian life and activities received slight attention from the scholastics.

[4]Pietism was a movement in the Lutheran and Reformed Churches which emphasized the devotional and personal elements of the Christian faith. It prospered in Germany, Switzerland, and Holland from the latter part of the seventeenth century until the middle of the eighteenth century. Philipp Jakob Spener was its first great leader and he was followed by August Hermann Francke. They emphasized the importance of Bible study, devotional exercises, and a new emphasis upon the role of the layman.

[5]The Great Awakening was a series of religious revivals which swept across the British Isles and the American colonies during the eighteenth century. It deeply influenced

doctrinal teachings as well as social and political thought. Emotional experiences were prominent in these revivals. It was a factor in the beginning of the modern missionary movement, the launching of several educational institutions, and social improvements. These included the first consistent attack against slavery in America. Its effects were felt in all the churches serving the colonies.

2

PIETISM, RENEWAL IN THE CHURCH

The Reformation was set in motion by Martin Luther's nailing 95 theses on the door of the Castle Church in Wittenberg, Germany, October 31, 1517. It burst upon the continent and Great Britain with explosive power. The teachings of Luther, Calvin, and the Anabaptists' brought life to the churches. Laymen were given the Scriptures and encouraged to experience the Christian faith as taught by Christ and the apostles.

However, within a century the emphasis of theologians and most pastors shifted to a struggle for orthodoxy and rigid rules for Christian behavior. Spiritual life in both pastors and laymen was ignored. Teachings about the new birth, justification by faith, the work and ministry of the Holy Spirit, spiritual gifts, and a holy life were seldom, if ever, heard. Scholastic tendencies of the church, especially among the Lutheran clergy, emphasized a fixed, dogmatic interpretation of Scriptures and demanded a rigid intellectual conformity. It was believed that pure doctrine and the celebration of the sacraments were sufficient for Christian living.

The Rise of Pietism

Since Pietism was a break with the scholastic practices of the church, it opened the door for the experience of emotions and the demonstration of Christian devotion. It also made possible the participation of laity in the life and activities of the church.

Two types of Pietism, Churchly Pietism and Radical Pietism, developed in Europe during the seventeenth and eighteenth centuries.

Churchly Pietism found its expression within the church. It sought to restore the church to the type of life and ministry demonstrated in the apostolic era. The Radical Pietists rejected the church and sought to establish new modes for the worship of God. They developed communal settlements, fanatical cults, and new church organizations. Among the Radical Pietists in America were settlements at Ephrata, Pennsylvania; Harmony, Indiana; Zoar, Ohio; Bethel and Amana, Missouri; and Aurora, Oregon. Excesses practiced by some of these communities brought disrepute to the entire Pietistic movement.

The biographer of Samuel Guldin, (1660-1745) a Swiss Pietist of the Reformed Church who spent most of his ministry in the middle colonies, wrote:

> [Churchly Pietists] stood between two fires, and were likely to be singed by both. Though their purpose was to revive the ancient churches in accordance with the spirit of the gospel, they were charged with heresy, and often unjustly persecuted and condemned. On the other hand, fanatics accused them of lacking courage to express their convictions.[2]

Philipp Jakob Spener

A leading voice in developing the Pietistic movement was Philipp Jakob Spener (1635-1705), a Lutheran. Born in Alsace, France, he was educated at Strassburg, where he was introduced to the writings and Scriptural expositions of the English Puritans and the Dutch Pietists. He furthered his studies in Geneva, Switzerland, where his early tendency toward a deep devotional life was strengthened.

Remaining a Lutheran, Spener became chief pastor in Frankfort, Germany, in 1666. By 1670, frustrated by the control exercised over his church by temporal authorities, he started holding small group meetings in his own home for Bible reading, prayer, discussion of the Sunday sermons, and social converse. Because these groups, along with designed instruction of children, were developed to deepen the spiritual life of his people, they were called *collegia pietatis*. From this identification the designation *Pietism* developed.

Spener issued his *Pia Desideria* in 1675 to give directions to those following his instructions. He proposed the gathering of little churches within the official church, *ecclesiolae in ecclesia,* in no way encouraging the development of a new denomination. He taught ways to develop the spiritual life of the individual and gave guidelines for preaching and teaching.

Because opposition developed in Frankfort, he was happy to accept a call to Dresden as the court preacher where opposition also quickly followed. The Saxon preachers rejected him; the two universities of the province, Leipzig and Wittenberg, would not recognize him; and Elector John George III was offended by his preaching. Therefore, when the invitation came to move to Berlin in 1691, he willingly made the move. Frederick III, Elector of Brandenbrug, who later became King Frederick of Prussia, supported him but was never converted to his practices and precepts. Spener died on February 5, 1705.

August Hermann Francke

During the 1680s the Pietistic movement spread to the University of Leipzig where a young professor, August Hermann Francke (1663-1727) was developing a scientific method of studying the Scriptures. In 1687 Francke experienced the new birth and soon visited Spener who instructed him in the basics of his new Christian life. Francke secured a large following in Leipzig even though opposition was headed by Johanna Carpzov (1639-1699), a professor of theology. His work at the university was limited by this opposition and he moved to Erfurt in 1690. Hostility to Francke caused him to be expelled from Erfurt in 1691, and he was promptly installed as a professor at Halle, a new university founded by the Elector of Brandenburg. Although not a full professor of the faculty until 1698, he dominated the methods, attitudes, and approaches of the school of theology. His organizational abilities and intellectual vigor kept Halle at the center of the Pietism until his death.

Francke organized a school for poor children in 1695 and later a preparatory school known as the *Paedogogium*. In 1697 he added a Latin school. These schools, which incorporated the teaching and spirit of Pietism, continued to expand until there were 2200 students at the time of his death. In 1698 he opened an Orphan House which numbered 134 residents by 1727. Believing that prayer and faith provided for these programs he created and expanded them without visible means of support. In 1710 Francke also established a Bible Institute for the publishing of the Scriptures which continued many years after his death. A zeal for missions at Halle was inspired by the enthusiasm and vision of Francke. In a sense the modern missionary movement started here. At least 60 foreign missionaries were sent forth from this spiritual center during the eighteenth century. Among them was the famous Christian Friedrich Schwartz (1726-1798) who laboured nearly 50 years in India.

The leading scholar among the Pietists was Johann A. Bengel (1687-1752). He was head of the theological seminary in Denkendor, Wurttenberg. His *Gnomon* of the New Testament was the outstanding commentary produced up to his time. John Wesley used it constantly and made it the basis of his *Notes Upon the New Testament* in 1755.

The Influence of Pietism

Pietism passed its zenith with the death of Francke. However, its influence has endured and the evangelical churches of the nineteenth and twentieth centuries have retained many of its teachings. The distinctive teachings of Pietists were centered around the new birth, the church, justification, the millenium, and the role of lay persons. Spener wrote:

> No unregenerated man can be converted or become born again without the Holy Spirit, but certainly the conversion, as well as the direction towards the same, are actions of grace by the Holy Spirit, and it is impossible that a man does anything of himself to prepare for the possessions of the Holy Spirit.[3]

In an age when the efficacy of the ordinances and the power of the church were paramount, these teachings approached heresy. They appeared to be an open attack upon the power and influence of the established church.

The Pietists drew heavily upon Puritan teachings regarding Christian life and behaviour. Restrictions regarding Sabbath activities were taught. Dancing, theatrical performances, parties, and any enjoyment of a social life were discouraged. Work, worship, spiritual exercises, prayer meetings, Bible study, and religious social life were encouraged to the practical exclusion of other activities.

Excesses and peculiarities of the Pietist movement marred and limited its growth. The movement produced few intellectual leaders. Most of the leaders were Churchly Pietists who saw Pietism as a means of revitalizing the church from within and dedicated their skills to this intent. The Radical Pietists were too visionary and their contributions faded away. Certain concepts of the movement have been rejected by the church at large. These concepts include an insistence upon a conscious conversion experience through struggle, an ascetic attitude toward the world, and a censorious attitude toward those not associated with the movement.

FOOTNOTES

[1]*Anabaptist* was a term applied in scorn to believers who held that infant baptism was not taught in the Scriptures and that baptism should be applied to adult believers only. The word *anabaptist* is taken from the Greek meaning "re-baptiser." A convert who was baptized in infancy must be rebaptized as an adult. They exerted considerable influence in Germany, Switzerland, Moravia, and the Netherlands. Although there were many similarities, they are to be distinguished from the Baptists, who were primarily English. They were persecuted by Protestants and Catholics alike for their teachings on separation of church and state, pacifism, and other social and economic reforms.

[2]Joseph H. Dubbs, "Samuel Guildin, Pietist and Pioneer," *Reformed Quarterly Review,* 1892, 39: 312.

[3]Philipp Jakob Spener, *Theologische Bedenken,* edited (by F.A.C. Hennicke, Halle, Gebauersche Buchhadlung, 1838) p. 21.

3

THE GREAT AWAKENING, FIRE ON THE FRONTIER

The darkness, desolation, and despair of religious life in the colonies were dispersed for a time in the 1730s and 1740s. This explosion of activity and new life became known as the Great Awakening. Hints of its coming were found in the pastoral ministry of Solomon Stoddard at Northampton, Massachusetts, in 1679. It arrived in a blaze of glory under the pastoral ministry of his grandson, Jonathan Edwards, and the evangelistic efforts of George Whitefield.

Other beginnings of the Awakening were experienced in New Jersey under the preaching of Theodore Freylinghuysen (1692-1747) and later under Gilbert, John, and William Tennent. It is believed that at least 300 persons came to faith in Christ during a six month period of time in 1735. Edward's report of the revival was published in England. One response to it was, "Never did we hear or read, since the first ages of Christianity, any event of this kind so surprising as the present Narrative hath set before us."[1]

However, the high tide of the Great Awakening came when George Whitefield visited New England and especially Northampton in the fall of 1740. For two entire years, believers were revived and the ungodly turned to the Lord by scores. Whitefield touched off this unusual work of the Spirit, but Jonathan Edwards was its true leader. It has been estimated that between twenty-five and fifty thousand were converted in New England and a similar number in the middle colonies.[2] Whitefield conducted great campaigns in most of the New England colonies, in addition to New Jersey, Pennsylvania, and Georgia. However, the full impact of the revival did not reach the German speaking population. Some effects were felt in the Shenandoah Valley of Virginia in about 1770 as recorded in the story of Martin Boehm's visit to the

Mennonites there.[3]

The influence of the Pietistic movement, the Great Awakening, and developments related to them were extensive. Although not exclusively responsible they

1. Brought about the elimination of slavery in England and about 120 years later in the United States.
2. Developed a Sunday School ministry in Christian education through Robert Raikes.
3. Gave great emphasis to missionary enterprises.
4. Helped implement prison reforms through John Howard.
5. Saw formation of tract and Bible societies for the distribution of the Scriptures in inexpensive editions for the common people.
6. Helped legislate child labor laws to eliminate grave injustices to young people.
7. Gave impetus to churches and Christian organizations, producing unprecedented expansion and growth.

FOOTNOTES

[1]A. Skevington Wood, *The Inextinguishable Blaze* (Grand Rapids, Mich.: Wm. B. Eerdmans, 1960), p. 61.

[2]Albert Henry Newman, *A Manual of Church History* 2 Vols. (Philadelphia: American Baptist Publication Society, 1944), 2:676.

[3]Henry G. Spayth, *History of the Church of the United Brethren in Christ* (Circleville, Ohio: Conference Office of the United Brethren in Christ, 1851), pp. 31-35.

4

RELIGIOUS LIFE AMONG GERMANS IN COLONIAL AMERICA

More than six decades passed following the English settlement of Virginia and Massachusetts before the Germans began coming to America. The opportunity for the Germans to achieve political, economic, and religious freedom came from an unusual source. William Penn (1644-1718), son of Admiral Sir William Penn, embraced the Quaker faith. In 1681 Penn secured from Charles II of England a grant of Pennsylvania, in return for release for a debt owed to Penn's father by the crown. Penn believed deeply in religious freedom. It was his desire that Pennsylvania be a refuge of those persecuted for religious or political reasons. Germans were especially encouraged to settle in the new colony. They began coming from western Germany and Switzerland soon after the establishment of Philadelphia in 1682.

The spiritual life of the German immigrants was disorganized and weak. Reports to the Pennsylvania and Maryland conference of the German Reformed Church indicated that in 1751 there were 46 Reformed churches and only six pastors. These pastors served 16 different charges leaving 32 churches entirely without pastoral care. Isolation was a debilitating factor for both pastors and churches. Congregations were exposed to the inroads of poorly trained, unworthy, and unordained imposters who preyed upon the churches. Excessive use of alcoholic beverages, gambling, and immorality marred the clergy. Reports of greed, wife abuse, and financial irresponsibility are found in official records. Facing this spiritual milieu, European denominations made positive contributions toward the organization of religious life among the colonists and upon new denominations born on American soil such as the Church of the United Brethren in Christ.

The Reformed Church

The Reformed Church came into existence as a part of the Reformation. Ulrich Zwingli (1484-1531) was a moving force for the revolt against the Roman Church in Switzerland. The changes brought about were religious, social, and political. Attempts to defeat opposing parties by both Catholic and Protestant factions created conflicts and wars. Zwingli, the "father" of the Reformed Church movement, was slain in a battle between Protestants and Catholics on October 11, 1531.

The preeminent theologian of the Reformation was John Calvin (1509-1563). He was raised in an influential home in Noyen, about fifty-eight miles northeast of Paris. A brilliant student, trained for law, he experienced a "sudden conversion" in the spring of 1532. He was soon at odds with the Catholic Church. He fled France and found sanctuary in Basel, Switzerland, on New Year's Day, 1535. He abandoned his humanist views and devoted himself to the study of the Scriptures and Christian doctrine, becoming a leader of the Reformation with the publication of his *Institutes of the Christian Religion* in 1536.

Calvin achieved distinction in Switzerland during his lifetime. As a tribute to Calvin, Williston Walker wrote:

> His influence extended far beyond Geneva. Thanks to his *Institutes,* his pattern of church government in Geneva, his academy, his commentaries, and his constant correspondence, he moulded the thought and inspired the ideals of the Protestantism of France, the Netherlands, Scotland and the English Puritans. His influence penetra; d Poland and Hungary, and before his death Calvinism was taking root in southwestern Germany itself.[1]

The Reformed Church in western Germany experienced discrimination, persecution, and war during the sixteenth and seventeenth centuries. French forces devastated much of western Germany known as the Palatinate during the last quarter of the seventeenth century. Suffering and starvation from an extended drought also caused masses of the population to become refugees. They settled in Switzerland, the Netherlands, England, and eventually the colonies.

Most of those coming to America settled in Pennsylvania, Maryland, and the Shenandoah Valley of Virginia. Religious freedom and a warm welcome were extended to the German immigrants by Pennsylvania. As a result the trickle that started soon after the founding of Penn's colony in 1681 became a flood by the 1760s. It is estimated that at least one half of these German immigrants were Reformed. The first German Reformed church in Pennsylvania was established in Philadelphia in 1727 by George Weis.

A Swiss-born Pietist, Michael Schlatter (1718-1790), was sent to America by the Synods of North and South Holland in 1746 because they believed "that through him they could organize the scattered Pennsylvanians."[2] He was an adventuresome, energetic young man. Records show that in the first three years of his ministry in the colonies he was seldom out of the saddle while traveling a distance of more than eight thousand miles and preaching well over six hundred times.

A conference, also known as a Coetus, was organized in 1747 by Schlatter along with four other active Reformed pastors. In 1751, with the recommendation of the Coetus, he returned to Europe to secure young men to help establish the work. He was also asked to raise money for the support of the churches and their schools. Success attended the mission. He returned in 1752 with 700 large Bibles, money to subsidize the work of the churches and their schools, and six young ministers. Among them was Philip William Otterbein.

Reformed churches prospered and the Coetus met annually to supervise the work. By the end of the century they believed that it was time to receive their independence, as enjoyed by the Methodist, Anglican, and Presbyterian churches. James Good recorded this development:

> In 1793 the coetus of the Reformed Churches of Pennsylvania was transformed into a synod. From being a church subordinate to and dependent on the Reformed Church of the Netherlands in Europe, it now becomes an independent body.[3]

The Reformed Church in the United States was approaching maturity and was prepared for growth and prosperity in the nineteenth century. However, while there was growth in the church, spiritual life, devotion, and Christian service deteriorated. J. W. Nevin reported in his twenty-eighth lecture on the *Heidelberg Catechism:*

> To be confirmed, and then to take the sacrament occasionally, was counted by the multitude all that was necessary to make one a good Christian, if only a tolerable decency of outward life were maintained besides, without any regard at all to the religion of the heart. True, serious piety was indeed often treated with open and marked scorn. In the bosom of the church itself it was stigmatized as *Schwarerei, Kopfhangerei,* or miserable, driveling Methodism. The idea of the new birth was treated as a Pietistic whimery. Experimental religion in all its forms was eschewed as a new-fangled invention of cunning imposters, brought in to turn the heads of the weak and to lead captive silly women. Prayer meetings were held to be a spiritual abomination. Family worship was a species of saintly affection, barely tolerable in the case of ministers (though many of them

gloried in having no altar in their houses), but absolutely disgraceful for common Christians. To show an awakened call on God in daily secret prayer, was to incur certain reproach . . . . The picture, it must be acknowledged, is dark but not more so than the truth of history would seem to require.[4]

Such a condition in the church was considered by many to be disgraceful and intolerable, and they sought to change the situation. Many of these loyal supporters of the church used their influence to develop Pietistic practices and to renew the church through revivals. The results of their efforts were seen in transformed lives and renewed spiritual life in a majority of the churches through the nineteenth and even into the twentieth century.

The Lutheran Church

The Lutheran Church became the official church of several German states and the Scandinavian countries as a result of the Reformation. During the seventeenth century, these churches became formal, sterile, and, in many instances, corrupt.

Pietism was a reviving force among the Lutherans, especially through the clergy educated at Halle. The University was the center of missionary activity for the church, and several of the pastors who came to the colonies brought this influence with them. They included Henry Melchior Muhlenberg (1711-1787) who arrived in Philadelphia in 1742. He was a man ". . . whose character and training fitted him to consolidate this vast body of raw material, and to lay the foundation for what was to become a great and influential denomination."[5] He was distinguished for his organizational and administrative abilities and ". . . may with propriety be regarded as the apostle of Lutheranism in America."[6]

The renewing power of Pietism permeated the life and teachings of Lutherans in the colonies.

It involved the hearts as well as the heads of many Lutheran colonists. It was marked by activity, enterprise, and concern for fellowmen. It is doubtful whether Lutheranism would have been established in the New World as effectively under the influence of the Scholasticism which preceded or the Rationalism which followed Pietism.[7]

However, the Lutherans stopped short of accepting the practices and demonstrations that were displayed in the Great Awakening and the revivals that followed.

John M. Boltzius, who ministered to the Lutherans in Georgia, described George Whitefield's visit to Savannah in 1740:

> He is a very warm person who is honorable toward God and man . . . . White-field preaches the gospel of Christ . . . with purity and great power. He does not speak from a written manuscript, as other preachers of the Anglican Church, but from the fulness of his heart.[8]

In contrast a year later Boltzius wrote: "More and more his manner and his unusual methods, of which I do not want to single any out displease me."[9] This response seemed to describe the relationship that existed between the German Lutherans and those who were influenced by the new life that was being infused into church and society. The flaming evangelists of the Methodists, Presbyterians, Baptists, and Congregationalists failed to exert much influence among the Lutherans.

The Moravian Church

The Moravian Brethren trace their history back to John Huss (1373-1415) in Bohemia. He was a priest and rector of the University of Prague. A forerunner of the Reformation, he was excommunicated by the Roman Catholic Church twice. By action taken against him by the Council of Constance, he was burned at the stake as a heretic July 6, 1415. Because of great persecution in Bohemia, his followers, commonly known at the *Unitas Fratrum* or *Unity of the Brethren,* fled to Moravia. During the next 300 years their fortunes moved from wide acceptance and prosperity to extreme persecution.

In June 1722 Christian David and a small band of the *Unity of the Brethren* came to the estate of Count Nicholaus Ludwig von Zinzendorf in Saxony, Germany. With his permission they established a community to be known as Herrnhut (The Lord's Watch). It was through this group of refugees and the wealthy Count that the modern Moravian Church came into existence.

Count Zinzendorf (1700-1763), one of the most distinguished church leaders of the times, was a descendent of an ancient Austrian family of nobles. His father died soon after his birth and he was raised by his grandmother, Baroness von Gersdorf, a devout woman who was also an ardent Pietist. Zinzendorf displayed deep piety and religious enthusiasm from his early days. Educated in Francke's *Paedagogium* at Halle, he went on to study law at Wittenberg. However, his main love and interest was Christ and His church.

August 13, 1727, is considered the modern Pentecost of the Moravian Church. On that date the whole church was moved by a spirit of love during the communion service. Augustus Gottlieb Spangenberg, the leader of the movement following Zinzendorf, wrote, "There were we baptized by the Holy Spirit Himself to one love."[10] From this day in 1727, with Count Zinzendorf as their leader, the Moravians sought to spread the gospel over the whole world. While establishing one of the great missionary movements of modern times, they also attempted to bring about a renewal in the established churches.

This desire for church unity led Zinzendorf to hold a series of convocations in the Philadelphia area in 1742. The goal of the synod was not organizational unity or the creation of a new creed. It was described as the "Congregation of God in the Spirit." Zinzendorf served as a bishop of the Moravian Church until his death in 1763. Although he was instrumental in renewing the ancient Bohemian Brethren, the *Unitas Fratrum,* he personally identified with the Lutheran church throughout his life. Moravian missions to the Indians were quite successful in the colonial days. However, many of these peace-loving Christian believers were massacred by the whites during the French and Indian War and the American Revolution. The modern Moravian Church is a result of the Pietistic movement of the seventeenth and eighteenth centuries. Its influence over other church leaders and denominations has been extensive.

The Mennonite Church

During the Reformation there arose, along with Luther and Zwingli, other teachers who held widely divergent views regarding the church and Scriptures. Among them were the Anabaptists. Often, because of their unusual beliefs and practices they were attacked and persecuted by both Protestants and Catholics. Anabaptist teachings included a rejection of infant baptism. They believed only adults should be baptized and many held that it must be by immersion.

Among the leaders of the Anabaptist movement was Conrad Grebel (1498-1526), a son of one of the leading families in Zurich, Switzerland, who was educated in the universities of Vienna and Paris. During the winter of 1524-25 he took the lead in teaching believers baptism and organizing churches of the regenerate. However, their baptism was not by immersion.

The following characteristics were generally stressed by the Anabaptists and are still practiced by their descendents:

1. Emphasis upon self-denial and brotherhood. This included tendencies toward communal practices.
2. Church membership should be restricted to the regenerate who give evidence of being true believers.
3. The belief that infant baptism is unscriptural and totally incompatible with the development of a church of regenerate believers.
4. Emphatic rejection of any connection of the church with the state.
5. Christians should not hold office in the government.
6. The taking of oaths was prohibited.
7. Waging warfare and bearing of arms is believed to be contrary to the gospel.
8. Capital punishment is considered anti-Christian.
9. Rejection of traditional theological systems, including Augustinian teachings as developed by the reformers.[11]

Menno Simons (1492-1559), a native of the Netherlands, was a converted Roman Catholic priest, who was a wise, peace-loving, and anti-fanatical leader. He brought maturity and responsibility to the Anabaptist movement and under his leadership it grew and developed the characteristics of a denomination. His followers were so devoted to him that they became identified as Mennonites.

Persecution and torture were the lot of these peace-loving followers of Christ. Because of this persecution they were dispersed throughout many areas of Europe and eventually the colonies. In 1683 William Penn, the founder of Pennsylvania, invited them to come to his new colony. Many of these Mennonites settled in what is now known as Lancaster County.

Jacob Amman, a leader of one of the more conservative elements of the Mennonites, led a division of the movement in 1693. A first contingent of his followers, known as Amish, came to the colonies in 1714. By the late eighteenth century many of the followers of Menno Simons and Jacob Amman had fallen into legalistic practices and ritualism without the spiritual life and spontaneity characteristic of their early days.

The Church of the Brethren

The Pietistic movement among the Lutheran and Reformed churches was a seedbed for many denominations and sects. Several of them have endured over the years. The Church of the Brethren was one of these new denominations. Alexander Mack was the leader of a small *collegium pietatis* in Schwartzenau, Germany. He led his group in a vigorous practice of Bible study, prayers, and self-denial. Following the Anabaptist tradition, they repudiated violence, war, taking of oaths, and control of outside forces. They renewed the practice of "love feasts"[12] and the ceremony of foot washing. The first contingent of these brethren, also known as Dunkers, came to Pennsylvania in 1719. Alexander Mack and others followed in 1729. They came to Lancaster County where they were prosperous farmers.

The Methodist Church

The Methodist Church was born in the evangelical awakening of Great Britain and the United States. Its progress was so great that it overshadowed, and in a sense dominated, the awakening.

One family name echoes through the entire history of Methodism. It is Wesley. The father, Samuel Wesley (1662-1735); the mother, Susanna Annesley Wesley (1669-1742); and the sons, John (1703-1791) and Charles (1707-1788), were intimately associated in the expansion of the evangelical movement.

Samuel Wesley was a country pastor of an Anglican church in Epworth, Lincolnshire, England, from 1695 until his death in 1735. An earnest but somewhat impractical man, he wrote books on the life of Christ and Job. Susanna was the dominant influence in the lives of the children. Of their household of nineteen children, eight of whom died in infancy, John was the fifteenth child and Charles was the eighteenth. In this large family Susanna still found time to supervise and train each at a specific time each week. Later, her insights and advice were highly regarded by John in his supervision of the societies under his care.

John and Charles were rescued from a burning rectory in 1709, an event that was buried deep in the minds of each of the boys. The mother often called her son John, "a brand plucked from the burning." Both boys were educated in London and Oxford, where John was chosen a Fellow of Lincoln College in 1726. John and Charles were part of a little club at Oxford that sought to develop their spiritual lives, help in Bible study, and seek opportunities of service. The group was nicknamed "The Holy Club" and then "Methodists," a description that has followed the brothers and their converts to the present time.

John was ordained an Anglican deacon in 1725 and a priest in 1728. He served as an assistant in his father's church at Epworth from 1726 to 1729. Both brothers sailed, in 1735, for the new colony of Georgia which had been settled by General Oglethorpe in 1733. The brothers became acquainted with Moravian missionaries on the voyage to Georgia and were deeply impressed with their spiritual lives and calm spirit. The Moravian leader, John Spangenberg, asked the brothers a disturbing question, "Do you know Jesus Christ?" John's answer, "I know He is the Saviour of the world," was not convincing. Spangenberg's response, "True, but do you know He has saved you?" deeply moved John Welsey. John and Charles were ineffective in their ministry in Georgia. They returned to England in defeat with John saying of himself, "I have a fair summer religion."

Charles experienced his "conversion" on May 21, 1738, while suffering from a serious illness. On Wednesday, May 24, a similar transformation came to John. He was attending a "society" meeting at Aldersgate in London when the preface to Luther's *Commentary on Romans* was read. He wrote about this dramatic, life changing event:

> About a quarter before nine, while he (Luther) was describing the change which God works in the heart through faith in Christ, I felt my heart strangely warmed. I felt I did trust in Christ, Christ alone, for my salvation; and an assurance was given me that He had taken away my sins, even mine, and saved me from the law of sin and death.[13]

Less than three weeks after his conversion, John departed from England to visit the Moravians and Count Zinzendorf in Germany. While Methodism shows a profound imprint of the Moravians, Wesley did not join them because of a difference of organizational concepts regarding the church and the lack of compatibility with Count Zinzendorf.

John and Charles Wesley preached in the "societies" in and about London as opportunities were presented. George Whitefield launched them into their greater ministry by inviting John to help him at Bristol where he had secured a large following. Although Wesley objected to any ministry outside of the churches and cathedrals dedicated for that purpose, he followed the example of Whitefield and preached in the open air. He immediately saw its benefits and the potential of reaching multitudes. The talents of John Wesley as an administrator were used to establish societies all over the country. Charles followed John in preaching, but his greatest ministry was the writing of hymns to be sung in their societies.

Methodism came to the colonies with Robert Strawbridge and Philip Embury. They established societies in Maryland and New York. Francis Asbury (1745-1816) was sent over in 1771 as a layman to assist in the growing ministry. He was ordained by a "conference" which was held in Baltimore in December 1784. One of the clergymen chosen to participate in his ordination was Philip William Otterbein, a Reformed pastor in Baltimore and a leader in evangelistic ministries among the Germans. The discipline, organization, and zeal that was demonstrated by the Methodist pioneers, especially Francis Asbury, influenced the German preachers who participated in the "great meetings"[14] of the day. The imprint and example thus given are reflected in the teachings, life, and organization of the United Brethren Church.

FOOTNOTES

[1]Williston Walker, *A History of the Christian Church* (New York: Charles Scribner Sons, 1946), p. 400.

[2]W. J. Hinke, "Philip William Otterbein and the Reformed Church," *Presbyterian and Reformed Review,* July 1901, p. 438.

[3]James I. Good, *History of the Reformed Church in the U.S. in the Nineteenth Century* (New York: The Board of Publication of the Reformed Church in America, 1911), p. 1.

[4]Drury, *History,* pp. 172, 173.

[5]Newman, 2: 563.

[6]Ibid., p. 564.

[7]F. Ernest Stoeffler, *Continental Pietism and Early American Christianity* (Grand Rapids, MI: William B. Eerdmans Publishing Company, 1976), p. 32.

[8]Ibid., p. 27.

[9]Ibid., p. 27.

[10]John R. Weinlick, *Count Zinzendorf* (New York: Abingdon Press, 1956), p. 79.

[11]Newman, 2: 153-155.

[12]The Love Feast, practiced by the Brethren, is still considered one of the most important activities of the church. It includes a foot washing service, a fellowship meal, and a communion service.

[13]Wood, pp. 110, 111.

[14]Great Meetings. See pp. 38f., 81, 82.

5

SPIRITUAL LIFE IN THE COLONIES, DEGENERATE, DEGRADING, AND DISMAL

On the continent, in Great Britain, and throughout the colonies, social, moral, and spiritual conditions were degenerate, degrading, and dismal during the eighteenth century.

"Morality and religion have collapsed to a degree that has never been known in any Christian country!" wrote the British churchman and philosopher, Bishop George Berkley, in 1738. He continued:

> Our prospect is very terrible and the symptoms grow worse from day to day . . . . The youth born and brought up in wicked times without any bias to good from early principle, or instilled opinion, when they grow ripe, must be monsters indeed. And it is to be feared that the age of monsters is not far off.[1]

This description of conditions in England could have been written of the colonies for they were in truth an extension of their European founders.

Increase Mather lamented the degeneracy of the church in his "The Glory Departing from New England." He wrote "Oh, New England, New England, look to it that the glory be not removed from thee, for it begins to go!"[2] Later, in 1721, he wrote: "Oh, degenerate New England, what art thou come to at this day?"[3] It is believed that the situation was no better in the remainder of the colonies.

According to A. Skevington Wood in *The Inextinguishable Blaze*

> The Church life of the day was dank and unattractive, not at all conducive to vitality and progress. Services were long and drab; they bore little relation to life and reflected the prevailing theological petrifaction of the day . . . . The spiritual

temperature of the churches dropped to zero.[4]

Jonathan Edwards described conditions:

Licentiousness for some years prevailed among the youth of the town; they were many of them very much addicted to night walking, and frequenting the tavern, and lewd practices, wherein some, by their example, exceedingly corrupted others. It was their manner very frequently to get together in conventions of both sexes for mirth and jollity, which were called frolics; and they would often spend the greater part of the night in them, without regard to any order in the families they belonged to.[5]

The colonial superintendent and missionary of the Lutheran Church, Henry Melchoir Muhlenberg, wrote to his superiors in Europe in 1749:

I must lament over some in our own church, however, and confess that many have the illusion that they are already converted if they have performed the *opus operatum* of external worship . . . although on other occasions they curse enough and horrify heaven, get drunk, and engage in worldly vanities . . . .[6]

Mullenberg also wrote his complaints in 1752:

The state and condition of some English and German neighbors here (in Trappe, Pennsylvania) groweth worse because Abr. de Haven continues to abuse the granted license by enticing one after another into a dissolute and wicked life. Surfeiting, drunkenness, playing cards and dice, fiddling, dancing, cursing, swearing, fighting, scuffling, and such like will hardly cease on the Lord's days! He has had, several Sundays in my absence, horse racing before, during, and after divine Worship.[7]

During this period of history alcoholic beverages were used instead of drinking water. Beer was regularly brewed at home and served at church work meetings, councils, and consistories. Only the abuse of these drinks was frowned upon.

While many of the colonists had a nominal relation to a church, they were superficial and without a vital religious life. There were 300,000 persons living in Pennsylvania in 1770, according to W. F. Dunaway in his second edition of *History of Pennsylvania*. Of the 100,000 who were German, 4000 were Mennonites, 1500 Dunkers, 2500 Moravians, 60,000 Lutherans, and 30,000 Reformed.[8] A reason for this identification with the church was the law regarding citizenship in the colonies. After waiting a brief period of time, an immigrant could renounce allegiance to his native land and swear allegiance to the King of England. In addition he had to present a certificate of baptism at this hearing. This may have been a declaration of interest but it did not provide an incentive to Christian living and service.

"After 1760 the religious life in the Colonies declined sharply," according to Behney and Eller in *The History of the Evangelical United Brethren Church.* They continued, "By the time of the Revolutionary War only about five percent (one in twenty) of the colonial population openly professed religious faith or admitted church relationship."[9] Social conditions of the eighteenth century were still primitive, oppressive, uncivil, and all aspects of life were affected.

Education of children was restricted to the privileged few. Children of the wealthy, clergy, and selected individuals were chosen for this honor. Most were limited to the barest of educational skills and learning. Children were put to work in shops, on farms, and in stores at an early age. Their only freedom came at night and during Sabbath days when they engaged in all types of destructive and exciting pleasures. Working conditions were oppressive and miserable. Laborers worked from sunup to sundown. They existed little better than animals in filthy, dismal, and oppressive conditions.

Slavery was still the curse of civilized, Christian nations. Many justifications were offered for this racial injustice. It was excused by some as a method of introducing the black Africans to Christianity. Often they were described as most happy and privileged. One slaveholder assured a friend that, ". . . the blacks were the happiest people in the world" and appealing to his wife, said: "Now, my dear, you saw Mr. T.'s slaves. Do tell Mr. Buxton how happy they looked."

"Well, yes," his wife replied, "they were very happy, I'm sure, only I used to think it so odd to see the black cooks chained to the fireplace."[10]

There is extensive documentation of the barbarities of the slave ships. The *Annual Register* in 1762 carried this report:

On Friday the men slaves being very sullen and unruly, having had no sustenance of any kind for forty-eight hours except a dram, we put one-half of the strongest of them in irons. On Saturday and Sunday all hands, night and day could scarce keep the ship clear, and were constantly under arms. On Monday morning many of the slaves had got out of irons and were attempting to break up the gratings; and the seamen not daring to go down the hold to clear our pumps, were obliged, for the preservation of our lives, to kill fifty of the ringleaders. It is impossible to describe the misery the poor slaves underwent, having had no fresh water for five days. Their dismal cries and shrieks, and most frightful looks, added a great deal to our misfortune; four of them were found dead, and one drowned herself in the hold.[11]

In 1788 a slave ship crammed 34 female slaves into sleeping quarters "measuring only 9 feet 4 inches in length, 4 feet 8 inches main breadth, and 2 feet 7 inches in height."[12] Slave ships planned for a death toll of at least 10 percent during passage. Horace Walpole, writing to Sir Horace Mann on February 25th, 1750, said:

> We, the British Senate, that temple of liberty and bulwark of Protestant Christianity, have this fortnight been pondering methods to make more effectual that horrid traffic of selling negroes. It has appeared to us that six and forty thousand of these wretches are sold every year to our plantations alone . . . .[13]

Those plantations were the American colonies.

Many of the colonists, arriving in the New World, were kidnapped, "indentured" workers, "redemptioners," or convicts. They were forced into unjust practices and oppressive social conditions. During the 18th century, thousands of the German immigrants came to Pennsylvania and Maryland to escape poverty, starvation, and religious persecution only to find disheartening conditions prevalent in their adopted land.

FOOTNOTES

[1] J. Wesley Bready, "This Freedom - Whence?" (New York: American Tract Society, 1942), p. 3.

[2] Wood, p. 54.

[3] Ibid.

[4] Ibid., p. 55.

[5] Ibid., p. 59.

[6] Stoeffler, pp. 25, 26.

[7] Ibid., p. 19.

[8] W. F. Dunaway, *History of Pennsylvania*, Second Edition.

[9] J. Bruce Behney and Paul H. Eller, *The History of the Evangelical United Brethren Church* (Nashville, TE: Abingdon Press, 1979), p. 27.

[10] Bready, p. 43.

[11] Ibid., p. 41.

[12] Ibid.

[13] Ibid., p. 42.

6

MARTIN BOEHM, A GOOD MAN

Martin Boehm was plain in dress and manners. When age had stamped its impress of reverence upon him, he filled the mind with the noble ideas of a patriarch. As the head of a family, a father, a neighbor, a friend, a companion, the prominent feature of his character was goodness; you felt that he was good. His mind was strong, and well stored with the learning necessary for one whose aim is to preach Christ with apostolic zeal and simplicity.[1]

This eulogy to Martin Boehm was delivered by Bishop Francis Asbury at Boehm's Chapel on Sunday, April 5, 1812. It revealed the way this patriarch of the Church of the United Brethren in Christ was viewed by his friends and co-workers. He was a *good man.*

Martin Boehm, the youngest son of Jacob and Barbara Kendig Boehm was born in the family home about five miles south of Lancaster, Pennsylvania, on November 30, 1725. His parents had come to Penn's colony in 1715 at the invitation of Martin Kendig, one of an earlier band of Mennonites to settle in the Pequea Creek area.

The Boehms were devout Christians dating back to Jacob Boehm I, who was associated with the Swiss Reformed Church. His son, Jacob Boehm II, came into contact with the Mennonites in Germany while he was serving as an apprentice journeyman. He was converted to the Mennonite teachings, and upon *returning* home to Switzerland, he was opposed by his family and arrested. A brother let him escape while escorting him to jail. He fled the country and settled in Holland. He had a son, Jacob Boehm III, Martin's father, who was born in Holland in 1693. Little more is known of the family until they settled in Pequea.

As far as can be determined, Martin's education was received in the home and church. In addition to the German language spoken by his people, he learned to speak and read English. His children had the advantage of a teacher who boarded "from house to house" and taught in the community. Martin Boehm was married to Eve Steiner, whose ancestors came to Pennsylvania from Switzerland. She was nine years younger than Martin and was a highly esteemed Christian mother.

Martin read extensively in addition to the Bible. He especially enjoyed Wesley's *Sermons* and Fletcher's *Checks to Antinomianism.* His library was distributed to his family, according to a will which was recorded in the Lancaster court house. It stated:

> I give and bequeath unto my beloved wife Eve such of my books as she may choose to take, to and for her properties, and all the remainder of my books I do give and bequeath to my four children (John, Jacob, Henry, and Barbara) to be equally divided between them, share and share alike.[2]

Family life in the Boehm home centered in their church and farming. Four of Martin and Eve's children died while still young. They were Martin, March 1758; Henry, January 1760; Maria, September 1765; and Abraham, January 1768. The last child, another Henry was born on June 8, 1775. He was to become a Methodist preacher and the story of his life, as recorded in his book, *Reminiscences, Historical and Biographical of Sixty-four Years in the Ministry,* gives most of the information available about Bishop Martin Boehm and family. Also, it relates some of the important events in the life of Francis Asbury, with whom Henry traveled for several years. Henry died in 1875 at age one hundred years, six months, twenty days.

In 1756 the Mennonite church at Byerland, Pennsylvania, where Martin Boehm's family were prominent members, determined that it was time to select a new pastor. Bishop Hostetter, their pastor, was becoming aged and infirm. According to Mennonite custom, candidates were nominated from the congregation and the pastor was chosen by lot:

> On the appointed day at a congregational meeting, the bishop leads the members in prayer and observation, and each candidate who is nominated selects a Bible standing in view. Each book contains a slip of paper but only one has the written message, "The lot is cast into the lap, but the whole disposing thereof is of the Lord" (Proverbs 16:33). The choice by lot falls on the one selecting the book with the writing. The selection is thought to be the Lord's choice. The ordination charge and act takes place at once, as the Bishop places his hands upon the new minister's head to symbolize the imposition of the new calling.[3]

It was in this manner that Martin Boehm was chosen to be their pastor. Bishop Hostetter died in 1761, and Martin Boehm, again by lot, became bishop of his church at age 36.

He felt that he was wholly unworthy of the pastoral position. Although he had often given testimony in previous years, now that he was a pastor, he was able to "stammer out a few words and then be obliged to sit down in shame and remorse."[4] He memorized Scriptures, planned his talks, but could not give them. After agonizing over his situation for weeks and possibly months, he came to a spiritual crisis. Henry G. Spayth recorded Boehm's experience in his own words:

> To be a preacher, and yet have nothing to preach, nor to say, but stammer out a few words, and then be obliged to take my seat in shame and remorse! I had faith in prayer, and prayed more fervently. While thus engaged in prayer earnestly for aid to preach, the thought rose up in my mind, or as though one spoke to me saying, "You pray for grace to teach others the way of salvation, and you have not prayed for your own salvation." This thought or word did not leave me. *My salvation* followed me wherever I went. I felt constrained to pray for myself, and while praying for myself, my mind became alarmed. I felt and saw myself a poor sinner. I was LOST. My agony became great. I was ploughing in the field, and kneeled down at each end of the furrow, to pray. The word *lost, lost (verlohren),* went every round with me. Midway in the field I could go no further, but sank behind the plough, crying, Lord save, I am lost!—and again the thought or voice said, "I am come to seek and to save that which is lost." In a moment a stream of joy was poured over me. I praised the Lord, and left the field, and told my companion what joy I felt.[5]

Giving his testimony and preaching became a joy to Martin Boehm. The congregation was moved, some of them to tears. He said, "This caused considerable commotion in our church, as well as among the people generally. It was all new; none of us had heard or seen it before."[6] Several in the community experienced a similar transformation, the first being his wife, Eve. They would ask him, "Oh! Martin, are we indeed lost?" Then he would reply, "Yes, man is lost! Christ will never find us, till we know that we are lost."[7]

During the next fifty years of Boehm's ministry many hundreds and possibly thousands entered into a similar regenerating experience. Large numbers, possibly the majority, remained in their home churches, choosing to continue as Mennonites, Reformed, Lutherans, or members of other denominations. Some chose to become "Boehm's people," seeking to promote the movement in local fellowships and churches.

In 1761 Martin Boehm, now bishop, was called to minister to the Mennonites who had settled in the Shenandoah Valley of Virginia. They were without pastoral supervision, and the influence of another movement was being felt. Upon arriving in Virginia he visited a family

named Keller. He learned that a daughter had attended services that
were being held by the "New Lights."[8] This term was one of the
designations of the followers of George Whitefield. The girl was in
deep distress and no words or arguments could cheer her or produce a
pleasant mood.

Boehm was introduced to the girl. He talked with her about her
condition. She sighed and began crying, asking if he, a stranger could
understand her feelings and sufferings. He replied, "Yes, I know this
my daughter, but I know Jesus came to seek and to save that which is
lost; do you believe in Jesus?"

"Yes, I believe there is Jesus Christ; but have I not offended him?
Will He not come and judge the world and me? Oh, that he would but
save me!"

"Come," said Boehm, "we will kneel down and pray." They knelt in
prayer and confession. Her agony was great and she cried out, "Lord,
save or I perish!"

"Yes, hold to that; He will save, and that speedily," and it happened.
Her sorrow was gone and she was filled with joy. The blessings of
salvation came to the whole family that night.[9] This is one of a few
recorded results of the Great Awakening among the Mennonites. It
made a deep impression upon Martin Boehm and influenced his
ministry among the German settlers.

Bishop Boehm soon became involved in holding *great meetings*. He
was assisted by several other revival preachers, among them some
converts from Virginia. These events were two and three day affairs
with several hundred in attendance at times. They were held in barns,
orchards, open air, and when possible in churches. They were attended
by Mennonites, Reformed, Lutherans, Moravians, Dunkers, and others from both the German and English speaking population.

These meetings generated considerable enthusiasm. Excitement
would move entire communities when they were held. Physical demonstrations, weeping, shouting, trembling, and trance-like states were
common. Atheists and mockers were often stricken down, spreading
fear throughout whole communities.

One such meeting was held at the Isaac Long farm home, about nine
miles north of Lancaster, on Pentecost Sunday, May 10, 1767. A large
crowd gathered filling the six-mow barn and running over into the
orchard nearby. Martin Boehm spoke in the barn while his Virginia
pastors were preaching in the orchard.

Boehm related his personal experience of salvation and how God
was blessing his ministry. Dominie William Otterbein, pastor of the
German Reformed Church in York, Pennsylvania, attended and was

deeply moved. Spayth recorded:

> Before he had time to take his seat, Otterbein rose up, and folding Boehm in his arms, said with a loud voice, *["Wir sind Brüder,"]*. At this sight some praised God aloud, but most of the congregation gave place to their feelings—weeping for joy.[10]

It is believed by many that this event led future followers to call the emerging church "The United Brethren in Christ." If it is not the direct or major reason for the name of the movement, it is symbolic of the spirit that prevailed among their followers.

Martin Boehm's ministry continued to expand. It led him into association with ministers of other denominations, including English speaking Methodists. He felt a spiritual unity with born again believers, without regard to their church affiliation. His closest personal friends were William Otterbein, a lifelong member of the Reformed Church and Francis Asbury, the pioneer bishop of the Methodist Church in the United States.

This broader ministry of Boehm brought him into conflict with his fellow Mennonite pastors. They did not approve of new religious practices. They were not comfortable with the evangelistic fervor and demonstrations of power that were experienced in the great meetings. They were disturbed by Boehm's ecumenical relationships, believing that they were compromising and corrupting.

A council of bishops, deacons, and ministers met with Boehm. They requested that he repent and desist from the error of his ways. He replied that he would repent of any error that he had committed in the sight of God but would have to follow his conscience and understanding of God's will. The breach was not healed. It continued to widen and when he met with his brethren again they demanded that he desist from his course. He replied, "If it could be shown he had done wrong, he would recall."[11] The council pressed the issue further and he was excommunicated sometime following 1775.

A report was issued to the Mennonite congregations that he had been expelled from their membership. John F. Funk in *The Mennonite Church and Her Accusers,* an 1878 publication, quoted extensively from the document explaining the actions of the church. He recorded five reasons for excommunicating Boehm: 1) his association with outsiders, especially those who approved the practice of war; 2) his saying that Satan is a benefit to mankind; 3) his preaching that the Scriptures might be burned without harm to the church of God; 4) his teaching that light comes from darkness and belief from unbelief; and 5) his feelings that the Mennonite ministers placed too much emphasis on the ordinances (baptism and communion) and this led people astray.[12]

Doubtless there was substance and validity for reasons one and five. They reflect a variant position from that accepted among Boehm's Mennonite brethren. Reasons number two, three, and four are vague and essentially unsubstantiated. They reflect opinions and interpretations of the church leaders rather than basic beliefs and doctrines of Mennonites. It is questioned that his ban would have been pressed in later times or other situations.

When Martin Boehm was interviewed at a later date regarding his relationship with the Mennonite church, he said:

> Many were brought to the knowledge of the truth. But it was a strange work; and some of the Mennonite Meetinghouses were closed to me. Nevertheless, I was received in other places. I now preached the gospel spiritually and powerfully. Some years afterwards I was excommunicated from the Mennonite church, on a charge truly enough advanced, of holding fellowship with other societies of different languages.[13]

He continued to wear the plain dress of the Mennonites. He also continued his ministry in the Rohrers Church on Mill Creek, Stoners Church, and Boehm's Chapel. The membership of these churches were principally Mennonites.

Martin Boehm was in attendance at several conferences of German preachers who were promoting ecumenical fellowship and revival efforts. The first was held at William Otterbein's home in Baltimore in 1789 and the second at the house of a Brother John Spangler, Paradise township, York County, Pennsylvania, in the year 1791. Spayth recorded fourteen members in the association in 1789 with seven in attendance. Records showed nine in attendance in 1791 but no account of the total number of ministers in the association was given.[14]

Boehm, at age 77, was elected a bishop of the United Brethren in Christ Church at its first official conference, at the home of Peter Kemp, near Frederick, Maryland, September 25 and 26, 1800. The other bishop chosen was William Otterbein, who served as chairman.

Two years later Bishop Martin Boehm united officially with the Methodist Church at the Boehm's Chapel. This act should not be considered unusual since William Otterbein was a member of the Reformed Church and a member of its official body, the Synod. Also the United Brethren Church was not considered an official denomination until the General Conference of 1815; therefore, membership was rather vague and undefined until that time.

Christian Newcomer withdrew from the Mennonite Church and

enjoyed close fellowship with the Boehms. He recorded in his journal at least 71 contacts with them. One of the interesting and inspiring reports was dated June 6, 1798:

> . . . this day I preached at Strasburg, . . . from thence I rode home with Br. Martin Boehm. After family prayers when we were just about to retire to bed, a son of Br. Boehm's, who lives about nine miles distant, arrived at the house of his parents. He had lately embraced religion, had found the pearl of great price, was yet in his first love, of course very happy, so much so, that he expressed himself in ecstasy of his enjoying heaven and the smiles of his Saviour and Redeemer here on earth. His mother, sister Boehm, was so rejoiced at the happiness of her youngest son, that she could not help shouting and praising God for the blessing; the father also got happy, and so we had a blessed time of it, 'til after midnight: glory to God; O! that many children may be the cause of such joy to their parents.[15]

This son was Henry who became a Methodist minister and traveling companion of Bishop Francis Asbury.

Martin Boehm's preaching was described by Spayth:

> . . . the plain, open, and frank expounder of God's word; being all animation, all life; often irresistable, like a mighty current carrying his hearers into deep water.[16]

Boehm was intimately associated with the beginning of the Church of the United Brethren in Christ. He was recognized as a pastor, leader, and administrator. Drury recorded his participation in the early conferences:

> Beginning with 1789 he was present at every conference of the United Brethren down to 1809, with the exception of those of 1806 and 1808, being present in 1809 for the last time. In 1800 and 1805 he was, with Otterbein, elected bishop.[17]

However, there is no official record of his attendance at the Conference in 1801. Spayth recorded that he ". . . was prevented by sickness from attending the Conference of 1801."[18] Further conference minutes report that he was the presiding chairman for the 1804, 1807, and 1809 conferences.

Age and infirmity prevented him from taking part in the conferences after 1809. Near the end of a long and productive life he related to his son, Henry:

> I can truly say my last days are my best days. My beloved Eve is traveling with me the same road, Zionward; my children, and most of my grandchildren, are made the partakers of the same grace. I am, this 12th of April, 1811, in my

eighty-sixth year. Through the boundless goodness of God I am still able to visit the sick, and occasionally to preach in the neighborhood: to His name be all the glory in Christ Jesus.[19]

Following a brief illness, he died on March 23, 1812. Spayth recorded the close of a noble and great life:

Death had . . . begun to show its effects by symptoms of increasing debility and weakness. He asked to be raised up in the bed,—said he wished to sing and pray once more before he left, which he did, with a clear and distinct voice. This done, he desired to be laid back on his pillow, and behold he was no more.[20]

A fitting memorial stands near his remains in the graveyard beside the Boehm Chapel, a Methodist church which had been built by his family and Christian brothers. It was located on property which was originally a part of the Boehm family farm. The memorial above his grave reads:

Here lie the remains of the Rev'd Martin Boehm, who departed this life (after a short illness) March 23rd, 1812, in the 87th year of his age. Fifty-five years he freely preached the gospel to thousands and labored in the vineyard of the Lord Jesus in Pennsylvania, Maryland, and Virginia, among the many denominations of Christians, but particularly the Mennonites, United Brethren and Methodists, with the last of whom he lived and died in fellowship. He not only gave himself and his services to the church, but also fed the Lord's prophets and people by the multitudes. He was an Israelite indeed in whom was no guile. His end was peace.[21]

FOOTNOTES

[1]Henry Boehm, *Reminiscences, Historical and Biographical, of Sixty-Four Years in the Ministry,* ed. Joseph B. Wakeley (New York: Carlton and Porter, 1865), pp. 373, 374.

[2]Abram W. Sangrey, *Martin Boehm* (Ephrata, PA: Science Press, 1976), p. 3.

[3]Ibid., p. 4.

[4]Spayth, *History,* p. 29.

[5]Ibid., pp. 29, 30.

[6]Ibid., p. 30.

[7]Ibid., pp. 30, 31.

[8]"New Lights" or "Separatist" churches were organized to serve those converted under the ministry of George Whitefield and his co-workers. These converts were previously excluded from church privileges and fellowship. Many felt that it was necessary to be separated from the ungodly elements that were active in the recognized churches. They also desired no affiliation with state-supported churches.

[9]Spayth, *History,* pp. 32-36.

[10]Ibid., p. 41.

[11]John F. Funk, *The Mennonite Church and Her Accusers.* (Elkhart, IN: Mennonite Publishing Company, 1875), p. 53.

[12]Ibid., pp. 54, 55.
[13]Henry Boehm, p. 379.
[14]Spayth, p. 59.
[15]Christian Newcomer, *The LIfe and Journal of the Rev'd. Christian Newcomer,* (Hagerstown, MD: F. G. W. Kapp, 1834), p. 40.
[16]Spayth, p. 60.
[17]Drury, *History,* p. 208.
[18]Spayth, p. 111.
[19]Boehm, p. 380.
[20]Spayth, p. 129.
[21]From a personal on site visit by Paul A. Graham, September, 1980.

7

GEORGE ADAM GEETING,
A DESIRABLE COMPANION

Another preacher in the movement that led to the development of the United Brethren Church was George Adam Geeting. This man, made in the mold of the Apostle John, was deeply loved by the church fathers, especially Otterbein.

Geeting was born February 6, 1741 in Germany and grew up in the Reformed Church. He was well educated, with some training in Latin. He came to the colonies in 1759, when he was eighteen years of age locating near the Little Antietam Creek not far from present day Keedysville, Maryland. A schoolteacher in his community during the winters, he quarried stone, dug wells, and farmed during the rest of the year. Soon after his arrival from Germany, Geeting became acquainted with William Otterbein. Otterbein was the pastor of the Reformed Church in Frederick and preached to the scattered German settlers in Geeting's community.

Geeting experienced conversion and became an enthusiastic supporter of Otterbein's ministry. He often conducted services in the schoolhouse reading the Bible expositions from a book of sermons. When Otterbein learned of this practice, he suggested that one of the men of the church remove the book from the pulpit while Geeting was praying, thus forcing the young man to speak extemporaneously. This project was successful, and Geeting became a powerful preacher of the Word.

Spayth said:

> . . . Guething was more like a spring sun rising on a frost silvered forest, gradually affording more heat, more light, till you could hear, as it were, the

crackling in the forest, and the icy crust beginning to melt and fall away, and like a drizzling shower ending in a clear and joyous day: such was Guething. He was the St. John of this clover leaf; always soft and mellowing; of good parts, having a well cultivated mind; in conversation cheerful, interesting and pleasing, and in every way a desirable companion.[1]

Widely known as a powerful preacher, Geeting would arise to speak to his audiences, exert a magnetic power, and the people would press around him. They loved him and his pulpit ministry to the end of his days.

His ordination by Otterbein and William Hendel in 1783 was considered somewhat irregular by the Reformed Coetus. The minutes of the Coetus of 1788 report that "Mr. George Geeting presented himself for examination and ordination, which was granted him after a long discussion, *pro* and *con.*"[2] He was listed as a regular member of the Coetus in 1791 and 1792, continuing up until 1804. At a meeting of the Synod in that year complaints were preferred against him on the basis of disorderly conduct. He was expelled from the Synod on a vote of twenty to seventeen and a note was included in the minutes indicating that he could be restored on giving evidence of true reformation. He was considered "highly fanatical" because of his revival practices and association with the United Brethren. No evidence is given suggesting that he was divisive, bigoted, or immoral, but rather that he was kindly, honest, and respected.

George Adam Geeting was deeply involved in the itinerating program of the United Brethren. Even though he had many responsibilities at home on the farm and with the local church, he traveled widely on church business in Pennsylvania, Maryland, and Virginia. Christian Newcomer recorded in his *Journal* many meetings that he shared with Geeting. During the years 1795 through 1802, Newcomer recorded 16 separate incidents when he participated with Geeting in the ministry of the Word. It is safe to assume that Geeting also made many trips outside the Antietam and Hagerstown communities without Newcomer. He was committed to the itinerant ministry of the emerging church.

Geeting served as the secretary of the early conferences of the United Brethren. It is recorded by Spayth that he served as chairman of the conference which was held in the Geeting home church, May 12-16, 1812. It is believed by his descendents that he was recognized as a bishop by the emerging church of the United Brethren. However, this honor cannot be substantiated by the minutes or reports of those participating.[3] Following the 1812 conference, the Geetings visited William Otterbein in Baltimore. Here Geeting gave his report of the actions of the conference and shared the good news about the success of the pastors and churches.

Because of his own illness, Geeting shortened their stay and started home, stopping for the night at an inn about thirty miles from Baltimore. He was unable to rest during the night and talked at length with his wife and Mrs. Snyder, the wife of the innkeeper, about the Christian's hope and immortality.

Shortly before morning he became silent. Then he said, "I feel as though my end has come. Hark! Hark! Who spoke? Who's voice is this I hear? Light! Light! What golden Light! Now all is dark again!" He asked to be helped from the bed. They did so. Then he sang a hymn. He prayed, giving thanks for God's abundant mercy toward him. Following the prayer he was helped into the bed, and in fifteen minutes he folded his hands and slipped away into eternity.[4]

For this founding father there remain three tributes: The United Brethren denomination, the Geeting Meeting House, and an inscription upon the gravestone in the cemetery hidden in the woods along the Little Antietam Creek.

George A. Geeting, Sen.
born in
Nassau SiegenLand
Neiderschelde, Germany
Feb. 6, 1741
& ended his Master's
labours & his life
June 28, 1812
Aged 71 yrs. 4 mo.
&22 days[5]

FOOTNOTES

[1]Spayth, p. 60.

[2]German Reformed Church, *Minutes and Letters of the Coetus: 1747-1792,* (Reformed Church Publication Board, 1903), p. 419.

[3]John H. Ness, Jr., *The Life of George Adam Geeting,* (A private publication by the Historical Society, Pennsylvania Conference, The Evangelical United Brethren Church, 1955), pp. 16-18.

[4]Spayth, pp. 129-131.

[5]Ness, p. 21.

8

PHILIP WILLIAM OTTERBEIN,
THIS MAN OF GOD

The Otterbeins, A Devout Family

Few families have equaled that of the Otterbeins for practical piety and service to the church. Charles Frederick Otterbein came to Dillenberg, Germany, in 1650, was appointed court trumpeter, married the daughter of Pastor Hitzfelt of Driedorf, and was a minister. His son, John Daniel, and a brother were ministers. Six grandsons and a brother-in-law were ministers. Four great-grandsons, who were children of John Henry, the oldest of John Daniel's sons, became ministers. Fourteen ministers in four generations is indeed a mark of distinction!

John Daniel was born September 6, 1696, in Herborn. A man of culture and learning, he was appointed principal of the Reformed Latin School in Dillenberg and was called to pastor the churches in Frohnhausen and Wissenbach. Valentine Arnold referred to him as "the right reverend and very learned John Daniel Otterbein."[1] The religious nature and devotion of John Daniel Otterbein is revealed in the baptismal register at Frohnhausen where he wrote: "I begin in the name of the Triune God and will continue this work to his honor, which must be the nature of all our private as well as public deeds and acts."[2]

He also gave expression to his spiritual devotion in the marriage register: "May the Truine God, to whom I have committed myself and all my possessions, grant that my beginning be pious, holy, and salutary, so that all my actions may redound to the honor of His name and the blessed edification of many."[3] Wilhelmina Otterbein, daughter of John Jacob Hoerlen, was a woman of rare spiritual and intellectual qualities. The wife of John Daniel Otterbein, she gave birth to ten children, seven living to adulthood and entering the service of the church.

An account of John Daniel and his family was printed in the Nassau *Chronicle* and *Vade Mecum* in 1802 by a Mr. Steubing:

> At Frohnhausen, in the principality of Dillenburg, the second quarter of the previous century, there was a minister who was much esteemed by his congregation.

> He was untiring in his efforts to fulfill the duties of his vocation; and in the circle of his family, which consisted of six sons and one daughter, he enjoyed every possible domestic happiness. Being formerly a teacher, he availed himself of every advantage by means of domestic instruction to prepare his sons for their future exalted career.

> His industry was so far rewarded that the oldest son was sent to the high school at Herborn, where he had already gained the confidence of his teachers, when death destroyed the father's well-conceived plans. The father died in 1742, without leaving any means, because the annual income was indeed not sufficient to meet even necessary expenses. The sufferings of the anxious widow were indescribable, yet they were not greater than her trust in God. She moved to Herborn because her sons could be educated much more cheaply there; and living was less expensive.[4]

Steubing's article continues with an account of Wilhelmina's sons, including Philip William:

> The following year already her oldest son received a charge from which he realized an amount equal to one-half of his father's salary. The family fared much better now. Four years later he received a parish. The second son, (Philip William), received a remunerative appointment by which he was able to assist in supporting the family and educating his younger brother. Six years later he went to a foreign land, where he was living after a number of years, happy and honored.[5]

The oldest son, John Henry, received his appointment at Herborn in 1744 when he was twenty-two years of age. In the following year he became vicar at the Reformed Church in Ockersdorf.

Philip William was educated at Herborn and appointed a teacher in 1748, six years after his father's death, when he was twenty-two years of age.

The third son, John Charles, was born May 14, 1728. He was a candidate for ordination in 1751, appointed a teacher at Herborn in 1752 and continued with the school to the end of his life. He was second pastor to the local church, co-rector of the school in 1780, and rector in 1790. He died May 4, 1807.

George Godfrey, the fourth son, was born January 14, 1731, and died September 10, 1800. He became pastor at Kecken in 1756 and at Duisburg in 1762. A widely read author, his works include three volumes on the *Heidelberg Catechism;* a book on practical Christianity; a book *Enoch* which he edited; a commentary on Romans; and textbooks for schools. Drury wrote of him:

> He was imbued with apostolic zeal, and was thoroughly convinced of the error of the spirit of his age. He stood associated with the leading minds of Germany. He felt the force of the course of events that ultimated in rationalism, but resisted with all his strength the on-rolling tide of ruin.[6]

John Daniel was born in 1736, completed his studies at Herborn by 1766, and was appointed a tutor in Berleburg in the same year. He became second pastor at Berleberg in 1771 and first pastor in 1795. J. Steven O'Malley stated in *The Pilgrimage of Faith:* "While George was waging his struggle in the cosmopolitan setting of Duisburg, a younger brother, Johann, was negotiating his way through the vagaries of sectarian Protestantism while serving as pastor in the relative isolation of tiny Wittgenstein-Berleburg."[7] He published a volume on the Heidleberg Catechism.[8]

The sixth son to live to maturity was Henry Daniel. He was born November 12, 1738, and died November 27, 1807. He pastored at Kecken, 1762, at Pfalzdorf, 1768, and at Mulheim on the Ruhr, 1771.

Some members of the Otterbein family who lived near Fulda emigrated to America and were established in various parts of the country.

William Otterbein, Teacher, Pastor, Missionary

Philip William Otterbein was born, June 3, 1726, in Dillenburg, Nassau, Germany. Although other dates have been suggested for his birth, this is the one entered in the Dillenberg church records and generally accepted. The records report:

> To John Daniel Otterbein, prime preceptor of the Latin School, and Mrs. Wilhelmina Henrietta (Otterbein) were born twins on the third of June early in the morning at two o'clock. The elder is a son, and the second is a daughter. Both were baptized on the sixth of June; godfather for the son was Philip

William Keller, steward to the court (and a close relative of the Otterbein family): the godmother of the second, the wife of Mr. John Martin Keller, butler to the court. The son was named Philip William and daughter Anna Margaret.[9]

The girl died in infancy. Philip William was educated by his father and in the schools in Herborn.

The Reformed school was a prominent institution of learning especially among the Protestants of Western Germany. Its distinctive was theological education. The school consisted of two sections—the paedagogium or gymnasium, which was made up of five classes and the academy. Students enrolled in the paedagogium studied two years and the subjects included: philsosophy, Greek and Roman literature, logic, mathematics, and history. After passing an examination on these subjects, the student entered the academy for a three-year course of study. These students were given the choice of medicine, jurisprudence, or theology.

Herborn was founded in 1584 by the leaders of the Reformed Church in the area. It has been described as an "academy," "seminary," "college," and "university." Drury wrote that it "approached, but did not entirely reach the standard of a university."[10] One of the first professors was Kaspar Olevianus (1536-1587), a teacher of theology and author of the *Heidelberg Catechism,* along with Zacharius Ursinus (1534-1583). Olevianus' service to the school was cut short by death after three years.

Moderate Calvinism described the theological position during the time William Otterbein was a student. The Pietistic influence was strong and many graduates carried the teachings and practices that were distinctive of this renewal movement to their pastorates and mission fields.

The educational situation at Herborn is described by Edwin H. Sponseller:

> The theological teachers during this period were John Henry Schramm, Valentine Arnold, and John Eberhardt Rau. Rau, who also had been born in Dillenburg, attained renown in oriental and rabbinical literature. The greatest influence exerted on Otterbein, however, came from Schramm and Arnold. Schramm was an apostle of the so-called *'Thaetige Christenthum,'* active Christianity. At Herborn he served as professor of practical divinity as well as being engaged in exegesis work. Schramm served one year as professor at Marburg, 1721-1722.[11]

Students in the academy were required to preach before their theological professors two times each week, and every Sunday afternoon a Bible study was held with one of them leading.[12]

Valentine Arnold showed special interest in William Otterbein because of his talents and spiritual dedication. A contributing factor to this concern may have been his friendship with William's father, the Reverend John Daniel Otterbein, who had also been a teacher and rector in the Latin school at Dillenberg. Because of Arnold's interest in the cause of missions, he was pleased to give his blessings and a recommendation to young William when he volunteered to accompany Michael Schlatter to America in 1752.

Following the completion of his course of study at Herborn, William (the name that both he and his family chose to use, rather than the given name Philip), went as a house-teacher in Burg, a "small dukedom lying northwest of Nassau about one hundred miles."[13] It is believed that he was a teacher in the family of a wealthy merchant in Elberfeld. He had not yet declared himself for the ministry, but it is evident that he was looking that way for this teaching experience was a step in that direction.

In 1748, at twenty-two years of age, he became a teacher in the Paedagogium at Herborn. To accept this position with his former instructors, he needed to pass an examination and take the rank and title of a candidate for the ministry. His examination was on May 6, 1748. He was approved by the faculty and was subsequently ordained in the city church at Dillenburg, June 13, 1749.

A translation of the ordination document which was presented to him in preparation for missionary service in the colonies follows:

To the Reader, Greeting:—

The reverend and very learned young man, Philip William Otterbein, from Dillenburg, in Nassau, a candidate of the holy ministry, and a teacher of the third class in this school, received of me, assisted by Cl. Arnold, professor and first pastor of the congregation at Herborn, and by the very Rev. Klingelhoefer, second pastor of the same church, on the 13th of June, 1749,—the rite of ordination by the laying on of hands, that he might perform the functions of vicar in the congregation at Ockersdorf. This I certify at his request; and to my much esteemed former hearer, who is now about to emigrate to foreign shores, I earnestly wish all good fortune and a prosperous voyage, and subscribe this letter as a testimonial of my neverfailing affection towards him.

JOHN HENRY SCHRAMM
Doctor of Theology and Superintendent
of the Church of Nassau, Herborn.

Seal

February 28, 1752[14]

William Otterbein assumed the duties of vicar at the Reformed Church in Ockersdorf in 1749 and preached frequently at the church in the small village of Burg. Ockersdorf, a town of about two hundred and fifty inhabitants was located about a mile and one half north of Herborn. Burg was about a ten minute walk from Ockersdorf. The duties included preaching once each Sunday at Ockersdorf, at a service on the first Wednesday of each month, on festival days, and a weekly prayer meeting. These prayer services reflect the Pietistic influence at Herborn. His position as preceptor required that he preach frequently in Herborn, since he was also considered a second pastor of the Reformed Church in that city.

Otterbein entered into his pastoral duties with energy and enthusiasm. This ministry was a forerunner of that which was developed more fully in America in the later years of his life. H. G. Spayth recorded the response of the villagers and friends:

> The zeal, the devotion, the earnestness, with which he met these new duties, suprised his friends, and astonished the hearers. In reproof he spared neither rank nor class . . . . While some approved and encouraged the young preacher, others would say—"No!"—such a sermon, such burning words, and from so young a minister . . . .

> His friends advised him to speak more cautiously, more calmly; to moderate his voice, his fervency, until he had become more exercised in the pulpit . . . . Opposition and clamor, however, had but a tendency to add force to his arguments, in directing his hearers from a cold formality, to the life and power of our holy religion . . . . Under preaching, some wept, in silence, till he himself could not suppress a tear. This increased the opposition, and the authority was privately solicited to arrest his preaching for a season; "Ah!" said his beloved mother, "I expected this, and give you joy. This place is too narrow for you, my son; they will not receive you here; you will find your work elsewhere." She was often heard to say, "My William will have to be a missionary, he is so frank, so open, so natural, so prophet like."

> "But missionary where? To what land, what people, mother, shall I go?"

> "Oh!" she would reply, "Be patient, preach us another sermon,—wait the Lord's time." And it came sooner than they could have wished.[15]

That call came through Michael Schlatter, a Reformed minister of St. Gall, Switzerland. Schlatter had returned from America in 1747 where he had been supervising the work of the German Reformed Churches under the sponsorship of the synods of North and South Holland. He was authorized to raise funds for support of the work and recruit young ministers to serve as missionary pastors.

Schlatter came to Herborn and issued a call for recruits. Six young men volunteered, among them Philip William Otterbein. He requested

testimonials regarding their fitness for this rugged work. Valentine
Arnold offered the following for Otterbein:

To the Reader, Greeting:—
The bearer of this, the truly reverend and very learned Mr. Philip William
Otterbein, an ordained candidate of the holy ministry, hitherto preceptor in this
paedagogium and now called as a preacher to Pennsylvania, was born June 4,
1726, in the morning between two and three o'clock, at Dillenburg, of honorable
parents belonging to the Evangelical Reformed Church and was baptized June
6.

His father was the right reverend and very learned Mr. John Daniel Otterbein,
formerly the highly esteemed rector of the Latin school at Dillenburg, but
afterwards a faithful, zealous preacher to the congregations at Frohnhausen and
Wissenbach, and who departed from time into eternity, November 16, 1742. His
mother is the right noble and very virtuous woman, Wilhelmina Henrietta, her
maiden name being Hoerlen. She is alive at this time as a widow. His godfather
was Mr. Philip William Keller, steward to the court of Nassau-Dillenburg, who
was a near relative.

The truly reverend Philip William Otterbein was well reared in the Reformed
Christian religion, and then received as a member of this church. He has always
lived an honest, pious, and Christian life; and not only by much preaching and
faithful declaring of the Word of God in this city as also at a near affiliating town
where he has been vicar for a considerable time, and at other places, but also by
his godly life, has he built up the church. Wherefore we do not doubt that he will
faithfully and fruitfully serve the church in Pennsylvania, to which he has been
called.

Therefore, to this end, we commend him to the protection of the Almighty,
whose care and leading we pray upon him; and we pray that he may give him
much grace from above, and the richest divine blessing in the work to which he
has been called, and to which he was so willing to go, and we wish him from the
bottom of our souls success. So done at Herborn, in the principality of Nassau-
Dillenburg, February 26, 1752.

V. ARNOLD
Professor and First Pastor[16]

The time had come for the fulfillment of his mother's premonitions
regarding his life's work. Informed of the plans and arrangements that
were being made, Wilhelmina Otterbein

. . . hastened to her closet, and after being relieved by tears and prayer she
returned strengthened, and taking her William by the hand and pressing that
hand to her bosom she said, 'Go; the Lord bless thee and keep thee. The Lord
cause his face to shine upon thee and with much grace direct thy steps. On earth I
may not see thy face again—but go.'[17]

He went with his mother's blessings, in the assurance of God's will for his future ministry.

Michael Schlatter and his band of young missionaries journeyed to Holland for their examinations, their outfits, and arrangements for passage. One of the six declined the appointment and turned back. He was replaced by a candidate from Burg, John Jacob Wissler. The other ministers were: William Stoy, John Waldschmidt, Theodore Frankenfeld, and John Casper Rubel.

After passing their examinations regarding theological, educational, and personal qualifications and delivering trial sermons, they were consecrated to missionary service. Those that had not yet been ordained received ordination by laying on of hands.

The band of missionaries sailed from Holland on April 15, 1752, and arrived in New York during the night of July 27 after a four month voyage. They were in the new world and prepared for missionary service.

Lancaster, 1752-1758

Michael Schlatter and his company proceeded on to Philadelphia after a brief stay in New York. A special meeting of the Coetus (conference) was held August 10-13. At this time Otterbein was recommended to the Lancaster congregation. A call was extended by the church and he accepted, with the understanding that he would serve them for a period of five years.

Lancaster was, next to Philadelphia, the most important settlement in the colony. There were five hundred homes and two thousand inhabitants. It was a respectable and wealthy place. The Reformed Church had been meeting in a large log building that would accommodate one hundred persons. It was constructed in 1736 in an area of almost unbroken forest.[18] The pulpit chairs, communion table, and some chairs that were used for pews in this log chapel were kept by the church and treasured for their historic value.

During Otterbein's pastorate a stone church was built, and the congregation prospered. His predecessors had left the church distracted and rent with divisions. His sincerity and enthusiasm were irresistible and the scattered elements were soon reunited. Although he brought order and discipline, there was no roll of church members, and there were irregularities. He desired to leave the pastorate in 1757 but consented to stay for one additonal year.

His success in the ministry of the church has been described by

Henry Harbaugh:

> Though the congregation at Lancaster had existed, with considerable prosper-
> ity, since 1736, it is evident that it was the labor, zeal, and influence of Mr.
> Otterbein, which, more than those of any previous pastor, gave it consolidation,
> firmness, and character. Previous to his time, its history was somewhat frag-
> mentary and weak. He was the instrument by which its strength was concen-
> trated and made permanent.[19]

During this pastorate in Lancaster, Otterbein experienced tensions,
pressures, and church problems that seemed to affect his spiritual life.
Although torn by conflict, he still preached with power. It is reported
that following one of his moving sermons on sin and the necessity of
repentance, a parishoner came to him asking for spiritual counsel. His
brief reply, "My friend, advice is scarce with me today,"[20] revealed some
of his own personal soul agony. It is believed that he found spiritual
power and personal peace following this event.

In later years a dear friend, Bishop Francis Asbury, asked Otterbein
a series of questions regarding his spiritual life and experience. Among
them was, "By what means were you brought to the gospel of God and
our Savior?" He replied, "By degrees was I brought to the knowledge of
the truth, while in Lancaster."[21]

The French and Indian War of 1754-1763 was in full progress while
Otterbein was at Lancaster. The Indians were encouraged in their
attacks upon the colonists, and, following Braddock's defeat in 1755,
panic gripped these frontier settlements. The Coetus meeting in Lancaster in 1757 set aside four days a year for fasting and prayer. William
Stoy, one of the six young men coming with Schlatter, wrote in a
Coetal letter in 1757:

> Cold horror shakes my body and an icy tremor runs through my very bones
> when I recall what I have seen myself . . . I have seen the savages slay the settlers
> and mutilate their bodies with tomahawks. They go and return unimpeded.[22]

At the meeting of the Coetus, June 8, 9, 1757, Otterbein discussed
the conditions existing in the Lancaster Church. The minutes record:

> (1) He declared he would not in the future bind himself to any congregation for a
> fixed time; (2) He complained of many grievances by which his mind during the
> time of his ministry had been vexed in various ways; (3) He desired that all
> disorderly customs be done away with as much as possible or changed in the
> future through the just and legitimate use of church discipline; (4) Finally he
> promised that if he be allowed to act in this matter according to the conviction of
> his conscience, and his hearers would obey them, he would further remain with
> them and discharge his pastoral office.[23]

The breach between the pastor and church was healed. The Coetus reported, "The congregation in Lancaster has not only promised to their pastor, whom they most earnestly longed to keep, the obedience owed, but also the desired correction."[24]

Otterbein atempted to improve the spiritual life of the congregation. He drew up a document in his own handwriting, which is still in the church records. It was signed by 80 men of the church. The text of this document follows:

> Inasmuch as for some time matters in our congregation have proceeded somewhat irregularly, and since we, in these circumstances, do not correctly know who they are that acknowledge themselves to be members of our church, especially among those who reside out of town, we, the minister and officers of this church, have taken this matter into consideration, and find it necessary to request that every one who calls himself a member of our church and who is concerned to lead a Christian life, should come forward and subscribe his name to the following rules of order:
>
> First of all, it is proper that those who profess themselves members should subject themselves to a becoming Christian church-discipline, according to the order of Christ and his apostles, and thus to show respectful obedience to ministers and officers in all things that are proper.
>
> Secondly: To the end that all disorder may be prevented, and that each member may be more fully known, each one, without exception, who desires to receive the Lord's supper, shall, previously to the preparation service, upon a day appointed for that purpose, personally appear before the minister, that an interview may be held.
>
> No one will, by this arrangement, be deprived of his liberty, or be in any way bound oppressively. This we deem necessary to the preservation of order; and it is our desire that God may bless it to this end. Whosoever is truly concerned to grow in grace will not hesitate to subscribe his name.[25]

This practice, which was rather common among churches influenced by Pietism, was continued in the church for seventy-five years. Although it had salutary effects on the congregation, there were those who considered it an attempt to introduce the Catholic practice of the confessional.[26]

During his pastorate at Lancaster, Otterbein was placed on committees of supply by the Coetus. This assignment made it necessary for him to conduct services in Reading, Conewago, York, and other appointments in the area. He was also given the honor of serving as chairman of the Coetus in 1757. He terminated his relationship with the Lancaster Church in October 1758, intending to visit his family in Germany. However, the French and Indian War made travel upon the Atlantic hazardous, and he postponed the trip.

Tulpehocken 1758-1760

The dangers of travel on the sea and the approach of winter made it advisable for Otterbein to accept a call to the Reformed Church at Tulpehocken.

The term Tulpehocken was applied to the settlement from the name of a creek that rises in Lebanon County, and flowing easterly empties into the Schuylkill at Reading. The name of the creek was itself derived from the name of a tribe of Indians. The settlement proper began in the eastern part of Lebanon County and extended twenty-two miles along Tulpehocken Creek to the vicinity of Reading. As the name of an old frontier community, the designation Tulpehocken was as well understood as that of Reading or Lancaster.[27]

The church continues today and is known as the Tulpehocken Trinity United Church of Christ. It is located about three miles east of Myerstown, Pennsylvania.

The church dates back to 1727 when John Philip Boehm began ministering in the community. It was organized in 1748 and was a prosperous church when Otterbein arrived. He ministered to the Reformed congregations at Host and Kimmerlings at the same time.

During his Tulpehocken pastorate, Otterbein increased the evangelistic practices that were distinctive of his ministry in later years. They seemed to be strange to his congregation but were common among the Pietists in Germany. His labors had a deep and lasting effect on many in the community.

Spayth gave details of Otterbein's pastoral ministry:

Not content with preaching on the Sabbath only, he made it his duty between the Sabbath days, to visit the families who attended his preaching, converse with them on religion, advise, admonish, reprove or encourage and cheer, as circumstances would demand; and then to sing and pray before leaving the house, Next to this, he would hold meetings on evenings in the week. On these occasions, his custom was to read a portion of Scripture—make some practical remarks on the same, and exhort all present, to give place to serious reflections. He would then sing a sacred hymn, and invite all by kneeling, to accompany him in prayer. At first and for some time, but few, if any, would kneel, and he was left to pray alone. This item in the history, although small, affords a glimpse of the low state of religion, and the moral darkness, united with ignorance, he had to contend with. After prayer, he would endeavor to gain access to their hearts, by addressing them individually, with words of tenderness and love.[28]

Although there was confusion, and even opposition to his innovations, many Reformed Church members and residents in the community became ardent supporters of Otterbein and his deeper spiritual ministry. Later several families became associated with the United Brethren Church. They included: the Kumlers, Browns, and Shueys. Their contributions to the church have been memorable. Records in the Tulpehocken Church listed William Otterbein as pastor from 1758 through 1764. The obvious reasons for this discrepancy in the record is that although he moved to Frederick, Maryland, in 1760 to pastor the Reformed Church in that community, the Tulpehocken Church did not find a replacement until 1764.

Frederick 1760-1765

Otterbein rejected a call to the Frederick, Maryland, Reformed Church in 1759. When the call was renewed a year later, the Coetus and the Synod of Holland urged him to make the move. In the fall of 1760 he transferred. Frederick, during this period of time was considered a frontier town, being somewhat off the main thoroughfare. The German population was growing rapidly and the Reformed congregation was "large and full of life, being made up of thrifty, substantial people."[29]

The congregation prospered both spiritually and materially during Otterbein's pastorate. "The congregation embarked on an extensive building program—a stone parsonage in 1761 and the 'third house of worship' in 1763 . . . . The house of worship built during Otterbein's pastorate was on the site where the Trinity Reformed Chapel now stands. 'The original stone walls of the tower on which the steeple rests, were built at that time, and are as firm and secure today as when first constructed.' "[30]

The Frederick church history recorded:

> Our third pastor, Reverend Philip William Otterbein, was to become the most widely known of Frederick Reformed ministers. Within his own denomination he was and remains a controversial figure, though not in a deprecatory sense; for in Baltimore, and interdenominationally, he won prominence . . . . From the earliest years of his ministry in Lancaster all through his long life he was an eminently respected and popular Reformed minister. This is attested to by many calls to churches which he received before he became stablished firmly in Baltimore in 1774.[31]

Otterbein's involvement in the revival movement had a deep impact upon the Frederick Church. He gave special emphasis to intimate personal religious experiences. He often held prayer meetings, somewhat along the line of the "little churches within the church" of the

Pietists in Germany. Many of his parishoners identified them with the practices of Whitefield's English preachers and later with Methodists. This labeling created a conflict between Reformed Church members who supported traditional church practices and Otterbein's followers.

The conflict grew in intensity:

> At one period, the excitment became so great that a majority of the church determined on his summary dismission; and to effect it most speedily, they locked the church door against him. On the following Sabbath, when the congregation assembled, his adherents, knowing that he had a legal right to the pulpit were disposed to force the door; but he said to them—'Not so, brethren, If I am not permitted to enter the church peaceably, I can and will preach here in the graveyard.' So saying, he took his stand upon one of the tombstones, proceeded with the regular introductory services in his usual fervent spirit, delivered a sermon of remarkable power, and, at its close, announced preaching for the same place on the succeeding Sabbath. At the time appointed, an unusually large concourse assembled, and as he was about to commence the services again under the canopy of the heavens, the person who had the key of the church door, hastily opened it, saying, 'Come in, come in! I can stand this no longer.' But this was not the only, or the last instance in which the doors of Reformed churches were locked against him.[32]

His predecessor at Frederick, John Steiner preached at neighboring communities in Maryland, Virginia, and Pennsylvania. No doubt Otterbein began his itinerant ministry at this time.

William Otterbein was married to Miss Susan LeRoy on April 19, 1762, in the Lancaster Reformed Church with the Reverend William Stoy officiating. He was nearly thirty-six years old and she twenty-six years of age. Miss LeRoy, one of five attractive daughters of the clockmaker on North Queen Street, had come with her family to Lancaster in 1754. Her family was of French Huguenot descent and had fled France when the Edict of Nantes was revoked by Louis XIV in 1685.[33] It is believed that her sister, Salome, during the French and Indian War, hearing the express rider hurrying through the streets of Lancaster and fearing an attack by the Indians, ran to the church and rang the alarm bell calling the frightened citizens together. Another of Susan's sisters, Elizabeth, married William Hendel, a close friend of William Otterbein and also a pastor of the Lancaster church. Salome married Charles Hall, a prominent figure in the Revolution and goldsmith. Anna Maria, who was reported to be a superior clockmaker, married Wilton Atkinson, a miller.

Otterbein received calls to pastor at Reading, Oley, and Philadelphia while ministering in Frederick. He declined each of these calls because of a feeling of obligation to the pastorate in Frederick. His correspondence with the Philadelphia church has been kept, and Drury recorded these letters in full in his *History of the United Brethren in Christ.* They revealed much of Otterbein's attitude, spirit, and character.[34]

York, 1765-1774

When an invitation came from the York congregation in 1765, he accepted the call. He transferred to the new location in September of that year. The town known as Little York in its early days was laid out in 1741. It grew rapidly and in ten years there were at least one hundred ninety houses. By the time of the arrival of the Otterbeins, it was a lively settlement, the chief city in Pennsylvania west of the Susquehanna River.

Three significant events occurred while Otterbein pastored at York. First was his attendance at a "great meeting" which was held at the Isaac Long home, located about nine miles north of Lancaster on Whitsunday, 1767. There is no definite record of the year when this event occurred. However, it is believed that it was held sometime between 1766 and 1768. Hence the year 1767 is generally accepted.

"Great Meetings" *(grosse Versammlung)* had become accepted religious and social events among the German colonists. An announcement would be issued with an invitation to meet at a home, grove, or barn and large numbers would assemble, usually for at least three days. They would spend the nights in neighboring homes, in barns, or in temporary shelters. Several ministers would preach or exhort and considerable excitement attended the events with intense confrontations between believers and antagonists.

Otterbein accepted an invitation to attend a meeting in Isaac Long's barn which had been arranged by Martin Boehm. Deeply moved by the sermon given by the farmer preacher, he arose at the close of the message and enfolded Boehm in his arms and cried aloud so that all could hear *"Wir sind Brüder!"* It is said that the sight of a formal Reformed clergyman and the simple Mennonite pastor engaged in a spiritual union moved the large crowd to tears. Some shouted their praise to God and all were melted into one. *This event brought together two noble men and launched a friendship that lasted throughout their lives. Its result was the formation of the Church of the United Brethren in Christ in 1800.* The barn where this historic event took place still stands and is used by descendents of the Long family. It is a visual reminder of the heritage of the church and its roots in colonial America.

Susan Otterbein's death on April 17, 1768, was a second critical event in Otterbein's life while he was pastor of the York Reformed Church. There were no children of the marriage and Otterbein never remarried. His love for his bride of six years is attested by a tradition that a few days before his death he requested a friend to bring him a pocketbook that had been made by the hands of his young wife. It is said that he gazed lovingly at the prized keepsake and then kissed it tenderly.

The third memorable event in the York pastorate was a return visit to his family and friends in Germany eighteen years after his departure for missionary service in 1752. Leaving in April 1770, he arrived in his homeland in late spring. He stopped first in Duisburg on his way to Herborn, where he visited his brother George Godfrey Otterbein. William told him of his spiritual pilgrimage and how he had come to a full assurance of salvation. George Godfrey listened intently:

> . . . rising from his chair embraced his brother, and as tears streamed down his cheeks said, "My dear William, we are now, blessed be the name of the Lord, not only brothers after the flesh, but also after the spirit. I have also experienced the same blessing. I can testify that God has power on earth to forgive sins and to cleanse from all unrighteousness."
>
> . . . My dear brother, I have a very strong impression that God has a great work for you to do in America.[35]

William visited other members of his family and in several instances ministered to their congregations. The most tender and moving of all was the time spent with his mother and John Charles at Herborn. He relived the joyous days of childhood, the stimulating experiences of school life at the university, his service as a teacher in the paedagogium, and his first pastorate at Ockersdorf and Burg.

Late in the winter of 1771 William took leave of his family, a very emotional experience. He would see his aged mother no more; she died seven years later. Although his brothers lived until 1800 and longer, he never returned to his native land, nor did they come to America. Once again he sailed from Holland and came to his adopted home. He resumed pastoral work at York where he was greatly loved and respected. He also renewed his itinerant ministry to the scattered settlements in Pennsylvania and Maryland.

Baltimore, 1774-1813

On May 4, 1774, Philip William Otterbein accepted a call to be pastor of Howard's Hill, a new Reformed congregation in Baltimore, Maryland. This congregation was the result of a division in the First Reformed Church of that city. First church had experienced conflicts, problems, and differences that resulted in a split that was never healed. A number of the members were influenced by the Pietistic revival movement which had come to prominence among the German settlers. They rejected cold formalism, unspiritual life, and what they considered immoral practices of many church members. They accused the pastor, John C. Faber, of being "not earnest enough in his conduct, and not energetic and active enough in his ministry."[36]

The dissenting group in the First Reformed Church was encouraged by a lay preacher, Benedict Schwope (1730-1810), who was associated with the Pipe Creek Reformed Church, about twenty miles northwest of Baltimore, near present day Westminister. Earlier in 1770, when Schwope had applied to the Coetus for ministerial standing, he had been opposed by Pastor Faber who was also without ministerial standing. The Coetus investigated their differences but was unable to produce a reconciliation. The revival group, led by Schwope, withdrew in early 1771 and immediately purchased lots on Howard's Hill near the waterfront. They erected a structure and began holding services in October 1771.

The Coetus continued efforts to achieve reconciliation without success. As a result, Faber resigned his pastorate at the First Reformed Church.

Although Schwope declared his willingness to leave the Howard's Hill pastorate in 1773, he did not until 1774. In the meantine Schwope was approved by the Coetus for ordination and became an active member of the Reformed Church Coetus for several years.

The Howard's Hill congregation and Schwope were acquainted with William Otterbein and found in him a kindred spirit. The Howard's Hill Church extended a call to him in 1773 when it appeared that Schwope would resign the church. The call was declined. Further appeals were made to Otterbein and he indicated that he would be willing to accept if the Coetus would approve. The Coetus declined, believing that William Hendel would be better able to accomplish a reconciliation between the churches. The First Reformed Church refused to accept Hendel and conditions did not improve.

In the spring of 1774 the Howard's Hill congregation renewed their call to William Otterbein, and he accepted without the approval of the

Coetus. He was given a mild censure and he wrote a letter to the Coetus stating that he felt at "liberty to accept a congregation according to his conscience, when, if not to the many, yet to a few, it may be regarded a means of edification."[37] The die was cast and Otterbein started a ministry that was to last thirty-nine and one-half years, until his death November 17, 1813. He was forty-eight years of age when he moved to Baltimore, in the prime of his life and ministry.

Benedict Schwope had become acquainted with Francis Asbury soon after Asbury arrived in America. Pleased to find one also interested in evangelical interests, he enlisted Asbury's help in influencing Otterbein's acceptance of the Howard's Hill church. Asbury entered in his journal on February 3, 1774, "This day I wrote a letter to Mr. Otterbein, a German minister, relative to settling in Baltimore town." Later he wrote, "Mr. Schwope came to consult me in respect to Mr. Otterbein's coming to this town. We agreed to promote his settling here."[38]

One month after Otterbein's arrival in Baltimore, Asbury entered the following statement in his journal, "June 4, 1774. Had a friendly [dialogue] with Mr. Otterbein and Mr. Schwope, the German ministers, respecting the plan of Church discipline on which they intend to proceed. They agreed to imitate our methods as nearly as possible."[39] Thus was begun a long and intimate friendship between two eminent churchmen, one German, one English, one Reformed, one Anglican. Their love, respect, and esteem for each other continued without abatement until the death of Otterbein. During the Methodist conference in Baltimore in March 1814, Asbury spoke in the Howard's Hill church. He reported this experience:

> By request, I discoursed on the character of the angel of the Church of Philadelphia, in allusion to P. W. Otterbein—the holy, the great Otterbein, whose funeral discourse it was intended to be. Solemnity marked the silent meeting in the German Church, where were assembled the members of our conference, and many of the clergy of the city. Forty years have I known the retiring modesty of this man of God; towering majestic above his fellows in learning, wisdom, and grace, yet seeking to be known only of God and the people of God; he had been sixty years a minister, fifty years a converted one.[40]

At Howard's Hill, Otterbein's ministry in Baltimore was attended with success. Favorable response from the Coetus is indicated in its minutes of May 11, 1775:

> After mature deliberations, the Coetus finds it advisable that Do. [Pastor] Otterbein continue his work in the congregation in Baltimore. It appears from his report that he labors with blessing and that the opposing party is becoming quiet.[41]

Even so, the church grew slowly at first because of the tensions of the Revolutionary War and the conflict with the old congregation.

One year after Otterbein's arrival the old building was either enlarged or replaced. By 1785 it became necessary for the congregation to erect a new structure of brick and stone. This is the building that remains to the present day. It is sixty-five feet long and forty-eight feet wide. An impressive high steeple was added at a later date. A small parsonage was built at about the same time. It is believed that Otterbein contributed a large portion of the cost of the church structure which was six thousand dollars.

The pastor and church felt a need for stability, strength, and a legal position for the congregation. In 1785 a book of order was prepared entitled *The Church Book of the Evangelical Reformed Church*. This material dealt with the organization of the congregation, the responsibilities of members and pastors, the moral and spiritual character of members including qualifications for participation in the sacraments, the establishment and maintenance of a German school, pastoral duties, and the duties of elders, deacons, and an almoner. It provided for ministry to associate churches in Pennsylvania, Maryland, and Virginia; legal arrangements for conveying property and other rights; suspension of members for immorality; resolving of conflicts in the church; and annual services for business and reading of the constitution and ordinances before the entire church each New Year's Day.

This document made it evident that Otterbein and the church had adopted a moderate Calvinistic position. In particular they rejected the traditional Reformed teachings of predestination and the impossibility of falling from grace (Article 13). The ecumenical spirit of openness to Christians of other persuasions was apparent. Article 6 read, "Persons expressing a desire to commune with us at the Lord's table, although they have not been members of our church, shall be admitted by consent of the Vestry."[42] Article 7 continued this position of openness to persons of other denominations.

These teachings by Otterbein and his followers brought them into conflict with several ministers in the Coetus. Nicholas Pomp, pastor of the First Reformed Church in Baltimore, led the opposition by writing a letter to church officials in Holland. He claimed that Otterbein was in error regarding his teachings about predestination and had been divisive in his ministry in Baltimore.

Otterbein responded with a letter to the deputies in Holland, June 15, 1788. He described the conflicts in the First Reformed Church, the division, the establishment of the Howard's Hill Evangelical Reformed Church, and his personal relationship to that congregation. He then explained his position regarding predestination. He wrote, ". . . to tell the truth I cannot side with Calvin in this case."[43] He was not censured by the Synods or the Coetus, remaining in the Coetus throughout his long life. His congregation on Howard's Hill kept a relationship with the Reformed Coetus for a number of years, perhaps as long as Otterbein lived. This relationship appeared to have become fragile when attacks upon their pastor were continued by the Reverend Christian L. Becker, pastor of the First Reformed Church of Baltimore. Becker succeeded in having Geeting expelled in 1804 but failed in his attack upon Otterbein.

Historical records do not show a formal separation from the Reformed Church by either Otterbein or his church in Baltimore during his lifetime. There is evidence of independent action by both that resulted in the church's eventual separation from the Synod. They include the formal association with the independent evangelical churches in Virginia, Maryland and Pennsylvania as recognized in the church constitution of 1784; a growing interchurch fellowship with other pastors and churches including the Methodists; a decreasing involvement in the Coetus and its activities; and the ordination of Christian Newcomer, Joseph Hoffman, and Frederick Schaffer— ministers of the United Brethren Church—without consent or approval of the Reformed Church.

The Supreme Court of the State of Maryland issued its opinion in 1846 that the Howard's Hill church was independent and held legal rights to its property. This ruling also confirmed its position with the United Brethren Church which had supplied its pastors from the time of Otterbein. Howard's Hill continued its relationship with the United Brethren, the Evangelical United Brethren, and is now considered one of the historic sites of the United Methodist Church. It is also the oldest church structure in the city of Baltimore.

The church property was purchased by a board of trustees as individual members and they retained the right to pass their interest on to their legal heirs. The congregation adopted its own constitution and by-laws and operated in what may be considered an independent congregational manner. They were considered Presbyterian in church polity. The official name of the church was "The German Evangelical Reformed Church." By using the name "Reformed" it was identified with the historic church. But the inclusion of "Evangelical" indicated an association with the revival movement.

William Otterbein's official church relationships were unusual. He retained throughout his life a loyalty to the Reformed Church of his family and childhood. He continued that relationship through his long

ministry of more than sixty years while ministering as a pioneer
preacher in the colonies and the new nation, the United States of
America. He is considered a leader among the founding fathers of the
Church of the United Brethren in Christ. His eminence as a preacher
and his administrative and organizational abilities have given him the
honor of being its first bishop.

Pipe Creek Conferences

An evidence of this growing interest in evangelical activities and
practices was verified in a discovery of the records of a series of
meetings with other Reformed ministers. These meetings were held in
1774-1776 and are called the Pipe Creek Conferences because the
minutes of the meetings were found at the Pipe Creek Reformed
Church about one hundred years after they were held. Six of the
twenty ministers associated with the Coetus joined together as "United
Ministers" to promote evangelical interests. The chairman was William Otterbein and the secretary was Benedict Schwope. Other ministers involved were: Jacob Weymer of Hagerstown, Frederick L.
Henop of Frederick, Daniel Wagner of York, and William Hendel of
Tulpehocken.

These meetings gave special emphasis to the function of class meetings in the churches. They were held for prayer, singing of hymns, Bible
study, and spiritual encouragement. Special attention was given to
family worship and harmony in the churches. Perhaps the most controversial action was granting Henry Weidner a license to preach on
June 4, 1776. This action was generally reserved to the Coetus. It may
have been a divisive event since one man present did not sign the
document.

There is no record of further meetings. This may be attributed to the
possible disagreement between the members regarding its authority to
grant a license to preach. Another factor that certainly was influential
was the Revolutionary War which started within weeks of the last
recorded meeting. It disrupted all social and religious activities for the
next six years.

The First Conferences

The evangelical movement among the Germans focused on the
"great meetings" for a number of years. They were interdenomina-

tional in nature and had existed for some time before the meeting of Otterbein and Boehm at Isaac Long's barn. Samuel Huber described them in his *Autobiography:*

> It was no uncommon thing then, for a brother farmer to give out an appointment for a "big meeting" to be held at his house. And it was expected, as a matter of course, that the people attending it should have something to eat while there. For this reason, provision for the people and provender for the horses, were prepared in sufficient quantities to meet the wants of the expected assemblage. It was not considered a strange thing among United Brethren, for the brother at whose house the meeting was held, to slaughter a few hogs, sheep, or calves, and, on extra occasions, a beef; and to have a quantity of bread—cakes—and pies baked, with bushels of potatoes and other vegetables ready for use.
>
> In addition to these preparations, one indispensable item in the farmer's utensils needed for such an occasion, was a large table, from ten to twenty feet in length, and from four to five feet in breadth. The top of it was made of good old tough oak or pine boards, from one to two inches in thickness. These were placed upon a frame, supported by feet made of oak or pine scantling, from three to four inches square. This table was then decorated with pewter and earthen dishes, with cups and saucers of the latter material, pewter spoons, iron knives and forks, together with large pewter and earthen dishes and bowls, which were placed on the center, as receptacles for eatables, and out of which the consumers were supplied.
>
> These "big meetings" were attended by crowds of people. Some came from a great distance. The hosts at whose houses the meetings were held, were not SCARED, when they saw carriages, wagons and vehicles of all sizes, then in use, drawn by four legged animals and loaded with saints and sinners coming to the meetings. Some came to see and be seen; others, to hear preaching. In many instances, from one to two hundred persons were entertained and fed during the meeting, together with their horses.[44]

These meetings were especially interesting to the preachers. Not only did they demonstrate their pulpit abilities, they heard other preachers and learned from them theology and the teachings of the Bible. They gave opportunities for counsel between ministers. It was during these meetings that Otterbein and Boehm outlined the responsibilities of ministers and systematic procedures for the work of the new churches.

Because of the growing need for supervision and organization, a conference for ministers was issued. It was held at the home of William Otterbein in Baltimore in 1789. The preachers attending were William Otterbein, Martin Boehm, George A. Geeting, Christian Newcomer, Adam Lehman, John Ernst, and Henry Weidner. Those associated with the movement, but absent, were Benedict Schwope, Henry Baker, Simon Herre, Frederick Schaffer, Martin Kreider, Christopher Grosh, and Abraham Draksel.

A second conference was convened in 1791 at the home of John Spangler in Paradise Township, York County, Pennsylvania. Three preachers absent from the first meeting were in attendance. They were J. G. Pfrimmer, John Neidig, and Benjamin Sauder. John Ernst was absent making a total attendance of nine ministers. No formal report of the proceedings is available. It may be assumed that instructions were given about class meetings, family worship, Bible teaching, and prayer. Although the constitution of Otterbein's church in Baltimore was available and the discipline and rules of the Methodists were well-known, these men did not establish a formal organization or provide for church membership. These two conferences prepared the preachers for the first organizing conference of the united fellowship in 1800. There were quite possibly other informal meetings of the ministers in the intervening years but no record of them is available, if they occurred.

Otterbein and Asbury

Francis Asbury and William Otterbein became intimate friends. This is indicated by an entry in *Asbury's Journal,* Tuesday, June 18, 1776. He wrote, "Returned on Wednesday to Baltimore, and spent some time with Mr. Otterbein. There are few with whom I can find so much unity and freedom in conversation as with him."[45]

Later he wrote, "I have had an agreeable conversation with my Mr. O., Maryland, January 27, 1777."[46] This friendship was especially meaningful to Asbury. The Revolutionary War was in progress; therefore, his English citizenship and relationship to the Anglican Church made him suspect in the colonies.

Asbury weathered the conflicts of the War of Independence and led the Methodists as they established their independence from English supervision in 1784. The conference where this was accomplished was held at the Lovely Lane Church in Baltimore. The sessions began on December 24 with Thomas Coke presiding. Following adoption of a resolution creating the Methodist Episcopal Church in the United States, Asbury and Coke were elected superintendents. A footnote in Asbury's *Journal* recorded:

On Christmas Day, the second day of the conference, Asbury was ordained deacon by Coke, assisted by Whatcoat and Vasey; the following day he was ordained elder; and on Monday, December 27, he was consecrated superintendent. William Philip Otterbein, a German minister and Asbury's friend, assisted in the consecration service. Nearly sixty preachers were present.[47]

A bit of humor can be found in the relationship of Otterbein and Asbury. Drury recorded that Asbury had written some verses of poetry which he showed to Otterbein for his evaluation:

Mr. Otterbein examined the verses carefully, and when Mr. Asbury asked him for his opinion, he replied: 'Bruder Asbury, I don't tink you was porn a boet." This honest expression was sufficient, and saved Mr. Asbury from having attached to his great reputation as a bishop the unenviable reputation of being the author of bad poetry.[48]

On Sunday, June 20, 1784, Asbury reported in his journal, "I attempted to preach at Newton. I raged and threatened the people, and was afraid it was spleen [rancor or ill humor]. I found, however, that Mr. O., a worthy German minister, had done the same a little time before."[49] These men recognized weaknesses and failures in their ministry.

William Otterbein, Man and Preacher

William Otterbein was distinguished in appearance. His manners and conduct commanded respect in both formal and informal situations. Henry Boehm, wrote in his *Reminiscences:*

In person he was tall, being six feet high, with a noble frame and a commanding appearance. He had a thoughtful, open countenance, full of benignity, a dark-bluish eye that was very expressive. In reading the lessons he used spectacles, which he would take off and hold in his left hand while speaking. He had a high forehead, a double chin, with a beautiful dimple in the center. His locks were gray, his dress parsonic.[50]

He lived a simple life in the parsonage in Baltimore. It was a small cottage of four rooms and stood close to the street near the church. He possessed a good library and spent much time in it. His knowledge of Latin was extensive, and he was familiar with Greek and Hebrew. He published no books and few of his works are available.

Among his works and letters extant is a sermon on Hebrews 2:14-15. The subject was "The Salvation—Bringing Incarnation and Glorious Victory of Jesus Christ Over the Devil and Death." It was preached in 1760 and printed by Christopher Sauer in 1763. It was a message dealing with salvation as provided by Christ's death, offering a new birth, and eternal life.[57]

Several letters writtern by Otterbein have been preserved. They were written to fellow pastors, elders in the church at Philadelphia, the deputies in Holland, a nephew, a former parishioner, and a cousin. His pastoral spirit, love, and compassion were revealed in these letters. His generosity and unselfish acts were common knowledge among neighbors, friends, and church members in Baltimore. The Howard's Hill Church was a beneficiary of his love and generosity both in life and at death. For some reason, perhaps known only to himself, it was reported that all his personal papers and notes were burned. According to Drury, John Hildt reported that this burning occurred in his presence during the last year of Otterbein's life.[52]

Otterbein preached with power and compassion. His sermons were filled with doctrine and Bible references. They were expository in the noblest sense. They were moving and unforgettable. Spayth wrote:

> While treating on the responsibilities of the ministerial office tears flowed in abundance,—preachers and people wept together. The discourse left impressions not soon to be forgotten.[53]

Thomas Winters, an early associate in the United Brethren movement and also a Reformed minister, related his impressions of Otterbein's preaching: "His preaching was sharp and powerful. He was a great friend of revivals, but of his own kind; he would have no noise; this he never could bear."[54]

Otterbein held a sacramental meeting (communion service) at Geeting's home along the Antietam on May 19 and 20, 1804.

> Father Otterbein was present, and preached on Saturday, from Isaiah 51:7, 8. On the Sabbath Bro. Otterbein preached again, from Psalms 72, with his usual energy, perspicuity, and divine power. Under preaching, and at the communion table, tears of sorrow and joy flowed abundantly, and the wells of salvation furnished a rich supply.[55]

The Revival Becomes a Movement

The awakening spread rapidly among the Germans living in Pennsylvania, Maryland, and Virginia. With William Otterbein and Martin Boehm as leaders, other men were willing to follow and devote their energies to it. Both Otterbein and Boehm inspired and moved congregations wherever they went.

Otterbein urged converts to remain with their own churches, if possible. It is reported that he often said, "I ask you not to leave your Church, I only ask you to forsake your sins."[56] Although Boehm was excommunicated from the Mennonite church early in his ministry, he did not affiliate with any other church until 1802 when he united with the Methodist church in his community.

The converts of this movement often met for fellowship and instruction. There was a spirit of unity among them that transcended denominational relations. There was love and mutual support. This spirit inspired the pastors to seek for ways to encourage and strengthen their efforts. A conference was held at the home of Peter Kemp near Frederick, Maryland, September 25 and 26, 1800. Since this meeting was the formal beginning of the Church of the United Brethren in Christ, its story will be the introduction to the next division of this history.

FOOTNOTES

[1]Drury, p. 47.

[2]Ibid., p. 32.

[3]Ibid.

[4]Ibid., pp. 32, 33.

[5]Ibid., p. 33.

[6]Ibid., p. 34.

[7]J. Steven O'Malley, *Pilgrimage of Faith: The Legacy of the Otterbeins* (Metuchen, NJ: The Scarecrow Press, Inc., 1973), p. 97.

[8]Daniel Berger, *History of the Church of the United Brethren in Christ* (Dayton, OH: United Brethren Publishing House, 1897), p. 25.

[9]Drury, *History*, p. 29.

[10]Drury, p. 36.

[11]Edwin H. Sponseller, *Crusade for Education* (Frederick, MD: Private Publication, 1950), p. 8.

[12]Drury, pp. 36.

[13]Ibid., p. 41.

[14]Berger, p. 31.

[15]Spayth, pp. 19, 20.

[16]Drury, pp. 47, 48.

[17]Spayth, p. 21.

[18]Elizabeth Clarke Kieffer, *Annals of the First Reformed Church* (Lancaster, PA: United Church of Christ, 1961), p. 5.

[19]Henry Harbaugh, *Fathers of the German Reformed Church in Europe and America* (Lancaster, PA: Springer and Westhaeffer, 1857), p. 57.

[20]Drury, *History*, p. 57.

[21]Ibid., p. 249.

[22]Kieffer, p. 13.

[23]*Minutes and Letters of the Coetus of the German Reformed Congregations in Pennsylvania: 1747-1792.* (Philadelphia, PA: Reformed Church Publishing Board, 1903) pp. 154, 155.

[24]Kieffer, p. 155.

[25]Drury, p. 56.

[26]Kieffer, p. 13.

[27]Drury, p. 68.

[28]Spayth, pp. 23, 24.

[29]Paul Rodes Koontz and Walter Edwin Roush, *The Bishops* 2 vols. (Dayton, OH: The Otterbein Press, 1950), 1:61.

[30]James B. and Dorothy Ranck, Margaret Motter and Katharine Dutrow, *History of the Evangelical Reformed Church, Frederick, Maryland* (Private Publication, 1964), pp. 36, 37.

[31]Ibid., pp. 34, 35.

[32]John Lawrence, *History of the Church of the United Brethren in Christ* 2 vols, (Dayton, OH: Sowers & King, 1861), 1:178, 179.

[33]King Henry IV of France issued an Edict at Nantes in 1598 defining the rights of French Protestants. It included full liberty of conscience, the privilege of private worship and public worship which were previously permitted, full civil rights, and royal subsidies for Protestant schools. Louis XIV declared that the majority of Protestants had converted to Catholicism and thus the Edict of Nantes was unnecessary. It was revoked in 1685 and repression and persecution of the Protestants flourished. Thousands fled abroad to escape the systematic destruction of their homes and lives, and several provinces were practically depopulated.

[34]Drury, *History*, p. 81.

[35]Ibid., p. 93.

[36]German Reformed Church, *Minutes*, p. 296.

[37]Ibid., p. 345.

[38]Francis Asbury, *The Journal and Letters of . . . .*, ed. Elmer clark, Editor-in-Chief, 3 vol. (London, England: Published jointly by Epworth Press and Nashville, TN: Abingdon Press, 1958), 1:105.

[39]Ibid., p. 114.

[40]Ibid., 2:753, 754.

[41]German Reformed Church, *Minutes*, p. 350.

[42]Drury, *History*, p. 125.

[43]Arthur C. Core, *Philip William Otterbein, Pastor, Ecumenist* (Dayton, OH: Board of Publication, The Evangelical United Brethren Church, 1968), p. 100.

[44]Samuel Huber, *Autobiography of the Rev. Samuel Huber, Elder of the Church of the United Brethren in Christ* (Chambersburg, PA: Printed by M. Kieffer & Co., 1858), pp. 212-214.

[45]Asbury, 1:190.

[46]Ibid., p. 229.

[47]Ibid., p. 474.

[48]Drury, *History*, p. 147.

[49]Asbury, 1:460, 461.

[50]Henry Boehm, *Reminiscences*, ed. Joseph B. Wakeley (New York: Carlton and Porter, 1895), p. 391.

[51]P. William Otterbein, "The Salvation—Bringing Incarnation and Glorious Victory Over the Devil and Death," in Arthur C. Core, *Philip William Otterbein, Pastor, Ecumenist* (Dayton, OH: Board of Publication Evangelical United Brethren Church, 1968), pp. 77-90. A sermon discovered by Mrs. Lucretia Mueller, Muncie, Indiana, in 1966. Translated by the Rev. Erhart Long.

[52]Drury, *History*, p. 226.

[53]Spayth, p. 87.

[54]Harbaugh, pp. 143-145.

[55]Spayth, p. 103.

[56]Harbaugh, p. 144.

DISTINGUISHED CHURCH LEADERS
ON THE CONTINENT

John Huss
1373-1415
Bohemia
Forerunner of
Reformation
Martyr

Martin Luther	Ulrich Zwingli	Conrad Goebel
1483-1546	1484-1531	c. 1498-1526
Germany	Switzerland	Switzerland
Founder of	Founder of the	Leader of Ana-
Lutheran Church	Reformed Church	baptist movement

Philip Melancthon	John Calvin	Menno Simons
1497-1560	1509-1563	1496-1561
Germany	France and	France and Friesland
Lutheran	Switzerland	Leader of
Theologian	Reformed Theologian	Mennonite movement

Philipp J. Spener	August Herman Francke
1635-1705	1663-1727
France and Germany	Germany
Lutheran	Lutheran
Leader of Pietistic	Leader of Pietistic
movement	movement

Count Nicholas L. von Zinzendorf
1700-1760
Germany - Saxon
Lutheran
Leader of Moravians

DISTINGUISHED CHURCH LEADERS OF THE COLONIES AND UNITED STATES

Theodorus J. Frelinghuysen
1691-1747
Holland and Colonies
Reformed

Heinrich M. Muhlenberg
1711-1787
Germany and Colonies
Leader and organizer of
Lutherans

Jonathan Edwards
1703-1758
Massachusetts
Congregational Church

George Whitefield
(see Great Britain)

Francis Asbury
1745-1816
England and Colonies
Pioneer bishop of
the Methodist Church

Michael Schlatter
1716-1790
Germany, Holland and
Colonies
Reformed missionary

William Otterbein
1726-1813
Germany, Pennsylvania
and Maryland
Reformed
Founder of United Brethren
Church

Martin Boehm
1725-1812
Pennsylvania
Mennonite
Co-founder of United
Brethren Church

George Geeting
1741-1812
Germany and Maryland
Reformed - early leader
of United Brethren
Church

Christian Newcomer
1749-1830
Mennonite
Pennsylvania
Pioneer bishop of
United Brethren
Church

Part Two

THE CHURCH
TAKES A NAME

1800-1841

Dr. Raymond Waldfogel

BIOGRAPHICAL DATA

Raymond Waldfogel was born April 7, 1926, to Fred and Bertha (Bates) Waldfogel in Fulton County, Ohio. His father, of Swiss/German background, was converted early in life and attended the Fountain Class, United Brethren Church, in the North Ohio Conference. His mother lived next door to the Inlet United Brethren Church, was converted, and attended services there, not far from Fountain Chapel.

The environment of the Waldfogel home and their church was such that encouraged conversion and faithful adherence to the principles of the Christian faith and practice as interpreted by the United Brethren. Raymond was converted as a child under the preaching of his pastor, the Reverend H.B. Peter and held junior and adult membership in Fountain Chapel. Raymond received his quarterly conference license from C. F. Mansberger (1946); and he received his annual conference license into the North Ohio Annual Conference from Bishop Ezra M. Funk (1949); and he was ordained by Funk in 1956. His entire pastoral experience has been in the North Ohio Conference. He pastored churches from 1950-1959. He was elected the one full-time superintendent (1959-1965), and one of three pastor superintendents (1965-1969).

His contributions as a member of many annual conference committees and denominational boards, as well as interdenominational activities in such organizations as the National Association of Evangelicals and the Huntington College Board of Trustees, have been appreciated. Having been elected as a delegate to the General Conferences of 1961, 1965, and 1969, he was then elected to serve as bishop (1969-1981). The church assigned him to serve as bishop of the West District (1969-1977) and as bishop of Central District (1977-1981).

Huntington College and Huntington College Theological Seminary awarded him the Bachelor of Arts degree (1950), the Bachelor of Divinity (1956), and the honorary Doctor of Divinity degree (1972).

Raymond married Wardena Mae Behrens, August 9, 1945, a United

Brethren from Claytonville, Illinois, Rock River Annual Conference. They have five children: James David, John Friedrick, Thomas Lynn, Susan Elaine and Douglas Joel.

Following his tenure as bishop, the Waldfogels pastor the Harvest Lane United Brethren church, Toledo, Ohio (1981-   ).

PERSPECTIVE

From my youth, I have heard much about the United Brethren Church, in particular, the events of 1889. I have supported the church as I knew it. However, curious minds probe into circumstances. It has been so with me in regard to our church, generally, and with specific reference to the happenings surrounding and following the General Conference of 1889. When I was asked to consider writing a section of the history covering the period of 1800-1841, I was humbled by the thought of doing so important a task. The decision to proceed with the project has been personally rewarding. My research has uncovered a wealth of material describing the spirit and vitality of the people known as the United Brethren in Christ. Matters from this early period relating to the formation of a new denomination, the writing of the Confession of Faith, the Discipline, and the Constitution, surely weave a tapestry upon which the later discussions can be viewed more clearly and with more meaning.

Raymond Waldfogel

9

CHARACTERISTICS OF THE
EARLY UNITED BRETHREN

The United Brethren entered into the nineteenth century with certain well defined characteristics. These characteristics were the factors that dictated the shape of the church throughout the organizational period.

Leadership by Strong Elder Statesmen

In 1800, the leadership of the movement was still in the hands of Otterbein and Boehm—no longer young men. Now in his seventy-fourth year, Otterbein had been in America since 1752. Boehm was in his seventy-fifth year. Nearly thirty-three years had passed since the great meeting at Isaac Long's barn. Twenty-six years had advanced since the first Pipe Creek meeting of the evangelistically-minded German Reformed ministers. Nine years had elapsed since the last formal conference at John Spangler's house. Although there were many informal organizational gatherings at the time of the great evangelistic meetings, there never had been more than a few formal conferences.

Otterbein and Boehm were the strong elder statesmen of the new and vigorous religious movement. No one knew for sure just how many people participated in the growing ministry. But, it was clear that if the movement was to continue without interruption, some further organizational leadership would be needed in order to channel the energy that was being generated and thus preserve the results of the expanding evangelistic efforts. Both Otterbein and Boehm continued to make frequent visits to the various preaching points in Pennsylvania, Virginia, and Maryland, giving leadership and counsel to the preachers. However, these efforts were not sufficient. For, by 1800, the ministers from the movement had extended their labors from Berks County in Eastern Pennsylvania to Augusta County in Virginia, and from Baltimore, Maryland, to Westmoreland County in Western Pennsylvania.

Concern About Moral Degeneration

Moral and spiritual decadence in America concerned Otterbein. Conditions demanded that the people be reached with a regenerating gospel. The Christian religion was held in scorn by many people and it was commonly thought that Christianity was outworn and would soon pass out of existence. Experiential religion was seen by many people to be weak and silly. Family worship was thought to be a farce and there were ministers who boasted that they did not practice it. Gross drunkenness was as common in the established churches among both ministry and laity as among the general population.[1] Only about five students at Yale were members of a church in 1795. William and Mary, the only college in Virginia at that time, was said to be a hotbed of unbelief. In 1810 it was said that nearly every educated young Virginian was a skeptic, and this was reported to be also true of professional men in all the states. In addition to all this, life on the frontier, where many of the German immigrants were going, was brutal. Most of the people were ill prepared for the rigors they faced, and because, for the most part, their former churches had not led them into the personal new birth experience, many fell to new lows of immorality.

Since the preaching of regeneration within the established churches was often nonexistent, the evangelistic movement outside the churches must have looked even more attractive as the time passed. At least, outside the established church structures, the United Brethren were free to combat the moral degeneration all around them. The United Brethren preachers, motivated by the Gospel, occupied a front line position as the apostles to the Germans. They labored in a field that was growing in numbers of people to be reached, and growing in effectiveness as people were lifted from the depths of sin to a new life in Christ.

Well-Articulated Doctrine

Although there is no book of doctrine from United Brethren sources dating at or near 1800, there was no misunderstanding as to their beliefs and practices. The rules of the Howard's Hill Church, Baltimore, Maryland, were written down and available. The meeting of preachers at Otterbein's parsonage produced both a discipline and a confession of faith that represented doctrinal and practical points of agreement.[2] A few points—baptism, foot washing, and church membership were still being hammered out in the arena of experience.

This confession of faith (1789) was no doubt produced largely by Otterbein, a scholar well trained in the churchly pietism taught in Germany. It was a statement based surely in his early teaching and confirmed by his own spiritual experiences. His faith plus his new life experience gave him that sufficient confidence and energy to initiate pietistic reforms within the German Reformed Church and to find opportunities for preaching that faith outside the church. Otterbein found in Martin Boehm a kindred spirit who had come to faith totally through the call of the church, the reading of the Bible, a personal awareness of his lost condition, a striving in agony over his lostness, and, finally, a conversion accompanied by release from the bondage of sin and a sense of great joy. This, a non-scholarly experience for Boehm, confirmed for Otterbein all that he had been taught and gave him further support for the confessional statements which he had drafted.

The most important tenet of the United Brethren doctrine was a teaching of the mystical union with God through Jesus Christ which caused spiritual regeneration. This personal experience changed the heart so radically as to produce a new person in ideals and desires, and therefore, in ethical conduct. Form and ceremony were nothing. Life and spirit were everything.[3] The practical evidence of this spiritual regeneration had to do with personal piety and with the continuing ministry of the Holy Spirit in the life of the believers. Therefore members were encouraged to gather weekly at mid-week informal meetings for worship and for cultivation of their spiritual life.[4]

Increasingly Lay-Oriented Ministry

The setting for Otterbein's ministry was the German Reformed Church and the growing revival movement outside Baltimore. At the 1789 conference, Philip William Otterbein and George Adam Geeting were the only German Reformed preachers present. Others were lay preachers from various places, none of whom had been ordained. The history of the early United Brethren Church is filled with the stories of men who, upon conversion, almost immediately became preachers. Most of them had very little schooling. They did have, however, that which was most important—an experience of their own conversion and a love for God that made them make extreme sacrifices in order to preach the Gospel.

These early itinerate preachers, with few exceptions, preached without pay, receiving only food and shelter for the man and his horse. In most cases they were farmers who could afford to itinerate. People to whom they ministered were widely scattered and the appointments would often require hours of travel by horseback over very difficult terrain. The circuits were large, sometimes requiring ten weeks to complete, and often had thirty or more preaching places. In between visits of the itinerating preacher, the class leader would hold meetings.

So eager were the people for the ministry of the itinerant, and so effective were their meetings, that frequently large crowds gathered and many were converted. Because there were many appointments to keep, the preachers, for want of time, often had to hurry away while sinners were still mourning under conviction of their sins.[5] Christian Newcomer may have been the first to accept and travel a circuit as an itinerant preacher for the growing evangelistic fellowship.

A Growing and Mobile Constituency

The field for the early United Brethren evangelists was constantly increasing. By 1775, nearly one-third of the population of Pennsylvania was German. Counties, such as Lancaster, York, Berks, Bucks, and Montgomery were occupied almost entirely by German immigrants and the wave overflowed into Frederick and Washington counties in Maryland. Comparatively few Germans came into the port of Baltimore. They settled first in Pennsylvania, then moved into Maryland, and from there they went in large numbers into the Shenandoah Valley in Virginia. Later, the Germans also moved into the western part of Pennsylvania, and then, along with others, poured into the states of Ohio, Kentucky, and Indiana. Still others moved into Canada. Wherever the German evangelists went in any of these areas, they found Pennsylvania German families, often relatives and acquaintances.[6]

So, the constituency for the United Brethren was a homogeneous, German immigrant population separated from other groups by language and customs, yet moving with the tide of people seeking new lands and new opportunities. By the beginning of this organizational period of United Brethren history, Newcomer along with Abraham

Troxel, had pushed into western Pennsylvania, and received there a positive response from the people.

FOOTNOTES

[1]Abraham P. Funkhouser and Oren F. Morten, comp., *History of the Church of the United Brethren in Christ, Virginia Conference* (Virginia Conference, 1919), p. 33.

[2]Daniel Berger, *History of the Church of the United Brethren in Christ* (Dayton, OH: United Brethren Publishing House, W. J. Shuey, Publisher, 1897), p. 138. The documents referred to are reproduced in footnotes 1 and 2, chapter fourteen.

[3]Funkhouser, p. 67.

[4]Henry G. Spayth, *History of the Church of the United Brethren in Christ*, 2 vols. (Dayton, OH: The Otterbein Press, 1851), 2:47.

[5]Ibid., pp. 84, 85.

[6]Paul Rodes Koontz, *The Bishops, Church of the United Brethren in Christ*, 2 vols. (Dayton, OH: The Otterbein Press, 1950), 2:218.

10

THE FIRST ANNUAL CONFERENCE

The year 1800 is significant to the United Brethren Church because the conference that was held became an annual conference and began the process of organizing the Church of the United Brethren in Christ. The conference was held September 25, 1800, at Peter Kemp's house, the homestead of Frederick Kemp in Frederick County, Maryland. The large stone house, located two and one fourth miles west of Frederick, was a regular preaching place and a home where Otterbein, Newcomer, and other preachers were often entertained. Peter was of German Reformed background and likely was engaged to some extent in preaching at this time although he was not listed as a preacher until the following year.

The Minutes

Minutes of the first annual conferences were apparently taken on loose sheets and kept by George Adam Geeting (Guething). They were not entered into a record book until after the conference of 1812, and only a short time before his death. The following is a copy of the record book from the first page through the minutes of the first conference. The introductory statements which precede the minutes were written by Geeting in 1812 after he had obtained the record book.

PROTOCOL
OF THE
UNITED BRETHREN IN CHRIST

"Sanctify them through thy truth: thy word is truth." Do it, Lord Jesus: for the sake of thy suffering and death. Amen.

This book was obtained the 13th (of May) 1812.

Here now follows what the United Brotherhood in Christ Jesus from the year 1800—the United till 1800—have done in their annual conference, how the preachers and church members should conduct themselves.

September 25, 1800, the following preachers assembled at the house of Frederick Kemp in Frederick County, Maryland: William Otterbein, Martin Boehm, John Hershey, Abraham Troxel (Draksel), Christian Krum, Henry Krum, George Pfrimmer, Henry Boehm, Christian Newcomer, Dietrich Aurand, Jacob Geisinger, George Adam Geeting, Adam Lehman.

Each person spoke first of his own experience, and then declared anew his intention with all zeal, through the help of God, to preach untrammeled by sect to the honor of God and (the good) of men.

1. Resolved that two preachers shall go to Smoke's and investigate whether D. Aurand should baptize and administer the Lord's Supper.

2. Resolved that yearly a day shall be appointed when the unsectarian (unpartheiische) preachers shall assemble and counsel how they may conduct their office more and more according to the will of God, and according to the mind of God, that the church of God may be built up, and sinners converted, so that God in Christ may be honored.

3. The meeting was opened with prayer, then a chapter read, a short discourse delivered by Brother Otterbein, and then again closed with prayer.[1]

Having just completed a three week tour of the Virginia circuit with Martin Boehm and his son, Henry, Christian Newcomer arrived home in Washington County, Maryland, on September 23. While the Boehms went by their own route to the conference, Newcomer attended an appointment on the 24th with Brother Draksel at Middletown. Then the two of them stayed overnight with Brother Jacob Baulus.[2] The three then rode to conference the next morning to find Otterbein, Boehm, and twelve other preachers there. In the words of Newcomer:

The Conference was opened with singing and prayer by Otterbein and Boehm; the former gave a powerful exhortation. Then were all the brethren present separately examined respecting their progress in the divine life, their success and industry in the ministry. 26th—This forenoon Father Otterbein preached from Amos 4: v. 12; Boehm spoke after him. After transacting some other business, the conference closed with prayer.[3]

Historian Henry Spayth lists the names of seventeen preachers who were absent.[4] Five of the ones in attendance were not listed as present or absent at the conferences in either 1789 or 1791. Eight of those listed as absent had not been listed with either of the conferences. This indicates vitality and growth even though no conference had been held since 1791. It also further demonstrates that a more formal approach to the administration of the work was becoming a necessity. The size of the staff of ministers and the scope of the work generally demanded it.

Regular Business

Spayth reports that additional circuits were formed in Pennsylvania, Maryland, and Virginia and that ten great meetings were to be held in the year that followed at the Antietam, at Andrew Mayer's, and other places, indicating that the conference planned and gave direction to their work.[5] One act of lasting significance was the decision that the conference would be held each year. No doubt this conference also followed the pattern established by earlier conferences in the granting of licenses to preach. It is shown that investigation was to be done in the case of Dietrich Aurand as to whether he should administer the ordinances.

Election of Bishops

In other business, a major action unrecorded in the minutes of the conference of 1800, was that of the election of bishops or superintendents. Perhaps secretary, George A. Geeting, thought it was unnecessary to record the election to the office of Bishop those persons who were already by general acceptance virtual bishops. That the action was actually taken cannot be doubted from the abundance of corroborating evidence. The historical statement from the early disciplines, probably written by H. G. Spayth, secretary of the first general conference, specifically stated that William Otterbein and Martin Boehm were elected as superintendents or bishops.[6] Henry Boehm, son of Martin Boehm and a recognized member of the Conference of 1800, made an entry in his diary stating that the election did occur at that time.[7]

Adoption of a Name

Though not given in the minutes, it is certain that the name, "United Brethren in Christ" was adopted at this conference. United Brethren had characterized the brethren as a distinct body of Christians for a considerable time, previous to the setting of the conference.

It was suggested, (and not without reason,) that the name "United Brethren," when used in papers of record pertaining to the church, in property, bequeaths, legacies or otherwise, might raise a legal inquiry as to who, or what Church was intended by "United Brethren," forasmuch as the Moravians, under Count Zinzendorf, in 1727, had formed their first society under and by the name "United Brethren," or *"Unitas Fratrum."* To avoid misapplication in consequence of the similarity of the name, which it was now too late to change—'in Christ' was added, and since then (the name) has been written and known as The Church of the United Brethren in Christ.[8]

Additional evidence showing that the name was adopted by this conference is given in the historical statement carried in the early Disciplines, with very little change until the present, which say that those who comprised the conference of 1800, there united themselves into a society which bears the name of the United Brethren in Christ.

Common Names in Use

Previous to this time there were various names used to identify the United Brethren.

Die Freiheits Leute (the Liberty People) was in a limited way early in use. A favorite text was, "Where the Spirit of the Lord is, there is liberty *(Freiheit)."* II Cor. 3:17. Other names were *Die Neue Reformirte* (the New Reformed), *Die Neue Mennoniten* (the New Mennonites), *Die Otterbeinianer (Otterbein's People), Die Boehmische* (Boehm's Followers). Here and there they were called by the names of particular preachers, and the followers of Felix Light were called *Die Lichtes Leute* (Light's People), and the followers of John Neidig, *Die Neidigs Leute* (Neidig's People). It should be remarked that, under the name *Die Allgemeine* (the Universal), there were many associates or followers of Martin Crider, Caspar Sherk, and Felix Light, who very slowly came fully within the ranks of the United Brethren. They stood midway between the Mennonites and the United Brethren. This explains the slow formation of the classes east of the Susquehanna.[9]

The minutes of the Conference of 1800, written by Geeting, make a reference to the Unsectarian *(unpartheiische)* preachers. This was a self-applied name in very general use. There were other common names given to the movement. Preceding the record of the minutes of 1800 is a brief prefatory statement which includes both "The United Brotherhood in Christ Jesus," *(Von Die Vereinigte Bruedershaft zu Christo)* and, "the United," *(die verinigte),* which was an abbreviation for "the United Brethren," *(die vereinigte Bruder).*

Other commonly used terms gave definition to the movement. The word society *(Gemeinde)* was an early term for a local group of adherents. It came to be used for a class and later for the denomination. The German New Testament term for the Christian Church is *Die Gemeinde.* The word translated Association, Connection, or society *(Gesellschaft)* was used in 1800. The Discipline of 1815 says that preachers united themselves into a society *(Gesellschaft)* which bears the name, United Brethren in Christ. Also used was the word *Gemeinschaft* which may be translated as society or communion. The use of the word church in the title of the denomination did not occur until it was recorded in the minutes of the Miami Conference of 1813.

FOOTNOTES

[1]A. W. Drury, *Minutes of the Annual and General Conferences of the Church of the United Brethren in Christ, 1800-1818* (Dayton, OH: Published for the United Brethren Historical Society by the United Brethren Publishing House, 1897), pp. 9, 10.

[2]Though not included in the list contained in the minutes as among those present, it seems certain that Jacob Baulus also attended.

[3]Christian Newcomer, with John Hildt, trans. and ed., *The Life and Journal of the Rev'd. Christian Newcomer* (Hagerstown, MD: F. G. W. Kapp, 1834), p. 74.

[4]Henry G. Spayth, *History of the United Brethren in Christ* (Circleville, OH: Published at the Conference Office of the United Brethren in Christ, 1851), p. 82.

[5]Ibid., p. 84.

[6]A. W. Drury, Editor, *Disciplines of the United Brethren in Christ, 1814-1841* (Dayton, OH: United Brethren Publishing House, 1885), p. 10.

[7]Henry Boehm and J. B. Wakeley, *The Patriarch of One Hundred Years; Being Reminiscences, Historical and Biographical, of Rev. Henry Boehm* (New York: Nelson & Phillips, 1875), pp. 55, 56.

[8]Spayth, p. 83.

[9]Drury, pp. 265-270.

11

A DECADE OF DEVELOPMENT

Conference of 1801

The annual conference met again at the home of Peter Kemp, September 23-25, 1801. Twenty ministers, including the bishops, were present. In this second annual conference the brethren addressed matters pertaining to the supply of available ministers who were willing to be appointed to the circuits. The first note in the minutes of September 24th indicated that there was ". . . hearty prayer that each one might be willing to preach the gospel and that he also be careful, and that he also walk as he preaches to others." The second entry of that day indicated that the preachers were examined as to their willingness to labor in the work of the Lord, according to their ability. The third item of the day indicated that the question was asked: "Who are willing to take charge of a circuit and preach at the appointed places?" There were ten who offered themselves, whose names were then listed in the minutes. Newcomer noted that many topics were discussed and that a general unanimity of love prevailed among the brethren.[1]

Two steps toward improvement of the ministry are indicated by the resolutions adopted: "That each preacher, after the sermon, shall hold conversation with those who would be converted . . . ." And, "That the preachers shall be brief and avoid unnecessary words in preaching and prayer; but if the Spirit of God impels, it is their duty to follow as God directs."[2]

Conference of 1802

Only thirteen preachers came to the Conference of 1802. That year the brethren dealt with the sensitive issue of whether or not a record should be made of the membership of the church. Out of twelve votes cast, nine were opposed.

It was decided that the preachers should establish prayer-meetings where they preached, if it was possible. A proposal was also presented relating to the collection of money for poor preachers, but nothing was done.

A matter regarding irregularities among preachers resulted in: "Resolved that if a preacher does anything wrong or scandalous, the nearest preacher shall go and talk with him alone. If he refuse to hear and heed, said preacher shall take with him one or two more preachers. If he refuse to hear them, he shall be silent till the next conference."[3]

An additional significant matter related to the bishops:

> Further, it is laid down as a rule *(vest Gesetzt)* that when one of our superintendents (or elders, *eltesten)* dies, namely Otterbein or Martin Boehm, who now are appointed to the place *(gesetzt sind)*, then shall another always be chosen in his stead. This is the wish of both, and all of the preachers present unanimously consent and are agreed that it be thus.[4]

The term bishop is not used in this action. It is apparent that the office and not the order was meant. A. W. Drury stated, "The United Brethren have always used the terms bishop and superintendents as equivalents."[5]

Drury also included a footnote statement in explanation of the circumstances which may have precipitated the above action:

> The following account from a later source purports to give more definitely the attending circumstances: "He (Otterbein) at this conference spoke as follows: 'Dear brethren, I am far advanced in years. My strength is failing. I do not expect to be with you long. My work will soon be finished and should I be called away by death, choose one from your number to take the place I now occupy. Be faithful to God. He is with us and he will be with you.' " The account proceeds. "Martin Boehm rose and uttered the same sentiments and made the same request."[6]

Conference of 1803

The Conference of 1803 met October 5th at the home of David Snyder, Cumberland County, Pennsylvania. In another step toward better regulation of the ministry, the conference appointed two preachers each in Virginia and Pennsylvania to supervise resident preachers and to place the preachers on the circuits in their respective states. The work in Maryland was left to the preachers living there to arrange. In other business, the recording of the names of members was again discussed. The conference gave each pastor the freedom to do according to his understanding, instructing them to love one another as brethren. Again, preachers were instructed to converse with awakened souls after the sermon as the circumstances might seem proper.

The subject of the growing work in western Pennsylvania was also discussed. Four years earlier, in 1799, Christian Newcomer had made a trip with Abraham Troxel (Drachsel) to western Pennsylvania. John George Pfrimmer had moved to Washington County, Pennsylvania, in 1801, and Matthias Bortsfield had moved there before 1803. Now, at this conference, Christian Berger, who also had recently moved to Washington County, was given an opportunity to speak to the conference about the work in his new location. His presentation resulted in the selection of Newcomer to further investigate the work in western Pennsylvania, this time in the company of Henry Crum.

The trip was begun on November 2, 1803, and was acclaimed a great success:

Sunday, November 13th—Today we had indeed a little Pentecost, from three hundred to four hundred persons had collected, more than the barn in which we had assembled for worship, could contain. I preached to them from Titus 3, with great liberty and effect, for the salvation of souls. The congregation was remarkable attending to the Word. Though it rained, those that had no shelter in the barn kept their stand in the rain without the least disturbance. It is indeed surprising, and to me somewhat mysterious, to behold the manner in which the power of God works here among the people. During the time of preaching, several persons fell to the floor, some laid as if they were dead, others shook so violently that two or three men could scarcely hold them; sometimes the excitement would be so great that I had to stop speaking for several minutes, until the noise abated; some few were praising God and shouting for joy. Bro. Chr. Berger addressed the congregation. When I had concluded my discourse in the German, I then preached in the English language, from I Peter 1:3, and the effect was again the same. At night I preached at Mr. Swartz's; here also several persons of both sexes fell to the floor, others were crying for mercy; so it lasted till after midnight.

14th—This day we had the best time; I spoke short and concise. Presently crying and lamentations began; one fell to the floor on the right and another on the left. I felt such pity and compassion for poor mourning souls, that my heart was ready to burst with sadness, and yet I was rejoiced to behold such a work of grace: God grant that it may prove a work which shall endure throughout eternity.[7]

Henry Spayth stated that after twenty years he met men and women in the West who had attended, who had espoused the cause of Christ at this meeting, and were still faithful servants of God with delightful memories of the happy scenes.[8] Many other successful meetings were reported on this trip.

One year after the trip, Abraham Troxel moved to near Mount Pleasant in Westmoreland County, western Pennsylvania. He became the chief representative and support of the church there, and his house became the center for activities of the United Brethren in that area.

Conference of 1804

The Conference of 1804 met October 3rd at the home of David Snyder in Cumberland County, Pennsylvania. This was the year of a prevailing sickness and mortality; consequently, only five preachers could attend. There was no business transacted except to establish that the next conference would be held in the spring on Wednesday before Whitsunday (Pentecost Sunday) near Middletown, Maryland.

Conference of 1805

Twenty-one preachers attended the meeting May 29, 1805, at the home of Jacob Baulus near Middletown, Maryland.[9] The salary of circuit riders was established at forty pounds yearly. It was also determined that "Preachers who preach where they desire, according to their inclination, shall have no compensation. When they receive money, they shall bring the same to the conference, to be given to the regular preachers."[10]

Again, the minutes do not record the election of bishops, but Newcomer's *Journal* leaves no doubt that, "Father Otterbein and Martin Boehm were elected presidents."[11] There is nothing to indicate the length of their terms, but each continued until death without further reported elections.

Conference of 1806

There was nothing in the business of the Conference of 1806 to attract our special interest. The usual kinds of business came before them. Five great meetings were planned for the following year. Neither of the Bishops were able to attend. Otterbein had been ill during the year which may explain his absence. The minutes do not indicate who may have been the chairman although some historians feel that George Adam Geeting may have been selected as chairman pro tempore.[12]

Conference of 1807

Bishop Boehm attended the Conference of 1807 and gave a short exhortation. Special attention was given to arrangements to serve the circuits in central Pennsylvania. Salaries were established for married preachers at forty pounds per year, and for unmarried preachers at twenty-four pounds per year.

George A. Geeting was authorized to compile and publish a hymn-book. Geeting, also as secretary, did not think to record the action in the minutes. The hymnbook indexing two hundred hymns, was printed in German the next year under the title, *Lobgesänge zu Ehren dem Heiligen und Gerechten in Israel, und zur Erbauung des Volks Gottes; wie auch zum Gebrauch für Jederman, der gerne selig werden möchte,* (Hymns to Honor the Saints and Allrighteous at Israel and to the Devotion of the People of God as well for the Use of Everyone Who Wants to Be Saved).[13]

Conference of 1808

The conference in 1808 considered the process by which a person could obtain a license to preach. It was determined that a candidate should be examined at a great meeting and have a good testimony. If two of the preachers should consider him to be worthy, they were to give him a certificate to preach for one year. Then he must appear at the conference for examination. In case he could not attend the conference, his certificate could be renewed at a great meeting. No doubt these were but extensions or revisions of those provisions already in practice. There is no reference to the name of the chairman given in the minutes, although some historians think that George A. Geeting was again selected chairman pro tempore.[14]

Conference of 1809

The annual conference met again May 10, 1809.

Prior to the conference, Christian Newcomer met with Methodist Baltimore annual conference in session in Harrisonburg, Virginia, early in March. While he was there, a committee was appointed to hold consultation with him, to ascertain whether any union could be effected between the Methodist Episcopal church and the United Brethren in Christ. The committee met with him, and after prayer and discussion of many different subjects, made their report to the Methodist conference. In the afternoon Newcomer was invited to participate in the conference session. After mature deliberation and discussion on their part, Newcomer received from the Methodist Conference a resolution in writing which he was to deliver to Otterbein in Baltimore. It was further agreed that a member of their body would attend the United Brethren conference in May and communicate their resolution.[15]

Following this Methodist conference, Newcomer went to Baltimore, and spent ten days in consultation with Otterbein and several Methodist brethren. Their conversation centered on the possibility of a closer union and harmony of the two societies. No specifics of their conversations were noted in *Newcomer's Journal.*

The Methodist brethren were present during the United Brethren Conference which followed and their letter was presented. This communication assumed a significant position in the consideration of the conference because its contents stated that after "mature deliberation" they (the Methodist Annual Conference) thought it proper to offer "terms, in order to establish a closer and more permanent union among us." There were three main points:

[Licensing of Ministers]
1. We think it advisable for your own good and prosperity that each minister or preacher who is acknowledged by the United Brethren should receive from your conference a regular license, which may introduce them to our pulpits and privileges and prevent impositions, as there are many who profess to be in union with you that are not acknowledged by you. And we would further advise that you favor each of our presiding elders with a list of the names of those ministers so acknowledged and licensed by you within the bounds of his district, that there may be no difficulties in admitting them to our privileges. And we would further observe that all our traveling ministers and preachers have their names printed in the minutes of our annual conferences, and our local ministers and preachers have credentials of ordination, or a written license, and we hope that you will admit none to your privileges calling themselves Methodist preachers but such as have their names on the minutes, or as are licensed as above mentioned.

[Church Discipline]
2. As we have long experienced the utility of a Christian discipline to prevent immorality among our people, we would earnestly recommend to you to establish a strict discipline among you, which might be a "defence of your glory." Our Discipline is printed in your language, and we would recommend it to your consideration, to adopt it, or any part of it that you in your wisdom may think proper, or any other form that you may judge best. And that under a discipline so established you make use of every Christian and prudential means to unite your members together in societies among yourselves. By these means we think your people will become more spiritual, and your labors be much more successful under the blessing of God.

[Church Membership and Fraternal Fellowship]
3. All those members among you who are united in such societies, or may hereafter be united, may be admitted to the privileges of class-meetings, sacra-

ments, and love-feasts in our church, provided they have a certificate of their membership signed by a regularly licensed preacher of your church. And to prevent inconvenience, we wish you to furnish each of our preachers with a list of the names of all such members as may be in the bounds of their respective circuits, that they may know who are your members.

In order further to establish this union, which we so much desire, we have given particular instructions to our presiding elders and preachers who have the charge of districts and circuits where the United Brethren live, to admit your preachers and members, as above specified, to our privileges, and also to leave a list of the names of your preachers and members in the bounds of their respective districts or circuits for their successors, that they may have no difficulties in knowing whom you acknowledge as preachers or members.[16]

The minutes of the United Brethren conference stated that the desire of the Methodists was approved, in regard to licensing preachers, because it was already a United Brethren practice. Preachers were allowed to give members of their churches a certificate of good standing in order that they might go to the Lord's supper with the Methodists. On the other matters, more time was needed. It was stated that the Methodists should have freedom to preach at all of the United Brethren meeting places.

This conference must have been a very difficult session for the United Brethren. *Newcomer's Journal* gives some of the emotion of the sessions:

10th—This day the session of our Conference commenced in the afternoon at Christian Herr's, in Lancaster County, and continued until 12 o'clock at night. Different subjects came up for consideration, particularly the case of a closer union and fellowship with our Methodist brethren: my wish and desire was, to have better order and discipline established in our society, and some of my brethren were of the opinion that this was unnecessary; that the Word of God alone was all-sufficient, and were therefore opposed to all discipline. I could plainly perceive, that this opposition originated in prejudice, therefore I sincerely and fervently prayed for the illumination of the Holy Spirit. The Lord answered my prayer, when I almost despaired of success, and had nearly determined to leave and withdraw from the Society; the brethren resolved, and a resolution was adopted in the Conference, to give a friendly and brotherly answer to the request and address of the Methodist Conference, and I hope that peace, unanimity, and concord, will be preserved and strengthened in the respective societies.[17]

An appropriate letter was composed and sent to the Methodists by Martin Boehm, George Adam Geeting, and Christian Newcomer. It contained the points noted above and concluded with a prayer that the

God of peace and love might unite the two societies still closer in the bonds of love and union in this present time and throughout the eternal ages.

Conference of 1810

In the Conference of 1810, the United Brethren considered another letter from the Methodists. Previously Newcomer and Boehm had gone to Baltimore to meet with Otterbein and together they attended sessions of the Methodist conference. The new communication was received first by the vestry of Otterbein's church, then relayed to the annual conference session. Since matters of a church discipline and the principles of a union between the two societies had been postponed for consideration by the next United Brethren conference, the Methodists thought it not proper to resume that subject in their new letter. Thankfulness was expressed that brotherly love still prevailed. The United Brethren resolved to respond to the Methodists, but this letter of response, however, was not preserved.

The exchange of letters seemed but a natural expression of a long friendship between preachers and members of both societies. Perhaps the words of Henry Spayth best describe the atmosphere of spiritual unity that existed.

These English men, called Methodists, found in the United Brethren the same spirit of grace, and truth and love; hence they were drawn, and flowed together. A mutual friendship and confidence ensued. This friendship, this pure disinterested love, was of great advantage to the cause of religion, and the extension of the reign of grace. These brethren when met, for a time, knew no difference,— had many happy seasons,—saw powerful conversions, and extraordinary displays of the outpouring of the spirit of God upon many people, as a result of their united labors.[18]

FOOTNOTES

[1]Christian Newcomer, with John Hildt, trans. and ed., *The Life and Journal of the Rev'd. Christian Newcomer* (Hagerstown, MD: F. G. W. Kapp, 1834), p. 85.

[2]References to the Minutes throughout this chapter may be found in a volume by: A. W. Drury, *Minutes of the Annual and General Conferences, 1800-1818* (Dayton, OH: Published for the United Brethren Historical Society by the United Brethren Publishing House, 1897).

[3]A. W. Drury, *Minutes,* pp. 14-16.

[4]Ibid., p. 16.

[5]A. W. Drury, *History of the Church of the United Brethren in Christ* (Dayton, OH: The Otterbein Press, 1924), p. 185.

[6]Ibid., p. 190.

[7]Newcomer, pp. 115, 116.

[8]Henry G. Spayth, *History of the Church of the United Brethren in Christ* (Circleville, OH: Published at the Conference office of the United Brethren in Christ, 1851), p. 98.

[9]The minutes state that the conference was held at the house of Christian Newcomer. However, Newcomer's *Journal* states that the conference was held at Jacob Baulus' place which was near Middletown, in accordance with the designation given in the minutes for 1804.

[10]Drury, *Minutes*, p. 18.

[11]Newcomer, p. 134.

[12]Samuel S. Hough, editor, *Christian Newcomer, His Life, Journal, and Achievements* (Dayton, OH: Board of Administration, Church of the United Brethren in Christ, 1941, p. 99.

[13]John H. Ness, Jr., *One Hundred Fifty Years, A History of Publishing in the Evangelical United Brethren Church* (Dayton, OH: The Board of Publication of the Evangelical United Brethren Church, 1966), p. 245.

See also the footnote in this volume on page 262 which contains the following excerpt from the preface of the Geeting hymnbook: "The here assembled songs are partly extracted from different hymn books and partly set up and established by God-loving book publishers. At our yearly conference of preachers I was commissioned to do such and to deliver the work over for printing. It now took place, and with no intention other as to the Adoration of God and to the devotion of those who read or sing hymns, though that they may be attracted to exercise the right Christianity to obtain the true Christian belief to the Lord Jesus. The work is designed for that. The Lord gave his blessing thereto. Amen.

In the name of the United Brotherhood in Christ.

George A. Geeting."

[14]Hough, p. 110

[15]John Lawrence, *The History of the Church of the United Brethren in Christ,* 2 vols. (Dayton, OH: Published at the United Brethren Printings Establishment, Sowers & King, Publishers, 1861), 1:347ff.

[16]Ibid., pp. 347-350.

[17]Newcomer, p. 175.

[18]Spayth, p. 81.

12

BEGINNING OF THE CHURCH IN OHIO

The Conference of 1810 ended on Friday, June 9. On the following two days, a sacramental meeting[1] was held along the Antietam,[2] in Washington County, Maryland. Following the sacramental meeting, Newcomer returned to his home nearby to make immediate preparations for a westward journey into the state of Ohio. This trip may have been authorized by the annual conference but not noted in the minutes. Christian Crum, who was to be his traveling companion, arrived at the Newcomer home on June 21, and they left the next day.

Newcomer needed Crum for general help in travel and preaching. By choosing a respected member of the church to go with him, Newcomer would have upon return another voice to give testimony to the growth of the church in the west. Christian Crum was well qualified for this purpose. He and his twin brother, Henry, grew up near Frederick, Maryland. Their parents belonged to the German Reformed Church; however, the brothers were both earnest, holy men and recognized itinerants in the United Brethren movement. They lived on farms not far from Winchester, Virginia. Great meetings were often held at their homes.

On June 22, Newcomer prayed with his family, commending them and himself to the care and protection of his heavenly Father. Bidding them farewell, the two preachers met Geeting in Hagerstown, had prayer at John King's, then rode to Mercersburg, Pennsylvania, where they lodged with Christian King.[3] Taking two weeks to travel through Pennsylvania, Newcomer and Crum conducted follow-up meetings in some of the same communities to which Newcomer had previously ministered.

At this point in history there were two possible trails from the East to southwestern Pennsylvania. One of these corresponded to what became the National Road, now U.S. 40, and the other corresponded to the Lincoln Highway, now U.S. 30. The latter was the better road at that time and was the one more generally taken by Newcomer and the immigrants moving westward.

From his home in Maryland, Newcomer passed through Mercersburg, Pennsylvania, to the foot of the Cove Mountain Range. At Fort Loudon he entered the Lincoln Highway, now U.S. 30, and traveled westward to McConnelsburg and Bedford. Several miles west of Bedford, Newcomer picked up and followed in part the road then known as the Glades Road or the West Newton, Mount Pleasant, and Bedford Highway, corresponding now to State Route 31. From West Newton the Glades Road went to Washington, Pennsylvania, and then to Wheeling, West Virginia, over the same route as the National Road.[4]

On July 6, 1810, Newcomer and Crum crossed the Ohio River and lodged overnight in Jefferson County, Ohio. The next day they went on into Belmont County stopping with Samuel Pickering, "a pious Quaker family." A famous Quaker meeting house long stood between these two counties not far from Mount Pleasant, Jefferson County. It is likely that they picked up the Zanes Trail at or near St. Clairsville. Zanes Trail, or Zanes Trace, the first wagon road in the State of Ohio, was opened in 1796. U.S. Route 40, and Interstate 70, now parallel that route from Wheeling, West Virginia through Zanesville, Ohio. From Zanesville it passed through Lancaster and Chillicothe, Ohio, and terminated at Marysville, Kentucky. Many immigrants, including many United Brethren, followed this road instead of going by boat down the Ohio River. In traveling the trail, Newcomer and Crum rode through Zanesville, and on July 10 they came to the home of Abraham Hiestand, east of Lancaster, Ohio, and lodged for the night. The next day they saw several acquaintances in Lancaster, then rode on to the home of George Benedum, a United Brethren minister living on the west side of Lancaster.

Preachers in Ohio

Hiestand and Benedum were known from their earlier work in the East. But they were not the only United Brethren preachers who had moved westward to Ohio. The first conference in the state of Ohio convened one month later, August 13, 1810, and the record shows a total of fifteen preachers present.[5] Several of these deserve mention for their contribution to the United Brethren expansion.

Abraham Hiestand came to Ohio in 1804 with his brothers—Jacob, John, and Samuel—from Page County, Virginia. In their early history the family had been Moravians.[6] Abraham, (listed as early as the Conference of 1800), John, and Samuel were United Brethren ministers. Samuel was later elected as a bishop.[7]

The coming of George Benedum fully launched the church in Fairfield and surrounding counties in Ohio. He was licensed to preach in 1794 and was present at the sessions of the annual conference in the east in 1803 and 1805. He seemed to have taken several years to make the complete transition to Ohio, for he was found in Pennsylvania by Newcomer in 1808 and he attended the Conference of 1809. However, it seems that he had some kind of residence in Ohio from about 1806,[8] having obtained title to land in Fairfield County, July 10, 1806.

Michael Creider had come to Ohio in 1795 to see the possibilities. He moved his family to Hopetown, near Chillicothe in 1796. He is listed as a member of the Miami Conference of 1810.[9]

Andrew Zeller, looked upon as the founder of the church in Ohio, was born August 15, 1755, in Berks County, Pennsylvania, and was converted to Christ about 1790 while living in Berks County. He settled on a farm near Germantown, Ohio, in 1806, a little more than a mile north of town on the west side of Twin Creek. There he built a log house which included a special room for religious meetings. A United Brethren class was organized at that house in 1806. Soon after his arrival in Ohio, he entered into the work of preaching and his home became the center for a large sphere of activity on the part of the United Brethren itinerants. About 1817 he built a larger house on the east side of the creek and a separate meeting house was also built.[10]

Daniel Troyer was also located near Germantown. He was born in Maryland and spiritually awakened under a sermon preached by Otterbein. He was in attendance at the conference in the east in 1805. In 1806 he came to Ohio. He was a man of power with a strong voice and great zeal.[11]

Thomas Winters settled in the Miami Valley in 1809. He had been licensed to preach by Otterbein in 1799, having previous connection with the German Reformed church. When the conference in Ohio was organized he was a member of it. He was a fraternal delegate to the Methodist Conference at Chillicothe in 1812. In 1813 he and Henry Evinger reported the formation of a circuit consisting of forty-seven appointments. The next year, however, he made the decision to return to the German Reformed church after several years of significant service.

Newcomer and Crum made many stops in Fairfield and Ross Counties, seeing many old friends and acquaintances from the East, who had entreated them to visit. Passing through Chillicothe and Pickaway Plains, they traveled to Montgomery County. A special addition to the German constituency was made there when, in 1805, ninety-six persons from Maryland settled a few miles east of Dayton.[12] These were mostly United Brethren people, known to Newcomer and Crum. They stopped at the home of Lewis Kemp, younger brother of Peter, who had moved to Ohio one year after his father's death.

From there they passed through Dayton and came to Andrew Zeller's house. Then they headed south toward Cincinnati making several stops on the way. In Cincinnati they visited Thomas King and Henry Gimbel who had come from Baltimore. They crossed into Kentucky and came to Newport where they were entertained by Jacob Bergman, a brother-in-law of Brother Geeting. They crossed back into Ohio and after several more stops, returned to Zellers' and to Kemps' for a two day meeting. They then rode to Michael Creiders' in Ross County, where the first meeting of the conference in Ohio convened August 13, 1810.

First Conference in Ohio

Newcomer must have been overwhelmed by the vision he saw for the work in Ohio. His entry for August 13, 1810, read:

> "To-day I held a little Conference with the Brethren; 15 preachers, (How I write?—preachers! indeed!—we are not worthy the appellation) were present: bless the Lord for the brotherly love and unanimity of mind which pervades throughout."[13]

The term, little conference, used by Newcomer, was one which often described a conference held to serve a local or temporary purpose. It is reported in Newcomer's *Journal* that another such conference was held several weeks later in western Pennsylvania. However, the conference in Ohio proved to be the first session of the Miami Conference and the seedbed for a work that grew rapidly. The preachers in Ohio seemed to expect that their conference of 1810 was to be the first in a regular succession of conferences. However, the conference in the East was under the impression that it was the only authorized conference to speak for the church, and no doubt they also considered the conference in Ohio as a 'little conference.'

Newcomer and Crum spent the remainder of August in Ohio,

crossing the river on the 30th. It had been nearly two months since they crossed that river in the other direction. Crum set out immediately for home, and, after a further week of meetings in western Pennsylvania, Newcomer returned to his home and found his family well.

Mrs. Newcomer's Death

Newcomer soon began the personal sorrow of his wife's prolonged illness and death. She became ill on the 9th of December and from that time until her death on April 22, 1811, his evangelistic activities were severely limited. With her death, of course, a great change came into his life. He wrote:

> I formed the resolution for some time, if it should be the pleasure of the Lord to take my companion from me, to break up housekeeping totally; this resolution I put into immediate execution, and moved this day to my son Andrew's, where I have my own room, and my board when at home at his table.[14]

Annual Conferences of 1811 and 1812

The annual conference in the East met May 22, 1811, at Joseph Knegi's. There were no unusual actions reported in the minutes. However, it is known that consideration was given to another letter suggesting definite steps toward union from the Baltimore Conference of the Methodist Church. The letter acknowledged receipt of a letter from the United Brethren following the conference of 1810. The Methodist letter stated that they understood the two societies to be fully agreed in respect of the necessity of union and a mutual endeavor to accomplish it. They had directed and instructed their presiding elders and preachers about the most expedient form of implementing the proposed union. They spoke of agreement on licensuring and certification for preachers and members. They stated that all their meeting houses were open to United Brethren preachers; their sacraments, love feasts, and class-meetings were open to United Brethren members with certificates of good standing. It was indicated that as soon as the presiding elders and preachers return to their fields following conference, this union shall have begun on their part. They expressed a hope to hear from the next annual conference of the United Brethren in the East.

Christian Newcomer replied for the United Brethren in a letter dated May 25, 1811:

Dearly Beloved Brethren in Christ:

We have received your affectionate letter bearing date of March 27, 1811, by our brothers Borg and Swertzwelder, with much joy and thankfulness, seeing therein that the God of love has united your hearts in love and harmony with us, to unite more and more together in the bonds of the gospel. We are certain, brethren, if we walk in the light as children of the light, we shall ere long be of one heart and one mind. Seeing likewise the blessed fruits of our union together in a measure already, and the glorious prospect before us, we do not hesitate a moment longer to give you the right hand of Christian fellowship again. We have now formed our members in classes, as much as possible. However, there are a number yet among us who have not yet joined with us in this privilege, so long delayed by us. We earnestly hope that you will instruct your traveling preachers to bear with such as much as the order of your church will admit. We would further inform you that we have drawn up some regulations, or discipline, among us, and shall endeavor, more and more, to put them into effect among ourselves and our members.

Any preacher or private member expelled from your church will not be received by us to the fellowship of saints in Christ, and we do hope that you will do the same in relation to those expelled by us, at least until sufficient reason be found of their repentance and good fruits.

We likewise hope that our mutual friendship and love to each other will be increased yet more and more, and that the intercourse, by letter and messengers from and to each conference, may be kept up yearly, through which medium difficulties may be readily adjusted, and more especially as such messengers or communications will be joyfully received by us and appreciated in the best possible way.

And, lastly, may the God of all peace and consolation, who has united our hearts together in the gospel, spread his militant church, by us, from pole to pole, and finally, when time is no more, make us, one and all, members of his church triumphant, to praise God and the Lamb forever. Remember us before the throne of God, is the earnest prayer of your affectionate brethren. Wishing you peace and prosperity in the kingdom and patience of our Lord Jesus Christ, we remain your affectionate brethren in the bonds of Christian fellowship.

Signed by order and in behalf of the conference.

May 25, 1811   Christian Newcomer.[15]

Newcomer did not go to Ohio in 1811, and as a result there was no session of the Conference held there that year. However, when the conference in the East met on May 13, 1812, two actions were taken with respect to Christian Newcomer and the work in Ohio. In one action Newcomer was to correspond with the brethren in Ohio or visit them to give counsel and exhort as he found best. In the second action, he was given authority to hold a conference in the Ohio district. Until this time the conference in the East had said or done nothing in regard to the work in Ohio or in regard to the conference formed there. With this action noted, it is now convenient to refer to the conference in Ohio as the Miami Conference. The conference in the East may be referred to as the Original Conference or the Old Conference.

This meeting of the Old Conference had further significance because Martin Boehm had died on March 23, 1812. Otterbein because of age and infirmity could not attend. Henry G. Spayth, who was present, reported that George A. Geeting was elected to preside and that Christian Newcomer was elected as temporary recording secretary.[16]

It is of interest to note that still further contact had been made with the Methodist Conference. In March, 1812, Newcomer had met with Bishops Asbury and McKendree in Leesburg, Virginia, where the Methodist Baltimore Conference was in session. There he received an invitation to attend the Methodist Philadelphia Conference and was informed that a letter from the Baltimore Conference would be sent to the United Brethren. In April he went to Philadelphia where the Methodist Conference appointed a committee of three to form a closer union with the United Brethren.

The Methodists of the Baltimore Conference wrote their letter on March 26, 1812, to say that they had instructed their preachers to deal very tenderly with the United Brethren who had not fully come into the measures of union, hoping and trusting that everything possible would be done to promote and extend the spirit and practice of discipline, it being evident that our mutual success depends upon union wherever the lines of labor between the two societies come together. The United Brethren Old Conference replied in a letter written by Newcomer, May 13, 1812, thanking the Methodists for the sentiments of their letter and informing them that the United Brethren had succeeded in forming class-meetings and extending discipline in many places.

The Methodist Philadelphia Conference wrote their letter April 25, 1812, to say that they knew about the friendly correspondence between the United Brethren and the Methodist Baltimore Conference. They stated that they were most willing to embrace the United Brethren as brethren in the kingdom of Jesus Christ and that they were ready to enter into the strictest union that the peculiar circumstances of the two societies would admit. George A. Geeting wrote the United Brethren reply to the Philadelphia Conference. He expressed the prayer that the discussions might terminate in a happy union. He informed them that two United Brethren messengers were to be sent to their next conference with whom they might consult concerning the contemplated merger.

The Miami Conferences of 1812

Newcomer started his second trip to Ohio on June 8, 1812, accompanied this time by William Ambrose, a preacher from Virginia. This year, two sessions were held in different locations, one in the Miami Valley and the other in the Scioto region.

The first session was held August 5 at Andrew Zeller's house, near Germantown, Montgomery County in the Miami Valley. It was resolved that a circuit would be formed. Thomas Winter, Henry Evinger, and Samuel Mau gave themselves to travel the circuit. Two brethren were elected as delegates to the conference of the Methodists at Chillicothe. A prayer and fast day was set to implore the prosperity and welfare of Zion. Zeller was elected presiding elder for two years. It was determined that the form of baptism be left to those who were to be baptized. Five preachers were given full status as ministers; three others were received as preachers.

The second session was held August 23 in Fairfield County in the Scioto district. Two preachers were received as full ministers, four were authorized to preach, and one to exhort.[17] A circuit was formed for which Samuel Mau and Jacob Lehman offered their services and were approved by the conference. George Benedum was elected presiding elder.

The Conferences of 1813

The Old Conference met on May 5, 1813, at Christian Herr's, Lancaster County, Pennsylvania. Martin Boehm's position as bishop had been vacant for over a year. This year, Christian Newcomer was elected to fill that position. Consequently, when he returned to Ohio later that year, he administered the work in the capacity of a bishop in the Church.

The Miami Conference met August 25, 1813, at Peter Site's home in Fairfield County. Eighteen preachers were present. Communications were read from several preachers. Matthias Bortsfield was granted full authority as a minister. The traveling preachers reported. Four preachers were granted full rights as preachers; six others were authorized to preach. Two were named as exhorters. Andrew Zeller and Abraham Hiestand were elected presiding elders for one year.

The matter of ordination and receiving of preachers was considered. It was deplored that too little order was observed. They considered whether it was proper to ordain preachers without the laying on of hands. It was determined to write a letter to Father Otterbein and ask him to ordain, by the laying on of hands, one or more preachers, who afterward would perform the same for others.

FOOTNOTES

[1]Great meetings were sometimes held in groves, yet they were not camp meetings, nor protracted meetings. According to the circumstances belonging to them, they were called great meetings, quarterly meetings, sacramental meetings, or two-day meetings. Frequently the crowds were such as to make the administration of the holy sacrament impractical on Sunday. In that case, the love-feast and sacrament were held on Monday. See the following references:

A. W. Drury, *History of the Church of the United Brethren in Christ* (Dayton, OH: The Otterbein Press, 1924), p. 165.

John Lawrence, *The History of the Church of the United Brethren in Christ*, 2 vols. (Dayton, OH: Published at the United Brethren Printing Establishment, Sowers & King, Publishers, 1861), 1:306, 307.

[2]John W. Schildt, *Drums Along The Antietam* (Parsons, W.VA: McClain Publishing Company, 1972), cover jacket.

The banks of the Antietam Creek and adjacent fields have heard the beat of the Catawba and Delaware Indians as they hunted, raided, and fought in the Valley of the Antietam.

Then the Valley heard the beat of drums belonging to British troops under General Edward Braddock as they marched westward to disaster.

Slowly settlers such as Chapline, Orndorff, Smith, Piper, and Mumma came to the Valley of the Antietam, cleared the forest, and built homes, farms, churches, and mills.

In the latter part of the eighteenth century the Great Awakening swept America. And along the banks of the Little Antietam at the Geeting Meeting House, the church of the United Brethren in Christ, the first American born denomination came into being.

Years later the Antietam heard the drums of the Blue and Gray as they pitched their "hundred-circling camps." Before it was over the soldiers faced "rows of steel," "fateful lightning," and "a terrible swift sword" at the Dunkard Church, at Bloody Lane, and at Burnside Bridge.

Eighteen thousand were wounded on the fields of Antietam. They were treated by Dr. Oliver, Dr. Dunn, Dr. Dimon, Clara Barton, and others by "dim and flaring lamps."

The tragedy and suffering of Antietam is found in the story of the homes, barns, churches, and schools of the Valley as they speak to us "in the evening dews and damps."

The Antietam has heard drums beating in honor of Presidents Abraham Lincoln, Andrew Johnson, William B. McKinley, Theodore Roosevelt, and Franklin D. Roosevelt as they came to visit and speak. Over these fields Dwight D. Eisenhower and John F. Kennedy have also walked.

Few areas of the United States have seen as much history as the Valley of the Antietam.

[3]Christian Newcomer, with John Hildt, trans. and ed., *The Life and Journal of the Rev'd Christian Newcomer* (Hagerstown, MD: F. G. W. Kapp, 1834), p. 188.

[4]Drury, pp. 290, 291.

[5]Ibid., p. 299. The fifteen preachers were: Christian Newcomer, Christian Crum, George Benedum, Abraham Hiestand, John Forshauer, Michael Kreider, Daniel Troyer, Thomas Winters, Andrew Zeller, Jacob Zeller, Lewis Kramer, Henry Evinger, Henry Hiestand, Frederick Klinger and John Pontius.

[6]The Moravians are a church with roots dating back to the supporters of John Huss (c 1369-1415), Bohemian martyr, who following his death formed the *Unitas Fratrum,* which can be translated, United Brethren. Count Zinzendorf organized some Moravian brethren who had sought refuge at Herrnhut in 1722. The first Moravians arrived in America in 1740. Their doctrine was similar to that of Otterbein.

[7]Drury, p. 308.

[8]Delbert R. Krumm, *A History of the Scioto, Southeast and Ohio Southeast Conferences* (Circleville, OH: The Ohio South East Conference, Evangelical United Brethren Church, 1958), p. 7.

[9]Ibid., p. 7.

[10]Roy D. Miller, *History of the Miami Conference of the Church of the United Brethren in Christ, 1810-1950)* (Published by the Ohio Miami Conference, 1970), p. 42.

[11]Drury, p. 320.

[12]Ibid., p. 307.

[13]Newcomer, *Journal,* p. 191.

[14]Ibid., p. 195.

[15]A. W. Drury, *Minutes of the Annual and General Conferences, 1800-1818* (Dayton, OH: Published for the United Brethren Historical Society by the United Brethren Publishing House, 1897), pp. 54, 55.

[16]Samuel S. Hough, editor, *Christian Newcomer, His Life, Journal and Achievements* (Dayton, OH: Board of Administration, Church of the United Brethren in Christ, 1430 U. B. Building, 1941), p. 142.

[17]The *Discipline* of 1815 gives useful definitions for the official members of the church. Accordingly, an exhorter was one who believed he had a call to exhort his fellowman and received a license to do so. The exhorter was to be distinguished from a preacher who was a regular minister of the Gospel. See: Lawrence, *History,* 2:50, 51.

13

LOSS OF EARLY LEADERSHIP

The United Brethren movement was entering into critical times. The minutes of the Original Conference of 1812 stated that Peter Kemp, John Hershey, Matthias Kessler, and Martin Boehm had died and within six weeks after the close of that conference, George Adam Geeting also died. Philip William Otterbein died in less than two years following the death of Martin Boehm. With the loss of these founding fathers in such a short period of time, one might wonder whether the movement could continue. Truly this was a period of change, the ushering in of a new era.

Peter Kemp

Peter Kemp died at his residence near Fredericktown, Maryland. The son of Frederick Kemp of the German Reformed, he was a strong supporter of Otterbein and the United Brethren movement. On September 23, 1778, he married Mary Lehman, daughter of the Reverend Adam Lehman.[1] Peter's house for many years had been the preacher's home. Otterbein, Newcomer, and other ministers were welcome. Peter entertained the original Annual Conference of 1800 and 1801 in his home. Licensed to preach in 1801, he was one of ten who volunteered to travel a circuit that year.

Sometime in the night of February 26, 1811, Peter Kemp was asked by a brother, whether or not the love of Christ was present with him. He answered, "Oh yes, bless the Lord, I shall soon be with Him." His strength slowly left him and he died between five and six in the morning while his family and friends were engaged in prayer around his bed.

Brother G. A. Geeting preached the funeral discourse.[2]

John Hershey

On March 4, 1811, John Hershey departed this life at his home, near Hagerstown, Maryland. He was born in Lancaster County, Pennsylvania, in 1741 and was of Mennonite descent. He married Magdalena Hoover. He was a member of the Original Conference and attended most of its sessions before his death. "Like Brother Kemp, Brother Hershey was a long, a loving, and a tried friend in the cause of that religion which he honored and adorned by his pious and upright manner of living in this world . . . ." Brother Hershey was a co-worker with Newcomer, Geeting, and Otterbein.[3]

Martin Boehm

In 1800, in his seventy-fifth year, Martin Boehm was still active in the ministry. In September of that year in company with his son, Henry, and Christian Newcomer, he entered upon a preaching tour into the Virginia circuit that lasted a month. Upon returning they all attended the first annual conference of the United Brethren where he was elected a bishop of the church.

Martin Boehm's participation in the United Brethren work, even in these later years, was active and important. As one of the co-founders of the movement, he was able to give direction and encouragement to those who were the new generation of leadership. In October 1802, he was involved in preaching on one of the circuits for at least a week prior to the convening of the annual conference. Two actions were taken at the Conference of 1802 which referred to him. The one appointed him to visit the circuits in Pennsylvania beyond the Susquehanna two times during the year. The other action was the one in which the rule was established that when one of the superintendents (bishops) died, another shall always be chosen in his place.

Boehm was one of only five who attended the Conference of 1804. He was re-elected as bishop in the Conference of 1805. Probably because of inability to travel easily, he did not attend the more distant conferences of 1806 and 1808. He was chairman of the conferences of 1807 and 1809, and in 1809 he, along with Geeting and Newcomer, signed the letter addressed to the Methodist Baltimore Conference as an official of the United Brethren Conference. He and Newcomer were the United Brethren representatives to the Methodist Conference meeting in Baltimore in March of 1810 when the letter was formerly presented. It was during this visit that Boehm was able to visit his friend Otterbein for the last time. On Sunday, March 11, Boehm preached with great power (his text was I Corinthians 4:20 "For the Kingdom of God is not in words . . . ."). On Monday they were invited to the lodgings of Bishop Francis Asbury, of the Methodist Church. Otterbein, Boehm, and Asbury each delivered a short address during this conference.

Martin Boehm died March 23, 1812, two years after that Baltimore visit. He was already buried when his son, Henry, arrived home. Not having known of his father's death earlier, Henry along with Bishop Asbury conducted a memorial service on the Sabbath Day, April 5, with a large crowd in attendance.[4]

George Adam Geeting

George Adam Geeting (Guething) had been associated with William Otterbein through all the formative years of the United Brethren Church. He has been called the first complete and well known product of the revival among the Germans. He stood next to Otterbein and Boehm as the chief exponent of the work.[5] Great meetings were often held in his neighborhood, at the Antietam, the Geeting Meeting-house, and Otterbein nearly always attended.[6] It is said that Otterbein and Geeting loved each other very much. That he held the respect of the United Brethren was indicated by the fact that he was chosen to preside at some of the conferences when the bishops could not be present. Geeting's was the counsel house for all the preachers. He was looked to for counsel, advice, and instruction. His word was received as law. His counsel was given in humility and love.[7] He was the keeper of the minutes of the annual conferences and these reflect his thinking on many subjects.

Soon after the close of the Conference of 1812, Geeting, with his wife, made an extended visit to his old friend Otterbein. He preached once more in Otterbein's pulpit. He had not felt well during his stay and shortened his visit and set out for home. The second night out he stopped at a public-house kept by Mr. Snyder, a place about thirty miles from Baltimore where he had stopped many times before.

In the morning he enjoyed a little rest and talked with his wife and Mr. Snyder about the Christian's life and hope. He became silent for a while and said that he felt as though his end had come. Then he said,

"Hark! Hark! Who spoke? Whose voice is this I hear? Light! Light! What golden light! Now all is dark, is dark again!"[8] Geeting asked to be helped out of his bed and they did so. He asked them to sing a hymn. When they had sung, he sank to his knees, and, leaning against the bed, he prayed fervently. He was helped into his bed again, and soon he died. This was June 28, 1812. Truly his passing from the scene created a void which others would need to fill.

Philip William Otterbein

Otterbein was still actively leading the United Brethren movement in 1800, although references in Newcomer's *Journal* suggest that his preaching tours outside Baltimore were less frequent. Otterbein was able to attend all of the annual conference meetings through 1805 with the exception of 1804. These conferences were held in Frederick County, Maryland, except those in 1804 and 1805 which were held at David Snider's in Cumberland County, Pennsylvania. He was elected bishop in 1800 and again in 1805, and continued to serve in that office without re-election until his death. Whenever he was in a meeting, the United Brethren looked to him for leadership. He preached with great effect whether he preached to the crowds of lay people, to the unconverted persons, or to the preachers. In the winter that followed the Conference of 1805, he became seriously ill; so ill that when Newcomer visited him he thought that in all probability he would never see him alive again.

I received the intelligence that Father Otterbein was very ill in Baltimore, and that in all probability he would not recover from his illness. 16th—This morning at 4 o'clock I set off for Baltimore; at night I reached the City, found Otterbein very ill indeed and in great pains; he requested me to pray for him. On account of his great weakness he could converse but very little: I lodged with Mr. Foltz. 17th—This morning Otterbein was somewhat better; we held a long conversation together, among other things he said, we should only prove faithful to the work which was so auspiciously began; the Lord would certainly be with us, and continue unto us his blessings. Towards evening his pains increased again, he inquired of those around the bed, whether I was present, being answered in the affirmative, I drew to him, and asked what he desired. "O! Christian," said he, "my pains are so severe and without intermission, that without the assisting grace of God, I must sink, for my strength will be shortly exhausted; do pray that the Lord may graciously lend me his assistance, and if according to his Holy will, to suffer my pains to moderate." We sung a few verses of a hymn; Bro. Ettinger, who was also present, and myself prayed and besought a throne of grace in his behalf; before we had concluded, the pains abated, and in a short time he fell into a slumber. 18th—This forenoon I continued with the old servant of God; the Rev. Mr. Dashield came also to pay him a visit. After commending him once more to the Divine favor in fervent prayer, I bid him in all probability a last farewell, and on reaching him my hand, he said, with great emphasis: "The God of Abraham be with thee and bless thee; remember me at a throne of grace." I departed, left the city . . .[9]

Otterbein recovered from that particular illness and was able to attend a meeting of the German Reformed Synod which was held in the spring of 1806. In regard to that meeting, it should be noted that he was asked particularly to attend.

Bending under the weight of four-score years, and leaning upon a long staff, which he carried to support him, he went with the committee. When he arrived, an opportunity was given him to speak. He arose and addressed the Synod in a most feeling manner, and strove to impress the minds of the ministers present with the importance of experimental religion,—of the new birth, and the great necessity of preaching it to the people distinctly and plainly, as men who must give account to God. After he had taken his seat, Mr. Becker, who, about that time, assumed the pastoral charge of the German Reformed Church in Baltimore, arose and opposed the views he had advanced, and answered him roughly. Mr. O. heard him through with his accustomed meekness, and then, taking his cane and hat, he bid the preachers farewell, bowed, and retired, never to return again.[10]

Because Otterbein had been unable to attend any United Brethren conferences outside of Baltimore since 1805, the Miami Conference agreed to send a letter on August 27, 1813, to Father Otterbein asking him to ordain by the laying on of hands one or more preachers who afterwards would be able to perform the rite for others. Newcomer found occasion to go to Baltimore on October 1st and learned that Otterbein had already received the letter from the Miami Conference. He found Otterbein very weak and feeble in body but strong and vigorous in spirit. He was glad for Newcomer's arrival, telling him that he was in receipt of the letter from the brethren in the West requesting him before his departure to ordain Newcomer by the laying on of hands. He added that he had always considered himself too unworthy to perform this solemn injunction of the apostle, but now perceived the necessity of doing so before he should be removed. He then asked Newcomer whether he had any objections. Newcomer indicated that he believed that solemn ordination to the ministry had been enjoined and practiced by the apostles; and if it was Otterbein's opinion that the act was necessary and beneficial, he had no objection. When Newcomer observed that Joseph Hoffman and Frederick Schaffer were present, he requested that Otterbein ordain them also. Otterbein readily assented and determined that the ordination would take place the following day.

The vestry and several other members of the Howard's Hill Church, Baltimore, assembled in Otterbein's house the next morning. He addressed them in so "spiritual and powerful a manner, that all beheld him with astonishment. It appeared as if he had received particular unction from above to perform this solemn act." After praying with great fervency, he called upon William Ryland, an elder of the Methodist Episcopal Church, who had been invited for the occasion, to assist him in the ordination. Thus three were ordained by the laying on of hands. John Hildt was a member of the vestry and the secretary who wrote out the certificates of ordination, in German and English, and they were signed by Father Otterbein.[11]

Otterbein was quite ill at the time of the ordination and had to deliver his address to the candidates sitting in an armchair to which it had been necessary to assist him. At one point he gave solemn injunction against being precipitate in the ordinations that it would fall upon them to confer. He again had to be assisted when he arose to place his hands on the heads of the candidates. When Newcomer and Hoffman took their departure the next day, his last words to them were: "Farewell. If any inquire after me, tell them that I die in the faith I have preached."[12]

For nearly six weeks following that ordination service, Otterbein's health continued to slowly fail. When it became apparent that the last hour had come, the Reverend Dr. J. D. Kurtz, of the Lutheran Church, a longtime personal friend, offered the last bedside prayer. When this was finished, Otterbein said, "Amen, amen! It is finished."

He then seemed to sink away, but rallying once more he said, "Jesus, Jesus,—I die, but Thou livest, and soon I shall live with Thee." Then he addressed those around him further, "The conflict is over and past. I begin to feel an unspeakable fullness of love and peace divine. Lay my head upon my pillow, and be still." In a few moments, the chariot of Israel had come. A smile, a fresh glow, lit up his countenance, and behold it was Death.[13]

It was 10 p.m. on Wednesday, November 17, 1813 when Otterbein died. On Saturday morning, at the Howard's Hill Church, the Reverend J. D. Kurtz preached the discourse in German from Matthew 20:8, using the words, "Call the laborers and give them their hire." Following this, the Reverend William Ryland of the Methodist Church spoke in English. Many people from many different churches in the city were in attendance in large numbers. Almost all of the ministers of the city were in attendance. The Reverend George Dashields of the Episcopal Church conducted the ceremony at the grave.

It is to be noticed that none of Otterbein's co-workers among the United Brethren took part in the funeral services. Frederick Schaffer took his place in the congregation as a mourner. Christian Newcomer, Joseph Hoffman, Christian Crum, and Jacob Baulus were in Pennsylvania trying to decide "whether a union could be effected between the societies of the United Brethren in Christ and the people known as the Albright Brethren."[14] When Newcomer arrived home, he found a letter informing him of the death of Otterbein. No Reformed minister took part in the services although Christian L. Becker was still serving as pastor of the German Reformed Church in Baltimore.[15]

When Bishop Asbury received the news of the death of his friend, he exclaimed, "Is Father Otterbein dead? Great and good man of God! An honor to his church and country. One of the greatest scholars and divines that ever came to America or was born in it. Alas, the chiefs of the Germans are gone to their rest and reward, taken from the evil to come."[16]

Otterbein was buried between Conway Street and the church, at the right of the entrance from the street. Two large marble slabs were placed over the grave, one placed directly over the grave on the ground and the second was supported by four pillars at the corners. This second slab contained an inscription to his memory.

> Here Rest the Remains
> of
> William Otterbein.
> He was born June 4th, 1726
> Departed this life Nov. 17th, 1813
> Aged 87 years 5 months and 13 days
> "Blessed are the dead which die in the Lord, for they
> rest from their labors, and their works do follow them."
> In the Ministry Sixty-two Years[17]

In 1913 these slabs were removed and the memorial was suitably renovated. Today one can read an upright pillar which adds the words:

> AND IN LOVING MEMORY OF
> PHILIP
> WILHELM
> OTTERBEIN
> FOUNDER
> AND FIRST BISHOP
> OF THE CHURCH OF THE

UNITED BRETHREN
IN CHRIST
JUNE 3, 1726
NOVEMBER 17, 1813

In March, 1814, the Baltimore Conference of the Methodist Church paid a special tribute to Otterbein. On the closing day, the conference assembled in Otterbein's church and Bishop Asbury delivered the memorial message.

FOOTNOTES

[1]Adam Lehman was one of the two leaders of Sam's Creek Class appointed by the Pipe Creek Conference May 29, 1774. He began to preach about 1777. He later moved to Frederick and died in 1823.

[2]John Lawrence, *The History of the Church of the United Brethren in Christ,* 2 vols. (Dayton, OH: Published at the United Brethren Printing Establishment, Sowers & King, Publishers, 1861), 2:377, 378.

[3]Henry G. Spayth, *History of the United Brethren Church* (Circleville, OH: Published at the Conference Office of the United Brethren in Christ, 1851), pp. 127, 128.

[4]Henry Boehm; J. B. Wakeley, *The Patriarch of One Hundred Years; Being Reminiscences, Historical and Biographical, of Rev. Henry Boehm* (New York: Nelson & Phillips, 1875), pp. 55, 56.

[5]A. W. Drury, *History of the Church of the United Brethren in Christ* (Dayton, OH: The Otterbein Press, 1924), p. 213.

[6]George Adam Geeting lived in Washington County, Maryland on the Little Antietam, about a mile from where it empties into the large Antietam. The meeting-house was probably built by the followers of Otterbein and was probably built before 1774 near Mr. Geeting's place. See Drury, *History,* p. 165.

[7]H. A. Thompson, *Our Bishops,* New edition (Dayton, OH: United Brethren Publishing House, 1904), p. 108.

[8]Ibid., p. 116.

[9]Christian Newcomer, with John Hildt, trans. and ed., *The Life and Journal of the Rev'd Christian Newcomer* (Hagerstown, MD: F. G. W. Kapp, 1834), pp. 141, 142.

[10]Lawrence, 1:260, 261.

[11]Newcomer, pp. 219, 220.

[12]Lawrence, 2:394.

[13]Ibid., 1:394, 395.

[14]Newcomer, p. 212. Jacob Albright began to organize churches under his care about 1800. A conference was held in 1807 at which time he was elected bishop, but he lived only a few months after that. The Conference of 1809 applied the name, 'The So-called Albrights,' to the Association. This was changed to the "Evangelical Association" in 1816. This association was an antecedent organization to the Evangelical Congregational Church with which the United Brethren are in federation (1984).

[15]Drury, p. 241.

[16]Ibid., p. 242.

[17]Thompson, p. 71.

14

DEVELOPMENT OF A CONFESSION OF FAITH AND A DISCIPLINE

Otterbein was aware of the value of a church creed. He seemed also convinced of the necessity of some simple disciplines to which the brethren could adhere that were consistent with the creeds and provided unity in expression. He well knew the faith and personal discipline of churchly pietism and did not hesitate to present them to the brethren. As a pastor at Lancaster he had proposed that disciplines consistent with his pietistic beliefs be observed by the membership as a condition of his continuance as their pastor. From the beginning of his pastorate, at Howard's Hill Church, Baltimore, Otterbein not only preached but put into written form the disciplines which were later adopted as part of the Howard's Hill Church rules. The minutes of the Pipe Creek conferences painted the picture of Otterbein and his associates as spiritual administrators of churches under their charge with a pietistic creed and discipline to guide them.

First Confession of Faith and Discipline

The interest in discipline continued to be revealed in Otterbein's relationship to the growing work among the Germans outside the German Reformed Church. The meeting that Otterbein held with the co-operating preachers in 1789 centered on a discussion of the continuation of their loosely structured work and of those procedures intended to make the work more effective. Historian Daniel Berger indicates that that meeting produced the first Confession of Faith of the United Brethren in Christ,[1] an antecedent to the Confession of

122

Faith of 1815. Early historians indicate that a discipline was also produced at that meeting, a condensed version of the Howard's Hill Church rules from Baltimore, re-written in more general language for a wider application.[2] The Confession of 1789 consisted of five articles, similar in language to the corresponding articles in the current Confession of Faith. The Confession and Discipline of 1789 were basically the documents that governed the United Brethren throughout the formative period until 1814, though they had not yet been formally adopted by the new denomination.[3]

Growth of the Church Idea

It is to be noted that the United Brethren had not spoken of themselves as a church, yet the Discipline of 1789 did use the word church, indicating that the idea may have been in the minds of some of those early leaders. When conferences began to be held annually, the idea of becoming a church became part of the climate leading to, and part of the reasoning behind the need for, a regularly adopted confession of faith and discipline. The concept of becoming a church was not uniformly received. Some in the church resisted this development, while others promoted it. Those persons such as Newcomer and Grosh who could readily appreciate the need for better organization of a widely scattered and growing work generally encouraged the adoption of a confession of faith and discipline. They were each early participants in the United Brethren movement. Grosh was of Moravian descent and lived in Lancaster County, Pennsylvania. He is listed as an absent member of the conference in 1789 and present in 1791. There were others, however, who were also part of the early United Brethren movement who were slow in accepting the growth of church characteristics. The Liberty People and the Unsectarian elements were not ready to adopt church forms, and their resistance was long and obstinate.[4]

Effect of Discussions with Other Groups

The close tie between the United Brethren and the Methodists may have encouraged the idea of better organization. The two societies had worked side by side from the beginning. Some families, even in the ministry, were represented in both societies. The preachers of both societies often shared the same pulpits. Those close ties made it quite natural that consideration should be given to a closer union between them.

However, since the Methodist work was a model of a well-organized and growing society, the subject of a discipline to better regulate the work of the United Brethren often came up in their formal and informal contacts with one another. Christian Newcomer began to pursue the matter. For several years he had attended sessions of Methodist annual conferences, sometimes with other United Brethren preachers, sometimes as an official representative of the United Brethren. He had frequent contacts with Bishop Asbury and other Methodist preachers. The Methodist conferences in return often sent fraternal delegates to United Brethren conferences.

When two Methodist preachers attended the United Brethren conference in May, 1809, the discussion which followed their presentation lasted long into the night. The subject of the discussion was the need for better order and discipline. Some of the brethren thought it was unnecessary to have more than the Word of God and were opposed to all other discipline.[5]

Serious attention was given to the formation of a discipline every year, beginning with 1809, until the first general conference in 1815. Correspondence between United Brethren and Methodist conferences report the progress. In a letter signed by Christian Newcomer shortly after the Conference of 1811, the Methodists were informed that:

> We have now formed our members into classes as much as possible. However, there are a number yet among us who have not yet joined with us in this privilege, so long delayed by us. We earnestly hope that you will instruct your traveling preachers to bear with such as much as the order of your church will admit. We would further inform you that we have drawn up some regulations, or discipline, among us and shall endeavor, more and more, to put them into effect among ourselves and our members.[6]

Throughout the period, Newcomer was in consultation with Otterbein, who because of the infirmities of old age was not able to attend these annual conferences. Progress toward the adoption of a confession of faith and a discipline was done with his knowledge and guidance. Another group with whom the United Brethren worked closely in this formative period were the Albright Brethren. Two weeks before the conference of 1813, Newcomer met with the Albright Brethren, April 21-24, at the Martin Dreisbach home. During Newcomer's stay among them they discussed the propriety and practicability of a union between the two societies. Newcomer laid the discipline of the United Brethren before them for examination; they made no objection to it. "On the contrary," he said, "they appeared to approve the same cordially. They delivered to me a written communication of the subject, addressed to the conference of the United Brethren; so I departed."[7]

The discipline that Newcomer laid before the Albright Brethren was no doubt the one that was generally accepted for use, dating from 1789. The United Brethren conference that followed began on May 5, and took up the subject of a church discipline. The Brethren were still "greatly divided in opinion, in respect to the discipline."[8] Even the next day they were still embroiled in a turbulent session so much that Newcomer said that they appeared not to understand each other. On the third day of the conference, having worked through those tense moments, they adopted a discipline and elected Christian Newcomer as a superintendent or bishop with specific duties and powers for a period of one year. The resolution adopted provided that the Confession of Faith and the Discipline of the United Brethren in Christ would be printed. The documents were to be revised and prepared for submission to the next annual conference. The organizational progress was fraternally reported by letter to the Baltimore Annual Conference of the Methodist Church.

If the adoption of a Discipline proved to be a problem for the United Brethren, it appears also to have been a problem for the Albright Brethren. Newcomer, Christian Crum, Joseph Hoffman, and Jacob Baulus met on November 11, 1813, with four brethren from the Albright societies to discuss whether or not a union could be effected. The consultation continued for two days and ended just five days before the death of Philip William Otterbein. The active leadership of the United Brethren, thus engaged, could not even be informed of the death of the patriarch of the church until after the funeral. No union could be effected because the Albright Brethren could not accept the right of local preachers to vote in conference the same as the traveling preachers.[9] Secondly, the Albright Brethren objected to the observance of the example of footwashing.[10] Newcomer recorded that a further unsuccessful attempt at union between the two societies occurred April 18, 1815.[11]

Discipline of 1814

According to early historians, when the United Brethren Original Conference of 1814 took up the matter of a Confession of Faith and Discipline, two separate documents were presented for consideration by Christopher Grosh and Christian Newcomer. At the conclusion of the conference one document, enlarged from what existed before, was tentatively adopted and signed by these two men.

The work of this Conference of 1814 was done with the knowledge that their elder statesman, Bishop Otterbein, was dead. At the time of Otterbein's death, Frederick Schaffer was in Baltimore, and, at the request of the Howard's Hill congregation, he consented to be their pastor. Since the congregation had held an independent position from its inception, its relationship with the United Brethren was somewhat different from that of other congregations. Prior to the Conference of 1814, the Baltimore congregation adopted resolutions stating: 1) They would connect themselves with the United Brethren to be supplied with their preachers. 2) They would provide support and salary for the preacher. 3) They would elect two members of the congregation to attend the conference as official representatives. When the conference met, a committee was formed to consider the statement of the Baltimore congregation. In place of Frederick Schaffer, Joseph Hoffman was appointed to preach there for one year with the possibility that he could remain for three years.[12]

The Original Conference of 1814 was in receipt of another letter from the Methodists. This letter called upon the United Brethren to keep the terms of union in view. Noting the harmonious sentiment, they thought it unnecessary to continue the ceremony of annual letters but left the door open for friendly relations. Though the letter left open the door of continued co-operative union, following the death of Bishop Asbury, these agreements came into disuse.[13] "The merging of the two societies into one was, as much from considerations on the one side as on the other, impossible, and was not thought of."[14]

Since 1810 there had been two annual conferences in the church. These were widely separated geographically. No bishop had visited in Ohio until after the Original Conference of 1813 had elected Christian Newcomer as bishop. The existing Discipline did not provide a strong bond of union. From the beginning, the original conference had transacted all business for the church. It was "under the impression that it was the first and last authority in the church in determining its policies and directing its work."[15] It is possible that the Eastern portion of the church was not fully aware of the rapid growth and importance of the work in the West. The West may have been unappreciative of the work done in the East, feeling that they should have some voice in the work. When Bishop Newcomer arrived in the West, he was elected as president of their conference.

When the Original Conference of 1814 adopted a confession of faith and discipline, they did not consult with the brethren from the West. However, it is likely that Bishop Newcomer, re-elected by the original conference for three years under provisions of the new Discipline of 1814, was requested to present this Discipline to the Miami Conference and to call attention to the contemplated plan for a general conference. There is no reflection of this in the minutes of the original conference, but both matters did come up in the Miami Conference that year. According to the minutes there, "The present order (or Discipline) of the Church was taken under consideration and protested against. It was moved and adopted that there shall be a convention, and that two members from each district shall assemble at Abraham Draksel's (home) in Westmoreland County."[16] The language used in the minutes seems to suggest that there was some disagreement with the proposals, but Newcomer noted that "We had considerable less difficulty than I had expected, and closed the session in great harmony and unanimity. Praise the Lord for it."[17]

If the Miami Conference did not approve "the present order of the church," their action in reference to a general conference was positive. They decided to divide the entire territory of the church into ten districts. First district, Baltimore; second, Hagerstown; third, Carlisle; fourth, Pennsylvania south of the Alleghenies; fifth, Pennsylvania north of the Alleghenies; sixth, Muskingum; seventh, New Lancaster, Ohio; eighth, Miami; ninth, Indiana and Kentucky; tenth, Virginia. Each district was entitled to two delegates.

Work proceeded through the year with further refinements of the Discipline in preparation for the General Conference of 1815. Newcomer was in Baltimore in December, and while there met with John Hildt for the purpose of revising Discipline.[18] Prior to general conference, the Original Conference met May 8-12 and business was conducted in a spirit of love and union. A date for prayer and fasting was set for August 8, 1815, and the first camp meeting authorized by the United Brethren was set to begin August 17, at Rocky Spring, Franklin County, Pennsylvania.

The First General Conference

The General Conference of 1815 convened on June 6 in Western Pennsylvania. Highways from the East and the various crossings of the Ohio River made this a desirable location. "The place of the meeting was a country schoolhouse, known as John Bonnet's, a very humble place indeed for the assembling of this body, whose counsels were to affect the faith and life of generations of devout followers. The location is about one mile east of Mount Pleasant."[19]

Only fourteen delegates attended the conference. Bishop Newcomer presided and Abraham Hiestand was elected as his assistant. Jacob Baulus and H. G. Spayth were elected as secretaries.[20]

As the brethren looked upon one another, they felt sadly the loss of the great leaders who had been transferred to the church triumphant. Good men indeed were they who sat at the head, but all missed the majestic personality of Otterbein, the saintly presence of Boehm, and the magnetic power of the eloquent Guething. Indeed, for a time, the conference in the absence of strong leadership, seems to have had rough sailing—more discord in the proceedings than harmony.[21]

Newcomer recorded in his journal, "This day the General Conference commenced at old Brother Draksel's; may the Lord have mercy upon us. Instead of love and unanimity, the spirit of hatred and discord seemed to prevail. May the Lord grant us more wisdom and grace."[22]

H. G. Spayth, one of the secretaries, wrote in his history:

Nor will we disguise the truth, the sky was not exactly clear. A heavy atmosphere would ever and anon press and swell the bosom, and then came ruffling breezes and sharp words. This could not last long. The darkening clouds which hung over the conference must be cleared away. A calm atmosphere and a clear sky could not be dispensed with. A pause ensued. The conference agreed to humble themselves before God in prayer. And such a prayer-meeting your humble servant never witnessed before nor since. Brethren with streaming eyes embraced and thanked God. From that hour to the end unanimity and love smiled joyously on that assembly.[23]

The following are the minutes of the General Conference of 1815, the first general conference of United Brethren in Christ.

This, the sixth of June 1815, the following preachers assembled for the General Conference near Mount Pleasant, Westmoreland county, Pennsylvania: Christian Newcomer, Abraham Hiestand, Andrew Zeller, Daniel Troyer, George Benedum, Christian Crum, Isaac Niswander, Henry Spayth, John Snyder, Abraham Mayer, Henry Kumler, Abraham Troxel, Christian Berger and Jacob Baulus. These persons were elected from the various districts to the General Conference. Brother Abraham Hiestand was chosen to assist the Bishop in the conference. The conference was opened with the reading of the fifth chapter of First Peter, then singing, and then prayer by the most of the members. Then proceeded to business. There was misunderstanding and prejudice on the part of some, but this was removed in part. A letter from Christopher Grosh, coming from their so-called conference, was read. It was evident therefrom that they had not considered the matter of which they wrote. Brother Newcomer was accused by Bonnet that he was untruthful. The matter was investigated by three presiding elders and it was found that there was only a misunderstanding. He was in nothing liable to accusation.

The Confession of Faith and the Discipline were considered, in some respects enlarged, some things omitted, on the whole improved, and ordered printed. Jacob Baulus, Secretary.[24]

The main work of the conference is recorded in the last sentence of the minutes. Although the Confession and Discipline were not printed until 1816, they are referred to as the Discipline of 1815. The minutes do not say that they were adopted by the conference. It appears they were to be presented to the Church for informal acceptance and use. Though the Discipline provided for a general conference every four years, this conference provided for another general conference to follow in only two years. It is noted that Newcomer's term as bishop was to last another two years.

There was no substantial change in the Confession of Faith from that which was adopted in 1789. The rules of Discipline that were approved made provision for general and annual conferences; the election, ordination, powers and duties of bishops; the election and function of presiding elders; the ordination and duties of elders; the method of receiving preachers, their office and duties, and procedures to be used in case of their immoral conduct; and members in general.[25]

"The difficulties in the conference were with reference to having a Discipline, or the extent to which a Discipline should go. Bonnet's accusation of Newcomer doubtless grew out of the feeling that the informal understandings as to association with the Mennonites and others has been disregarded."[26]

The result of this conference was more than a printed discipline. There had been a widespread feeling of doubt as to whether the church would be able to hold together after the death of Otterbein. Although there were recognized leaders, and still others who would be raised up soon, these were as yet largely untried. The church had derived strength from strong leadership and had not as yet a strong system of government. The itinerant system was not fully developed. Most of the preachers were local preachers and a very few were truly itinerants. The general conference seemed to provide a bond of union of the widely separated sections of the church and for a government and a working system which efficiently utilized the available preachers, thus encouraging growth.[27]

Although the General Conference of 1815 ended on a positive note and its effect was the preservation of the United Brethren for a much enlarged ministry in later years, some of the provisions adopted were implemented with difficulty at the local level for many years. "Large numbers of those who, by the attraction of divine love, formed themselves into United Brethren societies, refused to have their names recorded in a church book, and were slow to accept any discipline except the New Testament."[28] Daniel Eberly, in illustrating the slow, deliberate efforts to change this spirit at the local level, said that Jacob Erb had encountered resistance to organization of the local membership in 1827 in eastern Pennsylvania.

> Before he could proceed he had to get the consent of some of the older brethren. He found it necessary to go to Lebanon and present his case to Rev. Felix Light, who had the power of a bishop in that county. It was only after an earnest plea that he obtained a reluctant permission to proceed. The organization took place, at what was called Sherk's Old Meeting House.[29]

FOOTNOTES

[1]Daniel Berger, *History of the Church of the United Brethren in Christ* (Dayton, OH: United Brethren Publishing House, W. J. Shuey, Publisher, 1897), p. 138.

The text of the Confession of Faith adopted in 1789 is as follows:

"Article 1. In the name of God we confess before all men, that we believe in the only true God, Father, Son and Holy Ghost; that these three are one; the Father in the Son, the Son in the Father, and the Holy Ghost equal in essence with both; that this God created heaven and earth and all that in them is, visible as well as invisible, and sustains, governs, protects, and supports the same.

"Article 2. We believe in Jesus Christ; that he is very God and man, Saviour and Redeemer of the whole world; that all men through him may be saved if they will; that this Jesus suffered for us; that he died and was buried, rose on the third day, ascended into heaven, and that he will come again, at the last day, to judge the living and the dead.

"Article 3. We believe in the Holy Ghost; that he proceeds from the Father and the Son; that we through him must be sanctified and receive faith, thereby being cleansed from all filthiness of the flesh and spirit.

"Article 4. We believe that the Bible is the word of God; that it contains the true way to our souls' well-being and salvation; that every true Christian is bound to acknowledge and receive it, with the influences of the Spirit of God, as his only rule and guide; and that without repentance, faith in Jesus Christ, forgiveness of sins, and following after Jesus Christ, no one can be a true Christian.

"Article 5. We believe that the doctrine which the Holy Scriptures contain, namely, the fall in Adam and salvation through Jesus Christ, shall be preached and proclaimed throughout the whole world.

"We recommend that the outward signs and ordinances, namely, baptism and the remembrance of the Lord in the distribution of the bread and wine, be observed; also the washing of feet, where the same is desired."

Berger indicated that this conference of ministers entitled the document "The Doctrine of the United Brethren in Christ" but that the title was not part of the original draft.

[2]Henry G. Spayth, *History of the United Brethren Church* (Circleville, OH: Published at the Conference Office of the United Brethren in Christ, 1851), pp. 145-147.

According to Spayth, the disciplinary rules which governed the church from 1789 up to 1815 were these:

"(a) That no one, be he a preacher or lay member, can be a member of this Church, who should be found to lead an offensive life.—(I Tim. 3:1-3; I Cor. 5:13).

"(b) To keep the Sabbath day holy: and attend divine worship.

"(c) To attend class or prayer-meeting, once a week.

"(d) That none be received into the Church, who is not resolved to flee the wrath to come, and by faith and repentance, to seek his salvation in Christ, and be resolved willingly to obey the disciplinary rules which are now observed for good order, yet always excepted that such rules are founded on the Word of God, as the only unerring guide of faith and practice.

"(e) That a neglect of class and prayer-meetings by any one, after being twice or thrice admonished, without manifest amendment, (sickness or absence from home excepted,) excludes such from the Church.

"(f) Every member to abstain from all backbiting and evil speaking—(I Peter 2:1; James 4:11). The transgressor in the first instance, to be admonished privately, but the second time to be reproved in the class-meeting.

"(g) For as much as the differences of people and denominations end in Christ—(Rom. 10:12; Col. 3:11), and availeth nothing, but a new creature—(Gal. 6:13-16), it becomes our duty and privilege according to the gospel, to commune with, and admit professors of religion to the Lord's table without partiality.

"(h) That each member strive to lead a quiet and godly life, lest he give offense, and fall into the condemnation of the adversary—(Mathew 5:14-16).

"(i) All offenses between members, shall be dealt with in strict conformity to the precepts of our Lord—(Matt. 18:15-18).

"(j) Should a preacher or elder be accused of any known immorality, and upon the testimony of two or three creditable witnesses, he being present, the charge be proven against him, he will be immediately suspended, and until he gives proof of true repentance, and make open confession to the society, he remains excluded from the Church. The same rule shall be observed against members of the Church, who shall be found guilty of immoral conduct—(I Cor. 5:11-13; I Tim. 5:20)."

[3]Historian A. W. Drury expressed doubt that the creed and rules of discipline quoted above can be accounted for in connection with the Conference of 1789, but rather with some later development. While the date of their adoption may be in doubt, if indeed they were ever formally adopted, this writer has concluded that they were documents which characterized the movement during this entire period of time from 1789 until 1814 when the original conference adopted a Confession of Faith and a Discipline. However see: A. W. Drury, History of the Church of the United Brethren in Christ (Dayton, OH: The Otterbein Press, 1924), p. 158.

[4]Ibid., p. 275.

[5]Christian Newcomer, with John Hildt, trans. and ed., The Life and Journal of the Rev'd. Christian Newcomer (Hagerstown, MD: F. G. W. Kapp, 1834), p. 175.

[6]A. W. Drury, trans. and ed., Minutes of the Annual and General Conferences of the Church of the United Brethren in Christ, 1800-1818 (Dayton, OH: Published for the United Brethren Historical Society by the United Brethren Publishing House, 1897), p. 54.

[7]Newcomer, pp. 212, 213.

[8]Ibid., p. 213.

[9]Ibid., p. 221.

[10]Spayth, 143.

[11]Cooperative efforts with a successor to the Albright Brethren, the Evangelical Congregational Church, and the Primitive Methodist Church, have been initiated in recent

years. Since 1974 these denominations and the United Brethren in Christ have been working together in a federation of these autonomous bodies to assess the needs and resources available and to explore and implement procedures which would meet the needs and most economically use the resources. The General Conference of 1981 recommended that the United Brethren Church "aggressively pursue merger" with these two denominations. However, a Joint Statement Concerning Exploration of Merger was issued by the Administrative Council of the Federation as a result of their meeting held January 14, 1983 which concluded that ". . . the 3 denominations (should) discontinue the exploration of merger. The Joint committee further decided that attention be given to strengthening the structure and the program of the Federation."

[12]Drury, pp. 285, 286.

The Baltimore congregation reported the actions of their officers and members to the conference as follows:

"After the death of the deceased, William Otterbein, the elders and trustees of the Evangelical Reformed Church assembled to counsel with one another in what way the congregation in the future may best be preserved, the members of the same built up, the honor of God furthered through it. The greatest difficulty which they found was in the selection of a suitable preacher; one who, with the help and assistance of God, would carry forward the work begun by God through our deceased preacher, his faithful servant, William Otterbein, and declare the will of God pure and plain and without fear according to the Bible; in short, a preacher who does not preach for pay or money, but has on his heart more than all else the welfare and salvation of his hearers. Long before the death of our deceased father this was his greatest concern, but it pleased Divine Providence to take away this burden of his heart yet before his death, and to make evident that with him is counsel and help when one least looks for it. Through a special providence, Frederick Schaffer happend to come hither. He preached in our church, was by the deceased William Otterbein solemnly ordained to preach, and consented to serve this congregation since that time. We have reason to believe that the majority of the members are well satisfied with him, and that, with the help of the Lord, he labored among us profitably. The vestry would have no hesitancy in recommending said Frederick Schaffer as the preacher of the congregation, and expecting all else from the help and assistance of Jesus Christ, if they were not convinced that insurmountable difficulties stand in the way. In order, therefore, to avoid all difficulties and to preserve this congregation, the vestry have drawn up the following resolutions, which they herewith lay before the congregation for their approval or rejection:

"First. That this congregation connect itself with the United Brethren, so that from time to time we may by them be supplied with preachers.

"Second. That this congregation will provide for the support and annual salary of the preacher.

"Third. That the vestry elect two members of the congregation to make the United Brethren, in their conference, acquainted with these resolutions.

"After mature consideration, these resolutions were submitted to the members of the church present for acceptance or rejection. So, as the votes in the church-book to the names of those present show, the result was, thirty-five votes were cast for approval and only one for rejection. So the above resolutions were approved.

"A true copy.   John Hildt."

[13]Spayth, p. 115.

14Drury, pp. 202, 203.

15Ibid., p. 315.

16Drury, *Minutes*, p. 78.

17Newcomer, p. 226.

18Ibid., p. 230.

19Berger, p. 223.

20The minutes are unclear at this point. However, see a discussion on this subject in Drury, *History*, p. 318.

21Berger, p. 224.

22Newcomer, p. 234.

23Spayth, p. 150.

24Drury, *Minutes*, pp. 65, 66.

25A. W. Drury, *Disciplines of the United Brethren in Christ* (Dayton, OH: United Brethren Publishing House, 1895), pp. 11, 12.

"The Confession of Faith of the United Brethren in Christ

"In the name of God we confess before all men, that we believe in the only true God, Father, Son, and Holy Ghost; that these three are one, the Father in the Son, the Son in the Father, and the Holy Ghost equal in essence with both; that this triune God created heaven and earth, and all that in them is, visible as well as invisible, sustains, governs, protects, and supports the same.

"We believe in Jesus Christ; that he is very God and man; that he, by the Holy Ghost, assumed his human nature in Mary, and was born of her; that he is the Savior and Redeemer of the whole human race, if they with faith in him accept the grace proffered in Jesus; that this Jesus suffered and died on the cross for us, was buried, rose again on the third day, ascended into heaven, and sitteth on the right hand of God to intercede for us; and that he shall come again at the last day, to judge the living and the dead.

"We believe in the Holy Ghost; that he is equal in being with the Father and the Son; that he proceeds from both; that we are through him enlightened; through faith justified and sanctified.

"We believe in a holy church, communion of saints, resurrection of the flesh, and a life everlasting.

"We believe that the Bible, Old and New Testament, is the word of God; that it contains the true way to our salvation; that every true Christian is bound to receive it with the influences of the Spirit of God, as his only rule, and that without faith in Jesus Christ, true penitence, forgiveness of sins, and following after Christ, no one can be a true Christian.

"We believe that the doctrine which the Holy Scriptures contain, namely, the fall in Adam and the redemption through Jesus Christ, shall be preached throughout the whole world.

"We believe that the outward means of grace are to be in use in all Christian societies, namely: That baptism and the remembrance of the death of the Lord in the distribution of the bread and wine are to be in use among his children, according to the command of the Lord Jesus; the mode and manner, however, shall be left to the judgment of everyone. Also, the example of feet-washing remains free to everyone."

26Drury, *History*, p. 318.

27Berger, pp. 229, 230.

28Daniel Eberly, I. H. Albright, CIB Brane, *Landmark History of the United Brethren Church*, (Reading, PA: Behney and Bright Printers, 1911), p. 63.

29Ibid., p. 63.

15

EARLY CHURCH GROWTH

Following the General Conference of 1815, the Miami Conference concurred with the Original Conference plan for the prayer and fast day. The United States had just concluded the 'second war of independence,' the War of 1812, and with all the chaos and disruption, prayer was certainly an appropriate activity. But, there were other matters of more particular concern to the church that drove the brethren to prayer.

Early Concerns

Beginning about the time of Otterbein's death the German element in America began to give way to the English. Fewer Germans were coming to the United States annually. Further, since the English language was commonly used in law, in government, in literature, and in the schools, the German tongue rapidly became a secondary language, even in the largest German settlements.[1,2] As a result there was a growing need for English speaking preachers.

As noted in previous chapters, there was a longstanding fellowship between the United Brethren and Methodists, dating from the time of the close bonds between Otterbein and Asbury, which, in the more recent years, had resulted in agreements of co-operation between the two societies. It is easy to see how this fraternal co-operation and unity might work to the disadvantage of the United Brethren. The steady increase of the use of the English language meant that members and families, though they might have been United Brethren for years, would be lost to the movement. This would happen as English speaking children matured and assumed places of leadership in the church. They would require English preaching, and, not finding it with the United Brethren, would turn to the Methodists, who at that time were producing English speaking preachers in some quantity and with whom the long years of friendship had created the climate of easy transition.

Also, young preachers were enticed to enlist into the Methodist ranks. To the Methodists, the whole country was open, but the United Brethren work was confined to a few areas. The Methodist work was in the language in which young men had received their education. The Methodists itinerant system was far better organized and supported. There was a strong denominational feeling in Methodism which was still lacking in United Brethrenism. Historian Spayth noted that there never was a year "when the labors of our German fathers were not crowned with the conversion of numerous souls; yet, from causes already noticed, not only was no progress made in numbers from 1810 to 1820, but, undoubtedly, there was a retrocession."[3]

General Conference Work Approved

In both annual conferences, the actions of the General Conference of 1815, for the greater part, brought general approval among the brethren, with very little reaction. The Miami Conference ordained eight ministers in 1815. Christopher Crum was ordained by Bishop Newcomer first, then the two together ordained the others. When the Original Conference next met, they also proceeded to ordain four elders.

In 1816, the Old Conference strengthened their ministry by electing three presiding elders. The Miami Conference that same year elected five presiding elders for three districts of Miami, New Lancaster, and Kentucky-Indiana. John George Pfrimmer was presiding elder for the new Kentucky-Indiana District, and he took Bishop Newcomer on a tour into Indiana immediately following the conference sessions. The bishop then went on his own into Kentucky and reached the cities of Louisville, Frankfort, and Lexington with quite a few stops and meetings along the way. During this year, the Miami Conference collected forty-two dollars to begin a fund for the support of poorly paid preachers.

General Conference of 1817

When the second general conference convened on June 2, 1817, only twelve preachers came. Since the proceedings of the General Conference of 1815 seemed to have been well received, no extensive revisions were made to their previous work. A few items were added to the Discipline: 1) only the General Conference has power to elect bishops and revise Discipline; 2) each annual conference shall divide its territory into districts and the members shall elect two delegates to the next general conference; 3) two bishops shall be elected and both must be able to travel into all parts of the society and both shall attend all of the conferences or they cannot be re-elected; 4) the general conference shall determine the formation of new annual conferences.

Christian Newcomer and Andrew Zeller were elected bishops. A brief sketch of Andrew Zeller has already been given in connection with the work in Ohio. Though he was evidently preaching before he went to Ohio, he is not listed as present at any of the conferences in the East. However, in 1810 he is listed as one of the ministers in Ohio. He was elected presiding elder for two years in 1812 and again in 1814 and 1816. He was a delegate to the General Conference of 1815 and again in 1817 when he was elected bishop, serving as bishop for one term. He was a member of the General Conferences of 1825 and 1829. He died May 24, 1839, while the Miami Conference was in session.

In accordance with the provision for the formation of annual conferences, the Muskingum Annual Conference was formed by the General Conference of 1817. The first Muskingum Annual Conference meeting convened June 1, 1818 at the home of Joseph Naftzgar in the northern part of Harrison County, probably near Conotton, in eastern Ohio. Bishops Newcomer and Zeller were both in attendance, along with John G. Pfrimmer and Jacob Antrim from Miami Conference, and Jacob Lehman from the Original Conference. Regular members of the conference present were Abraham Forney, Matthias Bortsfield, Joseph Gundy, Christian Knagi, Jacob Winter, and John Crum. Bishop Newcomer gave an address, speaking on the origin of the brotherhood, and the reason for forming the Muskingum Annual Conference. He wrote in his journal for June 1: "This day we held our Conference here; this was something rather new and strange to some of the Brethren, and they appeared loathe to acquiesce and come under the rules of discipline; but they were soon convinced of their error."[4] Jacob Winter and John Brown were ordained. Three received licenses to preach.

The slower progress of the church in eastern Ohio can be explained by a look at the settlement of the state. Since the Ohio Company settlement at Marietta was made up of people from New England, few Germans were among the first settlers. German speaking people did not come in large numbers to Harrison, Tuscarawas, and Stark Counties until 1815. However, when Newcomer made his earlier journeys to eastern Ohio, he met a small number of German people, some of whom he had known before. Therefore, near the roads he traveled, United Brethren congregations sprang up, especially in the counties named. These classes had been in existence for some time when the first Muskingum Annual Conference convened.

General Conference of 1821

The third general conference convened at the Dewalt Mechlin home in Fairfield County, Ohio, May 15, 1821. This was the first of eleven successive general conferences to be held in the state of Ohio. Of the seventeen delegates, only three had served in previous general conferences. Nathaniel Havens and John McNamar of the Miami Conference were the first English-speaking delegates.

The actions of the conference resulted in several Discipline additions: 1) a resolution instructed preachers in towns and cities to give an account to the annual conference, to limit their salary according to their support and expenses, and to return any excess salary to the general conference to be expended for the support of the itinerant preachers; 2) circuit and assistant stewards were to be elected in each class and were to make quarterly collections, in money or produce, to be proportionably distributed among the traveling preachers; 3) where a person is recommended as a preacher or exhorter, the presiding elder was to examine him in the presence of the preachers; and should he be found competent in his standing and abilities, he may permit such brother to preach or exhort; and shall transmit his testimony and examination in writing to the annual conference.

A resolution on slavery was also enacted:

Resolved, That all slavery, in every sense of the word, be totally prohibited and in no way tolerated in our community. Should some be found therein, or others apply to be admitted as members, who hold slaves, they can neither remain to be members or be admitted as such, provided they do not personally manumit or set free such slave, wherever the laws of the state shall permit it, or submit the case to the quarterly conference, to be by them specified, what length of time such slave shall serve his master or other person, until the amount given for him or for raising him, be compensated to his master. But in no case shall a member of our society be permitted to sell a slave.[5]

Another item of importance, adopted by the conference but not included in the Discipline, dealt with making liquor. George Benedum moved that no preacher shall be allowed to carry on a distillery. William Brown moved to amend to strike out the word 'preacher' and insert the word 'member.' Then the matter was amended by substitution:

> Resolved, That neither preacher nor laymember shall be allowed to carry on a distillery; and that distillers be requested to willingly cease the business; that the members of the general conference be requested to lay this resolution before the several annual conferences; that it shall then be the duty of the preachers to labor against the evils of intemperance during the interval between this and the next general conference when the subject shall again be taken up for further consideration.[6]

Christian Newcomer and Joseph Hoffman were elected bishops. Zeller, although younger than Bishop Newcomer, retired because of age and infirmity. He found himself unable to perform the long journeys on horseback which were required of a bishop.

Joseph Hoffman was born in Cumberland County, Pennsylvania March 19, 1780. He was converted in 1801, licensed to preach in 1803, became an itinerant in 1805, ordained by Otterbein in 1813, and was chosen to fill the pulpit at Howard's Hill Church, Baltimore, in 1813. He had visited Ohio in 1817 with Henry Kumler, Sr., and bought a farm in Fairfield County. While on that first visit to Ohio, he attended the session of the Miami Conference in June 1817, at which time he assisted Bishop Newcomer in ordaining Andrew Zeller as bishop. The next year he moved his family to Ohio. He had been prevented from attending the first general conference because of illness but did attend the second general conference as a representative of the Original Conference. He was a member of the 1821 General Conference as a representative of the Miami Conference.

> Certain characteristics of Hoffman brought him to the favorable attention of the Conference. He was an able, scriptural preacher. He had a wide range of experience. He received ordination from Otterbein himself, and was Otterbein's successor in Baltimore. Both in the east and the west he had expended himself in his ministry without reserve. He was a logical choice, therefore, and was elected Bishop to serve with Bishop Newcomer.[7]

After his term as bishop, Hoffman returned to the work of an itinerant preacher and presiding elder. His ability and influence continued. About 1832 he moved his family to Dayton where he bought a ninety-four and one-half acre farm. He arranged rooms in his house where he could hold meetings, and soon organized a class of forty members. From 1838 to the end of his life, November, 1851, he lived near Lewisburg, Ohio.

Between the General Conferences of 1821 and 1825 the three annual conferences met regularly. The Original Conference of 1822 adopted the constitution for a benevolent society. It had become clear that the preachers could not give themselves continuously to the work of preaching and protect themselves and their families against poverty in the later years of their lives. John Snyder had presented a letter to the Conference of 1818 from the Howard's Hill Church as a result of their awareness of the problem. Their letter had to do with the raising of a fund to supplement the salaries of the preachers who preach in the frontier or western areas under the direction of the conference. It was not until 1821 that a conference committee was appointed to propose a plan to secure funds for the support of the itinerants. John Hildt and Jacob Baulus were appointed to be the committee and they recommended to the Conference of 1822 the constitution for the benevolent society. This constitution was adopted and the conference appointed a board of seven trustees for the society, three of whom were laymen. One could become a member of the society by payment of one dollar annually. For payment of ten dollars one became a life member. Only earnings from the invested funds could be used until the capital amounted to $20,000.

In 1822 the Muskingum Conference made some efforts to get more able and earnest preachers who would travel for the year. August 1 was set as a universal fast day. In 1823 an effort was made to get better support for traveling preachers because the brethren in Muskingum Conference labored under severe hardships. Another fast and prayer day was appointed.

In 1823, the Miami Conference held its session in Indiana for the first time. There were ten circuits formed with fifteen traveling preachers. In 1824 the Miami Conference approved a new hymnbook for use in public worship.

General Conference of 1825

The fourth General Conference met in Tuscarawas County, in Muskingum Conference territory, June 7, 1825.[8] The meeting was held at the home of John Jacob Shaup, on Crooked Run. Twenty-four preachers were present. *This conference made an addition to the last article of the Confession of Faith stating that it is not lawful for a preacher to condemn, whether in public or in private, the mode of baptism of another.*

The conference revised the book of Discipline in several points: 1) It was determined that since any newly elected bishop will already have been ordained as an elder, by the laying on of hands, a second ordination is unnecessary and unscriptural. The former rule on ordination of a bishop was thus annulled. It is also noted that ordination of deacons also ceased with this action. 2) The questions used for examination of candidates for the ministry were considered and changed. 3) Provision was made for annual conferences to elect presiding elders who should continually travel their districts and receive a pay equal to that of the other itinerant preachers. Bishops were to also be supported at the same rate. It was ordered that a public collection be lifted once a year for this purpose. Presiding elders, up to this time, had been selected mostly from among the list of local preachers. 4) Christian Newcomer and Henry Kumler, Sr. were elected bishops.

In other action, the General Conference of 1825 also decided to send two elders to each of three different Methodist annual conferences for the purpose of renewing fraternal relations which had been broken off earlier.[9] "To this well-meant effort, as might have been expected, there was no response."[10] It was also decided that if necessary, an English as well as a German secretary shall be elected at any annual conference. The Miami Conference was divided. The western part retained the name of the Miami Conference and the eastern part was called Scioto Conference. The dividing line extended north and south from near Hillsboro through the western part of Fayette county to the Black Swamp.[11]

Henry Kumler, Sr. was born January 3, 1775, in Brecknock Township, Berks County, Pennsylvania.[12] When he was sixteen years of age, he received instruction and united with the German Reformed Church. At thirty-five years of age, he bought a farm about four miles from Greencastle, Pennsylvania, and was converted about one year later in 1811. He attended his first annual conference in 1813 at Hagerstown, Maryland, was licensed to preach in 1814, and hosted the Old Conference of 1815 in his own home. He was elected delegate from the old conference to the first and second general conferences. "In 1815 he traveled a circuit himself in the region of his Greencastle home. The next year he rode 370 miles every four weeks, traveling the Virginia circuit. He received ordination at the hand of Bishop Newcomer in 1816, and served as presiding elder in 1817."[13] He moved to Butler County, Ohio, in 1819 where he built a house with a room large enough and furnished so that it could be used for religious services. There he formed a class which continued to meet for many years. He was a preacher and a presiding elder in Miami Conference and was elected as delegate from the Miami Conference to the General Conferences of 1821 and 1825.

The Scioto Conference was organized June 16-18, 1825, at the home of George Graul in Fairfield County, Ohio. Scioto Conference comprised an area in which the German population was "large enough to furnish a beginning for the German evangelists, but not dense enough to prevent an easy transition to the use of the English language."[14] The minutes of the first four sessions cannot be located. However, from the list shown in the minutes of 1829, it seems quite certain that there were at least twenty ministers, in addition to Bishop Newcomer, that were members of Scioto Conference that first year. Included were: Joseph Hoffman, John Russel, George Benedum, Dewalt Mechlin, Lewis Kramer, John Schmaltz, James Ross, William Stewart, Philip Kramer, Samuel Hiestand, William Ambrose, John Coons, Jacob Zeller, Jacob Adam Lehman, John Eckart, Nathaniel Havens, John Bauser, Joshua Montgomery, Joseph Dewitt, and John Dewitt.

After Scioto Conference was organized, the Miami Conference of 1825 listed five charges in Indiana and four in Ohio. Bishop Newcomer did not attend Miami Conference that year because to do so he would have had to stay over another month. He had already attended sessions of the Muskingum Conference, May 23, 24, the General Conference, June 7-10, and the organizing session of the Scioto Conference, June 16-18.

The Miami Conference learned in 1826 that three of its prominent ministers, Alfred Carder, John McNamar, and Aaron Farmer had become connected with the Freemasons. A strong resolution disapproving connecton with Freemasonry was passed. "All of the members of the conference, including the three just named, seemed to acquiesce in the action taken. Carder, however, withdrew from the church and soon ceased to preach."[15] The Old Conference also adopted a resolution against the membership of any of the preachers or members in the order of Freemasonry. Adopted in 1827, this resolution was similar to the one adopted one year earlier in the Miami conference.

Beginning the Sandusky Work

Jacob Baulus had moved from Maryland to the Black Swamp in Ohio near Fremont in 1822. Christian Newcomer visited him in 1823. While he was engaged in establishing his farm, he also established several classes and other preaching appointments. After seven years, in 1829, he attended the sessions of the Muskingum Annual Conference and reported on his work. Muskingum had four other circuits that year and appointed a presiding elder and an itinerant to each. Evidently based upon his report, they named Sandusky Circuit as a fifth circuit with Baulus as the presiding elder and John Zahn, a strong preacher from the old conference, as the itinerant preacher.

General Conference of 1829 convened in little more than two weeks from the close of the Muskingum Conference session. In a significant action, Sandusky circuit was attached to Muskingum Conference. During those years there seems to have been some overlapping of conference responsibility, especially in light of the previous general conference action in 1825 by which the dividing line between Scioto and Miami Conferences extended to the Black Swamp, the general area in which Baulus lived and preached. The Sandusky Circuit was some distance from any other work in Muskingum Conference, over one hundred miles from the nearest appointment on the Wooster Circuit. Baulus did not attend Muskingum Conference in 1830, and it does not appear that John Zahn had served on the circuit the previous year. Baulus, however, was renamed by the Muskingum Conference in 1830 as the presiding elder, and Israel Harrington and Jonathan Harrison were named as preachers.

Baulus is shown as a member of the Muskingum Conference in 1828-1830, but present only in 1829. In 1831 he is listed as an absent member of the Scioto Conference. The records show that he was the German "Clerk" for Scioto Conference. Scioto Conference listed the Sandusky Circuit as a district for the election of a delegate to the General Conference of 1833. Also in 1831, the Scioto Conference formed the Marion circuit with James Ross as the preacher in charge, who extended his work into Sandusky. Benjamin Moore was appointed to the Maumee mission, but in reporting his work the following year, he reported it under the name of Sandusky. The General Conference of 1833 cleared up this anomalous situation by the formation of the Sandusky Annual Conference.

Acting subsequently to the General Conference of 1833, the first session of the Sandusky Annual Conference was held May 12, 1834, at the house of Philip Bretz, on Honey Creek, in Seneca County, Ohio. Samuel Hiestand presided. There were sixteen preachers present, including Bishop Hiestand. No preaching assignments were included in the first minutes.

General Conference of 1829

The fifth General Conference convened at the home of Dewalt

Mechlin, Fairfield County, Ohio, May 15, 1829, with twenty-eight delegates present. Annual conference boundaries were changed. The Original Conference was divided into two parts to be known as the *Hagerstown Conference* and the *Harrisburg Conference.* Hagerstown Conference included all of the State of Virginia and the counties of Washington and Allegheny in Maryland. Harrisburg Conference consisted of the remaining portion of the Old Conference. Miami Conference was divided again, this time at the Ohio and Indiana state line, which line was then projected south through the State of Kentucky. The portion west of that line was to be known as the *Indiana Conference.* The east portion retained the *Miami Conference* name. This conference also assigned the Sandusky circuit to the Muskingum Conference as already noted.

A strong resolution disapproving Freemasonry was adopted to be inserted in the Discipline:

> Resolved, that in no way or manner, nor in any sense of the word, shall Freemasonry be approved or tolerated in our church, and that should any one of our Church members, who may now be a free mason, continue to attend their lodges, or as a free mason, attend and take part in their processions, or if he joins the free masons, such member, by such an act excludes himself from membership in our church.[16]

Seeking a union with the United Brethren, a representative from the Methodist Protestant Church was present at this conference. The conference replied that the membership of the church, and not the general conference, would have to make such a decision. It may be that the United Brethren were newly conscious of the limitations of the power of the General Conference as described in the Discipline, or it may be that they were too well satisfied with the prospect for the future of the church to even be interested in a union with another denomination.[17] Bishops Newcomer and Kumler were re-elected.

It is of special interest to note that this was the last general conference Bishop Newcomer attended. He was eighty years of age and still able to travel extensively. He had begun this conference season of 1829 by conducting the session of the Original Conference. He left on April 11 for the Muskingum Conference. He met the Scioto Conference on May 11 and began the General Conference of 1829 on May 15. Following general conference he conducted the Miami Conference, May 26-29, then he returned to his home. Before another year passed, the Lord called him to his eternal reward.

Annual Conferences 1829-1833

The Miami Conference of 1829 expressed an interest in religious periodicals, authorizing the publication of *Zion's Advocate* with Aaron Farmer, editor. Because of inadequate support, this paper had but a brief existence. This session still included the members of the new Indiana Conference.

The Original Conference remained substantially a unit until 1831. In March, 1830, it met for the last time at Shopp's Meeting-house, near Shiremanstown, Pennsylvania. Seventy-eight names were on the ministerial roll at that time, and fifty-seven were present. The minutes state that "love and unity reigned in the conference." It was determined that the Hagerstown Conference would receive the old protocol (minutes), and that the Harrisburg Conference should procure a new book. The record showed that Bishop Kumler gave William Brown two dollars with which to buy a new book for the Harrisburg Conference and indicated that he was to transcribe from the old into the new all important proceedings.

The first meeting of the Indiana Conference was held in the Stone-cipher Meeting-house about two and one-half miles south of Corydon, May 25, 1830, with Bishop Henry Kumler, Sr., presiding. There were twenty ministers present, including the bishop. There were thirty-seven ministers on the roll. The list of appointments for 1830 was as follows:

CIRCUIT	PREACHER IN CHARGE
Charlestown	Abiram Stacy
Flat Rock	James Griffith
Orange	Frederick Kenoyer
Coal Creek	John Hoobler
Wea	Josiah Davis
Tanner's Creek	John McNamar, Wm. Davis
White Water	Chandler Doud, Ober Nolan
Corydon	Crassy D. Key

For some reason Joseph Williams and John Denham were not reported as receiving appointments. Yet the salary report for the next year shows that each had served: Joseph Williams on the Illinois Circuit and John Denham on the Iriquois Circuit.

The first session of the Harrisburg Conference was held April 19, 1831. Thirty-two preachers were present and five applicants were received. The scope of the work was indicated by the list of appointments as given in 1833.

Huntingdon District	Ezekiel Boring, P E
Huntingdon Circuit	George St. Clair Hussey
	Jacob Ritter
Clearfield Circuit	John Potts
Juniata Circuit	George Gilbert
Chambersburg Circuit	James Niman
	John Hendricks

Carlisle District	Jacob Erb, P E
Carlisle Circuit	Jacob Snider
	Francis C. Wilson
Dauphin Circuit	Jacob Rupp
	John Smith
York County Circuit	Christian Shopp
Baltimore County Circuit	Frederick Gilbert
Baltimore	John Crack

Canada District	Gideon Smith, P E
Canada Circuit	Jacob G. Erb

The Hagerstown Conference convened in its first separate session on April 27, 1831, at Mill Creek, Shenandoah County, Virginia. Twenty ministers were present at the opening session. Early in the session, J. J. Glossbrenner, then not yet nineteen years old, was presented as an applicant for license to preach.

The first list of appointments showed the scope of its work:

Hagerstown Circuit	W. R. Rhinehart
	Jacob Glossbrenner
Mechanicstown	John Miller
	George A. Geeting, Jr.
Staunton and	John Zahn
Woodstock Circuits	Noah Woodyard
	John Haney
	Jacob Houk

General Conference of 1833

The sixth general conference convened at the Dresbach church on the line between Pickaway and Fairfield counties in Ohio, May 14, 1833. Bishop Kumler, Sr., presided. There were thirty-three delegates from six conferences.

The question arose again as to the difference in power between the general and annual conferences. It was determined that general conference had no power to change the *Confession of Faith* or in any way to change the meaning, spirit, rules, and regulations of the *Discipline*. Provision was made so that one or more bishops could be elected instead of only two.

In other orders of business: 1) It was decided that two delegates should be sent to the general conference from each annual conference. 2) A rule was adopted at this conference which has continued to the present, respecting the practice of affirming, rather than swearing, when testifying to the truth in a legal form. 3) It was made the duty of class leaders to appoint prayer and class meetings; and it was recommended that all the members of the church attend class meetings once every two weeks, and oftener if practicable. 4) It was decided that an itinerant preacher should not be allowed to travel more than three consecutive years on the same circuit, except by consent of the annual conference. 5) The term of appointment for presiding elders was reduced from four years to one. The bishops were still given the power to appoint presiding elders with the consent of the conference, although, in actual practice, they scarcely ever used that power. 6) A further action was taken regarding the manufacture and sale of intoxicating liquors on the part of any exhorter, preacher, or elder from and after the next annual conferences in 1834. This was a follow-up action of the previous general conference and was included in the *Discipline*.

Provision was made for a printing establishment by the General Conference of 1833, although this fact is not recorded in the minutes. Evidently the matter was turned over to the Scioto Conference to carry out, for the annual conference minutes of 1834 reveal that George Dresbach, Jonathan Dresbach, and John Russel were appointed as trustees to manage the concerns of the printing press, and that John Kunse (Coons) was named as treasurer, with power to vote as a trustee in the event of the absence of a trustee. Contacts were made to secure donations and subscriptions; and on April 12, 1834, the Publishing Board bought a printing press, type and other fixtures. The following month they bought a lot and two houses in Circleville, Ohio. Since W. R. Rhinehart had already begun publication of the *Mountain Messenger* at Hagerstown, Maryland, a few months before, the new board bought out the *Messenger* and employed Rhinehart to edit the *Religious Telescope,* beginning with the first issue dated December 31, 1834.[18]

The Harrisburg and Hagerstown conferences had each appointed committees in 1832 to have an English hymnbook printed. Scioto Conference also appointed a hymnbook committee in 1835. In the

Religious Telescope issue of October 21, 1835, an announcement appeared that a number of the new English hymnbooks had been printed and that these would be distributed soon. The hymnbook consisted of 393 hymns and had a total of 349 pages including an index.[19]

General Conference again changed annual conference names and boundaries. The name of the Hagerstown Conference was changed to the Virginia Conference. The name of Harrisburg Conference was changed to Pennsylvania Conference. That portion of the Muskingum Conference that lay in Pennsylvania was attached to the Pennsylvania Conference. The Sandusky Conference was created in northwestern Ohio. The Wabash Conference was set off from the Indiana Conference.

> It is the opinion of Mr. Spayth, who was a member of the general conference of 1833, and one of the secretaries, that the Wabash conference was set off from the Indiana conference at the same time. Mr. Hanby . . . entertains a different opinion. The minutes of the general conference contain nothing on the subject; and the question is one of small importance. It is a fact that the Sandusky conference was organized in 1834, and the Wabash in 1835, raising the whole number of annual conference districts to eight.[20]

Henry Kumler, Sr., was re-elected bishop. Samuel Hiestand and William Brown were also elected. Samuel Hiestand was born March 3, 1781 in Page County, Virginia, the youngest child in a family of seven sons and four daughters. His parents were devout members of the Moravian faith. Samuel made a profession of faith early in life, however, it was under the influence of George Benedum that he gained a real knowledge of his salvation. Five of the Hiestand brothers traveled to Fairfield County, Ohio in 1804. When George Benedum arrived in 1806, he and Abraham Hiestand immediately began preaching and became leaders of the United Brethren movement in Ohio. After Christian Newcomer visited them in 1810, Samuel Hiestand, known as Benedum's "apprentice," began itinerating with Benedum. He married Margaret Raudabaugh in 1808. He was licensed to preach in 1820 by the Miami Conference, was secretary of the General Conference of 1821, was a member of the General Conferences of 1825 and 1833, was elected bishop in 1833. He was re-elected bishop in 1837, and died October 9, 1838.

William Brown was one of five pastors of the Otterbein congregation who became bishops in the Church of the United Brethren in Christ. He was the third, following Otterbein and Joseph Hoffman. Brown was pastor in Baltimore from 1825 to 1828. From the days of his grandfather, the Brown family were followers of Otterbein. William was converted at the age of sixteen at a "great" meeting held on Abraham Mayer's farm, near Carlisle, and was granted a license to preach by the Original Conference in 1816 when he was twenty. In 1817 he traveled the Hagerstown Circuit; he traveled the Virginia Circuit in 1818 and 1819; he was on the Hagerstown Circuit again, in 1820; and he formed the York Circuit in 1823. He was an elected delegate to four successive general conferences beginning with 1821 and was a leader in the discussion leading to the adoption of resolutions pertaining to restrictions of the manufacture and use of intoxicants. He served four years as a presiding elder.

William Brown's father and other members of his family had moved to southwestern Ohio and Indiana by the time he was elected as bishop in 1833. He also moved to Indiana, but the time has been variously placed from 1833 to 1838. There is a record of two purchases of land by him in the eastern part of Bolivar Township, Benton County, Indiana, June 1833. After his term as bishop had ended, he gave the remaining years of his life to the development of the church on the frontier. As a member of the Wabash Conference from 1838, he traveled circuits and was a presiding elder. He died May 11, 1868.

The first session of the Wabash Conference was held at Rawling's Meeting-house, Park County, Indiana, beginning September 15, 1835, Bishop Brown presiding. There were eighteen preachers present, including the bishop, eight of whom were under forty years of age.[21] Appointments for the year included the Wabash District: Pine Creek, St. Joseph, Wea, Coal Creek, and Vermillion. Illinois District: Mackinaw Circuit.

FOOTNOTES

[1]John Lawrence, *The History of the Church of the United Brethren in Christ,* 2 vols. (Dayton, OH: Published at the United Brethren Printing Establishment, Sowers & King, Publishers, 1861), 2:18.

[2]Henry G. Spayth, *History of the United Brethren Church* (Circleville, OH: Published at the Conference Office of the United Brethren in Christ, 1851), pp. 157, 158.

[3]Lawrence, 2:98, 99.

[4]Christian Newcomer; John Hildt, trans, and ed., *The Life and Journal of the Rev'd. Christian Newcomer* (Hagerstown, MD: F. G. W. Kapp, 1834), p. 255.

[5]*Discipline,* 1821, Further Appendix, #4.

[6]Lawrence, 2:147, 148.

[7]Paul Rodes Koontz, *The Bishops, Church of the United Brethren in Christ,* 2 vols. (Dayton, OH: The Otterbein Press, 1950), 1:175.

[8]Newcomer, p. 301. Other historians and the minutes of the general conference all state that the General Conference of 1825 met on May 7. From Newcomer's *Journal* it appears that the general conference was actually held in June. *Journal* entries show that Newcomer was in western Pennsylvania for the Muskingum Conference May 23, 24. On

June 2, he attended a camp meeting in Harrison County and tarried there. On June 6, he rode to Michael Kohr's and stayed there for the night. On June 7, he came to John Jacob Shaup's on Crooked Run, for the General Conference, which continued through June 10.

[9]Lawrence, 1:366, 367.

[10]Lawrence, 2:162.

[11]The Black Swamp encompassed an area from Sandusky Bay throughout Northwest Ohio into Indiana on the west and Michigan to the north. It was drained by the Sandusky, Portage, Auglaize, and Maumee rivers. Through much of the Black Swamp, roads were beyond description and travel was exceedingly difficult. It was said that the sun never penetrated the dense forests there until settlers felled the giant trees for homestead use.

[12]Koontz, 1:182.

[13]Ibid., p. 185.

[14]A. W. Drury, History of the Church of the United Brethren in Christ (Dayton, OH: The Otterbein Press, 1924), p. 394.

[15]Ibid., p. 380.

[16]General Conference Minutes 1829 Translated and Unpublished (Huntington, IN: United Brethren Archives Microfilm).

[17]Drury, p. 345.

[18]Ibid., pp. 347-349.

[19]John H. Ness, Jr., One Hundred Fifty Years, A History of Publishing in the Evangelical United Brethren Church (Dayton, OH: The Board of Publication of the Evangelical United Brethren Church, copyright 1966), pp. 271, 272.

[20]Lawrence, 2:285.

[21]Augustus Cleland Wilmore, History of the White River Conference (Dayton, OH: Published for the author by the United Brethren Publishing House, 1925), p. 60.

16

CHRISTIAN NEWCOMER

Christian Newcomer kept a day-by-day record of his ministerial activities and wrote the story of his life during his last year. On December 16, 1829, his *Journal* showed that, after a five-week illness during which he was confined for most of the time, he received a visitor, John Hildt. Longtime friends and co-workers, they collated the manuscripts of the journal, and Hildt read the autobiography. It was clear that the journal would need to be transcribed into more legible writing because of the wear it had received from the many miles Newcomer traveled on horseback. "The original manuscript was written by Christian Newcomer, almost day by day, in any or all situations in which he happened to be placed; frequently with bad ink, which in some parts of the manuscript had faded by age and was nearly illegible; frequently with a bad pen, . . ."[1] After the death of Newcomer, a committee was appointed by the General Conference to examine the manuscript.[2] When they made their report, it was decided to proceed to publish the journal in English. John Hildt was appointed to transcribe, translate, and edit it for publication. The volume, *The Life and Journal of the Rev'd Christian Newcomer,* appeared in 1834 and included the autobiography.

Christian Newcomer was born in Lancaster County, Pennsylvania, February 1 (January 21 old style,) 1749.[3] His father's name was Wolfgang Newcomer, who had immigrated from Switzerland with his parents in childhood. His father married a Miss Baer, but she died after about a year. Two years later he married Elizabeth Weller, and Christian was the second of three sons born to this union. There were five daughters. His parents were both Mennonites and endeavored to lead a pious life. He recalled having "seen them both on their knees many a time before the bed, offering up their prayers or evening sacrifice to God, although in silence."[4]

While Newcomer was yet very young, the Spirit of God knocked at his heart's door. He did not know what it meant. He recalled that at the time he thought about death and eternity, heaven and hell, and that it was his desire to go to heaven. On one occasion he was present when his parents were talking about his grandmother.

> They said she was very melancholy and sad, in great doubts about the salvation of her soul, and in distress of being lost;—adding, that she ought not to do so, but cast herself on the mercy of the Lord her God. O what an impression did this make on my young and juvenile heart. Ah! said I to myself, if such persons as my pious grandmother (for I considered her a pious character) do lament and are in distress on account of their salvation, what will become of me? How shall I appear before the great Judge of all the Universe, to give account of all that I have done?[5]

This impression lasted for some time. There were many other inner struggles in his search for assurance of salvation. He was finally converted, but not long after the joy of his experience lessened. Fear returned and the confidence he had had in God was lost. It was at this time that he talked with an elder in the Mennonite society and asked his advice. He was told to be baptized, join the society, and take the sacrament. He did all of this, but still his Christian joy and inward comfort were not restored. For several years he continued in this state.

About this time his father died, and he came into possession of the family home. Previously he had not had to be concerned about such matters, but now he had to provide for a family. His mother and sister remained with him, but his sister married after about a year. His mother was a mid-wife and was frequently away from home. He married Elizabeth Baer on March 31, 1770, when he was twenty-one years old.

During the winter following his marriage, he became very ill. At this time the Lord gave him a clear vision of the situation with his soul, and he experienced a renewed desire for peace with God. As he was reading and reflecting on Revelation 12:10-12:

> At the latter clause of the 11th verse I made a pause, reflecting—"and they loved not their lives unto the death:" then reading again, "therefore rejoice, ye Heavens and ye that dwell in them;" the same instant a something (call it conviction or give it what appellation you please) whispered within me, "this is to say, all those who are in such a situation as yourself shall rejoice." In a moment the peace of God and pardon of my sins was manifested to my soul, and the spirit of God bore witness with my spirit, that God for Jesus sake had taken away the burthen of my sins, and shed abroad his love in my poor unworthy heart. O! thou

glorious Being; how did my soul feel at the time? only those who have felt and experienced the same grace, will be able to understand or comprehend what I am about to say. Yes, gentle reader! If at the time I could have called a thousand lives my own, I would have pledged them all, every one of them to testify to the certainty of my acceptance with God: my joy or rather ecstasy was so great, that I was in some measure as one beside himself; not to disturb those who were in the house locked in sleep, I ran out into the yard to give utterance to my feelings; there I gave glory and Hallelujahs to my Redeemer with a loud voice; my whole heart was filled with gratitude to God and the Lamb, unto him be all the praise and glory forever, Amen.[6]

Several weeks passed, perhaps the most happy weeks of his life. Now he felt a desire urging him to communicate this happiness of what God had done for his soul to others. But for fear that he would be considered insane, he did not follow his inclinations but went to speak with one of the Mennonite preachers who stood high in his estimation. When Newcomer related to him, with all the fervor of a new convert, what the work of grace had accomplished in his soul, the preacher could not understand him. Therefore his confidant felt that he had formed too strong an opinion in the matter, and that he might be in error in trusting in such an experience.

This response created severe doubt and discouragement in Newcomer's mind. He had loved this man and was exceedingly distressed that he could not understand what he was trying to say. Darkness overspread his soul, but it was not of long duration. He soon learned that the preacher had become severely ill. He made plans to visit him. During the visit they referred to their previous discussion and the preacher admitted that conviction had darted through his mind like a flash of lightning. Then he said, "My dear Christian, I do believe that by the power of our Savior Jesus Christ, sin can and must be destroyed in my heart if I shall be saved."[7] Newcomer rejoiced at these expressions. They were of one mind and prayed together.

After this experience the urge to preach became very strong. However, he declined because he felt himself unfit for the task. He many times felt compelled to tell his neighbors what to do to be saved, and they encouraged him to preach. Often the 'inward monitor' would reprehend him in his neglect. But he continued to resist solicitations and entreaties to preach, until ultimately like Jonah, he sought safety in flight. In the spring of 1775, he sold his farm and moved to the Beaver Creek community, about seven miles southeast of Hagerstown, Maryland.

In his new location he still refused to obey the call to preach the Gospel. The Revolutionary War began, and as a pacifist of the Mennonite faith, Newcomer could have nothing to do with war. Misunderstanding and disagreeable situations resulted.[8] At the same time he found himself without personal peace with God. Though he longed sincerely to be restored to God's favor, he became possessed with the thought that God would no longer strive with him. In short, despair had seized his soul.

He became ill with a fever and was weakened considerably. Expecting to die, he could recall that at a former time he had experienced forgiveness of sins and had enjoyed the love of God in his soul, but now he felt stripped of every comfort and consolation. In addition, something whispered continually in his ear saying, 'There is throughout eternity no mercy for you.'[9] This seemed to be repeated many times all day long, louder and louder. He spoke of this to his wife saying that he knew perfectly well that it was not so; that though he was very sick, and had no assurance of his acceptance with God, no love of Jesus in his soul—still he would trust in Him as well as he could—commit himself to God's hand, whether His will with him be for life or death, that it should be done as seemed good in His sight. He made a new promise to God to be more obedient if again restored to health. As his health was gradually restored, he had a desire to again be restored into the favor of God and toward that end he set upon a plan of devotion and prayer, wrestling as Jacob with God. A week later he again found the long lost treasure.

However, he still struggled with the call to preach, unable to surmount the obstacles, or conquer his diffidence, timidity, or disobedience. Yet, it was before the very neighbors from whom he had fled that Newcomer offered his first testimony to the saving grace of the Lord.

About this time I paid a visit to my friends and relations, at my former place of residence, in Lancaster County, Pennsylvania;—on the Sabbath day, I accompanied my friends to the meeting house, not with an intention to say anything, but on the contrary, with a resolution to be silent. Sitting for some time, listening with attention to the discourse and exhortations of several of their speakers, I could perceive distinctly that they still continued in the same ignorance and inexperience of religion as they were when I left them.

It now run like fire through my bones—I felt inwardly constrained to take up the cross; and whereas brethren (namely: the Mennonites,) gave the privilege or liberty to speak, I dared not remain silent any longer. I arose with a sorrowful heart, and spoke with tears in my eyes, to my old friends and acquaintances. I related to them, with all the ability in my possession, how I had oftentimes felt at meeting, when living yet among them; candidly stating my experience of the work of grace in my soul before I left them, as also what the Lord, in his infinite mercy, had done for me since my removal to Maryland. I also sincerely confessed to them, that the Lord had required of me, before my removal, to warn them of their danger, and that until this day, I had been disobedient to my Blessed Master.

I was so affected as to be hardly able to speak intelligible; but I stammered as well as I could, and endeavored to recommend to them the grace of God, in Christ Jesus; every person present, was sensibly touched—all shed tears, as well as myself; and I have no doubt, many were convinced that a form of religion, a religion whose habitation is only in the head, and is not felt in the heart, is insufficient to salvation.[10]

Following this testimony he received frequent requests to exhort and to speak in public meetings. These opportunities continued to cause some inward combat, but he always feared that he would lose the peace of mind which he now enjoyed should he be disobedient.

By this time he had already become acquainted with Otterbein and Geeting. Their preaching made a profound impression on him, and he was in complete agreement with their doctrines of repentance and conversion. He was drawn to them and joined their society.

He began to preach in 1777, and thus a new chapter began in his life which would continue until death. Opportunities to preach came rapidly and with urgency. Appointments were sometimes made for him without his knowledge, and he did not feel that he dared to refuse, even though it meant great sacrifices at home. Very quickly, Newcomer found himself to be an itinerant preacher first, and a farmer second. He was one of those who attended the conference at Otterbein's parsonage in 1789, and at John Spangler's in York County, Pennsylvania, in 1791. His first twenty-two years of preaching were in eastern Pennsylvania, Maryland, and Virginia. In 1799, accompanied by Abraham Troxel, he crossed the Allegheny mountains for the first time to preach to the German communities in Western Pennsylvania. This was the first of twenty-four round trips across those mountains. He was ordained as an elder by Otterbein on October 2, 1813, a few weeks before Otterbein's death. He was elected bishop by the Original Conference in 1813 and in 1814; re-elected by the General Conference of 1817 and by each succeeding General Conference through 1829, the year preceding his death. He was a minister fifty-three years and a bishop nearly seventeen years.

Something of the spiritual temperament of the man shows through these selections from his *Journal*. December 14th, 1821: "This day I rode, in a happy frame of mind, through wind and snow, from morning till night, without any refreshment."[11] October 2nd, 1826: "I crossed the Juniata River, came to a very steep mountain, and with difficulty gained the summit, where I kneeled down, and offered up praises and thanksgiving to my Lord and Master for all his mercies, and remembered all my brethren in the ministry at the throne of grace. I believe my offering was acceptable in his sight, for I felt his gracious presence in my soul! Glory, honor and praise be unto our God for ever!"[12] He was not a great preacher. He had an impediment that sometimes manifested itself in his speech. Otterbein was heard to say that when he heard him, he felt as if he wanted to help him.[13] Yet he always succeeded in feeding the flock, and in reaching the hearts of sinners.

After November, 1829, Newcomer seemed to be in declining health. At one time he was confined to his room for about five weeks. He made a few short trips following that. On March 1, 1830 he rode to Boonsboro and lodged with Michael Thomas. On the second it had been his intention to ride into Virginia, but finding the weather disagreeable, he returned home.

The Bishop made several entries in his journal after his return home. On March 4 he wrote, "This forenoon I tried to write in my journal, but alas! I find that I am not able to perform the task, so I lay down my pen, and the Lord alone knows whether I shall be able to resume it again. The Lord's will be done. Amen, Hallelujah!"[14]

Bishop Henry Kumler, Sr., from Ohio came by to visit with Newcomer during this period and they spent a few hours together. On March 12, 1830, Newcomer died. A few moments before his death he requested a young man present to pray. Then he,

> arose from his bed without assistance, and with those persons present in the room, presented himself at his bedside before that throne where he had formed a spiritual acquaintance with his blessed Lord and Master many years before. After the prayer was ended he again laid down, reclining his head on his pillow, drew breath but a few times, and calmly expired in the arms of his Savior and his God, in the full assurance of a blessed immortality. His whole countenance appeared to be a faithful mirror in which the serenity of mind and the peace within was depicted in faithful characters.[15]

The story of Newcomer's death was carried in the *Hagerstown Mail:*

> Nine days before his death he left home for the purpose of serving his Lord and Master in his official capacity, when his horse took fright, threw him and broke several of his ribs. He lingered and expired shouting praises to the God of his salvation. On Sunday following his remains were attended to the family burying ground near Beaver Creek, five miles from Hagerstown, attended by a concourse of persons amounting to upwards of one thousand people.[16]

The Bishop made several entries in his journal at about the time of this accident, and following it, but did not mention being thrown from his horse. Perhaps a person who knew horseflesh as he had for many years would not want to admit that he had been thrown. He had had a vigorous constitution that had enabled him to ride fifty-two miles in one day of his last trip west, in his eighty-first year.

Bishop Kumler preached the funeral discourse in German from John 16:22, and John Zahn followed, speaking in English from Deuteronomy 34:5. It was his desire that no stone mark his burial place, however, a suitable stone that now marks the probable place of his burial was erected later by the church.

FOOTNOTES

[1]Christian Newcomer, with John Hildt, trans. and ed., *The Life and Journal of the Rev'd. Christian Newcomer* (Hagerstown, MD: F. G. W. Kapp, 1834), p. iv.

[2]John H. Ness, Jr., *One Hundred Fifty Years, A History of Publishing in the Evangelical United Brethren Church* (Dayton, OH: The Board of Publication of the Evangelical United Brethren Church, 1966), pp. 260, 261.

[3]The date of Newcomer's birth was January 21 according to the Julian calendar. Various German states kept the Julian calendar until 1700, and Great Britain did not change to the Gregorian calendar until 1752. Birth dates and other important dates were often given in old style, that is, according to the Julian calendar, as well as in the new Gregorian calendar date. Thus, Newcomer was born February 1, 1749, according to the Gregorian calendar.

[4]Newcomer, p. 1.

[5]Ibid., pp. 1, 2.

[6]Ibid., pp. 6, 7.

[7]Ibid., p. 9.

[8]Ibid., p. 10. Newcomer wrote about his unpleasant experience: "About this time commenced the Revolutionary War, between this country and England, which also created considerable distress with me, being conscientiously opposed to war and bearing arms, I was thereby placed in many instances in disagreeable situations, respecting both my temporal and spiritual concerns; I desired to have nothing to do with the war, and be at peace, bearing good will to all mankind."

[9]Ibid., p. 11.

[10]Ibid., p. 13.

[11]Ibid., p. 278.

[12]Ibid., p. 309.

[13]John Lawrence, *The History of the Church of the United Brethren in Christ,* 2 vols. (Dayton, OH: Published at the United Brethren Printing Establishment, Sowers and King, Publishers, 1861), 2:210.

[14]Newcomer, p. 330.

[15]Ibid., p. 330.

[16]Quoted in, "Notes on the Death of Bishop Christian Newcomer" by Paul Holdcraft, *Religious Telescope* n.v. (December 4, 1943): n.p.

17

THE CONSTITUTION

The General Conference of 1837

The seventh general conference convened May 8, 1837 at Germantown, Ohio. Bishops Kumler and Hiestand presided. Bishop Brown was not present. W. R. Rhinehart was the secretary. Henry Kumler, Sr., and Samuel Hiestand were re-elected bishops and Jacob Erb was elected for his first term as bishop. William Rhinehart was elected editor of the *Religious Telescope* and William Hanby was elected book agent. A constitution for the management of the printing establishment was adopted.

Jacob Erb was born near Manheim, Lancaster County, Pennsylvania, May 25, 1804. His grandfather, Christian Erb, was born in Switzerland and was brought to this country when only three years of age. His maternal grandfather, Abraham Hershey, was also from Switzerland. His mother's name was Elizabeth, a sister to Christian and Abraham Hershey, early preachers in the United Brethren Church. Though the parents and grandparents were connected with the United Brethren Church, their earlier church connection was Mennonite.

When Jacob was six years old, his father purchased a farm in Cumberland County on the west bank of the Susquehanna River, midway between Wormleysburg and West Fairview. Here the parents established a preaching place for United Brethren preachers—the second such place in that part of the county—just as they had done in their Lancaster County home. Here, in his own home, Jacob was converted at the age of sixteen. His father died this same year, and his mother sold the farm and moved her family to Wormleysburg.

The year after his conversion, Jacob began to exhort. Soon, he answered the call to preach and joined the Original Conference in 1823. He traveled circuits in the conference, and in 1825 he made a trip to Canada, which was the first of several in other years. He was ordained in 1825 by Bishop Christian Newcomer, who was assisted by Bishop Henry Kumler, Sr. Jacob Erb had the spirit of Newcomer and Grosh in his desire to conserve the results of preaching and bring the converts and members of the society into organized congregations. When he was elected to his first term as bishop, he was nearly thirty-three years of age.

The item that received the most attention at the General Conference of 1837 was the adoption of a constitution for the church. This subject was unannounced beforehand. The draft had been prepared by William R. Rhinehart, but he was not a member of the conference. However, William Hanby presented the motion "That a constitution for the better regulation of the Church be adopted."[1] Hanby later described some of the rationale for the motion, stating that it was not intended to incorporate any new principle of church government, nor to reject any rules of discipline already in force. Rather, it was desired to put into one instrument all the fundamental principles upon which the government of the church rests. The constitution would define the duties and powers of the legislative and judicial church bodies, and set limits to those powers, securing to all members their just rights.[2] Daniel Berger suggested that the purpose for embodying the principles governing the church in a constitution was to give them the character of fundamental law, and to make any modification difficult.[3]

The constitution was adopted by a unanimous vote. However, the conference felt that it may have exceeded its authority in adopting Article IV, Section 2, the article on amendments.[4] John Lawrence said that "the conference did not regard its action as final or as at all binding on the church."[5] There had been no instruction to adopt a constitution. A circular letter was attached to the constitution and printed with it, part of which read as follows:

We are well aware that we have transcended the bounds given us by our Discipline, which (transcending of bounds) will be found in the Constitution, Article IV, Section 2, declaring that this Constitution can neither be altered or amended without a majority of two-thirds of a General Conference. If there had been a general notice given to the Church previous to the election of delegates, that there would be a memorial offered to General Conference, praying them to adopt a constitution, and to ratify it agreeable to Article IV, Section 2, then the General Conference would have had full power to have done so. The object of this circular is (feeling that the government of our Church is not as firm as it ought to be) to give notice to our Church throughout the Union that we intend to present a memorial to the nesct [sic] general conference praying them to ratify the Constitution now adopted, according to Article IV, Section 2.[6]

The feeling of doubt did not seem to apply to other aspects of the constitution. It was adopted and signed individually by all the members of the general conference in a solemn ceremony and served as a legal document for four years after 1837.

In other sections, the constitution provided: 1) that the delegates to general conference shall not exceed one for every five hundred members; 2) that no annual conference shall have the right to admit any new annual conferences; 3) that no rule shall be adopted by general conference so as to infringe on the rights of any as it relates to the mode and manner of baptism, the sacrament of the Lord's Supper, or the washing of feet; 4) that no rule or ordinance shall be passed in general conference so as to deprive local preachers of their eligibility of election to general conference, or of their vote in annual conference; 5) and that these last two provisions shall neither be altered or repealed without the unanimous consent of the whole conference.

In other business of the General Conference of 1837, the Benevolent Societies of Maryland and Ohio each reported. The amount of interest available for distribution to support preachers' salaries from the fund in Maryland was $168.95, and from Ohio, $100.00 was available. Trustees were elected to the printing establishment. It was determined that traveling preachers should receive the *Religious Telescope* free of charge. The copyright for the hymnbook was transferred to the general conference. Duties of book agents in the conferences were adopted. The number of delegates to the next general conference was determined for each annual conference.

After General Conference of 1837

The quadrennium following the General Conference of 1837 was one of growth in nearly all sectors. Growth was evident in the 1837 session of the Pennsylvania Annual Conference, so much so that no local church wanted to be host for the 1838 session. The conference had become large enough so that local facilities in most every community were strained for a meeting of this size that lasted for several days. Finally, Jacob Erb determined that he would entertain the conference at his own expense at Wormleysburg. When the conference met, ninety-eight preachers and over forty laymen were present. A consequence of this situation is that the conference decided to divide itself into two parts, resulting in the creation of the Allegheny Conference. The preachers were left to decide for themselves the conference to which they would belong. Their place of residence usually was the deciding factor. The Allegheny Conference had its first session at Mt. Pleasant, Pennsylvania on March 25, 1839.

Home missionary societies were formed by several annual conferences during the quadrennium, for the purpose of extending the work more effectually in the bounds of the conference districts. A Home Missionary Society was also formed by the Otterbein Church in Baltimore with the purpose "to send missionaries among the Germans in America."[7]

Another edition of 10,000 copies of the hymnbook had been ordered by the general conference. They had also ordered about 8,000 copies of the *Discipline,* 2,000 of these were to be in German. However, the trustees of the printing establishment were struggling financially and found it necessary to establish priorities. The English *Disciplines* were printed first. Arrangements were made to print the German *Disciplines* elsewhere, since the establishment did not have German type. The hymnbooks were printed a few at a time as money was available.

The Religious Telescope had quickly become known as a promoter of the opinions of its editor, William Rhinehart, and had earned much criticism for articles against slavery. Rhinehart, however, resigned in 1839, and between that time and the Conference of 1841, when one might expect much to be said on the subject of the adoption of the church constitution, very little was printed. H. G. Spayth and William R. Coursey wrote articles opposing its adoption on the grounds that the Bible and the providence of God had given existence to the church, had guided it until now, and would be able to keep it in existence in the future. Spayth's article said, in part:

> Human institutions and national compacts must necessarily have the elements of their agreement, for present and future action laid down in specific and fundamental principles called a constitution. But the church has the Scriptures for her light and guide in this matter, which is very explicit and full from first to last, for Bishops, Elders, Deacons, Teachers, Exhorters, members, young, old, rich, poor, bond and free.[8]

Expressing a favorable comment, Joshua Montgomery wrote:

> Let us have a constitution now while our church, laity and ministers, are disposed to be governed by the true spirit of Christ and his word, and then, should a part or all of us depart from this spirit, still no rule in discipline could be enacted contrary to the constitution until that constitution is altered.[9]

General Conference of 1841

The General Conference of 1841 met May 10 at Dresbach's church, in Ohio. Bishops Kumler and Erb were in attendance, Bishop Hiestand had died in the second year of the quadrennium. The subject of a constitution was brought up early in the session; however, it does not appear that the delegates referred at all to the constitution of 1837 or to the circular which gave notice to the church that it was intended that the 1837 constitution would be ratified. Based upon that circular, the General Conference of 1841 had the power to do one of two things—that was to ratify or to reject the constitution.[10] Instead, a vote was taken in favor of a constitution, and a committee of nine—one delegate from each conference—was appointed to draft a new one.

Historian A. W. Drury summarized something of the general atmosphere and perhaps some of the reasoning behind the action.

> In the first place, a very limited number had anything to do with the earlier instrument. Again, the circular often referred to was so involved and unintelligible in its wording as to seem to have reference to the body of the constitution itself, rather than exclusively to the article on amendments. Some saw in the confused state into which things had come an opportunity for a constitution of a different character. Thus, between those that desired no constitution and those that desired a constitution embracing different features, the constitution of 1837 went to the ground. William R. Rhinehart, who stood so closely identified with the constitution of 1837 had lost much of his influence, having been constrained to resign his position as editor of the *Religious Telescope* in the middle of his term. Some had objected to the constitution as stilted and grandiose in character.[11]

The discussion began on a motion that a constitution for the better government of the church be adopted. J. Montgomery spoke in favor of a constitution, saying that "the object of a constitution is to guard against apostasy; to sustain a balance of power between the ministry and the laity; that it is designed to establish points of polity which should stand unalterable."[12] There were statements by others, including J. J. Glossbrenner, who spoke in opposition to the above. When the vote was taken, it carried fifteen votes to seven. Glossbrenner was on the committee to draft the new constitution. Later, when asked "Why, if he was opposed to a constitution, he served on the committee to draft one, his answer was, "If there was to be a constitution I wanted to help to make it as good as possible."[13]

The constitution as drawn up was finally adopted by a wide majority. The safeguard against possible hasty amendment was transferred to the people of the entire church, requiring a two-thirds vote of the whole society. Pro rata representation in the general conference was eliminated. The provisions against secret societies and slavery were new to this constitution.

In other business of the General Conference of 1841, Henry Kumler, Sr. and Jacob Erb were re-elected bishops. Henry Kumler, Jr. and John Coons were also elected. William Hanby was elected editor of *The Religious Telescope*. It was ordered that the columns of *The Religious Telescope* were closed to the discussion of the slavery issue. This had come at the request of the Scioto and Sandusky conferences.

A German printing office was established in Baltimore and trustees were appointed. It was to be governed by the same rules which governed the other printing office. It was placed under the jurisdiction of the Pennsylvania Annual Conference between sessions of the general conference. Thus, the conference took over the publication of the German paper, *"Die Geschaeftige Martha"* (Busy Martha) and named Jacob Erb editor and financial manager. It was discontinued after about a year because of lack of support.

A Parent Missionary Society was formed for the purpose of extending the gospel on the frontiers and among the heathen in foreign lands.

A committee was formed to select theological works and other instructive books to be read by all young ministers that they may be educated and edified.

Henry Kumler, Jr. was the son of Bishop Henry Kumler, Sr., and the son-in-law of Bishop Andrew Zeller, thus uniting two distinguished United Brethren families. He was born at Myerstown, Pennsylvania, on January 9, 1801, the second of eleven children. The family moved to Lancaster County in 1810, where Henry grew up. When he was about eleven years of age, his parents were converted, and in the same year he also was converted at the home of his uncle. At the age of fourteen, he was chosen as class leader in the Greencastle Church. Through the performance of his duties he felt God was calling him to preach. Feeling unfit for the task, he confided in others, and was greatly moved by a sermon preached by the Reverend William Brown. He took courage and attempted to exhort. He received his license to preach in 1819 from Christian Newcomer. He moved to Butler County, Ohio, with his father's family just after he received his license. He was ordained by Bishop Newcomer, assisted by Bishop Joseph Hoffman, in 1822. In 1836 he was elected presiding elder in the Miami Conference and served in this capacity for five years. He was elected bishop in 1841.

John Coons was born of illiterate parents, and he himself was unable to read before he was twenty-four years of age. He was the son of a

German father and an English mother and was born October 27, 1797, near Martinsburg, Virginia. His family moved to Ross County, Ohio, when he was about ten years of age. In 1821 he was converted under the ministry of Jacob Antrim. That year he received a license to preach from the Miami Conference. He traveled circuits in Miami Conference and went with the Scioto Conference when it was formed. He received ordination as a deacon in 1824 from Bishop Joseph Hoffman, and was ordained an elder in the church in 1826 by Bishop Christian Newcomer, assisted by Bishop Henry Kumler, Sr.

He married Catherine Bookwalter in 1821, and eight children were born to this marriage. Catherine died in 1840, and after several years, John married Eleanor Windship. Seven children were born to this marriage.

John Coons represented Scioto Conference in the General Conferences of 1829 through 1841, when he was elected bishop. He served on the committee to draft the constitution of 1841. He was on the committee to select the theological works and other instructive books.

FOOTNOTES

[1]John Lawrence, *The History of the Church of the United Brethren in Christ,* 2 vols. (Dayton, OH: Published at the United Brethren Printing Establishment, Sowers and King, Publishers, 1861), 2:322, 323.

[2]William Hanby, *History of the Church of the United Brethren in Christ,* 2 vols. (Circleville, OH: Published at the conference office of the United Brethren in Christ, 1851), 2:250, 251.

[3]Daniel Berger, *History of the Church of the United Brethren in Christ* (Dayton, OH: United Brethren Publishing House, W. J. Shuey, Publisher, 1897), p. 261.

[4]A. W. Drury, *History of the Church of the United Brethren in Christ* (Dayton, OH: The Otterbein Press, 1924), p. 406.

[5]Lawrence, 2:323.

[6]General Conference Minutes of 1837, Unpublished (Huntington, IN: United Brethren Archives Microfilm).

[7]Hanby, p. 268.

[8]H. G. Spayth, "Important to the Church," *The Religious Telescope* n.v. (January 22, 1840): 6.

[9]Drury, p. 410.

[10]Berger, p. 268.

[11]Drury, p. 410, 411.

[12]Ibid., p. 411.

[13]Ibid.

MEMBERSHIP OF THE
FIRST ANNUAL CONFERENCES
1800-1810

	1800	1801	1802	1803	1804	1805	1806	1807	1808	1809	1810
William Otterbein	X	X	X	X		X					
Martin Boehm	X	X	X	X	X	X		X		X	
John Hershey	X	X	X	X		X	X		X	X	
Abraham Troxel	X		X								
Christian Krum	X	X		X		X	X	X	X		X
Henry Krum	X		X			X					
George Pfrimmer	X										
Henry Boehm	X										
Christian Newcomer	X	X	X	X	X	X	X	X	X	X	X
Dietrich Aurand	X										
Jacob Geisinger	X	X				X					
George Adam Geeting	X	X	X	X		X	X	X	X	X	X
Adam Leyman	X										
Jacob Baulus	X					X	X		X		X
Daniel Strickler		X				X					
Peter Senseny		X									
John Neidig		X					X	X			
David Long		X							X	X	X
Abraham Mayer		X		X		X		X	X	X	X
Frederick Schaffer		X		X	X	X		X		X	
Thomas Winter		X									
Ludwig Duckwald		X	X			X			X		
David Snyder		X	X	X	X	X		X	X	X	X

	1800	1801	1802	1803	1804	1805	1806	1807	1808	1809	1810
Peter Kemp		X	X	X		X	X		X		X
Matthias Kessler		X	X								
Abraham Hershey		X						X		X	
Michael Thomas		X	X				X				
Christopher Grosh			X	X						X	
William Ambrose			X			X			X		
Valentine Flugle				X							
John Winter				X							
George Benedum				X		X				X	
Matthias Bortsfield					X					X	
Lorenz Eberhart						X	X				X
Frederick Duckwald						X					
Christian Berger						X					X
Daniel Troyer						X					
Jacob Dehof						X					X
Joseph Hoffman							X	X	X	X	X
Isaac Niswander								X	X	X	X
Christian Smith								X		X	X
Christian Hershey								X		X	X
Henry Duckwald									X		
Adam Reigel										X	
John Snyder										X	
George Hoffman											X

165

NUMERICAL GROWTH OF PREACHERS
AND PREACHING APPOINTMENTS
1830-1840

	PREACHERS			CIRCUITS		
CONFERENCE	1830	1835	1840	1830	1835	1840
Old Conference	67			11		
Virginia		24	28		7	9
Pennsylvania		83	60		11	9
Allegheny			31			8
Miami	62	43	54	10	11	12
Muskingum	32	22	41	4	4	8
Scioto	18	25	65	6	5	15
Indiana		41	44		8	10
Sandusky			26			7
Wabash		13	38		6	12

Henry G. Spayth, *History of the Church of the United Brethren in Christ,* 2 vols. (Dayton, OH: The Otterbein Press, 1851), pp. 229, 241, 266.

Part Three

THE BEST AND
THE WORST OF TIMES

1841-1889

Mary Lou Funk

BIOGRAPHICAL DATA

As a teenager, Mary Lou Funk was converted in the Munson United Brethren Church, Fayette Circuit, North Ohio Conference, and became a member of the Fountain Church on the same circuit. Later, while associate editor of the United Brethren Publications (1957-1968), her membership was transferred to College Park Church, where she has served as a Sunday School teacher and is active in a women's missionary society. Following graduation from college she taught Bible classes in the schools of Bath County, Virginia. She has been a camp counselor at North Ohio and Rock River Camps, helped launch the Vacation Bible School program in United Brethren churches in Jamaica, and has been a member and secretary of the United Brethren Archives Committee since the 1960s.

Presently an elementary schoolteacher, she has a bachelor of arts degree from Huntington College and a master of science in education degree from Saint Francis College. She has occasionally been asked if she is related to the family of the late Bishop E. M. Funk. There is no known family tie, but she has been greatly influenced by the life and ministry of the bishop and values a spiritual kinship with his family. Her parents, Donald and Doris Funk, resided in Fulton County, Ohio most of their lives. She has three brothers.

PERSPECTIVE

This is a story of good and bad times in the United Brethren Church. From a high point of thousands of conversions and new members year after year, rapid geographical expansion, the beginning and development of institutions, and a noble record on dealing with moral issues, the denomination fell to a low of discord and division.

Through descriptions and accounts of nineteenth-century United Brethren and events of their lives, the writer hopes to give readers a sense of being there—for example, on the Oregon Trail as Jeremiah Kenoyer and ninety-seven others endured its rigors; in Lawrence, Kansas when Samuel Snyder paid the ultimate price; at the second session of Missouri Conference when one room of Josiah Terrel's home served as meeting room, dining room, and bedroom for conference members; at a campmeeting where Christopher Flinchbaugh left the pulpit to deal with hecklers; in the William Hanby home when even a five-year-old daughter felt the debt of the young printing establishment; with Mrs. S. K. Rike as she contemplated the role of women in the missionary ventures of the church.

The length of this history necessitated selecting events, subjects, and details the writer thought to be more important and representative of the history and life of the church. Much of interest had to be omitted.

Students of this period of United Brethren history cannot escape the search for understanding why United Brethren would divide. This account aims to explain what led to 1889 and to present some details of why the church divided, probed from sources from those years. Attempt has been made to present the Liberal as well as the Radical view. However, the writer admits to an emphasis on the Radical view. This emphasis is partly because of the noticeable lack of the Radical viewpoint in denominational histories by the other group of United Brethren.

Sources for this history and its background are primarily from the extensive collection in the United Brethren Archives. Quotations from official records and other sources of information from this period have been included to give some accounts in the words of participants or observers and statements of views in the words of those who expressed them. The writer is grateful to archivist Jane Mason for her encouragement and her assistance in locating materials and information. Also, I thank her and others for reading and criticizing the manuscript or parts of it.

Mary Lou Funk

18

THE MINISTRY

Following the Frontier

The influx of millions of European immigrants to the United States in the 1800s pushed the frontier westward. Many United Brethren preachers joined the migration, and the frontier became their mission field. Some also went north to Ontario, Canada. On horseback and often on foot, in all kinds of weather, these preachers traveled through mud, rivers, and dense forests to spread the gospel in new settlements. With the establishment of the church in new territories and states, along with the growth of the church in the eastern United States, the denomination grew from an estimated 25,000 members in 1841 to over 200,000 by 1889—eight times larger, and twice the national growth rate. Other churches also experienced large gains during this time.

Of all the United Brethren missions on the frontier, the mission to Oregon Territory stirred the church to more systematic, organized action on the frontier and in foreign lands. When sixteen families gathered at Council Bluffs, Iowa, in May 1853 to begin their long and arduous journey to Oregon, among them was thirty-three-year-old Jeremiah Kenoyer. He was a preacher and doctor, who, along with T. J. Connor, had been appointed to go with a colony of laymen to join other United Brethren families already settled there. Jeremiah was one of a family who in an unbroken line from 1800 to the present have been United Brethren. He exemplified the spirit that characterized those whom God used to enlarge the church in the face of great difficulties.

Jeremiah's maternal grandfather was J. G. Pfrimmer, one of the church fathers and a pioneer in establishing the church in Indiana.

171

Fredrick Kenoyer, Jeremiah's father, became an itinerant of the Miami Conference in 1827, and in 1830 a charter member of Indiana Conference. Following the western movement of settlers, he became a charter member of three other conferences—Wabash, Illinois, and Upper Wabash. In addition to being a successful itinerant pastor who organized many local societies, he also served as a presiding elder and was a delegate to the General Conference of 1837.[1]

At age seventeen Jeremiah was converted and joined the church. He was licensed by his quarterly conference and began preaching as a young man. From this period of his life there is an account of a time when he, in place of his father, traveled to a frontier settlement in Jasper County, Indiana, to fill an appointment:

> He was mounted. His horse was a pale sorrel with white mane and tail, badly crimped with burs, a very inferior animal, whose gait was seriously retarded by a stiff knee. The saddle was in keeping with the horse's knee, and the stirrups in keeping with the saddle—one of which was repaired with hickory-bark. An old, dilapidated blind-bridle comprised the head-gear. The dress of the minister was quite as ludicrous, and consisted of a coon-skin cap, an old-fashioned shingle-cape overcoat, and "jeans" coat, pants, and vest, with a pair of patched shoes. Add to this in your imagination the appearance of the man as somewhat homely, with dark hair and eyes, uncomely, heavy eyebrows, and you have a picture of our preacher. I must confess that I felt much chagrined at his uncouth appearance, and then thought that the newly-arrived could do more good in his father's cornfield.[2]

However, young Jeremiah "opened the services by singing in the most melodious and impressive manner . . . then followed with a prayer that seemed to open heaven," and delivered a sermon "of unusual power and tenderness . . . some wept and praised God, while many trembled. . . . Such eloquence and oratory were not expected from Father Kenoyer, much less from one so young." Three more services followed in the next two days. Fourteen united with the church, and Jeremiah organized a class. He

> . . . said he would visit and preach for us once a month if we would pay him one dollar for each visit, as he would have to ride twenty-five miles to reach us, and that he would necessarily have to use Saturday and Monday and would have to hire a hand to fill his place on the farm, which would cost him fifty cents per day. As for Sunday, he charged nothing for preaching on that day.[3]

At the organization of the Illinois Annual Conference in 1845, Jeremiah was granted an annual conference license to preach and appointed to a mission field on the Kankakee River. Two years later he was sent to Wisconsin Territory, "where the labors of this homespun, but marvelous, preacher did much toward establishing the church in this new field." While serving as presiding elder there, he was appointed as a missionary to Oregon. He had offered to go if $150 of his expense would be provided by the mission board, though the chief missionary, T. J. Connor, had an appropriation of $1000.[4]

With that meager amount, Jeremiah and his wife, Elizabeth, committed themselves and their seven children—the oldest age twelve and the youngest only a few weeks old—to a 2000-mile journey paced by slow-moving oxen over no well-defined road but merely a rough trail. Saturday, May 7, at ten in the morning, their wagon train, consisting of thirty wagons, ninety-eight persons, and about three hundred head of cattle and a number of horses, commenced crossing the Missouri River. By four o'clock all were safely on the western shore. "For the first time we felt we had left civilization—turned our backs to happiness while our faces fronted dangers, hunger, and fatigue," wrote Basil Longworth, one of the company. From his diary one gets a glimpse of the excitement, beauty, boredom, hardships, and weariness of traversing the plains, desert, mountains, and rivers of the Oregon Trail through heat, rain, hail, dust, and mud.[5] No United Brethren mission undertaking was more notable for the fortitude and endurance required of so many persons and animals.

When the Kenoyer family reached their destination, the home of a cousin in the Willamette Valley, they were penniless. According to grandson J. A. Kenoyer, they had to leave one of two milk cows with a ferryman because they had no money to pay him. He took them across only when they agreed to leave the cow until they returned with money for the crossing. When they arrived at the cousin's, two miles from the river, Jeremiah was holding up one side of the neck yoke in place of the cow at the ferry. Elizabeth's dress was worn to the knees from walking through brush. But they had survived the nearly five-months ordeal— even baby Louisa, who lived to age ninety-seven!

Settling in Yamhill County, Jeremiah split rails and chopped wood for their living, and preached week nights and Sundays in the homes of settlers. Milton Wright, who was associated with him two years as a fellow missionary, and other years as his bishop, said that he excelled as a preacher and revivalist.[6] To inform the church of the work in Oregon, letters from Jeremiah were published in the *Religious Telescope* (May 3, June 7, and August 30, 1854):

February 27, 1854 . . . Religion here is at a very low ebb, cold, dead formality prevails almost universally. . . . I have more calls for appointments than I can fill, situated as I am, having to travel afoot, and wade the mud and water . . .

May 7, 1854   I am now about 100 miles from home, hunting up the lost sheep. . . . We have had some good times but no general stir. People here know nothing about us, though they seem anxious to learn, and we have more calls than we can fill. I have traveled 150 miles and tried to preach twenty sermons in the last seventeen days. I have settled my family in the country on a half section of land,—I have fenced and broken about six acres, and put in a spring crop.

June 7, 1854   To give an idea of what we are doing in Oregon I will give them a leaf from my journal. . . . March 25, Preached at Salem, the capital of the territory; preached at night to a good congregation. March 26,   Preached at eleven o'clock. Had a good congregation, notwithstanding Bishop Simons, of the M.E. Church, preached in town at the same hour. Walked three miles into the country, and preached at three o'clock. Returned to town and preached again at night. I think that our prospects are fair for a good class at this place at no distant date, though the people that attend on preaching are mostly irreligious.

In 1856, missionary secretary John C. Bright, in his third annual report, said that from its beginning to June 1856 only $2450 had been appropriated for Oregon Mission. Then he added:

We see from the above, how much under God, can be done by humble, self-sacrificing men, with a little money, to promote the Kingdom of Christ. We do not hesitate to say, that we perform in proportion to the amount of money we use, as much, and perhaps more missionary labor than any other church in the land (unless we may except the Moravians). The reason is obvious. The itinerants of our denomination labor for souls. The untiring missionary, if not fully compensated on earth, will have a rich reward in heaven.[7]

Oregon Mission Conference was organized in 1855 and by 1861 had forty-eight preaching places, twenty-seven classes, and five hundred sixty-five members. The mission board tried to send additional reinforcements there, but had to report: "Attractive as is the Pacific coast, it seems harder to get men there as missionaries than to Africa."[8]

In 1868 Jeremiah Kenoyer and his family moved to Washington Territory, where to old age he continued as a pioneer itinerant and served as the leader in establishing and building up the Walla Walla (earlier called Cascade) Conference. He also played a role in going and sending workers from Walla Walla to Idaho Territory in the 1870s.

Three of Jeremiah's sons and a son-in-law became ministers in the church, and five grandsons also. Grandson Fermin L. Hoskins served as bishop 1905-1933 and then was elected bishop emeritus.

United Brethren work in California began about the time of the gold rush and was an attempt to give the message of salvation to transient mining people. Though some United Brethren families moved to California in the 1850s, they were scattered and not able to organize. Efforts to build a permanent work started with the arrival of Israel Sloan, who after being sent from Sandusky Conference as a missionary to Ontario, Canada, was then sent as a missionary to California in 1858. Having some financial resources of his own, he drew largely on these in order to continue full time in the work. His able ministry was sadly and abruptly ended in 1861 when he died as a result of injuries suffered when he was thrown from his pony while descending a steep mountain.[9]

For lack of funds and workers, the Pacific Coast conferences continued in mission status for several years. The area was designated as a bishop's district in 1861, but because of conditions arising from the Civil War, Bishop Daniel Shuck did not reach the coast until 1864.

Sandusky Conference, whose boundaries extended from northwest Ohio into Michigan, appropriated fifty dollars and sent Stephen Lee to begin United Brethren work in Michigan in 1849.[10] Within four years the Michigan Mission Conference was organized. In 1856, the missionary secretary's report paid glowing tribute to this young conference:

> Among the most prominent of our mission conferences we must place Michigan. So greatly has the Lord blessed the labors of his servants there that the conference has needed but little assistance from the Board comparatively. . . .
> The success in Michigan has been owing mainly, under the blessing of God, to the labors of a few self-denying itinerant preachers.[11]

Four years from its formation the conference was self-supporting. Appointments that year included Adrian, Hillsdale, Monroe, Jackson, and Kalamazoo. That year over 1000 conversions were reported, and 600 united with the church.

The General Conference of 1861 divided this growing conference into Michigan and North Michigan Conferences, and added territory in Ohio and Indiana to the Michigan Conference. These two conferences were renamed North Ohio and Michigan in 1869. With the progress of the work in Michigan, the General Conference of 1877 established a new conference in the north called Saginaw (named North Michigan in 1881). By 1888 North Ohio, Michigan, and North Michigan were all strong conferences. Their combined membership was nearly 12,000; itinerants numbered 125; local preachers 42; and there were 180 church houses.

Another area of the church that progressed quickly from mission status to self-supporting was Wisconsin, 1857-1861; in 1861 Fox River Mission Conference resulted from its division.

The Kansas Mission Conference, organized in 1857, did not receive strong support from the eastern part of the church. Then severe drought intensified difficult living conditions, and many people left Kansas in 1860. But most United Brethren preachers stayed. Their faith and persistence were rewarded. By 1867 there were 149 appointments, 86 classes, and 1918 members. The conference expanded and divided, and by 1882 there were four conferences (Kansas, West Kansas, Neosho, and Arkansas Valley) with 7427 members.

A pioneer itinerant in Ohio, Indiana, and Iowa, William Davis, in 1846 wrote in a letter to a friend:

> A few evenings ago, while sitting by my fireside, looking forward to the labor and exposure and privation which I must endure during the conference year which has just commenced, my mind was carried back to the past, whereupon I hunted up my old diary, by the aid of which I reached the following facts and conclusions: That I have been an itinerant minister in the United Brethren Church sixteen years; that I have traveled for ministerial purposes 54,200 miles; that I have preached (or tried to preach) 5,110 sermons; that I have received as an earthly remuneration $652; that the Lord has hitherto helped me; and that it would be wickedness to distrust so good a friend in time to come.
>
> My time has been spent chiefly on the frontiers, among poor people; and could I lead some of my rich brethren along Indian trails or more dimly-beaten paths to the cabins in the woods and introduce them to meanly-clad parents, surrounded by almost naked children, and let them worship and mingle their prayers, songs, and tears around the same altar, they too would love those poor brethren, excuse their scanty contributions, and of their abundance give something for the support of the missionary who, perhaps, with ragged clothes and naked knees (for I have preached with naked knees) is preaching on the frontiers. I do love the poor pioneer brethren in their cabins, and sympathize with the missionary who brings to them, at great personal sacrifice, the bread of life; and if after death my spirit should be permitted to visit my brethren on earth, I would fly on speedy wings to the suffering missionary and whisper consolation in his ears.[12]

Pioneer Preachers

United Brethren preachers came from humble backgrounds with few educational, cultural, or material advantages. But these matters were not highly regarded by them or by those to whom they ministered. "Grit, grace, and common sense" counted on the frontier. Lewis Davis, writing of some delegates of the General Conference of 1849, described them as "men of independent and resolute mold, devoted alike to their convictions and the interests of the church."[13]

On the subject of qualifications of the ministry, a leader of Allegheny Conference, Isaiah Potter, wrote in the *Religious Telescope* of January 12, 1853:

> [A minister] should be thoroughly furnished with information relative to the salvation of man. . . . Education is important to a minister's success, but not more so than deep humility, fervent zeal, a feeling sense of his responsibility, the value of souls, and a call to the ministry. I am decidedly opposed to licensing an ignorant man to preach the gospel; but not more so, than to license a literary coxcomb, or a phlegmatic drone. . . . We want men . . . who are intelligent, and who have at least a good common English education, and a pretty thorough knowledge of Bible doctrine; but they [United Brethren] require this no more than they do men of deep-toned piety, humble men, and men whose souls blaze with zeal like torches.

Candidates for the ministry and those who licensed them usually considered some educational attainments desirable, but many viewed with suspicion very much schooling for fear of dependence upon it rather than upon God.

Of the seventeen men who served as bishops during this period, only Ezekiel Kephart was a college graduate. Two others, Daniel Shuck and Milton Wright, each had one year of college. Of the earliest bishops of this period, John Coons did not have so much as a common school education and could not read until after his conversion in his early twenties. Bishop Jacob Markwood, recognized within and beyond United Brethren circles as a remarkable preacher, had no more than about twelve months of schooling. Jonathan Weaver, who served thirty-six years as a bishop, and authored ten books and numerous articles, as a boy had about three months of schooling a year for some years, and at age twenty-one attended a Presbyterian academy for five months. William Hanby, one of the church's first editors and historians, and bishop 1845-1849, had but a few months of schooling. David Edwards, a noted bishop who served in that office 1849-1876 and who was also a church editor, as a boy received instruction at home in reading and writing and attended school twelve months. The fame of Lewis Davis in the church for the establishment of the first college and later the theological seminary was born out of his intense desire that others should have the opportunities he longed for but did not realize. His self-education helped fit him for responsibilities as bishop and a leader both at Otterbein University and Union Biblical Seminary.[14]

In the early and mid-1800s the lack of school opportunities was often the reason for limited formal education. Many parents were satisfied when their children could read, write, and compute problems of everyday living. In 1870 the accumulated schooling of a lifetime received by the average person in the United States was three and a third years.[15]

After beginning their ministry, many United Brethren preachers studied independently or with the help of an experienced minister. Considering the hardships under which such study was done, the accomplishments are the more commendable. Most had very limited means for acquiring books, no special room for a study, limited time to study except while traveling or by a fireside where family activities and conversation had to be blocked out. In many cases study habits had to be developed. Writing materials were not the most accessible or convenient, so the memory was often taxed.

It was common for men to begin their ministry soon after they expressed the belief that God was calling them to preach. Official recognition and approval started when a local congregation recommended that a candidate be licensed by the quarterly conference. A year later he might be recommended by the quarterly conference to be licensed by the annual conference. At both levels he would be questioned regarding his conversion, call, beliefs, and subjection to church authority. An annual conference licentiate was on probation for three years, during which he was to study, if possible with the assistance of an experienced minister. The main subject was the Bible—its doctrine, biography, history, and geography.

Some conferences used particular missions or circuits to test a young preacher's determination. A West Virginia circuit covering four counties and part of a fifth was called "the college." It was often assigned to young men, and was considered necessary for graduating into the itineracy as a permanent member.[16]

John Russel, bishop 1845-1849 and 1857-1861, was efficient in enlisting and encouraging capable young men into the ministry. Soon after he was first elected bishop, he wrote a letter to a young minister which was later published in the *Religious Telescope*. In part, he wrote:

> Think not, Now I am a preacher I may be ranked among the apostles; rather think that you have barely entered upon the threshold of God's ministry. Also think it your duty to improve your mind, talents, self-knowledge and character, with all other graces calculated to advance a Christian minister. On the other hand, do not think less of yourself than you ought to think, but think soberly.
>
> If your retention is bad, do not crowd it. It is of as ill consequence to overload a weak memory as a weak stomach, so keep it free from trash. Take heed what

company you keep, what books you read, and what thoughts you favor. What you are determined to remember, think of before you go to sleep at night, and the first thing in the morning when your faculties are fresh. Habituate yourself to close and rational thinking. When you have started a good thought pursue it; do not presently lose sight of it. Manage your actions and thoughts in such a manner as if you were just going out of the world.

Take no text which you can not well handle, for it is ill in a child, when its parents send it to bring chips, to take hold of a big stick, and pout because it can not carry it.[17]

At the General Conference of 1845 the matter of a course of study was introduced, and an annual conference library for ministers was recommended. The General Conference of 1853 approved a three-year plan of study for licentiates. Successful completion of the course, including examinations, along with three years of experience as an active minister qualified a licentiate to be examined by his conference and voted on by the elders. If two-thirds voted favorably, he would be ordained by the laying on of hands by the bishop and two elders.

Ministerial associations or institutes were voluntarily organized by some of the annual conferences in the mid and later 1800s for the mental and moral improvement of the members and improvement in their methods of work. Members of these groups would meet for as long as a week at a time for discussions and lectures. To the novice these meetings were exceedingly helpful.

The *Discipline* listed a number of duties ministers were to perform. It also directed them to

1) Be diligent. Never trifle away your time; always be serious. Let your motto be "HOLINESS UNTO THE LORD!" Avoid all lightness and jesting; converse sparingly; conduct yourself prudently with women; and demean yourself in all respects as a true Christian. Be at all times averse to crediting evil reports; believe evil of no one without good evidence. Put the best construction on everything.

2) Speak evil of no one. Whatever may be your thoughts, keep them within your own breast till you can tell the person concerned what you think wrong in his conduct.

3) Let your business be to save as many souls as possible. To this employment give yourself wholly. Visit those who need it; and act in all things, not according to your own wills, but as sons in the gospel. For as such it becomes your duty to employ your time in the manner prescribed, in preaching and visiting from house to house, in instruction and prayer, and in meditating on the word of God. With these be occupied until our Lord cometh.

If an itinerant preacher ceased to be efficient and useful by neglecting his field of labor or by neglecting to read or study, the *Discipline* directed his annual conference to admonish him. If he did not reform, he could be dismissed from the itineracy or located (not assigned) indefinitely.

Poor as a Church Mouse

One year in the 1850s in western Ohio the spring and early summer rains prevented settlers from getting out a crop. Some of them had to live from day to day on the corn meal they earned for a day's labor. J. L. Luttrell, a United Brethren minister among these people, wrote in his Auglaize Conference history:

> We were as poor ourself as a "church mouse," . . . We were not receiving an average of twenty-five cents a day for our services on the work, and so were working every hour we could get off from the circuit, at anything we could get to do, that we might keep our family from starving.[18]

Even when times were better, not only Auglaize itinerants but other United Brethren itinerants received poor financial support. Bishop Jonathan Weaver told Auglaize ministers at the 1873 annual session that they might as well make up their minds to remain poor as long as they lived.[19]

According to *Discipline,* it was part of the business of annual conferences to inquire about what was collected for the salary of traveling preachers. At the White River session in 1847 in reply to the question about the preachers receiving their pay, the statement was made, "Not all in money, but in grace."[20] At the 1883 Arkansas Valley Conference (organized 1881) the average salary for the year was $136.[21] Bishop Kephart remarked, "Brethren, how do you get along? What do you live on?" Instantly one replied, "Live on? Why, Bishop, we live on sand and scenery!"[22]

A number of ministers and members of this period started out with the practice of preachers making their living at farming or some other occupation, and preaching in their spare time. This custom was hard to leave behind when the general conference took action to change to a full-time ministry supported by the church. In the 1840s the general conference put in the *Discipline* that an unmarried traveling preacher should receive an annual salary of $100, and a married one $200. This salary scale applied to bishops also.

A minimal amount was allowed for house rent and for children, and also travel expenses. Economic conditions of the country at that time did not contribute to the efforts for a full-time ministry. To add to the difficulty, these years were also the beginning of emphasis on money for meeting houses, missions, schools, and the publishing establishment.

Some ministers spoke and wrote with hopes of increased salaries; others seemed to have been content with their lot. If the quarterage (most were paid quarterly) was late or low, or flour and potatoes instead of money, they did not complain but found it another occasion to trust divine care and to remind themselves that their treasures were in heaven.

In the 1850s, a time of "peace and plenty," general conference set annual salaries at $150 for unmarried preachers and $300 for married ones. Beginning in 1869 a circuit or station preacher was to receive an amount agreed upon by him and the quarterly conference of the field to which he was assigned. A bishop was to receive $1000 plus travel and house. In many instances salaries paid were below the set figures, especially where the church was not well established or where the people were poor.

Telescope editor, John Lawrence, wrote in praise of United Brethren ministering to the poor, as Jesus had done. He stated:

> The great body of the people in the world are comparatively poor; and that church, all other things being equal, will be the most useful, will gather the most sheaves into the heavenly barn, which adapts its agencies and instrumentalities to the common people.

He lauded United Brethren inexpensive, plain meeting houses with seats as free as the gospel, and the self-sacrificing ministers whose salaries did not require the sale of pews to those who can pay an extravagant price. Not wanting to be misunderstood about ministers' salaries, Lawrence went on to say that if a minister gave himself wholly to his work, he should be paid as much as hard-working men in his community.[23]

Bishop John Dickson wrote a *Telescope* article (April 10, 1872) in which he said:

> From some observations we have set down *insufficient salaries* as one of the main reasons why we do not have a better supply of preachers. . . . In many instances it is impossible, with the most rigid economy, to be comfortable and decent, and keep out of debt, on their meager salaries.

Bishops, editors, and others, through the columns of the *Religious Telescope,* tried to inform and teach the church about ministerial support. Bishop David Edwards, under the title "Pay the Preacher," wrote, "God commands it. He has ordained that they that preach the gospel shall live of the gospel. 'Thou shalt not muzzle the ox that

treadeth out the corn.' "[24] Milton Wright, in a *Telescope* editorial,
"Support of the Ministry," (March 21, 1877) said that this is a subject
that requires line on line, precept on precept.

> It has been taught, but surely not learned. Certainly it is not well practiced. . . .
> Some think riches would hurt ministers. They might, but the danger is far off to
> most of them. . . . [A minister's] people would have him follow the example
> of Jesus, who was poor. Not all would follow him as he follows Christ in this
> regard.

It was a duty of members of the church, according to the *Discipline,*
to willingly and freely contribute to the support of the ministry, as the
Lord had prospered them. Each class had a steward who was to seek
pledges from members and then collect quarterly or oftener. This
officer was accountable to the quarterly conference. Bishop Weaver
went so far as to say that church members who did not give as God had
prospered them should be excommunicated.[25] Far from such discipline
were Mr. and Mrs. Singleton Buxton, who hosted a big meeting,
boarding and lodging all who came for the two or three days. William
Whetsel "always provided as carefully for his church dues as he did for
his taxes" and never allowed the salary of the preacher to go unpaid.[26]

It is difficult for twentieth-century North Americans to identify with
the plight of nineteenth-century "worn-out" or superannuated ministers, or disabled ones, for whom only a token effort was made in the
name of the Benevolent Fund and the Preachers' Aid Society. These
organizations were to give direct aid and to provide loans. At its
beginning the Benevolent Fund was a church-wide plan, but it was not
successful. Part of the reason was that money for it was to come from
proceeds of the printing establishment over and above contingent
expenses. But if the young printing establishment had such profits,
they were needed to maintain and develop the establishment. The
General Conference of 1853 advised each annual conference to adopt
the best means to care for superannuated or disabled ministers or their
widows and children. Unfortunately, the annual conference plans that
were inaugurated were not much more successful than the church-wide
plan.

Annual Conference—Frontier Style

Traveling to an annual conference session, like traveling a circuit,
was sometimes accomplished with pleasure and ease if the weather,
roads, horse, and rider were all quite fit. To add to the pleasure, a

group of ministers would meet and ride together at least part of the way—which might be 150 miles or more. Occasionally to break the monotony of a long trip, and for the profit of the group, they would ride slowly and close together while they sang, prayed, read Scripture, and even preached sermons. One minister commented, "It seemed that even our horses were cheered, especially by the singing."[27]

Annual sessions were usually scheduled to avoid severe winter weather and spring thaws. Nevertheless there were times when the roads or other circumstances made attendance by all an impossibility. In 1867 John Fetterhoff, age sixty-eight, walked the last six miles in mud "too deep for wagons" to the Ohio German Conference.[28] Bishops often traveled hundreds of miles under very arduous conditions until the building of railroads. In 1869, after chairing the California Conference business under a huge oak tree, Bishop Weaver traveled 600 miles by stagecoach over dusty, rough roads from California to Oregon.[29] Some of the early sessions of the Pacific Coast conferences were held without a bishop in attendance.

Bishop Edwards described the second annual session of Missouri Misson Conference:

> Every family in the neighborhood in which the conference was held was afflicted, except Brother Terrel's. They were "up," and able to keep the whole conference, which they cheerfully did, in truly primitive style, covering the floor with "United Brethren beds." To some who are unacquainted with frontier life, it might seem that they could not be happy, thus cramped, making one room serve for a meeting house, dining room, bedroom and parlor. But where love is, there is more true happiness in such a situation than in the most splendid palaces without it. We had a good time, God was with us.[30]

That same year, 1855, St. Joseph Conference session was held in the barn of a Brother Livengood near Elkhart, Indiana. Two years later Bishop Edwards met with five ministers in Samuel Snyder's sod house and organized the Kansas Mission Conference. The third session of Osage Conference, in Cherokee County, Kansas, November 1871, is described in part by J. R. Chambers:

> Bishop Dickson presided. It was very rainy, muddy weather, the faithful but *poor* preachers who had reached the place of meeting on horseback and in open wagons, were none too well dressed, either as to comfort, or looks, and presented a generally forlorn appearance. Reverend W. J. Shuey, the agent of the Publishing House, Dayton, Ohio, was present at this conference. He and the Bishop roomed together, in a small "early-day" Kansas house. To these men of the east the outlook was rather gloomy. On retiring to their room one night, speaking of the conference, Bishop Dickson was heard to heave a deep sigh, and

say,—*"Small potatoes."* Shuey heaved another sign, and echoed,—*"Few in a hill."*

Chambers thought these men did not "realize and appreciate the possibilities of the great West."[31]

Wherever the annual sessions were held, the business centered around the examination and stationing of preachers (appointments were changed every one, two, or three years, the *Discipline* limiting the time at one appointment to three consecutive years or fewer, except by special approval). Sometimes conferences had to conduct the painful and delicate business of bringing charges against ministers, making investigations, and occasionally expelling a minister. A series of questions in the *Discipline* served as the agenda for the annual sessions during this period of history:

> 1) Have any of the preachers died during the last year? 2) Who are the candidates for the ministry? 3) Are any to be ordained to the office of elder? 4) What has been collected for contingent expenses and the salary of traveling preachers? 5) Has reckoning been made with the traveling preachers? 6) Have they received their dues? 7) Who are willing to travel the ensuing year, without reserve? 8) Who are the Presiding Elders? 9) Where are the preachers stationed this year? 10) No preacher shall arbitrarily form a mission, or circuit within the embrace of any circuit, or Presiding Elder's district. 11) Where shall our next conference be held? 12) Is there anything else to be done? 13) Is all that has been done entered upon the record?

When the denominational mission board and Sabbath school board became organized, questions were added in relation to missions and Sabbath schools.

Spontaneous humor sometimes broke the tension or monotony of business. R. W. Braddock of Erie Conference had a habit of sitting on the front seat and speaking a great deal. This irritated the bishop and other members. One time he began, "If it please the Chair," and, without waiting for the bishop's acknowledgment, started to go on with his speech. But Bishop J. J. Glossbrenner interrupted, "And what if it doesn't please the Chair?" Startled, Braddock sat down—but missed his seat, much to the amusement of the conference.[32]

The General Conference of 1877 made lay representation in annual conference optional provided that two-thirds of the ministers approved. Lay representatives were to have all the privileges and rights of ministers except voting on reception or expulsion of preachers, the passing of licentiates in the reading course, and the election of presiding elders.

During the 1800s a practice began which lasted about a century—

that of concluding the annual session on Sunday with devotional and often missionary services. Many lay people came to hear the bishop preach and to learn of the stationing of preachers. These services were often held outdoors because of large attendances. Nearly 3000 people assembled in a grove near Jay City, Indiana, for the Sunday services of the August 1873 Auglaize Conference.[33]

Questions on Baptism and Doctrine

In the time of Otterbein and Boehm, they and their associates agreed that the ordinance of baptism should be practiced, and that the mode—immersion, pouring, or sprinkling—should be left to the individual being baptized. The General Conference of 1815 affirmed these agreements in the last paragraph of the Confession of Faith, which was revised and ordered printed by this conference. Water baptism was considered an outward form symbolizing the inner baptism of the Holy Spirit. Water baptism or any particular mode of baptism was not to be a test of Christian fellowship among United Brethren. The General Conferences of 1853 and 1857 reaffirmed that liberty of mode be allowed and that there be respect for one another's choice of mode.

From the days of Otterbein and Boehm, some practiced infant baptism and others did not. Like the mode, the matter of candidates for baptism was also to be left to the judgment and understanding of each individual—such was the decision of the General Conference of 1857. Writing on this subject in *Unity with God* magazine, Bishop David Edwards, editor, expressed his views:

> As to infant baptism, we neither advocate nor oppose it strongly. If religious parents desire to consecrate their children to God in this way, what harm is there in it—especially if they teach them that on consecrating themselves to Christ in riper years they are at liberty to be re-baptized if their views of Bible requirement demand it. We have neither time nor disposition to contend with any one about forms. Let us have the living power, which the best of forms do but faintly shadow forth.[34]

Depravity

The General Conference of 1841 voted to ask ministerial candidates about their knowledge of depravity. At the next general conference a motion to remove this topic from the examination of candidates was lost by a vote of 20 to 6. The General Conference of 1853, after a discussion extending over parts of four days, voted 23 to 19 to substitute "Do you believe in the doctrine of natural, hereditary, complete depravity?" along with an explanatory amendment offered by Bishop Glossbrenner:

> 1. By *depravity* is meant, not guilt, nor liability to punishment, but the absence of holiness, which therefore unfits a man for heaven. 2. By *natural* is meant that man is born with this absence of holiness. 3. By *hereditary* is meant that this unholy state is inherited from Adam. 4. By *complete* is not meant that a man or child cannot become more unholy, or that he is irrecoverably unholy, nor that he is a mass of corruption, but that this absence of holiness must be predicated of all the faculties and powers of the soul.[35]

Lewis Davis, a bishop-elect of this conference, wrote of the discussion:

> A few of the members of the General Conference objected to the doctrine of "total" depravity as held by the orthodox [reformed] church. It was affirmed by those who held this view that before the promise man was totally depraved, but not afterward. That is to say, the death of Christ had so far affected the moral nature and condition of man as to make it improper to use the term "total" as applied to human depravity. There was no differences of opinion respecting the nature or extent of the atonement. The common ground of belief was that Christ did so die for the whole human race as to make salvation attainable for all men. It was also agreed that man in his present condition is, in fact, deeply depraved and sadly in need of Christ's salvation. The only question in dispute related to the extent of man's depravity under Christ's remedial scheme.[36]

The decision of the general conference gave satisfaction to some but not to others, particularly some ministers of the western and the German areas of the church who were classed as "partial" depravity men.[37] Articles on depravity frequently appeared in the *Religious Telescope,* as they had since 1845. "A brisk theological skirmish was kept up in many places during the four years which intervened between the General Conferences of 1853 and 1857; and when the last-named conference convened, preparations were made, on both sides, for a pitched battle," wrote John Lawrence, a member of both conferences.[38] However, the *Discipline* revision committee, made up of one delegate from each annual conference, came to agreement and offered a substitution. By a vote of 57 to 1 the amended substitution was adopted:

> Do you believe that man, abstract of [changed to *apart from* in 1873] the grace of our Lord Jesus Christ, is fallen from original righteousness, and is not only entirely destitute of holiness, but is inclined to evil, and only evil, and that

continually; and that except a man be born again he cannot see the kingdom of God?

Immediately after the report of the committee there was a general call for the question. Following a brief discussion and the vote, the conference arose and sang the doxology as an expression of thanksgiving and joy at the relatively quick and harmonious settlement of this matter.[39] As to why the question on depravity adopted in 1857 was so generally approved and continued in the *Discipline* with only the minor change in 1873, Halleck Floyd offered this explanation:

> Some regard the statement as an abstract view, that man is in fact a subject of grace; while others regard it as a statement of fact that man is in fact abstract of the grace of God, and hence those of differing views were quieted by the statement, each one being allowed the liberty of his own particular view. Under that statement ministers holding to different views on depravity have remained in the church, because the church has allowed liberty of conscience in the interpretation of that statement.[40]

Holiness

The United Brethren who was most often and most favorably spoken of in connection with the doctrine of holiness was David Edwards, bishop from 1849 until his death in 1876. "He was a kind of authority in most parts of the church on the subject of sanctification," wrote Lewis Davis in his biography of Edwards. "The favorite theme of Mr. Edwards was holiness of heart and life. If there was any one subject that wholly absorbed him, it was this. Hence his tongue and pen were alike busily employed in its advocacy."[41] Of Edwards' preaching and writing on this topic, Davis said:

> It is doubtful if the particular doctrine of entire sanctification has ever been stated more clearly, more profoundly, and in a way less liable to objection, than as stated by him. One of the proofs of this is that he carried with him, in this movement, so many of the best minds of the church, and that, of those who were not convinced, so few ventured to oppose him.[42]

In reply to "What is holiness?" Edwards said:

> It is not a mere emotion or passion, neither does it exist in any external act or ceremonies; but it is a moral state and habit—a condition of purity and rectitude. It is not a grace, but the assemblage of all the graces necessary to form the Christian character. It is, in a word, the moral image of God, who is said to be "glorious in holiness," and whose nature is love. The heart that is full of love is

full of holiness. Yet it abhors sin as the "abominable thing that God hates." Such is holiness.[43]

At the age of twenty-nine, after ten years as an itinerant minister in Scioto Conference, Edwards was elected editor of the *Religious Telescope*. During his four years as editor, the paper frequently included editorials and articles on holiness. In an editorial "Sanctification— When Obtained?" Edwards wrote:

> Among Protestants we know of but four different views on this question. Some say that sanctification is attained at the moment of justification, others that it is a gradual work, others that it is attained at death, and others, still, that it is obtained at any moment subsequent to justification, when it is sought by unwavering faith. We are not prepared to say that the reception, as to time, is absolutely limited to any of the above methods. We have reasons to believe that there are examples of persons receiving it in all of the ways mentioned. To adopt any of the above views as an absolute standard, and to deny this grace to all who do not receive it precisely in the same manner as to time, would be assuming a position not warranted by scripture nor sustained by experience.[44]

In 1846 Edwards compiled from various authors a little book which had quite an extensive sale, *The Perfect Christian or Condensed View of the Doctrine of Bible Holiness.*[45] In the introduction Edwards stated that no doctrine of the Bible has been the subject of controversy, misrepresentation, and misunderstanding more than the doctrine of Christian perfection.

From 1853 to 1857, while serving as bishop, he edited *Unity with God,* a denominational magazine which had as one of its purposes to advocate "entire regeneration and sanctification of heart and life, exemplified in all the holy and living forms of an experimental and practical Christianity."[46] A *Unity with God* magazine editorial of Edwards, May 1854, aimed at reform in the teaching of this doctrine:

> The time, manner and means of obtaining it, and the inward evidences of its reception have too often constituted the whole burden of our teachings upon this subject. . . . The whole truth must be insisted upon, and the genuine fruits required by the Bible as evidence of a state of holiness must be as clearly and repeatedly taught as the abstract theory and experience have been heretofore.

Edwards also lamented "the general silence of the pulpit" upon the theme of Christian holiness. If it was mentioned, he thought such references were "casual and indefinite allusions to it."

Edwards also wrote:

> This is the end—other gospel doctrines and duties the *means* to lead us forward

to this, man's really *true state*—Hence Christians are commanded to leave the principles or *beginnings* of the doctrine of Christ, and to go on unto perfection. . . . It is necessary to make the subject of holiness a distinct and definite theme, in order to lead the church forward to its attainment.[47]

. . . . Without holiness, the heart remains deeply selfish and unlike God. The unity and strength of the church of Christ in the world depend much upon the progress of holiness. All her weakness and divisions originate in her want of purity. . . . There must be a waking up to the subject of holiness in the churches, among ministers and members, if we would have another general revival. . . . The cause of missions, too, will be promoted in proportion to the revival of the spirit of true holiness. . . . He who promotes holiness advances every true interest of the church of Christ.[48]

Daniel Berger, who was personally acquainted with Edwards, wrote in his United Brethren history, "As a result [of Edwards' emphasis on holiness] the spiritual life of the church was greatly quickened both in the pulpit and the pews, . . ."[49]

Edwards experienced entire sanctification in January 1845, after about ten years of studying and praying about this doctrine. William Hanby, co-author with Henry Spayth of the first history of the denomination, said that the year of Edwards' experience "was replete with revivals of religion in almost every portion of the church." Many obtained what Hanby called "this glorious rest—this freedom from selfish and anxious cares." Hanby himself "consecrated his all to God" in "child-like faith." From then on he "enjoyed a constant peace, a sea of glory unknown before."[50]

In a report to the *Religious Telescope* (August 28, 1861) about the annual session of White River Conference, Edwards spoke of the ministers' entire consecration to God and that a number of them "expressed an unusual hungering and thirsting for righteousness."

A book by Miami Conference minister Chester Briggs, *Present and Entire Sanctification,* was published in 1854 under the authorization of the trustees of the printing establishment. *Holiness or The Higher Christian Life* by Jacob Hoke, a lay evangelist of Chambersburg, Pennsylvania, was published in 1870 by the printing establishment. This small book was a revision of articles which had recently appeared in the *Religious Telescope.*

In the 1870s and 1880s holiness received considerable attention in the columns of the *Religious Telescope.* In an editorial note, April 12, 1876, Milton Wright noted:

We have admitted to our columns quite a free expression of views on the subject of sanctification; and these have differed widely. We presume that it is a subject on which persons can not express themselves so as to be as easily understood by some people as upon other subjects. We hope (and shall insist) that our brethren avoid getting into direct controversy on the subject. A wrangle on almost any other subject would be more appropriate. Let us seek holiness, not wrangle about it. What has appeared in our columns from time to time for the past year satisfies us that it would be better that many should be candid students on the subject, rather than dogmatic teachers. In the investigation of this grand subject we all need much grace.

About a year later (March 14, 1877) Wright wrote an editorial "Spirituality of the Church":

. . . What do we mean by spirituality? We mean the indwelling, cleansing, illuminating, strengthening power of the Holy Spirit. . . . There is too much disposition to try to reach heaven and induce others to do so without either they or we attaining to any high degree of spirituality. This diluting of the saving power of God is corrupting and weakening to the church militant. . . . It is not so much that technical holiness about which some make so much ado, as it is that holiness—that spirituality—which has no graduating standard this side of the gates of eternal glory. . . . A little less display of holiness parchment and a little more address to the work yet to be attained would in some cases be very refreshing.

In 1874 at the Mt. Zion Campmeeting, six miles north of Chambersburg, Pennsylvania, Bishop Edwards gave counsel to a number of ministers and a few laymen who met under the branches of a large tree and determined to form an association for the purpose of promoting the cause of holiness.[51] This organization was named the Pennsylvania Conference Holiness Association. Holiness associations were formed in some other conferences, and annual holiness campmeetings were held. A union meeting attended by representatives from seven or eight annual conferences was held in June 1883 at Petersburg Camp, near Fostoria and Bucyrus, Ohio, under the auspices of the Sandusky Union Holiness Association "for the purpose of organizing a general association for the promotion of scriptural holiness in the United Brethren Church." Officers chosen were from Pennsylvania, Ohio, and Indiana. The *Highway of Holiness,* a monthly magazine that the Pennsylvania Conference Holiness Association had published since 1875, was transferred to the general association. The newly formed association declared this doctrinal basis:

That the work of soul purification commenced in regeneration may be perfected by an act of consecration and faith, or that the carnal mind or inbred sin may be entirely destroyed from the soul by the power of the Holy Spirit by virtue of the cleansing blood of Jesus. We discard the views which are sometimes ascribed to the advocates of entire sanctification, as self-perfection, or Adamic or angelic perfection, or a perfection that precludes either growth or decline, or the liability to err or fall. The views we hold are those found in the books placed in the hands of our preachers by the General Conference, as Watson, Fletcher, Upham, Ralston, Wakefield, and others. For a concise statement of this doctrine, we recommend tract No. 7, published by the association, entitled, "The Carnal Mind, or Entire Sanctification Theoretically Stated."[52]

From 1880 on there were indications that some United Brethren considered the different beliefs regarding sanctification divisive. The secretary of the Sandusky Association reported in the February 1880 *Highway of Holiness* on their 1879 semi-annual meeting. In the report he said:

Much as some of our dear brethren think we are dividing the church by this movement, yet we love her, and pray for her day and night. We are glad to see that the fruit of this work is noticeable in both Quarterly and Annual Conferences. Notwithstanding many of our brethren oppose it.

J. K. Alwood, of North Ohio Conference, wrote and published in 1880 *Twenty-eight Objections Against the Doctrine of Double-Birth Perfection Commonly Called the Second Work Sanctification Together with a Clear Statement of the Bible Doctrine Concerning Christian Perfection.* In the preface Alwood said he had studied this doctrine for twenty-five years with more attention to it than any other. At first he embraced the "second-work theology," but after a careful study of God's Word he abandoned that theology about fifteen years before he published this book.

"Let There Be No Strife" was the title of an article by Bishop Kephart in the January 30, 1884, *Religious Telescope:*

At the present stage of religious growth in our church, as in many others, quite a diversity of opinions obtains relative to the doctrine of Christian holiness. Out of this diversity of opinions some of the most bitter strifes among brethren have sprung, resulting in the rupture of whole societies. . . . The dispute does not appear to be about the doctrine of holiness as such, for all concede that a Christian must be holy, but about the "how" and the "when."

In an editorial of the April 1885 *Highway of Holiness,* B. G. Huber wrote of "the little the church . . . has done for us in this work." He charged that the *"Religious Telescope* as readily publishes articles *against* the special holiness work, as *for* it, on the flimsy excuse that it is a paper for the *whole* church."

Robert Mason, in a biographical account of his father, Harold C.

Mason, a United Brethren bishop in the 1920s and Huntington College president in the 1930s, pointed out: "Although standard reference works in the history of American Protestantism do not make the point, Father has told me that the issue of the 'second work' was centrally involved in the church division of 1889." Emmet Carlton Mason, Harold Mason's father, was active in North Ohio Conference in 1889.[53]

Floyd W. Atkinson, whose father lived through the church division, wrote in the *Christian Conservator* (June 29, 1949):

> According to my father and grandfather, the question of eradication as taught by the Wesleyan doctrine of sanctification had a high point of controversy before the division and was the main factor that brought about the division . . . . According to my father, the Wesleyan faction went with the liberal group."

Mason's account also indicated that the Wesleyan faction were Liberals. Atkinson noted that the new Confession of Faith adopted by the Liberals included a separate article on sanctification:

> We believe that sanctification is the work of God's grace, through the word and the Spirit, by which those who have been born again are separated in their acts, words, and thoughts from sin, and are enabled to live unto God, and to follow holiness, without which no man shall see God.

Lewis Davis, professor of theology from the beginning of Union Biblical Seminary, 1871, until his retirement in 1885, did not approve of this article and refuted it in his pamphlet "The New Creed."

FOOTNOTES

[1]Elizabeth Kenoyer Davis, comp., *Preachers—Farmers—Pioneers: The Kenoyer Family in America, Descendants of John and Elizabeth Kenoyer from Germany* (n.p., 1971), pp. 5, 6, 8.

[2]Lydia Sexton, *Autobiography of Lydia Sexton, from 1799 to 1872* (Dayton, OH: United Brethren Publishing House, 1882), p. 219.

[3]Ibid., pp. 220-222.

[4]*Christian Conservator*, September 26, 1906.
The first money for the Oregon mission was raised from the Rocky Springs Circuit, Pa., by J. M. Bishop as follows: "John Jones promises to raise a steer worth $20 to $25 available in three years; John Crider, Henry S. Crider, Benjamin S. Huber, Sr., John Huber, Jacob Carmany, J. M. Bishop, each one hog worth an average of $5, available next fall; John Bashore, $2." A. W. Drury, *History of the Church of the United Brethren in Christ* (Dayton, OH: Otterbein Press, 1924), p. 436.

[5]*The Diary of Basil N. Longworth, Oregon Pioneer: From Ohio to Oregon by Ox Team, 1853-1854* (Portland, OR: Historical Records Survey, n.d.).

[6]*Christian Conservator*, September 26, 1906.

[7]*Third Annual Report of the Board of Missions of the United Brethren in Christ* (Dayton, OH: United Brethren Printing Establishment, 1856), p. 40.

[8]*Eighth Annual Report of the Board of Missions of the United Brethren in Christ and the Proceedings of the Annual Meeting.* (Dayton, OH: United Brethren Printing Establishment, 1861), p. 6.

[9]W. M. Weekley and H. H. Fout, *Our Heroes or United Brethren Home Missionaries* (Dayton, OH: Home Missionary Society, 1908), pp. 273-281.

[10]Ibid., p. 122.

[11]*Third Annual Report of the Board of Missions,* p. 32.

[12]John Lawrence, *The History of the Church of the United Brethren in Christ,* 2 vols. (Dayton, OH: United Brethren Printing Establishment, 1868), 2:275, 276.

[13]Lewis Davis, *The Life of Rev. David Edwards,* 3rd ed. (Dayton, OH: United Brethren Publishing House, 1883), p. 101.

[14]Henry A. Thompson, *Our Bishops,* rev. ed. (Dayton, OH: United Brethren Publishing House, 1903), pp. 589, 476, 531, 280, 429, 452, 341, 363, 390-393.

[15]A. M. Schlesinger, *Political and Social Growth of the United States, 1852-1933,* rev. ed. (New York: Macmillan, 1933), p. 239.

[16]A. P. Funkhouser; Oren F. Morten, comp., *History of the Church of the United Brethren in Christ, Virginia Conference* (Virginia Conference, [1919]), pp. 80, 81.

[17]Thompson, pp. 296, 297.

[18]J. L. Luttrell, *History of the Auglaize Annual Conference of the United Brethren Church, from 1853 to 1891* (Dayton, OH: United Brethren Publishing House for the author, 1892), p. 417.

[19]Ibid., p. 182.

[20]*Religious Telescope,* February 10, 1847.

[21]Bernard L. Cook, John E. Branson, *Seedtime and Harvest: A History of the Kansas Conference of the Church of the United Brethren in Christ, Part I 1853-1882 and Part II 1883-1914* (Theses presented in partial fulfillment of the requirements for the degree of Bachelor of Divinity, Bonebrake Theological Seminary, 1942, 1943), p. 65.

[22]Weekley and Fout, p. 248.

[23]*Religious Telescope,* April 22, 1857.

[24]Davis, pp. 165, 166.

[25]Jonathan Weaver, *Ministerial Salary: An Address Delivered Before the Ministerial Association of the Virginia Annual Conference at Rohrersville, Md., Feb. 12, 1873* (Dayton, OH: United Brethren Publishing House, 1873), p. 14.

[26]Luttrell, pp. 252-260.

[27]Thompson, p. 310.

[28]John Fetterhoff, *The Life of John Fetterhoff* (Chambersburg, PA: United Brethren in Christ Print, 1883), p. 166.

[29]Henry A. Thompson, *Biography of Jonathan Weaver* (Dayton, OH: United Brethren Publishing House, 1901), pp. 163-166.

[30]*Third Annual Report of the Board of Missions,* p. 42.

[31]J. R. Chambers, *History of Osage-Neosho Annual Conference, Church of the United Brethren in Christ, 1870 to 1901* (photocopy of manuscript in Kansas State Historical Society Archives), pp. 5, 6.

[32]S. Paul Weaver, *History of the Erie Conference of the Church of the United Brethren in Christ* (n.p., 1936), p. 83.

[33]Luttrell, pp. 181, 182.

[34]Davis, p. 157.

[35]*Religious Telescope,* May 18 and 25, June 1, 1853.

[36]Davis, p. 146.

[37]A. W. Drury, *The Life of Bishop J. J. Glossbrenner* (Dayton, OH: United Brethren Publishing House for John Dodds, 1889), pp. 146, 147.

[38]Lawrence, 2:415-417.

[39]*Religious Telescope,* May 27, 1857.

[40]*In the Supreme Court of Illinois, Northern Grand Division, March Term, 1893, Jacob Kuns, et al. vs. J. W. Robertson, et al., Abstract of Record* (Pontiac, IL: Lowry and Clark, printers, 1893), pp. 191, 192.

[41]Davis, pp. 292-294.

[42]Ibid., p. 79.

[43]Ibid., p. 94.

[44]Ibid., p. 96.

[45]Lawrence, 2:344.

[46]Davis, pp. 149, 150.

[47]*Unity with God,* January, 1854.

[48]Ibid.

[49]Daniel Berger, *History of the Church of the United Brethren in Christ* (Dayton, OH: United Brethren Publishing House, 1897), p. 301.

[50]Henry G. Spayth and William Hanby, *History of the Church of the United Brethren in Christ,* 2 parts (Circleville, OH: Conference Office of the United Brethren in Christ, 1851), pp. 295-298.

[51]Davis, p. 296.

[52]*Religious Telescope,* July 11 and 18, 1883.

[53]*Asbury Seminarian,* Spring-Summer, 1961.

19

WOMEN IN THE CHURCH

Keeping the Home Fires Burning

Stephen Lee in 1848 joined the Sandusky Conference and was appointed to Bean Creek Circuit in northwest Ohio. A daughter, who was then a young girl, described the travel conditions when in a one-horse buggy the family went to this assignment:

> We had, oh, such a time! The mud was deep, and the last few miles the ground seemed to be covered with water. It was wade and splash all the time. A few days after reaching our destination we all took the ague, and a good deal of the time we could hardly carry water enough to drink, as we had to carry it a quarter of a mile.

The pay was meager, and the circuit was large, requiring Lee to be away from home most of the time. There were periods when the family was in destitute circumstances. The next year Lee was appointed to open a mission in Michigan. During his second year in Michigan, he made a tour of seven weeks to open up work in Jackson County. Because he had no communication with his family, he did not know of the death of his little daughter until he arrived home.[1]

In his *Twenty Years on Horseback, or Itinerating in West Virginia,* W. M. Weekley wrote:

> Too much cannot be said for the faithful wife of the itinerant. But alas! her worth, I fear, is not appreciated by the church as it deserves to be. People watch and criticise her, to be sure, as they do but few other women, but as a rule she is not accorded a very large place in the achievements of her husband. Indeed, I sometimes fear the minister himself does not realize her true relation to his

success in soul-winning. God only knows her anxiety and heart-yearnings as she struggles with the problems of the home in the absence of her husband. . . .

The fact is, many a successful preacher today would be out of the work but for his devoted wife. . . . Said one of these noble helpers: "Husband, I know we are poor. Our carpets are old and faded, and our furniture is scant and plain. I know our dear children are barefooted, and can't go to school; but I want you to keep on preaching."[2]

One of the earliest books by a United Brethren included advice for the wives of traveling preachers. Author Jacob Ritter, a presiding elder in Allegheny Conference, advised wives to economize, discipline the children ("make your word law amongst them"), talk to them about their father's work, and give them Christian training.

When your husband returns home, let him find things in order, and meet him with all the affections of a lovely wife, and should it so happen that your husband had to labor amongst the poorer class, and become almost or alto-gether pennyless [sic], remember the gospel must be preached to the poor; and do not fret yourself about what you shall eat or drink, or wherewithal ye shall be clothed.[3]

The Milton Wright family through modest inheritances and wise investments fared better financially than many families of United Brethren itinerants. Nevertheless, the Wrights practiced frugality, and this ability to make wise use of what was at hand contributed to the invention of the airplane by sons Wilbur and Orville. Susan (Koerner) Wright, daughter of a wagon and carriage maker, was described by her children as one who "could mend anything." She even built a sled for the two oldest boys, Reuchlin and Lorin. Sadness invaded the Wright home when she became ill with tuberculosis in the 1880s. Wilbur became his mother's close companion and nurse while he was recovering from a serious hockey injury.[4] During this time of illness, Bishop Wright traveled to the Pacific Coast for nearly six months of each year. He indicated in his diary how difficult it was to leave his family for months at a time.

When Jeremiah Kenoyer went from his home in Oregon to begin mission work in Washington Territory, it was hard for him to leave his family alone. Indians in their area would sometimes get drunk and become mean. One time when Jeremiah was gone, a group of drunken Indians tried to enter the Kenoyer home. Several dogs guarded the house, and members of the family armed with guns stood at the doors all night and part of the next day. After the Indians slept and became partly sober, they left without harming the family.[5]

Mrs. Israel Sloan did not know for weeks that her itinerant husband was critically injured when thrown from his pony while descending a steep mountain, nearly 200 miles from home. She did not receive word until he was near death, and reached his side only shortly before he died.[6]

One laywoman spoke out in the *Religious Telescope,* April 26, 1876, in behalf of wives of itinerants. She said that owning a home of their own was almost impossible because often an itinerant's pay scarcely met current expenses; and if a house was provided it was often uncomfortable. She wrote sympathetically of moving every year or two to a new community, enduring all the necessary labor and fatigue involved in moving 25 to 150 miles.

Often the itinerant had to find a house to rent, for parsonages were few. Renting was difficult—either suitable houses were not available in a good location, or the family could not afford the rent asked. The *1884 United Brethren Year-Book* reported 1246 itinerants and only 398 parsonages.

Reminiscing on his itinerant days of the 1800s, J. E. Hott wrote about the itinerant's wife:

A minister . . . knows only too well how much depends on the minister having a good wife. If she is a fashion plate she spoils all the girls; if she is extravagant in habits of living, a poor charge will not support her; if she is an untidy housekeeper, she cannot be sent to refined and cultured people; if she is a gossip from house to house, she will keep the charge in an uproar of turmoil and confusion and so on indefinitely. On the other hand if she is a quiet, devout, sympathetic Christian, and well-skilled in household and domestic affairs, her husband can leave her for a few days in a home of an outsider while he goes to a remote appointment and on returning will find that, that family is forever bound to the cause of Christ and the church with hooks of steel. May God bless our preachers' wives with this spirit and influence.[7]

Ahead of the Times

Women in the 1800s in the United States did not have the right to vote in political elections or hold any political office except in isolated instances in local communities. In some states a married woman could not hold claim to earnings or property, not even an inheritance or gift from her father. On July 19, 1848, a woman's rights convention at Seneca Falls, New York declared that a woman was "denied the . . . facilities for obtaining a thorough education, all colleges being closed against her."[8]

The first colleges in the United States did limit enrollment to men.

But when colleges in the Midwest opened, many of them admitted women students, beginning with Oberlin College in 1833. From the opening in 1847 of Otterbein University, the first United Brethren college, all the denomination's schools allowed equal privileges to women. This included Union Biblical Seminary, which opened in 1871. According to Henry Garst, who wrote a history of Otterbein University in 1907, this school had "the honor of being the first to throw open its doors to young women without limitations or restrictions of any kind." Otterbein also had at least one woman on its faculty from its beginning.[9] The General Conference of 1853 authorized a new magazine, *Unity with God,* and directed that among its purposes it should advocate the cause of education for both sexes.

That the United Brethren fathers of higher education went against the general precedents and spirit of the time is in harmony with the attitude of the church in according women a high place. Women offered prayers and testified in United Brethren meetings, as well as providing hospitality for meetings in private homes, and lodging and meals for traveling preachers. Some women served as local church officers. All women who were members of the church could vote for local officers and general conference delegates, and for the granting of quarterly conference licenses to preach and exhort.[10] United Brethren women gained distinction in being among the first to organize for foreign mission work. The General Conference of 1881 discussed the purposes of the National Woman Suffrage Association and the Women's Christian Temperance Union and expressed approval of both movements. In 1869 Muskingum Annual Conference passed a female suffrage endorsement.

A few United Brethren women, as early as 1841, believing God was calling them to the gospel ministry, requested counsel from the church on the matter. The *Discipline* contained nothing about licensing women. A committee of the General Conference of 1845 concluded: "We do not think the Gospel authorizes the introduction of females into the ministry." Some annual conferences commended certain women to the church as helpers in the work of Christ. Perhaps the most noteworthy of these was Lydia Sexton. In her autobiography she told of being encouraged to preach by her presiding elder, other ministers, and members. In 1851 her quarterly conference granted her license to preach. It seemed to her and others that God blessed her preaching, and so when her quarterly conference in 1859 wanted to recommend her to Upper Wabash Annual Conference, she consented. The annual conference voted to "recommend her to the churches as a useful helper in the work of Christ."[11]

Until 1869, when she moved to Kansas, Lydia Sexton preached in the Midwest, especially Indiana. John Fetterhoff, a United Brethren preacher who began his ministry in 1818, wrote in his journal for October 5 and 6, 1867:

Heard Lydia Sexton preach in the school. Sunday the 6th she preached again at 11 o'clock. She is a warm-hearted speaker, and a great revivalist. She has traveled extensively and has held many protracted meetings, and at nearly all of them had great success. Great has been the fruit of her labor. She has taken hundreds of souls into the church.[12]

She began the work of chaplain in the Kansas State Penitentiary in 1870, at the age of seventy-two. She served there for a few years with notable success. When her autobiography was published in 1882, she was in southern Kansas ministering to refugees from Louisiana and Texas.[13]

By 1889 the sentiment in the church for regularly licensed women preachers was such that the general conference revised the *Discipline* to say, "There shall be no discrimination between men and women in the matter of granting credentials."

FOOTNOTES

[1]W. M. Weekley and H. H. Fout, *Our Heroes or United Brethren Home Missionaries* (Dayton, OH: Home Missionary Society, 1908), pp. 121-125.

[2]W. M. Weekley, *Twenty Years on Horseback or Itinerating in West Virginia* (Dayton, VA: n.p., 1924), pp. 90-92.

[3]Jacob Ritter, *Sixty-Odd Skeletons in the Form of a Sketch Book* (Harrisburg, PA: Clyde & Williams, 1845), p. 209.

[4]Fred C. Kelly, *The Wright Brothers* (New York: Random House, 1943), p. 14.

[5]Gladys Calvert, comp. *History of the Idaho Conference Church of the United Brethren in Christ* (n.p. [ca. 1966]), p. 116.

[6]Weekley and Fout, pp. 278-280.

[7]*Christian Conservator*, September 17, 1913.

[8]Arthur M. Schlesinger, *New Viewpoints in American History* (New York: Macmillan, 1934), pp. 138, 139.

[9]Henry Garst, *Otterbein University, 1847-1907* (Dayton, OH: United Brethren Publishing House, 1907), pp. 79-84, 67, 307.

[10]Ibid., pp. 79, 80.

[11]Lydia Sexton, *Autobiography of Lydia Sexton, from 1799 to 1872* (Dayton, OH: United Brethren Publishing House, 1882), pp. 211-215, 234, 239, 240, 400-403.

[12]John Fetterhoff, *The Life of John Fetterhoff* (Chambersburg, PA: United Brethren in Christ Print, 1883), p. 170.

[13]Lydia Sexton, pp. 613-655, iv.

20

UNITED BRETHREN MEETINGS

Meeting Places

For more than half a century United Brethren meetings took place in homes, schools, barns, and outdoors more than in church houses. In these early years the great concern was evangelism, not church membership. But with a growing emphasis on membership, circuits became smaller, ministers spent more time where they had regular appointments with organized classes, and the need for church buildings became more significant.

Virginia, one of the first states where United Brethren preaching began, had but three United Brethren church houses in 1850.[1] Miami Conference of southwest Ohio was organized in 1810, but no church was built until 1851.[2] Following the Civil War a noticeable increase in church construction began. United Brethren churches generally fit the guidelines in the *Discipline:*

> Let all our meeting houses be built plainly and neatly, with free seats, and not more expensive than necessary. . . . [Trustees] shall at no time proceed with the building of a house of worship beyond the means, either in hand or sufficiently secured, so as to avoid involving our houses of worship in any way in debt . . .

The General Conference of 1869 authorized a Church-Erection Society and placed it under the management of the board of missions and the bishops. Donations for an interest-free loan fund were solicited throughout the denomination. The results for the following quadrenniums were:

200

Years	Offerings	Returned on loans	Churches assisted
1873-77	$ 7,499	$ 383	26
1877-81	6,215	1,123	16
1881-85	5,253	3,416	43
1885-89	12,325	9,548	69

By 1889 the society had a working capital of nearly $22,000.[3] The *United Brethren Year-Book* for 1888 reported the following statistics on church houses: 776 in 1857, 1247 in 1867, 2003 in 1877, and 2641 in 1887. The number of organized churches listed for 1887 was 4396.

The Preaching

Whenever a preacher was present at a meeting, the sermon highlighted the event. The one great theme of United Brethren preachers was repentance, being saved from sin through the death and resurrection of Christ, and possessing the witness of the Spirit to the new birth. A second dominant theme was living as a child of God in contrast to the way of the world.

David Edwards, bishop from 1849 until his death in 1876, perhaps represented United Brethren preaching at its best. His biographer, Lewis Davis, said that as a preacher Edwards was regarded "as having few equals and no superior" in the church. When not conducting annual conferences, he traveled and preached almost incessantly. Davis wrote that the power of Edwards as a preacher came from "a marked solitariness with God, a vital communion with Christ, a thorough dependence upon the Holy Spirit, a mind and heart completely yielded to the authority of the Scriptures." Davis described Edwards as systematic, clear and logical, and with a talent for description and dramatics. At an outdoor meeting, speaking of Elisha smiting the Jordan River, Edwards seized an umbrella hanging from a tree and imitated the act, as he exclaimed, "Where now is the Lord God of Elijah?" Several persons rose to their feet and looked to see the waters part.[4]

Edwards reminded fellow preachers, "It is fully as much our duty to commend the good as to reprove the evil." He thought that, on the whole, United Brethren preachers paid too little attention to pulpit preparation. "Let no one say," he remarked, "that by devoting so much time to mental preparation the Holy Spirit's influence will be discarded. This need not, must not be. A proper preparation for the pulpit will always include the preparation of the heart."[5]

Another whose preaching was considered outstanding by ministers within and without the church was Jeremiah Kenoyer. Milton Wright described his preaching:

> The rise and fall, and all the modulations of Mr. Kenoyer's sonorous voice, could hardly have been excelled. This, and the magnetism of the man of God behind it, was the secret of much of his great success. In language, he was peculiarly direct and powerful, and barring a few careless incorrections in the use of verbs and pronouns, his language was ready for the printer. But his thought and pathos were the crowning excellence of his sermons and exhortations. For his exhortations, of irresistible power, were as systematic as a good sermon.

Wright also told of a sermon he heard Kenoyer preach in 1858 at the church's school in Sublimity, Oregon, "in which he ground into the very dust the proslavery prejudices which spurned a quarter-blood negro from the school by simple protest; and yet it was so masterful as well as kindly done, that no one could be seriously offended."[6]

Of United Brethren preaching in general, Bishop Jonathan Weaver said: "The preachers were lame in philosophy, and knew nothing of the higher criticism; but on the cardinal doctrines of the gospel they were giants. They would preach on the judgment and future rewards or punishments until one would think the day had come."[7]

The Music

Music in United Brethren meetings was like many other aspects of the denomination—plain and simple. Often only the minister and a few others in a meeting had a hymnbook. Classes or societies did not provide hymnals; members purchased their own copies. The denominational printing establishment published hymn and song books. Until the 1870s these contained only words. Tunes were memorized by listening to others sing. If available, a tuning fork was used to set the pitch. When many in a congregation did not have hymnals, the minister or leader would "line" the hymn—that is, read two lines, sing them, read two more lines, sing them, and so on to the end of the hymn.

Musical instruments were not accepted until 1869, and even then the *Discipline* advised against them. For a number of years after 1869 they were not widely used because they were controversial. Some opposed them, not as sinful in themselves, but because of a distaste for them. Choirs were viewed as instruments were—both were associated with cold, formal, mechanical worship. In 1885 the *Discipline* was revised to eliminate advising against choirs and instrumental music.

Class, Quarterly, and Protracted Meetings

When preachers were at other appointments on a circuit, classes met and a layman, quarterly conference preacher, or a licensed exhorter was in charge of a class or experience meeting. These meetings consisted of singing, extemporaneous prayers and testimonies, reading of Scripture, and sometimes exhortations. There were no liturgies in these meetings or in preaching services. The only forms or ceremonies followed were for weddings, burials, church dedications, and ordination of elders. Formulas for these were published in the *Discipline*.

Quarterly meetings were held four times a year for business, preaching, and holy communion. The sermon of the presiding elder at quarterly meeting was often much anticipated. Attendances were often very large, especially in fair weather.

The practice of uniting Christians of diverse church memberships at the communion table was a characteristic of United Brethren. This practice probably stemmed from the early years when different denominations were represented in the fellowship.

Evangelistic or revival meetings, often referred to as protracted meetings, were the heart of United Brethren meetings. Through these the main mission of the church was accomplished. Presiding elders and bishops frequently went from one such meeting to another, preaching daily or almost daily for weeks at a time. In communities where cold, formal religion had prevailed, the contrasting United Brethren meetings frequently aroused curiosity and sometimes opposition.

Campmeeting—Rowdies and All

Most United Brethren campmeetings in the mid-1800s were circuit ones, appointed by presiding elders, and held on some member's farm. Homemade tents housed many who went for the week. Each family took food for themselves, guests, and horses. Campfires provided heat for cooking. Preaching, praying, and singing went on much of the day and evening. Many were converted at these humble meetings. Some of these persons would have attended no other church meetings, so campmeetings were viewed as an important means of evangelism.[8]

Some rowdies attended—not to be converted, but to break up the meetings. One presiding elder confronted a crowd of them from the pulpit. After telling them they were a "pack of sneaking cowards, and did not have a single trait of a gentleman," he dared them to do another thing to disturb the congregation. Cowering before the brave preacher, the roughs crept away into the darkness.[9] The preacher who could best handle such ruffians "was quite as popular as the pulpit orator," wrote J. E. Hott.[10]

One minister known for his ability to master unruly elements was Christopher Flinchbaugh. He was described as a man of "gigantic proportions and Herculean strength." On one occasion after suffering some disturbances from two ruffians, he stopped preaching and kindly requested them to be seated or withdraw from the congregation. With an oath they told him to mind his own business. This was too much. Flinchbaugh hurried to them, seized the man who uttered the oath— the other having fled—ushered him to the edge of the camp, and dealt him a blow or two. The intruder promptly promised to leave and not interfere again. Returning to the pulpit, Flinchbaugh exclaimed in his German brogue, "That is the way I cast out devils," and then he proceeded with his sermon.[11]

Negative features of campmeetings, as viewed by "A Friend to Camp," were described in the July 23, 1856, *Religious Telescope:* the expense and time; persons who took advantage of the hospitality of less able campers; participation more from a sense of duty; extremes in fashionable dress and too much cooking and feasting; a religion that is good only during campmeeting; hucksters competing for campers' attention; and preachers selling patent medicines.

But the general opinion of United Brethren campmeetings was that they were times of spiritual seed-sowing and harvesting, and that over the years many thousands were converted at them. Many who attended were non-United Brethren who came by invitation or out of curiosity. When church houses were few or too small to hold large congregations, campmeetings were a favorite means of reaching masses of people in the summer. They were also a "powerful means of uniting and strengthening the church," wrote *Religious Telescope* Editor Lawrence in the July 22, 1857, issue. Often the Lord's Supper and baptismal services were held in connection with campmeetings, and sometimes converts united with the church. Summer quarterly business meetings were also often conducted at the campgrounds.

Campmeetings grew out of the great meetings in barns but were more denominational and more self-supporting rather than depending on the generosity of farm hosts. In the later 1800s some annual conferences formed camp associations, and the campsites were made more permanent with the purchase of land and the erection of buildings.

In Indiana a campmeeting was held annually from 1835 to 1860 at Rawling's campground in Parke County. For United Brethren and others it was a center of attraction for scores of miles in all directions.[12] Pennsylvania was noted for several campmeeting sites where successful meetings took place for many years. One which was usually very largely attended was Mt. Zion, also known as Orrstown, six miles north of Chambersburg. John Fetterhoff told of the Greencastle Circuit campmeeting in 1873 being attended by hundreds on Sunday. "They could not all get inside the circle of the tents. It was supposed that ten or fifteen hundred were outside."[13] In western Pennsylvania the Bigler campmeeting of 1888 was reported in the September 12 *Religious Telescope* as having a crowd of 10,000 people.

Such large crowds tested vocal powers. Through years of preaching and singing at outdoor meetings, many preachers developed an ability to make themselves heard quite a distance. Michael Long, Sandusky Conference, was one with a powerful voice which distinguished him as the "great campmeeting preacher." A gentleman who lived not far from a campground in Sandusky County, Ohio, told this story:

> A stranger called at my home one day about eleven o'clock to inquire the way to the campmeeting, which was then in progress. I told him to listen, and, on being silent for a moment, the voice of Michael Long, in the full exercise of its powers, came wafted upon the breezes. I told the stranger to follow the sound through the wood, and he would find the campmeeting about three miles distant in that direction.[14]

On the last evening of a very good campmeeting on Bath Circuit, Virginia Conference, Benjamin Stickley preached on the second coming of Christ, with a voice that could be heard a great distance. While listening, Jacob Bachtel, the presiding elder, remarked, "That sermon can almost be heard in hell."[15]

Sabbath Schools

Instruction of children, begun in the early years of the church, became widespread in the latter half of the nineteenth century. The General Conference of 1849 directed preachers to organize Sabbath schools and the printing establishment to furnish suitable books for them. In the 1850s the *Discipline* went further in authorizing sermons on the importance of Sabbath schools, the proper organization of these schools in each society, soliciting funds for a Sabbath school library, and offerings for missions. Reports to annual conferences were to include Sabbath school statistics.

Children's Friend was first issued May 6, 1854. Subscriptions for this biweekly paper soon reached 10,000.[16] Small books for children about persons, places, and incidents in the Bible were also available in the 1850s. Often a school would have a circulating library of these books.[17] David Edwards, John Lawrence, and W. J. Shuey were selected by the General Conference of 1861 to compile a book of Scriptural questions and answers for the use of families and Sabbath schools. *Youth's Scripture Compend,* a thirty-four page pamphlet of 141 questions and answers arranged in fifteen lessons was first published in September 1861. By 1865 nearly 7000 copies had been printed. A revision of the pamphlet was printed in 1871.[18]

The bishops' address to the General Conference of 1861 included this paragraph:

> The interests of Sabbath schools should not be overlooked. Most of the annual conferences, if not all, report an increasing interest in this blessed cause. But very much yet remains to be done. The number of schools should be greatly increased, and many of those already in existence need to be improved, so as to have a more direct bearing on the religious instruction and the early conversion of the children.

Some of the improvements needed were to make them year-round schools, to provide for teacher training, to involve parents, and to provide suitable literature.

By the 1870s Sabbath schools were coming into their own and receiving wide support. A denominational Sabbath School Association and a board of directors administered the work. Some annual conferences began holding Sabbath school conventions, and some ministers instituted teachers' meetings on their fields.

When the National Sunday School Convention introduced the Uniform Lesson Series in 1872, the United Brethren Publishing trustees adopted this series. Soon a full-time editor of Sunday school literature became a necessity.

The decade of the 1880s witnessed the organization of the Home Reading Circle, a three-year reading course, in 1880, and the Bible Normal Union in 1886 for the training of teachers and leaders in United Brethren Sunday schools. Some of the former emphasis on campmeetings with much preaching was shifted to Sabbath school assemblies or summer schools for Bible study and training for Christian work.

FOOTNOTES

[1]A. P. Funkhouser and Oren F. Morten, comp., *History of the Church of the United Brethren in Christ, Virginia Conference* (Virginia Conference, [1919]), p. 51.

[2]*Religious Telescope,* February 2, 1876.

[3]W. M. Weekley, *Twenty Years on Horseback or Itinerating in West Virginia* (Dayton, VA: n.p., 1924), pp. 132, 133.

[4]Lewis Davis, *The Life of Rev. David Edwards,* 3rd ed. (Dayton, OH: United Brethren Publishing House, 1883), pp. 194, 140, 241, 244-246.

[5]Ibid., pp. 92, 167.

[6]*Christian Conservator,* September 26, 1906.

[7]Henry A. Thompson, *Biography of Jonathan Weaver* (Dayton, OH: United Brethren Publishing House, 1901), p. 370.

[8]Lewis F. John, *The Life of Ezekiel Boring Kephart* (Dayton, OH: United Brethren Publishing House, 1907), pp. 97, 98.

[9]Zebedee Warner, *The Life and Labors of Rev. Jacob Bachtel of the Parkersburg Annual Conference, United Brethren in Christ* (Dayton, OH: United Brethren Publishing House, 1868), p. 93.

[10]*Christian Conservator,* July 16, 1913.

[11]W. M. Weekley and H. H. Fout, *Our Heroes or United Brethren Home Missionaries,* 2 vols. (Dayton, OH: Otterbein Press, 1911), 2:135-137.

[12]Augustus C. Wilmore, *History of the White River Conference of the Church of the United Brethren in Christ* (Dayton, OH: United Brethren Publishing House for the author, 1925), p. 61.

[13]John Fetterhoff, *The Life of John Fetterhoff* (Chambersburg, PA: United Brethren in Christ Print, 1883), pp. 238, 226.

[14]Weekley and Fout, 2:179.

[15]Warner, pp. 92, 93.

[16]Davis, p. 161.

[17]Adam B. Condo, *History of the Indiana Conference of the Church of the United Brethren in Christ* (Indiana Conference, [ca. 1926]), p. 113.

[18]John H. Ness, Jr., *One Hundred Fifty Years, a History of Publishing in the Evangelical United Brethren Church* (Dayton, OH: Board of Publication of the Evangelical United Brethren Church, 1966), p. 359.

21

INSTITUTIONS OF THE CHURCH

Over the Hump and Established:
United Brethren Publishing

Sitting with knitted brow, evidently in more than usual concern for "the debt," William Hanby turned to his five-year-old daughter. She had slipped to his side and laid down what was to her young heart treasure enough to remove the dark shadow that hung over their household. Looking at the five copper cents, Hanby asked, "What is it for?" "To pay the debt," his daughter replied. The debt of the not quite ten-year-old United Brethren Printing Establishment at Circleville, Ohio, was looked upon by the Hanby family as a personal calamity.[1]

Hanby held responsibilities at the establishment in the humble, difficult beginning years. Forty years later the growing business would be out of debt and paying dividends to the annual conferences. But for Hanby, his family, and others, it was a day-to-day struggle to keep the business alive.

The General Conference of 1837 appointed twenty-nine-year-old Hanby to serve as treasurer and book agent of the infant publishing concern of the church. At the same conference, Hanby helped draft a constitution for the establishment, which had been in operation about two years. When the first editor, William R. Rhinehart, resigned in 1839, that responsibility was added to those Hanby already had. This economy measure on the part of the trustees required almost super-human effort of Hanby.

To begin the publishing venture the church went into debt. This debt grew as the years passed, for the circulation of the church paper, the *Religious Telescope,* grew slowly. Editor Rhinehart's ardent views on temperance and slavery were too strong and controversial for many United Brethren of the 1830s.

Hanby, now treasurer, editor, and book agent, faced several difficult tasks: liquidating or at least reducing the debt; editing a paper that would have wide appeal over the church; managing the printing and mailing; handling the accounts; and supervising *Telescope* promotion, subscription sales, and the small book trade through agents (all itinerant ministers, some laymen, and for a few years one or two traveling agents). Hanby worked to put the business on a cash basis and to discontinue credit because many credit accounts were not paid. Hanby "probably saved the *Telescope* office from a disgraceful wreck," wrote John Lawrence, who succeeded Hanby as editor in 1852. Lawrence also credited Hanby with doing much to establish order in the business affairs of annual conferences during a quadrennium (1845-1849) as bishop between his first and second stints at the printing establishment.[2]

As editor, Hanby declared his antislavery and total abstinence views. He backed up his words with action. Keeping a pledge of total abstinence, he cast one of the first votes for prohibition. He took part in the underground railroad when the laws of Ohio imposed a heavy fine and imprisonment for assisting fugitive slaves. In Hanby's editorial column of January 15, 1845, there appeared a brief news item about a Maryland minister being sentenced to six years in the penitentiary for aiding slaves in their escape. Hanby's vote was one of the first seven cast in Pickaway County for the Free-Soil candidates.[3] His son Benjamin wrote the words and music of the song "Darling Nellie Gray," which had the kind of influence for antislavery sentiment that Harriet Beecher Stowe's novel *Uncle Tom's Cabin* had. His daughter Amanda (Mrs. J. K. Billheimer) was the first woman missionary to Africa for the church.

Other contributions of Hanby include compiling a songbook and hymnals and writing the first church history of the period 1825-1849. Playing a role in the beginning of Otterbein University, the first college of the church, he remained one of its loyal supporters the rest of his life (at one time all his property was liable for its debts). Hanby also initiated action which led to the beginning of the Ohio German Conference.[4]

Along with Hanby the printing establishment trustees were credited for its survival and growth. Two Dresbach brothers, successful farmers who lived near Circleville, served as trustees for twenty years—from the beginning of the establishment until 1853. Since Circleville was within the bounds of Scioto Conference, this conference supervised the business of the establishment between general conferences. Scioto

Conference appointed the trustees until 1853.

The growth of the establishment resulted in a move in 1845 from a four-room frame dwelling to the basement of the Circleville United Brethren Church, which had been built with this expectation. A power press was purchased in 1850. For the first several years handpower instead of steam was used to turn the wheel of the press. But even so, printing was much easier and faster than before. Two days labor of two men was cut to a few hours. This efficiency allowed for the job printing of two local newspapers. Bindery machinery was also purchased. At first the only books published were *Disciplines* and song or hymn books. Before the bindery equipment was purchased, books had to be taken to Cincinnati or Pennsylvania for binding. This new equipment temporarily increased liabilities more than the trustees or agent desired, but it was hoped and planned that in the long run the greater volume of printing would more than take care of the cost. This pattern was to continue. New facilities or equipment to expand or facilitate the publishing periodically resulted in temporary financial setbacks and concern by trustees or general conference lest the debt get out of hand. Questions arose from some at general conferences as to why no money was available to pay a dividend to "worn-out" preachers or their widows, one of the stipulated purposes of the establishment. Editors Lawrence and Hanby expressed the opinion of many when they declared that the first purpose was to furnish papers and books for the church so cheaply that its people would not be tempted to buy elsewhere. A dividend could not be paid when major expansion or improvements were needed that took all available capital.

The General Conference of 1849 considered a move to Cincinnati, but this idea was defeated by a large margin. However, in the General Conference of 1853 the issue came up with more urgency, for the business had outgrown the basement of the Circleville Church. This time a majority voted to relocate in Dayton, Ohio, thinking a larger city would have more conditions favorable to growth. One factor that may have influenced the voting was the guarantee from a Dayton committee of four that the move would not cost more than forty dollars. However this committee, except for one member, did not pay any of the difference between forty dollars and the total cost of $347.08.[5]

The move to Dayton was made in late summer 1853. The equipment was loaded on wagons at Circleville and taken to the canal. Canal boats transported it to Columbus. From there, by train the equipment was taken to Xenia, and two Conestoga wagons pulled by oxen took it the last lap of the journey. Overseeing the move was the new agent

Solomon Vonnieda, who remained with the establishment for nearly thirty years. First he served as agent, then as editor and bookkeeper. A lot with two buildings, on the northeast corner of Main and Fourth Streets had been purchased for $11,000. By the fall of 1854 a new four-story office building, 40 by 90 feet, was completed at a cost of $15,000. From 1853 to 1857, thirty-three persons were employed in all the work of the establishment.

With experience and better equipment the editorial and printing quality of the publications improved. With enlarged facilities and more equipment, the scope of materials published gradually enlarged. More church periodicals were added (and a few discontinued). With the growth of the church membership, the circulation of most of the periodicals grew, even though many of them had their ups and downs. In several quadrenniums the *Religious Telescope* was the greatest source of profit.[6]

The General Conference of 1861 approved a General Benevolent Fund of $30,000 to be raised by annual conferences and loaned to the printing establishment. The interest paid was to be used to support "worn-out" preachers or otherwise as annual conferences might direct. Only about $5000 was raised.

The Civil War years brought sharp rises in wages and materials, and consequently financial difficulties for the establishment—even near bankruptcy. Soon after William J. Shuey became assistant agent in 1863, he studied the indebtedness and proposed a plan of asking for direct gifts from individuals and annual conferences. He reasoned that if the church wanted a publishing business such support was necessary. A Publication Fund was approved by the General Conference of 1865 and Shuey was elected agent. The amount of $42,500 was apportioned to the annual conferences, which in turn were to apportion the amounts to their classses. By 1869 about $18,000 was received and used to reduce short-term obligations.

A three-story building adjoining the first one was built in 1869 and paid for by 1873. In spite of a depression in the 1870s, the establishment made a profit and the indebtedness was reduced further. Going into the 1880s the debt was completely eliminated and many improvements were made. For the first time in the history of the establishment, in 1882 and 1884 dividends of $5000 were distributed to the annual conferences. During the same quadrennium adjacent property was purchased, and in the next four years a four-story building was erected on this new property. Profits from 1881-1885 totaled more than $61,000, and nearly $51,000 from 1885-1889.

Lewis Davis Achieves His Goal:
United Brethren Schools

As far as Lewis Davis was concerned, the time had come for the starting of a United Brethren school. And he was determined to persuade others that it was a necessity. It was a good thing he possessed a strong perseverance. Some fellow churchmen shared his views, but many did not. Some openly opposed the idea, while others were hesitant to advocate it. Furthermore, probably no United Brethren of that time had an understanding of the complexities and requirements of beginning and maintaining such an institution. And there was no standing in line to give financial support. The circumstances were indeed adverse.

Born of a poor Virginia farm family, Davis had only about eighteen months of education beyond the common schools. As a young man he attended an academy at New Castle, Virginia. In 1845, at age thirty-one, he was, however, on his way to becoming a self-educated man, and was known for his habits of reading and study.[7]

The formal beginning of the first United Brethren college occurred when the General Conference of 1845 (with some persuasion by Davis from the sidelines, for he was not a member of that body)[8] passed this resolution by a vote of 19 to 5:

> Resolved, that proper measures be adopted to establish an institution of learning. Resolved, therefore, that it be recommended to the attention of the annual conferences, avoiding, however, irredeemable debts.

Miami Conference, at its 1846 session, decided to found a college at Bluffton, Indiana, or at such place as agreed upon, and to ask the cooperation of the conferences in central and northern Indiana. This did not materialize. In October of the same year the Scioto Conference, convened in Pickaway County, Ohio, received a delegation representing a Methodist school at Westerville, Ohio. The conference was offered the buildings, grounds, and all other property of the school for $1300. Lewis Davis and two others were appointed to visit the property and examine it.

They reported favorably and the school became the property of Scioto Conference. It was named Otterbein University and opened with eight students September 1, 1847. Davis was appointed to solicit funds and to seek the cooperation of other conferences. Reporting through the December 30, 1846 *Religious Telescope* on his early efforts, he wrote: "I feel, dear brethren, that I am engaged in the cause of Christ; if I did not I should at once desist. . . . I feel willing to endure with patience all the opposition I may meet with. . . . Our motto is, we WILL by grace succeed." He was the first to give, and though his gift was only fifteen dollars, in his circumstances it was a generous beginning.

Bishop John Russel, presiding at Sandusky and Muskingum Conferences in 1847, openly opposed the appeal of Davis for these conferences to join Scioto in supporting the school at Westerville. Russel and many other United Brethren believed in the highest mental culture, but they did not think "the church should descend from the lofty business of saving souls to manage institutions of learning."[9] They feared that young men would come to think that a formal education was their main preparation for the ministry. They looked at ministers of denominations which were coldly formal and lacking in evangelistic fervor, and they imagined that literary institutions would become theological institutions which would lead United Brethren away from the spirituality and piety which had always characterized them. However, Davis successfully guided Otterbein University "through the shoals of ignorance and the quicksands of poverty."[10] He succeeded because he "could live by devouring defeat," said A. W. Drury, who knew Davis personally.[11]

Once Otterbein University was a reality, keeping it going and building it up was as heroic a struggle as getting it started. And it was President Lewis Davis, often serving as a general-purpose man, who was "always coming in to perform the impossible."[12] (Some of the years he was president he was also a bishop of the church.) "It was a great undertaking, and grandly did he meet it," was the evaluation of Henry A. Thompson, who became president in 1872.[13]

By 1853 it appeared that the enthusiasm of United Brethren for schools needed some caution. The general conference of that year adopted this recommendation: "That our people be advised not to encourage at present, the being of more than three literary institutions, within the present bounds of our church." But by 1857 there were five. Again the general conference asked the church "to concentrate her efforts." The organization of many colleges in the United States prior to the Civil War and of public high schools in the last half of the nineteenth century made United Brethren education-conscious. So despite the cautioning of general conference, additional annual conferences started new schools (some of high school level, called academies or seminaries). These conferences thought their young people would be more apt to attend a United Brethren school if it were near their homes.

Consequently the limited funds for education could not be stretched to reach the financial needs of all these institutions. They suffered threatening debts, had inadequate libraries and facilities, and the faculties were often understaffed, overworked, and underpaid. The country generally suffered financial crises in the 1860s and 1870s. Money was scarce, and this scarcity affected the giving of the church as well as the ability of students to pay tuition. Nevertheless conferences which had schools did not wish to give them up, though they considered the colleges more important to continue than the institutions of high school level.

In retrospect, Davis and others could see many mistakes in the educational history of the church, yet significant progress and contributions had been made. Davis did not live to see the schools debt-free. However, he did have the pleasure in the General Conference of 1881 to report that the church then had fourteen institutions of learning, including one theological seminary, and a very efficient board of education; that over 18,000 students had received instruction under the auspices of the church, and over 500 had been graduated from these institutions; that in buildings, grounds, libraries, cabinets, and endowment funds these institutions were worth between $700,000 and $800,000.[14]

By 1889 about ten schools were either discontinued or united with other institutions. The board of education report to the General Conference of 1889 included these statistics: 1 theological seminary, 9 colleges, 7 schools of high school grade; total property value—$846,857; debts—$262,000; aggregate of library volumes—22,425; 69 professors and 68 other teachers; 1888-89 total attendance of students—2747; college graduates during quadrennium—190.[15]

Theological Educational

With educational institutions multiplying within and without the church and the level of education rising in many communities, gradually it became accepted by many United Brethren that ministers should be college trained. The General Conference of 1865 recommended "that the trustees of our different schools take into advisement the propriety of connecting with their schools, as soon as possible, Biblical classes, embracing the course of reading recommended in our Discipline."[16] Hartsville College, Hartsville, Indiana, became the first school to offer courses in theology. Milton Wright was elected to teach these courses in 1868 by White River and Indiana Conferences, the two conferences supporting Hartsville at that time.

The bishops' address to the General Conference of 1869 on the

subject of education included: "The standard of ministerial qualifica-
tion is being gradually but surely elevated. It cannot be raised too high,
provided it is not substituted for the necessary preparations of the
heart."[17]

To avoid proliferation of theological schools, as had happened with
colleges, a board of education, established by the General Conference
of 1869, carried out the desire of that conference to found a biblical
institute under the control of the general conference. Union Biblical
Seminary, which all annual conferences were asked to support with
funds and students, opened in the fall of 1871 with Lewis Davis as
senior professor. (Davis continued in this position until his retirement
in 1885.) The other two faculty members were G. A. Funkhouser, a
graduate of Allegheny Theological Seminary, and J. P. Landis, a
graduate of Lane Theological Seminary.

In the early years classes were held in basement rooms of the new
Home Street United Brethren Church (named Summit Street in 1873)
in Dayton, Ohio. Eleven students from five conferences enrolled the
first year. Three years later the seminary graduated eight students. In
1878 a three-story brick building was erected on the northwest corner
of First Street and Euclid Avenue on about five acres of land donated
by John Kemp, a minister who served for several years as the school's
financial manager. Tuition and room-rent were free to all students.
The third story of the new building served as a dormitory for twenty-
five students. In 1888, the enrollment was thirty-nine. By 1889 the
seminary had graduated 116 students out of an accumulated enrollment of 282. Besides graduates employed in the ministry, there were
three college presidents, one theology professor, one editor, several
professors and teachers in colleges and academies, and five foreign
missionaries.[18]

Expanding Horizons—Foreign Missions

West Africa

Stones from John Newton's slave pens on Plantain Island[19] served as
a main source of stone to build a United Brethren Training School at
Shenge, Sierra Leone, West Africa in 1886-87. A gift of $5000 paid for
the school. A native of Sierra Leone, Daniel Flickinger Wilberforce,
became the head of the school.[20] An ordained minister who had been
educated at Dayton, Ohio, he had successfully ministered in Sierra
Leone for nearly ten years. This school for training African converts to
be teachers and preachers, along with the prospects it held, made 1887
a high year for the mission after thirty years of struggle to get

established.

The General Conference of 1853 organized the Home, Frontier, and Foreign Missionary Society to more efficiently extend the gospel into new areas. John C. Bright, a delegate from Sandusky Conference who was credited with stirring the conference to this action, served as secretary until compelled to relinquish the post because of failing health in 1857. Meeting in September 1853, the new society "determined to establish a missionary station on the Big Boom River in the interior of Africa, at an early period."[21] In January 1855 three Miami Conference ministers—D. K. Flickinger, W. J. Shuey, and D. C. Kumler, a medical doctor as well—set sail from New York for Africa. They made expeditions along the coast and up some rivers, looking for a site for a mission, finally settling on Shenge, on the coast about sixty miles southeast of the capital, Freetown.

Bright reported $5500 expended on the mission by mid-1857. The next quadrennium expenses paid amounted to $7349.67.[22] From 1857 to 1866, six missionaries went to Africa, including two women who accompanied their husbands, Mrs. J. K. Billheimer and Mrs. Oliver Hadley. J. K. Billheimer served the longest, making three trips to Africa. His second and third terms were cut short by ill health, as was true of other missionaries in their first terms (and for the most part their only term). Conversions were few. One who became a Christian in the early years was Lucy Caulker, daughter of a chief who opposed the mission until near the end of his life, when he became a Christian. Another, Thomas Tucker, who stayed with the mission following his conversion, advanced from laborer to foreman to captain of the mission boat. Finally he became a minister of the gospel.

When the General Conference of 1869 convened, not a single missionary was on the field. Oliver and Mahala Hadley had just returned home. While in Africa, Hadley wrote in his diary of "a great concern . . . for the poor blind wandering creatures about us. It seems very hard to reach them. . . . I cannot speak their language and have no reliable interpreter. . . . O shall my eyes ever see the salvation of God come to one of these poor blind benighted creatures."[23] When the Hadleys left Africa, a native minister, J. A. Williams, carried the responsibility of the mission, as he had done before when all missionaries left. However, the mission treasury was empty, and within a year Williams died.[24]

Because of the Civil War in the United States, money was scarce during most of the 1860s, and this shortage affected collections for missions. What was received was divided between the mission board and annual conferences by a vote of the annual conferences each year.

During this financial bind a non-United Brethren of Kentucky gave $4200 to the mission board because of the church's antislavery position.[25]

Within days of his return home, Oliver Hadley died. His death, the illness of missionaries, and the few converts made some United Brethren favor abandoning the mission. Both a bishop and a prominent layman publicly opposed the African mission.[26] In numbers of converts, the home and frontier missions had far greater success. However, some thought that to give up the work in Africa would have a blighting effect on the home and frontier missions, and that the church would rally to keep the African mission going. Some favored using the men and means to evangelize freedmen of the South instead of Africa, or of trying to evangelize another foreign field. Several favored beginning a mission in Germany. The final action on the matter by the General Conference of 1869 was to refer the decision to the board of missions. Financially, prospects were a little better, for the conference made it a requirement that annual conferences give the mission board one-fourth to one-half of missionary monies collected.[27]

With one exception, the board voted to stay in Africa.[28] Thinking that perhaps African descendants in America could tolerate the climate and conditions of Africa better than white missionaries, the board sought suitable candidates. Joseph and Mary Gomer, from a small Negro United Brethren congregation in Dayton, Ohio, were assigned the leadership of the mission in 1870. In the next years there were more conversions, and the number of preaching places increased. Converts began to assume positions of increasing responsibility. Other missionaries, Negro and white, were recruited and sent to Africa; however, the Gomers were the mainstay of the leadership for two decades.[29]

The first United Brethren churches in Africa were organized in 1876 at Shenge and Bompetook. Missionary Secretary D. K. Flickinger organized a mission district in 1880. Gomer wrote in 1881: "Five new members have been received into the church at Shenge, and the Sabbath is well observed here and elsewhere where our schools are located. To compare ten years ago with the present, it does not seem like the same place."[30] To the General Conference of 1881 it was reported that the mission had four stations and chapels, over forty appointments, 112 church members, and 164 seekers of religion.[31] About a year later the American Missionary Association transferred to the United Brethren mission board their Mende mission, with headquarters at Bonthe, about sixty miles south of and contiguous to the United Brethren Sherbro mission at Shenge. The Mende people were one of the largest tribes in Sierra Leone, and the Mende mission the oldest established of the American missions in West Africa. The Association gave annual subsidies for the next several years amounting to nearly $39,000. The Freedmen's Missions Aid Society, of London, England, also gave the United Brethren board $13,000.[32] By 1885, including the Mende mission and the work of the Woman's Missionary Association in Africa, 320 towns were being reached, church membership was 1547, and from 2000 to 2500 on the Sabbath regularly received instruction in the divine Word from forty preachers and teachers.[33]

With the growth and development of the mission in Africa an increasing indebtedness occurred. It came to the point where there was some retrenchment, and again some entertained the thought of selling out. Flickinger was convinced the need was to persuade the North American church members to each give an average of twelve and one-half cents annually for foreign missions, and to give themselves in prayer for mission work.[34] There was no action to sell the mission. Rather, the General Conference of 1885 encouraged mission giving, authorized the building of the training school—if it could be accomplished without further indebtedness, elected Flickinger missionary bishop for Africa and Germany, and approved the employment by the mission board of a business manager if the board thought it practical and financially safe. In addition, in 1885 the mission board began support of a Chinese mission in Walla Walla, Washington, which Walla Walla Conference began in 1884.

The bishops' address to the General Conference of 1889 stated that the accumulated deficit of the missionary society in 1887 was $60,000. Of that deficit, $50,000 was secured, with $40,000 of it cash in hand. The missionary secretary reported that the church membership in Africa was 4720.[35]

Through most of the struggling and successful years of the mission up to 1889, D. K. Flickinger served as missionary secretary or missionary bishop. A part of his responsibility was editing the *Missionary Telescope* (later the *Missionary Visitor*). He demonstrated an indefatigable interest in and persistent efforts on behalf of the mission, visiting it eleven times. He weathered much criticism and did not allow it to deter him.

Germany

In 1869, at a time of great uncertainty about the church's mission in Africa, Christian Bischoff, a member of the Ohio German Conference, and his wife commenced mission work in Bavaria, Germany, their native land. Many United Brethren were of German stock, so it was natural for them to send missionaries to Germany, where evangelical Christianity was little known. In Bavaria religious intolerance prevailed; citizens were required to support state churches. These large costly churches stood nearly empty Sunday after Sunday, for there was little offered there to feed the soul.[36]

Because non-state churches were denied many privileges granted to the state churches, the progress of the mission was hindered. It was hard to rent suitable halls for preaching, so funds were needed for building. A lack of means and of additional missionaries also limited the work. Finally the civil authorities prohibited United Brethren missionaries from holding meetings for public worship.

Amidst talk in America of abandoning the mission in Germany, work was begun north of Bavaria. Here there was a little more success.[37] On December 10, 1879, Flickinger organized a mission district, with 235 members in eleven classes, and thirty-four preaching places.[38] In the secretary's report to the General Conference of 1889 it was stated that the mission "goes on as well and rapidly as could be expected with the money expended and the number of missionaries employed."[39]

A Vision from a Raspberry Patch: the Woman's Missionary Association

Three months after women representatives from many of the annual conference areas had adopted a constitution and elected officers, these women were not sure their new Woman's Missionary Association was going to be approved and recognized by the general conference. Several church leaders were opposing it. The board of the Home, Frontier, and Foreign Missionary Society had encouraged the women's society, but the general conference was the body that could give official recognition from the denomination.[40] The conference would not meet for another sixteen months. The women were hopeful, for the General Conference of 1873 had commended the women's missionary societies that had organized in a few annual conferences—Ohio German, California, and Miami being the first ones.[41] That general conference had also encouraged the organization of societies in all the annual conferences.[42]

However, in addition to opposition from individuals, the Virginia Conference passed a resolution "That in the opinion of this conference a church of less than 150,000 members has no need of two boards of missions." Virginia did say that if a woman's board was approved by the general conference that "we insist that it be auxiliary to the parent Board" and that there should be a common treasury.[43]

The secretary of the Home, Frontier and Foreign Missionary Society, D. K. Flickinger, favored the women's organization. But he recognized opposition from "some leading men in the church, including two bishops, a president of a college, and some members of the Board of Missions." Flickinger said opposition "was not only strong, but unkind at times."[44]

In response to opposition, Mrs. S. K. Rike, of Dayton, Ohio, wrote a letter which was published in the February 2, 1876, *Religious Telescope:*

> . . . We read and hear through returned missionaries of the woeful, *woeful* estate of heathen women and children. We contrast our condition with theirs until our hearts run over with feeling that the lines have fallen to *us* in pleasant places. *We* have a goodly heritage; but how can we help them? . . . .
>
> Born of this gratitude, these yearnings, these prayers, are the thoughts: first, can not I do something more? True, I join with my husband or father in paying the yearly assessments gladly. . . . Christ has done so much for me, a woman, that I want to give him something of my very own, something which I must deny myself for the sake of giving. . . .
>
> This summer I visited a friend in the country. Her raspberries were delicious. I saw she was enthusiastic. "After supper I want to show you where they grow." There they were, two short rows of them, but all trimmed up square and supported on either side by a rough railing. "Two years ago," she went on to say, "I wish you had seen them; nothing but a jungle—little fruit and of poor quality. I asked John to let me have that for myself. He laughed at me—said all the farm was mine, for that matter, and I had enough to do already; but I might try my hand. I borrowed a book that tells you how to trim, enrich, mulch and all that and then went at it. The first year it was hard work. You see most all my bushes were cut away, and many a time when I could have rested in the house, there was that raspberry patch. But the next year—oh, the leaves, the flowers, the fruit! I sold forty quarts!" "But," I said, "you could not do all the work." "Oh, when the men saw how beautifully they were doing, they got interested, and suggested the fence, and built it, too." I do not think it ever occurred to the dear lady that she was working against her husband or the best interests of the farm. There is many another wild jungle which might be made to blossom as the rose if we could become enthused. . . .
>
> We disclaim all ambitious rivalry, all pretensions to an independent head. One head for one body is enough; but two arms and two feet are not bad. We shall work in harmony with our faithful tried right arm. Should serious differences arise, never fear; our innate desire to always appear to the best advantage will dictate that we yield cheerfully and gracefully.

Among the women themselves there were those who expressed doubts about their ability to organize and carry out the purpose of the society. But others, including returned missionaries Amanda Billheimer and Mahala Hadley, were optimistic and ready to try.[45] (The earliest of the women's missionary boards among denominations in the United States was formed in 1868.)[46]

When the General Conference of 1877 opened, the bishops' address set a favorable tone:

> The Woman's Missionary Association, though yet in its infancy, is likely to become a power for good in the missionary field. Our sisters have a mind to work. The field is large enough, and the demand for laborers sufficiently urgent, to enlist the combined efforts of all who love our Lord Jesus Christ. Paul made honorable mention of women who labored with him in the gospel; and so now we commend to you for recognition this association, trusting that you will be able to give such direction and encouragement as in your judgment may seem necessary.

On the seventh morning of the conference, Mrs. Rike, recording secretary of the WMA, was invited to read the WMA address to the conference. The address described the WMA as a "homeless orphan" wishing to be adopted as the ward of the general conference. Repeating some of the reasons for a women's organization that she had given in her letter in the *Telescope,* she called for the sanction of the general conference. She told them that the women wanted to have schools for children, and had already established one at a village about seven miles from the United Brethren mission at Shenge, in Sierra Leone.

The address suggested that the WMA appeal to the Sabbath schools to give an offering the first Sunday in each month to help support schools in Africa. This suggestion was approved by the general conference, the WMA constitution was ratified, and officers confirmed.

Upon the advice of missionaries and the board of missions, the WMA set to work to establish schools in a heavily populated area of Sierra Leone where there was no missionary work. The location was up the Bompeh River, about fifty miles from Freetown and about sixty miles from Shenge. Four schools were established, and public services were held. In the late 1880s a chapel and a girls' home were built.

In addition to the work in Africa, the WMA began supporting a pastor at Coburg, Germany, in 1880, and in 1882 undertook the responsibility of a night school for Chinese in Portland, Oregon. Moy Ling had started the school and continued as a teacher and interpreter. From twenty students the enrollment soon grew to 157, and a Sunday school was organized. In the first five years, 500 different Chinese attended the school, and fifty-nine professed faith in Christ and joined the church. By 1885 five of these students had gone to China, where it was hoped they would become missionaries to their countrymen.[47]

The WMA address to the General Conference of 1885 indicated a benefit in the homes of WMA members from their organization: "a greater spirituality, a more systematic beneficence, a better training for the children." Many men of the church recognized the accomplishments of the WMA, and sometimes in annual and general conferences included speeches and resolutions commending the WMA.

From the beginning the WMA experienced growth and progress in the organization and in its mission work. By 1881 one woman was employed full time in correspondence work and organizing. That same year a sixteen-page monthly, the *Woman's Evangel,* was begun with a subscription list of 1200. The publication was self-supporting from the start, and the circulation grew to 2900 by 1889. In 1877 there were three branches and 18 local societies; 1880—30 branches and 150 locals with 3000 members; 1885—37 branches, 302 locals, and a membership of about 5000. By 1889 the membership was 8202. That same year seven American and fourteen native missionaries were employed; the church membership in the mission congregations was 939; and property was valued at $26,500. From 1875 to 1880 monies collected by the WMA amounted to $11,531.97. From 1885 to 1889 the average annual income was $10,000.

Young women and children were encouraged to become active in mission work by joining a Gleaner's Band or a Young Women's Band, both sponsored by the WMA. The first Gleaner's Band was organized by Mrs. G. P. Macklin at Fostoria, Ohio, in 1879; the first Young Women's Bands at Westerville and Circleville, Ohio, in 1883. In just fifteen years the women of the church had become a recognized force for spreading the gospel. The children's and young women's work was a step in ensuring the future of the Woman's Missionary Association.

FOOTNOTES

[1]Henry A. Thompson, *Our Bishops,* rev. ed. (Dayton, OH: United Brethren Publishing House, 1903), p. 344.

[2]John Lawrence, *The History of the Church of the United Brethren in Christ,* 2 vols. (Dayton, OH: United Brethren Printing Establishment, 1868), 2:253.

[3]Thompson, pp. 341, 352-355.

[4]Ibid., pp. 345-347.

[5]John H. Ness, Jr., *One Hundred Fifty Years, a History of Publishing in the Evangelical United Brethren Church* (Dayton, OH: Board of Publication of the Evangelical United Brethren Church, 1966), p. 348.

[6]Ibid., p. 370.

[7]Thompson, pp. 390-393, 397-399.

[8]*Hartsville College Index,* November, 1890.

[9]Thompson, p. 302.

[10]Ibid., pp. 413, 414.

[11]Augustus W. Drury, *History of the Church of the United Brethren in Christ* (Dayton, OH: Otterbein Press, 1924), p. 626.

[12]Ibid., p. 622.

[13]Thompson, p. 405.

[14]*Proceedings of the Eighteenth General Conference of the United Brethren in Christ* (Dayton, OH: United Brethren Publishing House, 1881), p. 179.

[15]*Proceedings of the Twentieth General Conference of the United Brethren in Christ* (Dayton, OH: United Brethren Publishing House, 1889), p. 187.

[16]*Proceedings of the Fourteenth General Conference of the United Brethren in Christ* (Dayton, OH: United Brethren Printing Establishment, 1865), pp. 23, 24.

[17]*Proceedings of the Fifteenth General Conference of the United Brethren in Christ* (Dayton, OH: United Brethren Printing Establishment, 1869), p. 12.

[18]*Proceedings of the Twentieth General Conference,* p. 82; *1888 United Brethren Year-Book,* pp. 31, 33.

[19]John Newton became a Christian while engaged in the African slave trade. Then he became an evangelist. Out of his experience he wrote the hymn "Amazing Grace."

[20]Daniel Kumler Flickinger, *Fifty-five Years of Active Ministerial Life* (Dayton, OH: United Brethren Publishing House, 1907), pp. 180-182.

[21]Drury, p. 587.

[22]Lawrence, 2:395.

[23]Oliver Hadley, Diary, pp. 115, 133, United Brethren Archives, Huntington, IN.

[24]Drury, p. 590; Flickinger, pp. 84, 90, 100.

[25]Flickinger, pp. 67, 68.

[26]Ibid., pp. 91-96, 86-89.

[27]*Proceedings of the Fifteenth General Conference of the United Brethren in Christ,* pp. 33-38, 47, 173-175, 182-184.

[28]Flickinger, p. 93.

[29]Ibid., pp. 100, 106, 110, 200, 201, 107.

[30]Ibid., p. 145.

[31]*Proceedings of the Eighteenth General Conference of the United Brethren in Christ,* p. 28.

[32]Flickinger, pp. 156, 157, 182, 189.

[33]*Proceedings of the Nineteenth General Conference of the United Brethren in Christ* (Dayton, OH: United Brethren Publishing House, 1885), p. 8.

[34]Flickinger, p. 126.

[35]*Proceedings of the Twentieth General Conference of the United Brethren in Christ,* pp. 11, 40.

[36]Flickinger, pp. 146, 147.

[37]United Brethren Church, *Twenty-third Annual Report of the Board of Missions for the Year Ending March 31, 1876* (Dayton, OH: United Brethren Publishing House, 1876), pp. 16, 17.

[38]Flickinger, pp. 140, 141.

[39]*Proceedings of the Twentieth General Conference of the United Brethren in Christ,* p. 39. In 1880 the Woman's Missionary Association began a work in the city of Coburg, Germany, a city of 14,000 people. In 1889 the WMA turned this over to the mission board. Following the United Brethren division in 1889 the Liberal United Brethren controlled the mission in Germany. The highest the membership reached was about 1000. In 1905

the Methodist Episcopal Church took over the membership and property. In the 1870s and 1880s there were United Brethren missions to German immigrants in Toledo, Ohio, and Philadelphia.

[40]United Brethren Church, *Twenty-second Annual Report of the Board of Missions for the Year Ending March 31, 1875* (Dayton, OH: United Brethren Publishing House, 1875), p. 11.

[41]Drury, p. 598.

[42]*Proceedings of the Sixteenth General Conference of the United Brethren in Christ* (Dayton, OH: United Brethren Printing Establishment, 1873), p. 76.

[43]*Religious Telescope,* March 1, 1876.

[44]Flickinger, pp. 126, 130, 131.

[45]*History of the Woman's Missionary Association of the United Brethren in Christ* (Dayton, OH: United Brethren Publishing House, 1910), p. 9.

[46]Drury, p. 598.

[47]*Proceedings of the Nineteenth General Conference of the United Brethren in Christ,* p. 252.

22

POSITIONS ON MORAL ISSUES

Slavery and Racial Discrimination

When August 21, 1863, dawned at Lawrence, Kansas, Samuel S. Snyder, a United Brethren minister, was milking his cow. Suddenly the morning stillness was broken by the sound of horses approaching. One of the riders called to Snyder, "Are you the owner of that house?" Snyder replied that he was. The two riders then shot him three times.[1] Snyder was one of about 150 Lawrence citizens killed in a four-hour raid of shooting and burning by a Rebel band led by a young Confederate guerrilla leader, William C. Quantrill. It was thought that these raiders had carefully planned to kill every antislavery advocate in Lawrence, stronghold of Kansas abolitionism, and that the two who came to Snyder's were specifically sent to find and kill him.[2]

Only three months earlier Missionary Secretary Flickinger had included this statement to the board of missions:

> For more than forty years we have refused membership to slaveholders; because of this many have turned from us, and we have been subjected to much opposition and injustice, especially in the slave states. No one now doubts the wisdom of our fathers in preferring right to members and popularity. The progress the nation is making in breaking the shackles of the enslaved is a reward for all that has been suffered and for the sacrifices we may yet have to make before the struggle ends.[3]

During every one of Snyder's nearly ten years in Kansas, the towns and countrysides, especially near Missouri, were never free from skirmishes and war over slavery. When Kansas Territory was opened to white settlers in 1854, Congress voted to let the settlers of a new state or

225

territory decide whether it would allow slavery. Kansas became a
symbol of the nation's struggle over slavery. The goals of United
Brethren missionaries to Kansas were to "aid in founding the church
and free institutions."[4]

The *Religious Telescope* carried news of happenings in Kansas
Territory and reports from the church's missionaries there. An August
27, 1856 item stated that "the presses of *all* the Free State papers in
Kansas are in the bottom of the Missouri River." The *Telescope*
reported Kansas citizens being murdered, tarred, feathered, and
beaten, and of homes being burned. Snyder wrote that "Free State men
were daily found hung from trees or shot to death."[5] One biography of
Snyder said that because of his pulpit utterances and newspaper
articles against slavery, his life was threatened almost daily.[6] In 1856 his
horse was stolen.[7] Another United Brethren minister in Kansas, John
S. Gingerich, also had horses stolen, and he was attacked at a religious
service.[8]

A resolution of the Ministerial Alliance of Lawrence, Kansas,
appeared in the May 7, 1856, *Religious Telescope:*

> *Resolved,* That as preachers of the gospel, *we* will not be deterred by any
> prohibition, threatening, or reviling, from the supporters of this iniquity of
> slavery, from testifying to it in the name of the Lord Jesus, deciding with the
> Apostles, whenever forbidden so to do, that we ought to obey God rather than
> man.

When Bishop Edwards went to Missouri Mission Conference for
the first time in 1855, "he found himself surrounded with slavery.
Anti-slavery views had penetrated the country to the very smallest
extent."[9] Edwards reported to the mission board of the missionaries in
Missouri:

> They have made no compromise with slavery, nor pro-slavery influ-
> ences . . . . anti-slavery ministers and churches in a slave state are lights in a
> dark place.
> I am more than ever convinced that anti-slavery churches ought to sustain
> missions and plant churches in the South; for upon the subject of slavery there is
> a vast amount of ignorance even among the most intelligent. Every effort is
> made to exclude every ray of light upon this subject . . . . the teaching and
> practice of the church, of nearly every denomination, go to sustain the peculiar
> institution as it exists among them.[10]

United Brethren missionaries in Kentucky and Tennessee also suffered
persecution, and proslavery opposition hindered the success of their
work and tried to drive them out.[11]

While other churches became entrenched in defense of slavery, the United Brethren stand against it became more pronounced. The Constitution of the church declared that involuntary servitude shall not be tolerated in any way. From 1841 a section of the *Discipline* stated: "All slavery, in every sense of the word, is totally prohibited, and shall in no way be tolerated in our church. Should any be found in our society who hold slaves, they cannot continue as members unless they do personally manumit or set free such slaves." Prior to 1841 the *Discipline* allowed for delay of freeing slaves until remuneration for raising or buying them was satisfied; annual conferences were made the guardians of any such slaves and were responsible for the contract of simple justice between owner and slave. In 1849 a paragraph was added which made ministers accountable for carrying out the *Discipline* on slavery among their members.

At the General Conference of 1849 the Virginia Conference was called to account for connection with slavery, the charge based on acknowledgment of the members of Virginia Conference. A question of whether there could be slaveholding cases of peculiar character that might not be included by the *Discipline* rule was raised at the General Conference of 1853. But all twelve cases described were prohibited, and the conference declared that immediate emancipation should take place. The thought of the conference was that no entering wedge of slavery should be allowed. The bishops were instructed to carry out the letter of the *Discipline*. A magazine authorized by the General Conference of 1853 had as one of its objects "to show that slavery . . . is sinful, necessarily sinful, under all possible and conceivable circumstances."[12]

Some United Brethren leaders and pastors went further than keeping their own church in line and in declaring to others the unpopular position of United Brethren. In the fashion of Paul publicly rebuking Peter (Gal. 2) and the Galatian church (ch. 3), these United Brethren rebuked proslavery churches and church members. In the new magazine, *Unity with God,* David Edwards, editor, wrote in the fourth issue (Feb. 1854):

It is by no means a pleasant task to speak of the evils of the churches, but there are times and circumstances when it must be done by every one worthy the name of a "watchman" on the towers of Zion. The present position of all the great and influential churches of this land on the subject of slavery is so glaringly inconsistent, and so destructive in its tendencies, that it ought to be exposed everywhere, until for shame, if for nothing else, they are led to cease tolerating such an abomination in their midst. Infidels and heathens ought to be informed that a slaveholding Christianity is not of God,—that it is a corruption of Christianity which neither God, angels nor good men can tolerate for a moment, any more than they can robbery and oppression in any other form. The absurdity of Christian churches, which acknowledge Jesus Christ as their leader, and the New Testament for their rule of life, taking sides with the manstealer, and receiving him to the Christian fellowship without requiring him to "break every yoke and let the oppressed go free," is so manifest that it seems like offering an insult to any man's intellect and moral sense to attempt to prove it. . . . The melancholy proof is too abundant, that all the old and large churches of America have, for gold, numbers or popularity, compromised the great principles of justice and gospel equality taught by Jesus Christ . . . Conferences, Synods and Assemblies, the Pulpit and the Press, have in many instances, either by a timid and shameful non-interference, or by open avowal, taken sides with slavery. A few weak and timid resolutions declaring slavery to be an evil, is no more felt by it than a gnat on an ox's horn while the slaveholder is not treated as a sinner and excluded from the church. . . . The churches of America have the power, if they would use it, to break off the chains from every slave in the land.

While editor of the *Religious Telescope,* John Lawrence wrote a pamphlet "A Short Treatise on American Slavery," and then a 224-page book, *The Slavery Question,* which was for "the common people—the people of plain sense—who are not offended at plain talk and plain facts."[13] Lawrence believed that if the workingmen of the free and slave states could be aroused into action, slavery would be ended. By 1857 this book was in a fourth edition.[14] It used no "mealy words" about the churches and slavery, calling the powerful churches of America "apologists of oppressors, . . . and the only reliable bulwark of American slavery."[15] Lawrence quoted the great abolitionist Frederick Douglass, "The dealer gives his blood-stained gold to support the pulpit, and the pulpit, in return, covers his infernal business with the garb of Christianity."[16]

Among United Brethren annual conferences there were instances of rebuke—of Congressmen who helped pass proslavery legislation, of United Brethren ministers with proslavery views (even to the point of revoking licenses), of members who refused to subscribe to the *Religious Telescope* because of its uncompromising stand against slavery. (As the battle lines over slavery became more distinct, the *Telescope* was banned and burned in slave states.)

The bishops stated in their address to the General Conference of 1857:

We would earnestly recommend that there be no change in the Discipline touching secret societies, and slavery. And we see no good reason why these subjects should be agitated at this session. It is fondly hoped that the time is not far distant when we will not only be practically free from these evils, but that there will be none found to advocate them in our connection.

The church stood firm in its position on slavery, even though within it there was scattered opposition to the abolitionist view. Like many others in both the North and South, some United Brethren thought the South should be left alone; they also feared that abolitionism would lead to war; they feared the consequences of four million slaves suddenly freed. Auglaize Conference experienced a schism over the church's strong antislavery stand.[17] In northern states, including Ohio and Indiana, where the denomination was becoming strong, turmoil over slavery was commonplace in the years preceding as well as during the Civil War. An Ohio United Brethren minister of those times said:

> All was commotion in Church and State, and the possibility of building up the Church seemed small. Especially was this true in the U.B. Church, for we were known to be "black abolitionists," and all sorts of charges were made against us as being dangerous to the welfare of society.[18]

When the General Conference of 1861 convened, the Civil War had begun. Both the bishops' address and the resolutions on the state of the country revealed the solemnity of the hour. One of the resolutions adopted declared that "it is the duty of all the patriots of the United States to use all lawful and Christian means to arrest and stop the secession movement."[19] When the call to arms was issued by President Lincoln, many United Brethren responded, including a number of ministers—even some from Virginia. One hundred seventy-one persons affiliated with Otterbein University as alumni, students, or veterans who enrolled upon their return from military service, participated in the War.[20] In contrast to almost every college in the United States, Otterbein welcomed colored students. However, the number who attended was very small, and in some years none were enrolled. Prior to and during the War this school was noted as a center of antislavery sentiment and agitation. Leading antislavery champions of the country, including Frederick Douglass and Wendell Phillips, spoke at Otterbein University. The home of President Lewis Davis was an underground railroad station. Across the street from Otterbein College is the home of William Hanby, now a state memorial. A son, Benjamin R. Hanby, wrote the words and music of the ballad "Darling Nellie Gray." He was inspired by the story of a fugitive slave who died in the Hanby home.[21]

Western College in Iowa, another United Brethren school, had a greater proportion of students enlist in the Union Army than any other college in the country.[22] There were 7000 military subscriptions to the *Religious Telescope,* which was sent free to any United Brethren in the service who requested it.[23] The editor, John Lawrence, resigned during the War, enlisted in the army, and became a chaplain of a colored regiment. After the War, he was appointed judge of a freedmen's court in Nashville, Tennessee.[24] During the War, annual conferences regularly passed resolutions against slavery, and in support of the Union and President Lincoln. "The church was patriotic in the highest degree," wrote Lewis Davis. "In some conferences the feeling for the Union was such that to be a Democrat was to be regarded with suspicion, or pressed out of the church; while to be a secessionist was to receive no quarter."[25]

United Brethren in Virginia were caught "between a rock and a hard place." To stay in Confederate territory was to be called "Rebel" by many in the North. To be in sympathy with the Union and yet remain in Virginia for the sake of family and church was to risk being accused as a traitor by many in the South. Some United Brethren ministers were arrested, three at least were imprisoned for not taking the oath of allegiance to the Confederacy.[26] For four years Virginia Conference met in two parts, the northern part in Maryland and the southern in Virginia. Bishop Markwood, though a Virginian, was an out-and-out antislavery man and fled the South when a $1000 reward was offered for his arrest.[27] Bishop Glossbrenner, also a Virginian but moderate on slavery, remained in Virginia except for attending the northern Virginia Conference and going to Pennsylvania in 1863.[28]

A misson among freedmen was authorized by the board of missions in 1863. Three members of the board went to Washington, D.C., to arrange with government officials, including President Lincoln,[29] for transportation and supplies for missionaries to open a mission in Vicksburg, Mississippi.[30] This evangelistic and educational mission was continued for about two years, and then it was turned over to the Freedman's Mission.[31] The most lasting United Brethren work among freedmen was within the bounds of Virginia Conference.

When, at the General Conference of 1865, Bishop Edwards received and read the news of the capture of Jefferson Davis, the conference broke out in applause and then arose and sang the doxology. That conference adopted twelve resolutions on the state of the country. The most controversial one favored "placing every inhabitant of the land, black and white, on an equality before the law, and hereby pledge our influence and efforts to secure the complete enfranchisement of the Negro, with all the rights of an American citizen."[32] In reference to that resolution, in 1866 Bishop Weaver wrote an article "Public Sentiment" in which he declared that United Brethren were unlike many men and churches who are controlled by public sentiment, who have the same relation to moral reform that the weathercock does to the wind. His article indicated that annual conferences endorsed the action of the general conference.[33]

When the African Methodist Episcopal Church sent a letter of fraternal greetings and a delegate to the General Conference of 1877, the United Brethren reply included this statement:

> Though we do not boast as to numbers or wealth, we do remember that when four millions of your race were in bondage in this land we were among the first and most earnest pleaders for your liberty; and when the last chain was broken we were among the first to ask that your people be made equal before the law.[34]

When rights of the Negro were disregarded, United Brethren protested. Milton Wright, editor of the *Religious Telescope,* in 1876, decried the public indifference to election frauds in some of the southern states.[35] The mission board, at its 1879 meeting, deplored "the unjust discrimination becoming so general in this country against Negroes, Chinese, and Indians." A *Religious Telescope* article of June 11, 1884 by I. L. Buchwalter was prophetic:

> . . . I fear that if our Government does not soon take decisive measures to put a stop to the present shot-gun policy of the South, by which thousands of colored citizens are disfranchised and the innocent blood of multitudes is shed without fear of punishment, there will yet be another struggle for human rights, perhaps marked with blood, before the work of this great reform is fully completed.

Intoxicating Drinks

The first official United Brethren actions against alcoholic beverages came early in the history of the denomination and in advance of the public sentiment and action. The United Brethren rule became most comprehensive and prohibitive—making the church, in effect, a total abstinence society. When temperance enthusiasm in the United States waned during the Civil War, and temperance legislation enacted by all northern states except New Jersey fell by the wayside, with only Maine remaining "dry" by 1868, the United Brethren did not compromise their stand. When liquor manufacturers and retailers entered politics to advance their interests, the church did not retreat. A national temperance convention in 1868 at Cleveland, Ohio, attracted fifty United Brethren delegates.[36] Many United Brethren promoted temperance in their communities and worked for prohibition legislation. By the 1880s some states were "dry" again.

In 1841 the United Brethren *Discipline* forbade preachers and laymen from distilling and vending ardent spirits. The prohibition was extended in 1849 to include use as a beverage.[37] Failure to comply with this rule meant expulsion from the church. The term "ardent spirits" was changed to "intoxicating drinks" (to include both distilled and fermented beverages) by the General Conference of 1873. The Committee on Resolutions and Reform of the General Conference of 1877 included this statement in their report:

> . . . We believe there is no one thing which is more effectually hindering the advancement of Christ's kingdom than the use of intoxicating liquors and the traffic in them. It weakens and finally destroys the body. It enfeebles, it benumbs, and often crazes the brain. It blunts the moral sensibilities and disqualifies for the reception of religious truths, and finally sends its victim to a drunkard's grave, and a drunkard's hell. It is the chief source of poverty in our land; the principal cause of its ignorance and idiocy; the producer of nine-tenths of the crime, and the great burden of taxation resulting therefrom. It is the great destroyer of the objects of civil government, and ought to be repulsed by the strong arm of the law. That all laws for the regulation of such a wrong are in violation of the divine law, and promoters of evil doings. Not only should our people totally abstain, and teach their children and others to do so, but in their capacity as Christian citizens they should vote for such persons only as are temperate themselves, and will agree to use all proper means for the prohibition of this unholy traffic. That we emphatically pronounce against the use of fermented and intoxicating wines for sacramental purposes . . .[38]

In 1881 there was added to the *Discipline* a statement forbidding the signing of petitions for license to sell intoxicating drinks, becoming bondsmen for persons engaged in selling liquor, or renting and leasing property in which to manufacture or sell intoxicating drinks. The General Conference of 1885 adopted a report which urged action to secure constitutional prohibition, both state and national, favored instruction in schools on the effects of alcohol, pledged cooperation with other efforts to overthrow the liquor trade, and praised the Women's Christian Temperance Union. Otterbein University became a temperance center, and among the temperance leaders who spoke there were Frances E. Willard, Susan B. Anthony, and Elizabeth Cady Stanton. Two United Brethren college presidents, Charles H. Kiracofe and Henry A. Thompson, ran for state offices on the Prohibition Party ticket, and Thompson was the vice-presidential candidate on the Prohibition ticket in 1880.[39]

Tobacco

Tobacco in various forms, but especially chewing tobacco, was used by a number of United Brethren ministers and laymen during this period. However, objections were raised and the use declined. Bishop Edwards would sometimes tell those who were addicted to this habit to take their tobacco out of their mouths before entering God's house, and lay it by the fence. "I can assure you," he chided, "that neither the hogs nor the dogs will carry it off."[40]

At annual and general conference meetings, there was usually a motion to the effect that there be no use of tobacco during session hours. Illinois Conference, in 1865, pledged themselves "to keep agitating against the sinfulness of chewing and smoking tobacco." Many United Brethren considered chewing or smoking tobacco an offensive and unsanitary habit, and unbecoming, particularly by a minister. Some also objected to the tobacco habit because of the money it required.

Tobacco was called "a narcotic poison," and this was elaborated on in the report of the committee on resolutions and reform at the General Conference of 1877. All United Brethren, especially ministers, were entreated to abstain from the evil habit and the bad example. The 1881 moral reform report stated: "Christians should avoid all filthiness; hence we earnestly advise all our brethren to avoid and discountenance the use of tobacco . . ."[41] The 1885 report rejoiced in "a growing sentiment against the use of tobacco," and young men looking toward the ministry were to be most earnestly advised to abstain from its use. Those already in the ministry who used the narcotic were advised to stop. To the questions for ministerial candidates, this was added to the *Discipline* in 1885: "Will you abstain from the use of tobacco?"

Divorce and Other Issues

The General Conferences of 1877, 1881 and 1885 adopted resolutions against divorces granted for "many minor, and some very trifling offenses," and against solemnizing marriages of persons divorced for such offenses. The one justifiable cause for divorce was adultery. The foregoing points, with some elaboration, were added to the moral reform chapter of the *Discipline* in 1885. Other subjects sometimes included under the moral reform report at general and annual conferences were Sabbath observance, church fairs, gambling, dancing, and extravagances in dress.

Secret Societies

A moral issue which sparked a controversy that led to division in the denomination was membership in secret societies. The Constitution, adopted in 1841, prohibited such membership: "There shall be no connection with secret combinations." This and other parts of the Constitution were protected by Article IV: "There shall be no alteration of the foregoing constitution, unless by request of two-thirds of the whole society."

From 1841 to 1849 the *Discipline* stated:

> Freemasonry in every sense of the word shall be totally prohibited, and in no wise tolerated in our Society. And should any of our members continue to attend their lodges, or join as a member in any masonic procession, or otherwise join a masonic fraternity, he shall, for so doing, be excluded from our church.

This was much the same as what was in the *Discipline* from 1829 until 1841. It reflected the position of the church founders. The General Conferences of 1849 and 1861 revised the *Discipline* on secret societies to clarify "secret combinations" and to outline the procedure for dealing with offenders.[42] These revisions were attempts to ensure conformity to the Constitution, and were made with almost unanimous approval. When two prominent Virginia ministers in 1851 announced in the *Religious Telescope* that they could not and would not carry out the *Discipline* on slavery and secret societies, other annual conferences passed resolutions censuring this conduct and urging Virginia Conference to correct these abuses.[43]

For enlightenment on secret societies, *Religious Telescope* editor John Lawrence wrote *Plain Thoughts on Secret Societies*. The denomination's book committee commended it, and about 5000 copies were produced in at least four printings, the first in 1851.[44] Lawrence warned:

> I dare not, as a sinful man, appear in the presence of a holy God, except as I am sheltered and screened by the righteousness of the One Mediator; but no prescribed prayer or other ceremonial of these secret societies makes mention of any such Mediator. . . . whatever has the least tendency . . . to confound the distinctions between the church and the world, ought to be avoided with the most scrupulous care.[45]

A few other antisecrecy books by non-United Brethren writers were published by the United Brethren Printing Establishment between 1850 and 1880. In addition, a magazine authorized by the General Conference of 1853, *Unity with God,* had as one of its aims: "Freemasonry in all its forms and aspects will be freely and fearlessly discussed. It will be shown that all secret, oath-bound societies are anti-social and anti-Christian."[46]

The *Religious Telescope* carried articles on the subject also. A few weeks before the General Conference of 1857, in the March 11 issue, Lawrence editorialized on "What shall be done with members of secret societies who profess religion at our protracted meetings?" He believed in making clear to them the denominational stand on secrecy and that a condition of membership in the church was adherence to this position. To those who could not give up the fellowship of the lodge for the fellowship of the church, Lawrence said, "Bid him go in peace to the Methodists, or to any other denomination which entertains views of secret societies different from ours." He cautioned the church against weakening its stand when several lodge men were converted and were prospective church members, or of thinking "we can convert them to our principles after we have received them." To do so, he warned, would be degrading and would end in strife, bitterness, loss of members, and other evils. Lawrence could see no difference between opening the church to converted slaveholders and opening it to those who retained their lodge membership. He declared:

> We believe that the church has the first and the highest demands upon men, and that he who is not willing, if need be, to waive any and every earthly interest for the sake of the church, is not likely to be of very much use in it nor to it.
>
> If our position is right, and we believe it is, let us adhere to it, if the heavens fall.
>
> . . . if God is with us he will sustain us in a rigid adherence to principle; and if he is not with us, neither secrecy, slavery, nor rum will secure to us his presence.

A serious blow to the church and its record of opposition to Freemasonry, in fact to the integrity of its ministry, came in the late 1850s in Sandusky Conference. It was suspected that some ministers were Freemasons. At the 1857 annual session each member was asked, "Are you a member of any secret society?" Each said, "No." However, soon after the session it was learned that several, including some of the leading ministers, were Freemasons. At the 1858 session they were asked to confess and promise to cease their connection with Freemasonry. When the conference made it clear that it intended to maintain the law, they confessed and were forgiven. At the General Conference of 1861 an impeachment for maladministration was entered against Sandusky Conference. After hearing testimony and explanations, the general conference, by a vote 58 to 3, passed a resolution sustaining the action of Sandusky Conference. Bishop Edwards spoke on the issue:

> For years we have met this wily foe of secrecy, seeking to make its way into the

church at every crevice. . . . I am clearly of the opinion that to clandestinely go into the lodge and conceal it from the church is a crime I hardly have language to characterize properly.[47]

By 1861 Freemasonry, after a downfall to about 5000 members, had revived and grown to 200,000 members. Following the Civil War, Masonry and other secret orders flourished.[48] With widespread growth and acceptance of these orders, opposition to them became unpopular. This led in 1867 to the antisecrecy forces uniting to form the National Christian Association Opposed to Secret Societies. Several United Brethren annual conferences sent delegates to its 1868 national convention at Pittsburgh, and Bishop Edwards was elected president.[49] His opening address at the 1869 convention expressed anticipation that the antisecrecy cause would grow in strength and influence like the antislavery cause did.[50] Soon after its organization the National Christian Association began to publish the *Christian Cynosure.* At that time opposition to secret societies was meager. But by the late 1870s, the editor of the *Cynosure* named thirty-six church papers which were antisecrecy. And some secular newspapers and magazines, including the *New York Times,* the *Philadelphia Press,* and *Harper's Weekly,* on occasions condemned secret societies.[51]

Within his own church Edwards faced a minority who favored leniency toward secret societies, thinking this necessary to succeed in large towns and cities, where these societies were popular. Those holding this view came to be known as "Liberals." At the General Conference of 1869 a minority report on secret societies presented the views and recommendations of this group. The majority report held to the traditional restrictive position and aimed to make more certain that the law was enforced. Delegates debated these reports the sixth and seventh days and half of the eighth. On this topic the bishops had said in their address to the conference:

. . . It seems to us that the question is *not* whether a change in the law would increase our numbers and wealth, but would it tend to increase our spirituality and power for good? Could we do more for Christ and his spiritual kingdom if that law were removed? There was a time in the history of this church when it was said that we could do more for God and his cause if we would expunge our rule against slavery. The majority did not think so; and now we have reason to be grateful that we stood firm. The same may be true if we remain steadfast in our opposition to secret societies.

The majority of the delegates shared the views of the bishops. The vote was 72 to 25 to adopt the majority report.

From 1869 the two sides became more polarized, and voting for officials seemed to reflect the positions on the secrecy issue. Liberals became more vocal and grew in number as the years passed. They favored limiting the Constitution's "no connection with secret combinations" to oath-bound societies, or changing the Constitution to only *advise* against such connection. However, the "Radicals" or "Conservatives," who wanted to maintain the constitutional prohibition against secret societies, continued to hold the balance of power in the General Conferences of 1873 and 1877.

The *Discipline* could be changed by action of a majority of a general conference, but changing any part of the Constitution was not so simple. An explicit interpretation of Article IV *(There shall be no alteration of the foregoing constitution, unless by request of two-thirds of the whole society.)* was requested of the bishops by the General Conference of 1873. This interpretation was to be given after the close of the conference and published in the *Religious Telescope*. But the bishops could not agree on an interpretation.[52]

Liberals chafed under the restrictions of the Constitution and *Discipline* and the frustration of not knowing how and when the Constitution could be changed. Some extremists openly encouraged disregard of the secrecy law. They argued that it was against the spirit of the gospel, it limited the influence and growth of the church, and if enforced would divide or destroy some congregations.

In the revision of *Discipline* at the General Conference of 1877, majority and minority reports on the secret combinations section were read. The discussion of these reports was confined to a part of an afternoon and an evening. Presiding Bishop Glossbrenner "urged economy of time. He said a week's discussion would not make any converts." The majority report, signed by Milton Wright and Nicholas Castle, both of whom at this conference were elected bishops for the first time, by J. W. Hott, who succeeded Wright as editor of the *Religious Telescope,* and by M. L. Tibbetts, was adopted by a vote of 71 to 31. For the next eight years the *Discipline* read:

> We believe that secret societies are evil in their nature and tendency; that they employ solemn oaths and obligations for evil and unworthy ends; that they bind men together in brotherhood with wicked and unholy persons, and bring them into fellowship not consistent with the teachings of our Lord and his apostles; that they tend to produce jealousies and alienations in the Church of God; that they employ the forms of religion in unwarranted services and ceremonies, not in the name of Christ nor founded on the merits of his atonement; that they enjoin under oaths and solemn obligations obedience to laws and regulations unknown to the civil government within which they are organized, or to any government divinely ordained; that they pervert the Holy Scriptures to foolish

and unholy uses; that their ceremonies encourage many of their adherents in hopes of eternal life without a truly evangelical faith; that they are contrary to that openness of conduct and guilelessness of character enjoined by the word of God, and that Christians should not be connected with them, for the apostle expressly says: "Be ye not unequally yoked together with unbelievers; for what fellowship hath righteousness with unrighteousness? and what communion hath light with darkness? and what concord hath Christ with Belial? or what part hath he that believeth with an infidel?" "Wherefore come out from among them and be ye separate, saith the Lord, and touch not the unclean thing, and I will receive you, and will be a father unto you, and ye shall be my sons and daughters, saith the Lord Almighty."

1. Any member or preacher who shall connect himself with a secret society shall be regarded as having thereby declared that he prefers such society to the fellowship of our church, and shall be considered as having withdrawn from the church.

2. No person shall be permitted to join our church while holding membership in a secret society.

3. If any member or preacher, at the time of the passage of this rule, be connected with a secret society, and does not discontinue such connection within six months thereafter, his failure to do so shall be regarded as a refusal to comply with the condition of membership as found in our Constitution (Article II, Section 7), and his severance from the church shall be entered on the church records.

Other paragraphs dealt with what to do in cases of denial or concealment of connection with a secret society, in cases of withdrawals, and with the duties of pastors to instruct, warn, and reclaim. The final paragraph was:

Provided, That in case a member has been deceived and thereby drawn into any of those societies commonly called minor orders, he may be borne with for a reasonable time, if there be reason to believe that he may be reclaimed; but the time shall not extend beyond twelve months in any case.

One delegate stated that such a law would "not be enforced," and that he would "be no party to it." Another opponent called the majority report a "damnable paper," and "the most infamous document ever offered to this church."[53]

Following the adoption of the majority report, a protest, signed by twenty-two delegates, was read:

WHEREAS, The General Conference has this day adopted an antisecrecy law, which, in its mode of operation, in our opinion, stands directly opposed to the enlightened sentiment of Protestant christendom, the reason, conscience, and practice of this church and of the Bible; therefore we, the undersigned, enter our most solemn protest against such sentiment, and wash our hands of the consequences to this church resulting from the passage of this law.[54]

The General Conference of 1881 did not change the section on secret societies, and it adopted a moral reform report which included this resolution: "That our opposition to all secret combinations remains unabated; and our Christian efforts for their final overthrow shall be exerted until that end is accomplished."[55]

At the General Conference of 1881 the Liberals championed the cause of pro-rata representation (representation according to the number of members) and won by a narrow margin, 60 to 57. This ensured a Liberal majority in the General Conference of 1885, because the eastern and central conferences, which had more members, had many Liberal leaders.

Bishop Weaver, in the February 25, 1885, *Religious Telescope* argued for a change in the secrecy law, to one that only advised against connection with secret orders. The church needed this change to reach people in large towns and cities, he said. If the church could succeed in urban areas, Weaver reasoned, it would consequently gain the needed improvement in ministerial support and financial help for its institutions. "We are living in another age," he said, "with vastly different surroundings, and our ecclesiastical machinery must be adjusted to meet these days, and not the days of our fathers." He maintained he had not changed his views of secret societies, just his idea of how to deal with them.

Earlier Weaver had supported the secrecy law. In 1862, three years before he was first elected bishop, he published a pamphlet "A Lecture on Secret Societies." Scriptures were presented in opposition to secret societies, and arguments against compromise, cooperation, or leniency with these societies. He declared:

> . . . It is impossible, as it seems to me, from the nature of the two things, to be a consistent member of Christ's Church, and at the same time a consistent member of a secret society. He must violate the rules of one or the other of the institutions.

The pamphlet pointed out that the denomination had stood against lodgery, and still it "steadily increased in number, . . . two hundred percent stronger now than . . . twenty years ago." Weaver stated further that "those who think it is not incompatible with the gospel to be a member of a secret society, can find a home in churches that do not make it a test of membership."

The bishops' address to the General Conference of 1885, written by first-term Bishop E. B. Kephart, recommended that the conference determine if the whole subject of secret societies could be transferred from constitutional law to legislative enactment—which would allow any general conference to revise the secrecy rule in any way it chose. The address also recommended that the prohibitory feature of the legislation be limited "to combinations secret and open, to which the church believes a Christian cannot belong." In case the conference decided that this constitutional question was beyond their control and in the hands of the whole society, the address recommended submitting the proposition to a vote of the whole church and "let a two-thirds vote *of those voting* be the authoritative voice of the church on the subject." (The emphasis is added.)

The Liberal majority acted upon these recommendations in spite of resistance and protest by Radicals. When the General Conference of 1885 adjourned, the *Discipline* section on secret societies had been revised to read:

> A secret combination, in the sense of the constitution, is a secret league or confederation of persons holding principles and laws at variance with the word of God and injurious to Christian character, as evidenced in individual life, and infringing upon the natural, social, political, or religious rights of those outside its pale.
>
> Any member or minister of our church found in connection with such combination shall be dealt with as in other cases of disobedience to the order and discipline of the Church, . . .

Those voting for the change numbered 76; voting against it were 38 members of the conference, including Bishops John Dickson and Nicholas Castle. Six did not vote. Those against it preferred the much more specific and prohibitory section it replaced. They believed it would open the church to all kinds of lodge members, and that there would be little that could be done to stop their joining the church. Further, they thought it violated the Constitution ("there shall be no connection with secret combinations").

William Dillon remarked of the new secret society section: "The heart and life of that law was taken out, leaving nothing but a change-able swivel, and unconstitutional at that."[56] The *Dayton Daily Journal* of May 25, 1885, said this of the revision: "It strikes the death blow to what has always been one of the fundamental restrictions of the United Brethren Church. . . . the law as passed by this conference completely revolutionizes the church idea on this matter."

In connection with his vote on the section, Bishop Glossbrenner said:

It is known to the ministers of this church, east and west, north and south, that I have been recognized as a modificationist, for years, although I did not impose my views upon those with whom I associated. But these were my views, and for these of course I received some frowns and some sneers. But as regards Freemasonry, I never did and never can recognize it as an institution worthy of admission into the Church; but this law gives me and my Church the privilege of determining by the word of God whether that institution is contrary to the principles of Christianity or not, and with that view I say *yes.*[57]

Bishops Weaver and Kephart also voted *yes.* But Bishops Castle and Dickson voted *no,* with these explanations:

Castle—Fearing that this definition of the committee may be susceptible of a construction, in the light of the amendments offered, contravening the meaning of the constitution, I will have to answer *no.*

Dickson—As I understand, the paper as amended on last evening permits every Mason, admitted to be such, to be a *bona fide* member of the United Brethren Church, if the society wishes it so—with that understanding, and I think it is very clear—I say *no.*[58]

The two factions were characterized by the *Dayton Daily Journal* in its May 25, 1885, issue:

The liberals are men of advanced thought, men of religious progression, men who believe that the framers of the church constitution were not incapable of mistake. The radicals—and we speak from a disinterested standpoint and with no disrespect to them—seem to be men of one idea, namely, that it is an utter impossibility to mix Christianity and organized secrecy. So firmly has this idea taken possession of them that the magnificent oratory of the opposition was powerless to move them. . . . Many of the liberals are young men, men of education, of argument—the radicals are principally men whose ages are in keeping with their antiquated ideas, yet they are thoroughly earnest and sincere in the belief that this conference has made a grievous blunder.

Some, no doubt, saw the actions of this conference as a step toward union with the Evangelical Association, which had only an unwritten law against secret societies. A fraternal delegate from that church attended the United Brethren General Conference of 1885. A resolution favoring the union of these two denominations had been passed by the general convention of Liberals in Dayton in 1878.

By actions of the General Conference of 1885, the rift in the church became very pronounced. Other antisecrecy churches indicated their disapproval of the action of the general conference. The *Lutheran Standard* noted:

The United Brethren have permitted false notions of expediency to triumph over righteousness in their action on secretism. Once that denomination had a noble record on the subject; but it has been giving way to a craving for popularity, and finds the lodge too mighty a power to put under its feet. Its declarations against secretism do not amount to much while the door is thrown open for the admission of secretists. If these do not despise it for making concessions and turn all the more against it until it yields everything, they will be very likely to enter in and take possession, forcing the opposition to keep silence or leave the house. For those among the "Brethren" who were convinced of the sinfulness of the lodge the case has become distressing. Whether they will have the grace to stand up for the right and rather to suffer than yield to the encroachments of lodgery, time will show.[59]

FOOTNOTES

[1]*Religious Telescope,* September 2, 1863.

[2]Bernard L. Cook and John E. Branson, *Seedtime and Harvest: A History of the Kansas Conference of the Church of the United Brethren in Christ, Part I 1853-1882 and Part II 1883-1914* (Theses presented in partial fulfillment of the requirements for the degree of Bachelor of Divinity, Bonebrake Theological Seminary, 1942, 1943), pp. 18, 19.

[3]Daniel Kumler Flickinger, *Fifty-five Years of Active Ministerial Life* (Dayton, OH: United Brethren Publishing House, 1907), pp. 72, 73.

[4]*Third Annual Report of the Board of Missions of the United Brethren in Christ* (Dayton, OH: United Brethren Printing Establishment, 1856), p. 44.

[5]Cook and Branson, p. 6.

[6]W. M. Weekley and H. H. Fout, *Our Heroes or United Brethren Home Missionaries* (Dayton, OH: United Brethren Home Missionary Society, 1908), p. 226.

[7]*Religious Telescope,* October 15, 1856; *Third Annual Report of the Board of Missions,* p. 46.

[8]Cook and Branson, p. 6.

[9]Lewis Davis, *The Life of Rev. David Edwards,* 3rd ed. (Dayton, OH: United Brethren Publishing House, 1883), p. 163.

[10]*Third Annual Report of the Board of Missions,* pp. 41, 42.

[11]Ibid., p. 44; Flickinger, pp. 63, 55; Weekley and Fout, pp. 136, 137; Davis, pp. 237, 238.

[12]*Proceedings of the Eleventh General Conference of the United Brethren in Christ* (Circleville, OH: United Brethren Printing Establishment, 1853), p. 28.

[13]John Lawrence, *The Slavery Question,* 2nd ed. (Dayton, OH: Conference Printing Establishment of the United Brethren in Christ, 1854), p. iii.

[14]*Religious Telescope,* April 29, 1857.

[15]Lawrence, p. iv.

[16]Ibid., p. 168.

[17]J. L. Luttrell, *History of the Auglaize Annual Conference of the United Brethren Church, from 1853 to 1891* (Dayton, OH: United Brethren Publishing House for the author, 1892), pp. 89-99.

[18]*Autobiography of Rev. James G. Baldwin* (Dayton, OH: United Brethren Publishing House for East Ohio Conference of the United Brethren in Christ, 1912), p. 52; J. K. Alwood's "life was threatened because he preached against human slavery." *Christian Conservator,* February 17, 1909.

[19]*Proceedings of the Thirteenth General Conference of the United Brethren in Christ,*

1861 (microfilm of manuscript journal), pp. 299, 300.

[20]Harold B. Hancock, *The History of Otterbein College 1930-1972* (n.p., [ca. 1972]), p. 6.

[21]Delbert R. Krumm, *A History of the Scioto, Southeast and Ohio Southeast Conferences* (Ohio Southeast Conference, Evangelical United Brethren Church, 1958), p. 16; Henry Garst, *Otterbein University 1847-1907* (Dayton, OH: United Brethren Publishing House, 1907), pp. 136-144; "The Ohio Story," a tape recording about Hanby and "My Darling Nellie Gray" (Ohio Bell Telephone Co., n.d.); in his thirty-three years, B. R. Hanby, a United Brethren minister, and a teacher, wrote eighty songs, hymns, and minstrel airs, among them, "Who Is He in Yonder Stall?" and "Up on the Housetop."

[22]Augustus W. Drury, *History of the Church of the United Brethren in Christ* (Dayton, OH: Otterbein Press, 1924), pp. 626, 627.

[23]John H. Ness, Jr. *One Hundred Fifty Years, a History of Publishing in the Evangelical United Brethren Church* (Dayton, OH: Board of Publication of the Evangelical United Brethren Church, 1966), pp. 356, 364.

[24]Drury, p. 565.

[25]Davis, p. 223.

[26]Marion R. Drury, *The Life and Career of James William Hott* (Dayton, OH: United Brethren Publishing House, 1902), p. 51.

[27]Henry A. Thompson, *Our Bishops,* rev. ed. (Dayton, OH: United Brethren Publishing House, 1903), pp. 439, 441.

[28]Augustus W. Drury, *The Life of Bishop J. J. Glossbrenner* (Dayton, OH: United Brethren Publishing House for John Dodds, 1889), pp. 177-185.

[29]In his *Fifty-five Years,* Flickinger wrote, "We spent three-quarters of an hour with the President. The President was in his shirt sleeves, and much care worn, yet took ample time to consider all we said to him." pp. 73, 74.

[30]After the Union victory at Vicksburg, Negroes by the thousands went there, hoping to go from there up the Mississippi River to the North.

[31]Flickinger, pp. 72-74.

[32]*Proceedings of the Fourteenth General Conference of the United Brethren in Christ* (Dayton, OH: United Brethren Printing Establishment, 1865), pp. 10, 11.

[33]Henry A. Thompson, *Biography of Jonathan Weaver* (Dayton, OH: United Brethren Publishing House, 1901), p. 131.

[34]*Proceedings of the Seventeenth General Conference of the United Brethren in Christ* (Dayton, OH: United Brethren Publishing House, 1877), p. 172.

[35]*Religious Telescope,* April 12, 1876.

[36]Thompson, *Biography of Jonathan Weaver,* pp. 150, 151.

[37]This action in 1849 was taken "with the utmost enthusiasm and without a single dissenting voice." Drury, *History of the Church of the United Brethren in Christ,* p. 433. In 1845 a motion was adopted to keep the *Discipline* section on ardent spirits as it was instead of including a prohibition of *use* as a beverage. The vote was 14 for, 7 against, and 5 not voting.

[38]*Proceedings of the Seventeenth General Conference of the United Brethren in Christ,* pp. 161, 162.

[39]Garst, *Otterbein University,* p. 150; O. W. Pentzer, *Hartsville College 1850-1897* (Columbus, IN: O. W. Pentzer & Son, 1928), p. 11.

[40]Davis, p. 224.

[41]*Proceedings of the Eighteenth General Conference of the United Brethren in Christ* (Dayton, OH: United Brethren Publishing House, 1881), p. 185.

[42]"Freemasonry in every sense of the word shall be totally prohibited, and there shall be no connection with secret combinations. A secret combination is one whose initia-

tory ceremony or bond of union is secret. And any member found connected with such a society shall be affectionately admonished twice or thrice by the preacher in charge, and if such member does not desist in a reasonable time he shall be notified to appear before the tribunal to which he is amenable, and if he still refuses to desist shall be expelled from the church." *Discipline,* section on secret societies, 1849-1861.

"We believe that secret societies are evil in their nature and tendency; (a secret society is one whose initiatory ceremony or bond of union is a secret;) and any member or preacher of our Church who shall be found connected, in any way, with such a society, shall be dealt with, as in case of other immorality, according to sections eighteen and nineteen of Discipline, respectively." *Discipline,* section on secret societies, 1861-1869.

[43]Davis, p. 131.

[44]Ness, *One Hundred Fifty Years,* pp. 323, 324.

[45]John Lawrence, *Plain Thoughts on Secret Societies,* 3rd ed. (Circleville, OH: Religious Telescope Printing Office, 1852), pp. 199, 215, 216.

[46]*Proceedings of the Eleventh General Conference of the United Brethren in Christ,* p. 28.

[47]Davis, p. 202.

[48]Clyde S. Kilby, *Minority of One, A Biography of Jonathan Blanchard* (Grand Rapids, MI: Eerdmans, 1959), pp. 168, 169.

[49]*Religious Telescope,* June 27, 1883.

[50]Davis, pp. 237, 264.

[51]Kilby, p. 183.

[52]*Board of Bishops Minutes* (manuscript).

[53]*Proceedings of the Seventeenth General Conference of the United Brethren in Christ,* p. 157.

[54]Ibid., p. 160.

[55]*Proceedings of the Eighteenth General Conference of the United Brethren in Christ,* p. 185.

[56]*Proceedings of the Nineteenth General Conference of the United Brethren in Christ* (Dayton, OH: United Brethren Publishing House, 1885), p. 237.

[57]Ibid., pp. 235, 236.

[58]Ibid., p. 236.

[59]*Christian Conservator,* July 15, 1885.

23

DISCORD AND DIVISION

Resistance to the Secrecy Law

Discord over "the vexed question" of secret societies surfaced in and between every general conference from 1869 to 1889.

White River Conference showed one of the first signs of organized resistance to the secrecy law of the church. In June 1869, representatives from a few churches met in a convention and declared that the secrecy rule was "impractical and injurious." Consequently a few members of the conference withdrew or were expelled.[1]

In September 1873, some members of East Pennsylvania Conference began the *United Brethren Tribune* in the interests of the Liberal viewpoint on lay and pro-rata representation in general conference and on the secrecy law. The *Tribune* advocated making the law much less severe or repealing it, and in the meanwhile ignoring it.[2] The *Religious Telescope* and several annual conferences denounced the *Tribune,* which was renamed *United Brethren Observer* in March 1876, and apparently discontinued in 1879. Another prominent Liberal publication was the *Monthly Itinerant* (1876-1888), from East Pennsylvania Conference.[3]

Pennsylvania Conference in 1876 by a vote of 24 for, 15 against, and 4 neutral, adopted a statement on the secrecy question:

> Resolved, that as a conference we favor the abrogation of our present law (on secret societies) and the passage of one more in harmony with our practice and the holy word of God, and more compatible with the magnanimous spirit of our church and nation.[4]

Bishop Edwards was stationed on the East District of the church in

1873 "that he might correct, if possible, the very general disregard of the restrictive rule on secret societies that prevailed in some of the conferences." The last annual conference attended by Edwards before his death, June 1876, was the conference in West Virginia in March of that year.

> At this session he ruled against sending before the committee an applicant for license to preach, who was understood to be connected with the Odd-fellows. His ruling in the case was appealed from, and the appeal sustained by the conference. . . . The bishop understood it to be a deliberate attempt to set at naught the rule of the church on secret societies.[5]

A convention of Liberal ministers and laymen from several annual conferences met at Harrisburg, Pennsylvania, July 11 and 12, 1877. The two prime subjects were what course to pursue to counteract the influence of the secrecy legislation of 1877, and how best to promote pro-rata representation in general conference. In a letter to this convention, William McKee of Miami Conference, who had been missionary treasurer 1869-1873, wrote of the church making changes "Peaceably if it can, forcibly if it must, through the constitution or over it." The convention resolved: "We firmly believe that duty . . . requires at our hands to decline to enforce or execute said [secrecy] law, . . ." and "That we respectfully claim the right to control our contributions for general church work until such time as a just and fair representation shall be obtained."[6]

Another Liberal convention had been held at Westerville, Ohio, May 30, 1877. Ministers of the East Allegheny Conference met for the same reason on June 28, 1877. The Westerville and Allegheny conventions adopted this resolution: "That we pronounce an earnest judgment against the recently enacted secrecy law, and therefore shall proceed in the treatment of members who may belong to secret societies as our judgment may dictate with a view to saving souls."[7] The Allegheny convention also adopted this preamble:

> Whereas, the late general conference convened at Westfield, Ill., May 10th, 1877, refused to grant the just request of a modification of the present unjust system of representation, a system which gives a conference of 500 members as much legislative authority, as a conference having 9,500 members. And whereas, such an unjust system of representation can never command the respect of an enlightened judgment, and is entirely repulsive to the affections of our hearts. And whereas, delegates representing the rural districts, who are not acquainted with the circumstances affecting the cities and manufacturing centres, have unwisely and unrighteously passed the Tate law on secrecy.[8]

Many of the recorded speeches and letters to these conventions included plain avowals to ignore the church's law on secrecy. Sandusky Conference minister D. R. Miller said that many in Ohio felt they had to decide between nullification and destruction, and, therefore, chose the former. Isaac Crouse, of Sandusky Conference, and general secretary of the Sabbath-School Association 1865-1877, agreed with Miller about the losses that would result from enforcement of the law. He proposed that annual conferences singly or unitedly take action by making a declaration of principle and purpose to reform the law, and that some plan be made to consolidate the strength of sympathetic laymen.[9]

However, an Allegheny Conference minister cautioned that because "in the membership of our congregations we have too many who are in sympathy with the law policy—not the late law so much as the former—" there should not be too much haste in acting.[10]

A contrasting convention of 134 ministers and laymen of Pennsylvania Conference took place November 13-15, 1877 at Salem Church, near Chambersburg. Its purpose: "To rebuke and counteract the spirit of nullification in this Church and to express a hearty approval of the proceedings of the late general conference."[11] This convention warned: "The spirit [of subversiveness], if unrebuked, would encourage and give a precedent to minorities on all questions, in all time to come, to nullify and thereby bring certain and speedy disintegration to our beloved Zion."[12]

In the sessions of Pennsylvania Conference immediately following these conventions, the presiding bishops and a majority of the members of the conference acted in sympathy with the Liberal conventions. Ministers who objected to the secrecy law not being enforced and who encouraged the separation of law-abiding members were censured, put on probation, and ordered not to preach to congregations that had separated from Liberal classes. One of these ministers was suspended for one year and expelled the next. At the same time a minister who was a Mason was given an honorable dismissal.[13]

Ministers in Sandusky Conference in favor of modification of the secrecy law were invited to a council the evening preceding the 1877 annual conference session. At this meeting it was resolved that the secrecy law should not be enforced, because, they said, it was "unwise, unjust, and not in harmony with the spirit of the Gospel of Christ," and if enforced "would produce results seriously detrimental to the interests of this conference and the Church generally."[14]

A Liberal convention of ministers and laymen from thirteen conferences—mainly conferences in Ohio, Pennsylvania, Virginia, and West Virginia—and three delegates at large, including Bishop Weaver, met May 21-23, 1878, at Dayton, Ohio, in the First United Brethren Church. Pro-rata representation, lay representation, and the secrecy law were the main topics considered. A West Virginia minister called the work of the convention "that of liberating our common Zion from the fetters that have been bound about her by a few men in the church."[15] Z. Warner, a leader in Parkersburg Conference and one of the first to publicly oppose a secrecy law, declared:

> [General conference] may become an irresponsible despotism, whose oppressive acts may precipitate rebellion. Men are not bound to accept and be held by everything that may be the polity of the church they join. Much less are they bound by what the church may afterward do or require.[16]

The convention appointed a central committee of three ministers and four laymen and instructed the committee to appoint for each bishop's district an executive committee who were to appoint sub-committees in each annual conference to promote reforms sought by Liberals.

H. A. Thompson wrote in his biography of Bishop Weaver that in 1878 a number of annual conferences passed strong resolutions opposing secrecy and against nullification and revolutions in the church. Thompson no doubt was referring to the conferences in Weaver's district, which included ones in Michigan, Indiana, and Illinois.[17]

Bishop Weaver defended his adherence to the laws of the church in an 1880 *Religious Telescope*. Then he went on about the dissension in the church:

> For more than ten years I have witnessed with deep concern a growing restlessness in the church. Men of long standing in our denomination have changed their views, not so much in regard to secrecy itself, as in reference to the manner of dealing with it. Without attempting to conceal or exaggerate the matter, the fact is before us that there are two parties in the Church. Another fact is, that there is danger of a rupture. I have heard men on both sides of this question say, "Let it come; we are ready." I do not feel thus; we are not ready. There is too much at stake. Those who remain near at home, whose duties do not require them to travel throughout the whole church do not, and cannot know the extent of this restlessness. To prevent what I most dread, I have counseled moderation on both sides.[18]

Developments 1881-1885

Attempts were made in the General Conference of 1881 to amend the *Discipline* to make more explicit the duties of bishops and ministers to enforce all the laws, and to require that none be elected as presiding elders who did not uphold the laws. A spokesman for the Liberals, William McKee, declared:

> Once for all, these brethren ought to learn that they can not enforce such measures. The conference will not heed them. Some of the conferences, at least, have taken their position on this vexed question; and they will not recede from said position. You can not coax them, or frighten them by threats, or bind them by additional laws. . . . You have not the power to thrust these measures on the conferences that do not approve them. . . . [19]

In the General Conference of 1881 the most significant legislation relating to the dissension in the church was the adoption of a modified pro-rata representation. This meant a change from general conference delegates representing territory—which, some argued, was more unifying for the church—to representing numbers of members. Liberals hailed this plan as saving the church from a practice that was unfair to the older conferences, which had the largest memberships and gave the most money.

The most significant election of 1881 was the replacement of Bishop Wright of the Radical persuasion by Ezekiel Kephart of the Liberal persuasion. Before the year ended, Wright, in addition to his work as presiding elder in White River Conference, began editing and publishing on behalf of the Radical cause. Earlier, Radicals in Pennsylvania had organized the United Brethren Association and began, in 1879, publishing the *United Brethren in Christ* to articulate their views.

Pleading for "charity and sweetness of spirit" in the "struggle on the secrecy question," Bishop Weaver, in a *Religious Telescope* article in 1882, said, "Many things have been said and done that were not in harmony with the mood and spirit of Christ." He advised, "Stand firmly by the long-established principles of our Church." Then he went on:

> A man may be sound in principle and wrong in method. Concerning any matter not clearly defined in the Word of God, we may be mistaken. . . . It seems to me that any method, however wise it may seem to be, which does not aim at the salvation of the soul is not of God.[20]

A young North Ohio minister, W. H. Clay, in rebuttal of the argument that many secret orders did not have the objectionable character of Freemasonry, wrote a tract "The Lodge in the Light of the Word." This was first issued in 1884. Clay concluded that, after its downfall in the 1830s, Masonry had reestablished itself through subsidiary orders: "The least secret order . . . makes way for others . . . so stealthy and effectual has been the march of lodgery

upon the churches that for the most part they are helplessly enslaved."
Edwards, Davis, Wright, and others also believed that there was an
interrelatedness of secret societies.

In 1883 and 1884, twenty of the forty-six annual conferences passed
resolutions to maintain the secrecy law. These were reported in the
Religious Telescope.[21] Allegheny Conference, in 1884, passed a resolution asking the next general conference to modify or annul the law.[22]

In the June 11, 1884, *Religious Telescope,* Lewis Davis called for
maintaining the secrecy law, and for church authorities to insist that
the rule be enforced and opposition to it cease. "If this cannot be done,"
said Davis, "church authority among us is little more than a rope of
sand."

"The Outlook," an article on the church controversy, by Bishop
Weaver, appeared in the February 25, 1885, *Religious Telescope.*
Weaver said he had canvassed the church east and west and was of the
opinion that nine-tenths of the members, ministers and all, were
opposed to secret organizations. But, he added, he had found "a
difference of opinion concerning the best manner of dealing with
them." He said he did not think the present secrecy law was or would be
enforced by a good many of the ministers. He thought this law seemed
not to rest upon the principles and spirit of the gospel of Christ. His big
objection seemed to be that the *Discipline* provided restoration after
other offenses, but not after joining a secret order, except the minor
orders. He said this confused members and divided the denomination.

Much of Weaver's article presented Liberal arguments against the
secrecy law: the law antagonized lodge members and all who were in
sympathy with the lodge, and so shut the church out of large towns and
cities. Consequently the church was denied influence and money
needed to support its institutions and ministers. To meet the changing
times, Weaver said, it was necessary to modify the secrecy law. He
favored submitting a proposed change to the membership and letting
two-thirds of those voting settle the issue. Two-thirds of those voting
was, he thought, a reasonable construction of Article IV of the Constitution. That spring Weaver wrote: "I hold it is the prerogative of any
general conference subsequent to 1841 to change, modify, or rescind
any part of the constitution that was put there by the General Conference of 1841."

Two weeks before the General Conference of 1885, Editor Hott
wrote in the *Telescope:* "Our whole statement of law is destined to be
changed. . . . Those whose hairs are gray may oppose it, if they will,
but it will be of no avail."

Clearly there were two factions in the church. Debate in this general conference would be crucial in winning any fence-riders. Lewis Davis was known as one of the strongest debaters at general conference for years. He was described by H. A. Thompson, biographer of the bishops, as "an open, fair antagonist, but his sledge-hammer blows were blows the opposition did not care to meet." The Liberals knew, wrote William Dillon,

> that they could never carry their retrogressive ends while Dr. Davis had a chance to perforate their secular gew-gaws. Their line of tactics to prevent his election to General Conference [in 1885], which was accomplished by means that will never bear the light; an example of which, we had certain information.[23]

The Conflict Grows in the 1885 General Conference

The bishops' address, at the opening of the conference, made it clear that the Liberals had a plan to get what they wanted, and that they were going to be bold and daring, as some of them had been for several years. The address, mainly the work of Bishop Kephart, stated that the church expected this conference to put to rest the perplexing subject of secret societies and bring peace to the church. To that end the bishops recommended: 1) that the conference decide if the Constitution was in the hands of the conference; 2) if so, that the subject of secret societies be expunged from the Constitution and brought into the field of legislative enactment; 3) that the prohibitory feature of the secrecy law be limited to combinations to which the church believes a Christian cannot belong; and 4) if the Constitution is not in the control of the general conference, but in the hands of the whole church, that the conference submit propositions two and three to a vote of the church, and a *two-thirds vote of those voting* decide the matter.

Through their address and committee appointments, the bishops called for a consideration of the fundamental documents of the church. Bishop Dickson, however, on the afternoon of the second day, made this statement:

> . . . I was not at the meeting of the Board of Bishops when this address was adopted, and did not see it until it was in print with my name affixed to it. Of course, not being there was my own fault. But after reading it I can say I heartily concur with all that there is in it with the exception of what pertains to the constitution and confession of faith being acted upon by the Church. I do not concur in that at all. I think it would lead to serious difficulty in the Church. I just give my views why I dissent. I will not argue it, sir. Perhaps it is enough for me to say here that I never have and never will concur in that part of the address.

Committee No. Six of this general conference and its reports resulted in the most controversy in the history of the denomination. It was intended that the committee and its work would settle the conflict in the church, but instead the conflict was heightened. To this thirteen-member committee the bishops gave the responsibility to deal with the revision of the Confession of Faith, the Constitution, and the secret combinations section of the *Discipline.*

On the afternoon of the sixth day the committee reported. The main points of the report were: 1) the Constitution was never ratified; 2) its legality and binding force as organic law was and had been questioned; 3) the article on not changing or doing away with the Confession of Faith, and the article calling for a request of *two-thirds of the whole society* to alter the Constitution "are in their language and apparent meaning so far-reaching as to render them extraordinary and impracticable as articles of constitutional law." 4) "The general conference has a right to institute measures looking to the amendment, modification, or change of the Constitution at any time when it is believed that a majority of our people favor a modification thereof." 5) The Constitution was not in harmony with the wishes of the church members. 6) A church commission was to be elected to prepare an amended Confession of Faith that would preserve unchanged in substance the present Confession, so far as it was clear. Also the commission was to formulate an amended Constitution that would preserve the general usages and distinctive principles of the church as sustained by the Word of God. The proposed amended documents agreed on by a majority of the commission would be voted on by the membership. *If two-thirds of those voting gave their approval this would ratify the proposed Confession of Faith and Constitution.*

A minority report of Committee No. Six was given by J. G. Mosher and William Dillon. Their conclusions were:

1. The constitution we now have in the Discipline, and have had for forty-four years, is the constitution of the Church of the United Brethren in Christ, and every member legally received into the Church for years has consented to be governed by the same. It was declared legal also by the General Conference of 1849, and to it our legislation has conformed, and under its directions our officers have been elected and the General Conference formed according to its provisions.

2. This constitution makes no provision for the General Conference to alter or change it without first securing the consent of the members of the Church by a two-thirds vote, as required in Article IV of the constitution, and to take any other method would not be legal.

3. It is our view that this question as to the constitution should be determined before we revise Section 3 of Chapter X [secret combinations section].

Consideration of these reports continued for about a day and a half. The legality and authority of the Constitution was a major topic of debate. Liberals argued that it had only legislative authority, and hence could be changed by the general conference. Radicals contended that the Constitution was fundamental authority and could be changed only according to its provision. Some Radicals believed that it was intended that the Constitution be very difficult to change, that only *two-thirds of the church members could change it,* and that until the constitutional provision for change was tried, it was not fair to call the provision impracticable.

During the discussion, Milton Wright indicated a willingness to change the Constitution: "We are ready to adopt a change when we see and believe that the people want it. You may formulate it and send it down to the people, and, with a constitutional majority, it becomes a part of our organic law."

A strong objection to the church commission plan was that the general conference would be delegating power to a twenty-seven man commission to formulate a new Confession of Faith and a new Constitution. Opposers said the general conference could not delegate this power to the commission. Radicals said the general conference should formulate and decide on proposed constitutional changes to be submitted to the people. Liberals insisted there was not time to do so during the conference. In addition to the five bishops, the commission was to be made up of ministers and laymen elected by the general conference. The Constitution said: "All ecclesiastical power herein granted to make or repeal any rule of discipline is vested in a general conference." And membership in general conference, as prescribed by the Constitution, was limited to ministers who had been elders in their conferences at least three years. Radicals also objected that the general conference would have no opportunity to approve or disapprove what would be submitted to the church for vote.

The commission plan provided that *two-thirds of those voting* would be sufficient to adopt the proposed Confession of Faith and proposed Constitution. Liberals defended this, arguing that the general conference had the authority to interpret and construe the *"two-thirds of the whole society"* of Article IV of the Constitution to mean *two-thirds of those voting.* All in all the commission plan was, in the words of Milton Wright, "one of disputed legality, and on that subject there was allowed scarcely any discussion at all."[24] As to what was published in the proceedings of the General Conference of 1885 of speeches against the commission plan, Halleck Floyd later testified that the published speeches were "simply short extracts and frequently very unsatisfactory."[25]

When the vote was taken on the majority report of Committee No. Six, 78 delegates voted *yes;* 42 voted *no.*

Since there had been no request sent to general conference to change the Constitution or Confession of Faith, Radicals thought Liberals were putting the cart before the horse. They thought the plan should have been to determine first if the membership generally wanted a change or changes, and if the desire for change was strong, then formulate proposals at general conference and submit them to the members for their vote. Thirty-one delegates entered a protest against the adoption of the majority report of Committee No. Six:

> WHEREAS, We have assembled with this General Conference in good faith to promote its interests, and legislate in harmony with the constitution of the church; and
>
> WHEREAS, We believe that this body in its action in forming a commission for the revision of our confession of faith and the constitution of the Church has transcended its constitutional authority, and instituted an illegal plan (not the one provided in the constitution) for change, and legislated a rule not in harmony with the constitution, but equivocal and capable of varied construction in order, as we think, to make it ineffectual and worthless; therefore, we determine to stand by the constitution and never to submit to any change therein, unless it is effected in harmony with its provisions; and we hereby earnestly and solemnly protest against all such action.
>
> Halleck Floyd, Milton Wright, J. M. Kabrich, W. H. Clay, J. L. Luttrell, Wm. Dillon, J. W. Lilly, H. T. Barnaby, W. H. Chandler, J. K. Alwood, A. B. Powell, G. A. Bowles, J. H. Grimm, H. A. Long, B. H. Mowers, A. W. Geeslin, D. B. Sherk, J. Fry, J. Breden, R. H. Watson, W. S. Spooner, A. J. Newgent, D. A. Beauchamp, William Miller, J. Noel, F. J. Crowder, Daniel Shuck, David Shuck, Geo. Plowman, John Riley, W. P. Caldwell, J. G. Mosher, J. N. Lemasters, and L. L. Hager.

In view of the size of the vote for adopting the work of Committee No. Six, Milton Wright's election as bishop of the Pacific Coast district surprised many. *Religious Telescope* editor, J. W. Hott, probably would have been elected, but after the first two ballots, which he led by a considerable margin, he said he could not go to the coast because of his wife's health. The *Dayton Daily Journal* (May 27, 1885) said: "A number of liberals excused themselves for voting for him [Wright] by stating that his election would send him clear across the Rocky Mountains, where he could not disturb them." Wright would spend about six months of each of the next four years on the coast, and the remainder of time at his home in Dayton, Ohio.

One of the last acts of the General Conference of 1885 was the adoption of this resolution: *"Resolved,* By the General Conference of the United Brethren in Christ, here assembled, that the General Conference of our church is, and is hereby declared to be, the highest judicial authority of our church." This was described by the *Dayton Daily Journal* (May 29, 1885) as "the liberals clinching their grand success. . . . This was evidently done to head off any move the radicals might hereafter make on the secret organization matter, regarding the constitutionality of the action of the conference."

A *Religious Telescope* editorial following the conference indicated that the policy of the church organ would be in recognition and support of the actions of the conference: "The Commission for the revision of the Constitution and Confession of Faith of the Church is now a fact in our Church, and it is to be so regarded by all."

Radicals Form Constitutional Association

The Radicals responded to the conference and the *Telescope* policy by organizing a Constitutional Association, a united effort to uphold the Constitution and Confession of Faith, and to protest the commission plan. The association published the *Christian Conservator,* beginning in July 1885, with William Dillon as editor. By 1889 its circulation reached about 3000, one-fourth that of the *Religious Telescope.* The association held general conventions annually, 1885-1888. These were not largely attended on account of distance and expense, but at each successive one the interest and attendance grew. At the 1888 convention 245 attended. The first general convention in Hartsville, Indiana, August 1885, was attended by 80 persons. At this convention the signatures of 5000 persons were displayed, protesting the commission plan. By November the number of signatures was about 9000.[26] The convention resolved to "consider the law of 1877 [on secret combinations] still in force." Another resolution exhorted those in sympathy with the convention to be generous in supporting local interests and institutions of the church "so far as they are established and run on a loyal basis." The Hartsville convention also resolved:

> That the method proposed in the commission act by which to change the Constitution is a plain violation of its own provisions in language and in spirit; that it clearly disregards the guaranteed rights of the people in taking such a step without their knowledge or request; and that, in our opinion, said act is revolutionary and schismatic. For these reasons, and such as these, we solemnly declare that we will not cease to resist the commission act by all constitutional and lawful methods known to the denomination.

Liberals Proceed with Commission Plan

Despite Radical resistance and protest, the Liberals went on with the commission plan. Soon after the general conference adjourned, the publishing house issued a fourteen page tract "The United Brethren Commission, Reasons for Its Creation, Its Constitutionality," prepared by Bishop Weaver. The last paragraph contained these sentences: "The commission ordered by the General Conference will meet and do its work. There need be no question about that."

Of the twenty-two men the general conference elected to the commission, three were leading laymen, and seven of the ministers chosen were not members of the general conference. All twenty-two were Liberals, in spite of earlier Liberal speeches declaring that the commission would be non-partisan. The bishops wanted to nominate Lewis Davis, but he could not conscientiously consent to serve. Bishops Wright and Dickson refused to serve on the commission. On June 16, 1885, Wright wrote to Bishop Weaver:

> . . . In reply, permit me to say, that entertaining very unfavorable views of the legality of the Commission, and unpleasant apprehensions of its results on the peace and unity of the church, I do not wish any part in its arrangement, or my name attached to its appointment.[27]

Twenty-five commission members met for a week in November 1885 at Dayton, Ohio. They were divided into three committees: Confession of Faith, Constitution, and plan of submission to the church. The *Religious Telescope* announced that in all probability the meetings would not be open to visitors. At the opening the chairman announced that they would sit with closed doors, and the commission acquiesced. But when Lorin and Wilbur Wright, sons of Bishop Wright, learned that Liberals who were not commission members were attending, they went to the last of the meetings. Wilbur wrote in detail of the last day and printed his account in an eight-page pamphlet, "Scenes in the Church Commission During the Last Day of Its Session." It was advertised in the *Conservator,* and several thousand of them were circulated.[28]

Wright's pamphlet discredited the work of the commission. It stated that Judge Shauck, a member of the commission, gave as his opinion that the commission could not legally call an election, that only the general conference could do so. This caused excitement in the meeting. Some wanted to adjourn and go home. One favored calling a constitutional convention. Another thought the next general conference should call the election. Finally they decided to have an election in 1888 as a "feeler." It would be held at the time of election of general conference delegates.[29] If the courts judged it illegal, the results would be taken to the next general conference as a petition.

The pamphlet also told that Judge Shauck gave it as a legal opinion that courts would uphold that a simple majority could adopt a revised Constitution and Confession of Faith.

According to Wright's pamphlet, when the commission came to adopting their proposed Constitution, "a heated discussion occurred" when the clause on secret combinations was considered:

> Some were for expunging it from the constitution altogether. Others, while agreeing with these in sentiment, were afraid of the people. They said, we must go slow; the people are not ready for it yet; we must first educate the people up to it. When it became evident that they were agreed in nothing but their opposition to the clause as it stands in our present constitution, they finally adopted a form for the clause which says nothing, but would leave the whole matter for the General Conference to fight over every four years. . . . There was also some disagreement as to how this clause should be submitted to the church. Some desired to submit their work entire; others wished a separate vote taken on the clause on secrecy and lay delegation. . . . In order to get lay delegation, [some argued] the people would willingly accept the secrecy clause. They would "swallow the bitter to get the sweet." . . . Bishop Weaver said he had carried two law conferences by promising that the secrecy clause should be submitted separately. This plan they at length adopted.

The pamphlet also stated that the work of the commisssion was changed after that body's final adjournment, and that this did not conform with a stipulation of the general conference that there be a final vote on the work *as a whole.*

At the close of the commission meetings, Editor Hott, a member of the commission, asked what he would be permitted to publish. "He was authorized to make a general statement but forbidden to publish the minutes of their proceedings," Wright stated in his pamphlet.

In January 1886 the revised Confession of Faith and the revised Constitution began to be published and circulated. Bishop Weaver prepared a thirty-nine page pamphlet with the revised documents and related comments. He argued that many changes had been made in the *Discipline* over the years to meet changing conditions—some of them by men who had changed their minds with the passing of time, so why not change the Constitution and Confession.

Secrecy

Bishop Weaver insisted that in regard to secret combinations the church should be able to discriminate, but it could not because of the clause in the Constitution. It was his opinion that discrimination would have saved the church a lot of problems. In his pamphlet he declared that even the disciplinary rules on secrecy, that many thought were too restrictive, were more lenient toward secrecy than the church had ever been toward slavery; therefore, he concluded, the church did not look upon secret combinations as it did upon slavery. He asserted that secret orders were injurious, not beneficial, to the Christian. But just as the church tolerated members who were proud, covetous, or committed other sins, so it should tolerate members who joined a secret order; and just as the church warned members of other evils which it considered injurious to Christian character, so it should advise against secrecy. He stated that "the general belief seems to be that more souls will be saved in the end by moderation than would be by an arbitrary law excluding them all. Something must be allowed for education and the different views persons may take on the same subject." He favored expelling a member from the church only if Christian character were affected by membership in a secret order and the person did not heed instruction and admonition. This procedure he considered to be the apostolic method.

Amending the Constitution

In the revised Constitution the way to change that document was a marked departure from the 1841 Constitution. The revision stated:

> Amendments to this constitution may be proposed by any General Conference—two-thirds of the members elected thereto concurring—which amendments shall be submitted to a vote of the membership throughout the Church, under regulations authorized by said conference.
>
> A majority of all votes cast upon any submitted amendment shall be necessary to its final ratification.

Lay Delegation

Another change in the revised Constitution provided for lay delegation to general conference. But at the same time lay members lost their constitutional right to vote for general conference delegates. The revised Constitution said the mode of election was to be determined by the general conference.

As early as 1849 there was a request for lay delegation. But the number requesting this was small. The fact that the delegates were elected by a popular vote of the members gave "a degree of lay influence and lay control which is not possessed by those churches which [have] a lay delegation. No other church having an itinerant ministry elects its delegates by a popular vote of the whole church," stated a report adopted at the General Conference of 1857. Further, the Constitution gave lay persons the right to petition.

A petition from two Sandusky Conference members asking for lay delegation in annual and general conferences was considered by the General Conference of 1861. That conference recognized that the constitutional restriction on general conference membership made lay delegation in that body impossible unless the Constitution were changed. It was admitted that lay representation in annual conference could be granted, but because "no considerable portion of the laity" requested it, and "such an arrangement would increase a burden without any result of good," no action was taken to allow lay representation.

At the General Conference of 1869 the committee on lay representation recommended that an amendment to the Constitution to allow lay delegates to general conference be submitted to the people for their ratification or rejection. However, due to the fact that only about 500 names were on the petitions, the conference, by a vote of 55 to 32, passed this resolution: "Inasmuch as there is no general desire expressed in favor of lay representation, we do not deem it expedient at present to take action in regard to it."

The General Conference of 1873 considered 43 petitions for lay representation in general conference. These petitions were from various annual conferences and were signed by 1836 persons. A few delegates argued that there was no general desire for this, and that a lot of the sentiment for it had been worked up by ministers, some having circulated petitions. These delegates preferred waiting to act when a majority of the people took the initiative to request it. In 1869 and 1873 lay delegation was also objected to, on the basis that it would make the general conference too cumbersome and costly. (The sessions were nearly two weeks long.) But it was decided at the General Conference of 1873 by a vote of 91 to 12 to submit to the people a constitutional amendment for lay representation in general conference. A plan for submitting the amendment to the membership was not given in the Constitution, and since there was not time at the conference to perfect one, the matter was referred to the Board of Bishops. The conference also asked the bishops to give an explicit rendering of Article IV of the Constitution and publish this in the *Religious Telescope.*

The Board of Bishops' minutes recorded their decision:

> . . . Whereas, after prayerful consideration of the subject they found them-
> selves unable to agree, and believing that they had not the power in this reference
> to agree on a compromise, there seems to be no other course left us, than to refer
> it back to the General Conference to decide.

Consequently no vote was taken on the proposed amendment—the
only effort to amend the Constitution until 1885.

Between 1885 and 1889 in the controversy between the Liberals and
Radicals, the issue of lay representation in general conference was not
emphasized, according to Halleck Floyd, a Radical leader. "I do not
remember that any objection was made to 'Lay Delegation' on principle in the *Conservator*," he testified in the 1890s.[30]

Confession of Faith

By adopting the majority report of Committee No. Six, the General
Conference of 1885 asked the commission to revise the Confession of
Faith. "That a new confession of faith and new improvement of our
constitution need to be made, there is no question," said J. W. Hott at
the conference. Bishop Weaver, in his 1885 pamphlet on the commission, stated: "Many of our most intelligent ministers and members
have for many years been impressed with the belief that our confession
of faith and constitution might be, and indeed should be, improved."
In the *Religious Telescope* of January 22, 1890, an anonymous writer
declared, ". . . the more progressive portion of the United Brethren
Church a few years ago saw that revision of their creed and constitution was a necessity."

A Liberal leader, A. W. Drury, wrote in his history that "there was
no immediate urgency in regard to the Confession." Radical leaders
Lewis Davis, Milton Wright, and others said that expressions of
dissatisfaction with the Confession were not made prior to the General
Conference of 1885. J. P. Landis, professor at Union Biblical Seminary, testified:

> Prior to 1885 there was no serious disturbance in the ranks on doctrinal
> questions. There was some talk that the creed ought to be better arranged and
> more specifically worded. It was a subject of conversation among young men in
> the theological schools more so than among the lay membership who are not
> ordinarily capable of considering such questions very far. The lay membership
> was not agitated over the creed.[31]

The General Conference of 1833 adopted a restrictive rule: "Nothing shall be done by the said conference, which would in any wise affect or change the article of faith. . . . " The General Conference of 1845 passed a resolution: "That in view of the Constitution this General Conference has no right to revise, alter, or amend the Confession of Faith as it now stands."

To help convince the church that it was all right to revise the Confession in the 1880s, some leading Liberals claimed that changes were made by the General Conferences of 1837, 1841, and 1857. But in the journals of the general conferences for those years there is not a word authorizing any change of the Confession, except in 1857. The official report of the proceedings of this conference shows that the change from "this respect" to "these respects" in the last clause was merely to correct a "misprint" in the English translation from the German. There are slight verbal discrepancies in the Confession as printed in the *Disciplines* of all these years. But there is no evidence that the general conference had anything to do with it. It was the work of the editors of the *Discipline* and the printers.

In his 1885 pamphlet on the commission, Bishop Weaver wrote: "It is of the utmost importance that articles of faith should set forth as clearly and fully as possible all the leading doctrines of the church." In the May 2, 1888 *Religious Telescope* he emphasized "omissions" in the Confession:

> [The old Confession] leaves out some very important points. The wonder is that some of our modern critics do not sit in judgment upon these omissions. Nothing is said on the Christian sabbath, nothing concerning the future destiny of the wicked, and nothing to show what we believe on the doctrine of depravity. You will find these doctrines scattered throughout the Discipline, but not in the Confession of Faith, where they properly belong.

An address of the bishops to the church on the commission, January 1, 1886, identified "five new articles" in the new creed: "justification, regeneration and adoption, sanctification, the Christian sabbath, and a future state." So, by admission, nearly one-half of the "revised" Confession was new. In total length it was about one-third longer than the old. It was entirely new in form.[32]

After insisting that the old Confession needed changing by addition and clarification, Liberals, apparently to appease those who doubted the wisdom and legality of the new Confession, and to have a stronger legal property claim, insisted that there was no essential change. They denied that there was anything in the new not stated or implied in the old Confession, or that there was anything in the new that conflicted with the old. J. P. Landis, who succeeded Lewis Davis as professor of systematic theology at Union Biblical Seminary, in testifying for the Liberals in a litigation case in the 1890s, said, "The old creed is not silent on any of the cardinal doctrines of the Bible."[33] This testimony was exactly opposite of what Committee No. Six and a majority of the General Conference of 1885 affirmed.

Bishop Weaver in legal testimony in the 1890s said:

> . . . The Apostles' Creed is pronounced by authorities, the creed of creeds, and yet it is silent on many of the cardinal doctrines of the Bible, and yet theologians and creed builders allow that all fundamental doctrines of Christianity are either expressed or implied in the Apostles' Creed.[34]

Lewis Davis wrote in his pamphlet "The New Creed" that Otterbein "loved the simplicity, brevity and clearness of the Apostles' Creed and drew largely from it."

Liberal historian Berger wrote in the 1890s of the old Confession as "brief, simple, comprehensive, and really beautiful, lacking in some essentials of a compact statement of Christian doctrine, and yet worthy of a most honorable place among the creeds which have been framed through the ages to express Christian belief." He also described the creed as "so clear and beautiful in its expression, and so comprehensive in its grasp . . . " This is in agreement with Davis in his "The New Creed" where he characterized the old Confession as "remarkably clear and comprehensive." Berger also referred to the old creed as "this excellent utterance of the Fathers."[35]

A. W. Drury, in his biography of William Otterbein, described the old Confession as

> . . . simple and majestic. It impresses by what it includes, by what it omits, and by its doctrinal savor. It rests on the Apostles' Creed and the New Testament, and adds only those necessary specifications in regard to the application and mission of the gospel that even the simplest of the later creeds have been compelled to include.[36]

Yet the *1888 United Brethren Yearbook* called the new Confession "a decided improvement of the original." Conflicting Liberal statements about the creeds seem to confirm what some Radicals believed was the reason for revising the Confession and the whole Constitution—to becloud the secrecy issue by adding others.

Lewis Davis led the Radicals in discussing the proposed new creed— "a subject too important to be passed over lightly or superficially," he said. Having been professor of systematic theology from the beginning of Union Biblical Seminary in 1871 until his retirement in 1885, he was considered an able spokesman. He contended "that the work of the Commission shows a *new* confession of faith, and not an 'amended' one." He pointed out that this was not expected, nor called for by the commission act. Such action he termed "arrogant proceedings," a trampling in the dust of the constitutional guarantee of the rights of the members of the Church. Davis charged that the commission act was unlawful, "without warrant, or precedent." And that the commissioners compounded illegalities by disregarding instructions given by the general conference.

Davis said that, in examining the new creed,

> . . . no one can tell without the most careful study, what part is original and what borrowed. Of the thirteen articles . . . eight are left in this mixed condition. In this part of their work the old Confession of Faith is freely drawn from, but its contents are so changed and interwoven with other theological opinions, . . . that no one but an expert can determine where the one begins and the other ends. Is this the way to "amend" a document already existing and in force?[37]

Davis admitted that "no creed is perfect, and, of course we do not claim that the one bequeathed to us by Otterbein is an exception to this rule." But Davis questioned that it needed "tinkering," and whether the commissioners had more scholarship and were better theologians than Otterbein.

As for the Liberal concern that the old Confession was "silent" on some of the cardinal doctrines of the Bible, Davis wrote: "But is this not true of creeds in general? It certainly is. A creed is a brief exposition of a *few* important points, and nothing more. It should not be expected to include all the 'cardinal doctrines of the Bible.' " He said Philip Schaff, creed authority, held that a creed need include "only such points as are deemed sufficient, or as have been disputed." Continued Davis, "This is the sensible view, and the one now generally accepted."

The new articles of justification and sanctification Davis categorized as Calvinistic, and not believed by most of the church. He protested against the article on regeneration because it did not clearly include regeneration of the intellect and will. He did not approve of the removal of several phrases, including: "following after Christ," "the forgiveness of sins," "the communion of saints." The substitution of "dead" for "body" in the phrase "the resurrection of the body" displeased him, as did some other substitutions.

When, in 1890, Davis gave testimony for litigation cases, and affirmed what he wrote in "The New Creed," the *Religious Telescope* editor tried to dismiss Davis' views with this disparaging remark: "His objections are not only the merest quibbles, but are unscriptural."[38]

Bishop Wright was charged with not trusting future general conferences when he wrote "A Creed on Wheels." This was a tract on the importance of protecting the creed from changes. He and others were critical of the new Constitution, Article I, Section Ten:

> The General Conference may—two-thirds of the members elected thereto concurring—propose changes in, or additions to, the Confession of Faith; *provided,* that the concurrence of three-fourths of the annual conferences shall be necessary to their final ratification.

"There is not the slightest limitation to changes, either in the doctrine or in the wording of the confession," warned Wright. He conceded that "sweeping changes are improbable." Yet, he cautioned, ". . . it is possible to make very radical changes in doctrine. And if a creed is thus put on wheels, departure, sooner or later, from some fundamental truth is even probable."

The new Constitution did have a restriction regarding the creed in Article II, Section One, a part of which seemed to contradict the part which provided for changes: "The General Conference shall enact no rule or ordinance which shall change or destroy the Confession of Faith; and shall establish no standard of doctrine contrary to the Confession of Faith."

Wright argued that the 1841 constitutional restriction regarding the Confession of Faith and the one made by the General Conference of 1833 were sensible rules: "Men wish to know whether this church is built upon a solid or upon a shifting foundation. If our creed were upon wheels, it would argue that we are not certain that we are right on fundamental doctrine." Another point of his was "there are no questions that so agitate and disturb Christian churches as those concerning articles of doctrine."

Wright also noted that, according to the new Constitution, the lay members of the church—unless they were among the small number who were general or annual conference delegates—would have no voice in future changes in the creed. He spoke frankly when he wrote:

> To disfranchise the people on all change of faith, shows the utter hollowness of this professed regard for the people's right of franchise. But they flatter the people about the right to vote that they may wheedle them into voting for the new "constitution," and the new "constitution" proposes henceforth to disfranchise the people on the most sacred and important questions.

At the 1886 convention of the Constitutional Association this resolution was adopted:

That inasmuch as the history of church creeds demonstrates the fact that no church has ever materially changed its symbols of Faith, and maintained its organic union, we lay at the door of the liberal majority of the late General Conference the responsibility of whatever evil result may ensue.

Voting

By a *yes* vote of *two-thirds of those voting,* the new Constitution and Confession could be adopted, according to the General Conference of 1885. Bishop Weaver *(Religious Telescope* February 25, 1885) argued that two-thirds of those voting was a "reasonable construction" of Article IV, and that a vote of two-thirds of all members would never happen.

Bishop Wright in the April 7, 1886, *Religious Telescope* presented three views of Article IV: two-thirds of those voting, two-thirds of all members, and

> . . . two-thirds majority of a *large vote*—say, one-half or two-thirds of all enrolled—would indicate sufficiently the will of two-thirds of our people concerning any proposed change, and that if our people really desired such proposed change there *would be a large vote.*
>
> Probably somewhere in this medium lies the most reasonable solution of this disputed question. It seems unreasonable that changes in the constitution should be decided by the request of *less than one-tenth* of the whole Church, or that, on the other hand, members, hardly to be found by any process, should prevent all change.

Because Radicals objected to the interpretation—*two-thirds of those voting,* and because they considered it unlawful for the commission to make the proposed changes, plus the fact they objected to the proposals—many thought they should not vote on the proposed changes, but instead should petition the General Conference of 1889. To vote would destroy the authority of the Constitution, they thought. Some annual conferences passed resolutions disapproving of the commission plan, its proposed changes, and of voting. Other conferences did the opposite.

Some individuals, who in 1885 appeared to be in the Radical camp, by 1888 decided that the best course was to vote—in spite of the "constitutional technicalities," and then abide by the vote. After all, they reasoned, the general conference decided this plan. Some of these persons expressed regret that Radicals put so much emphasis on opposing the methods of change. Radical leaders were accused of causing a boycott of the election and thereby perhaps defeating that for which they were contending.

On the question "Will Voting Save the Church?" Wilbur Wright wrote:

> There are many in the church who, while they recognize the unconstitutionality of the commission act and the illegality of the "feeler" election, yet hope that by voting the church may, in some way, be saved from division. How these hopes can be fulfilled it is difficult to see. An election can settle our trouble only when both sides agree to be bound by the result of the vote. This would not be the case now. The radicals believing the election illegal and even rebellious, will not even vote, much less will they submit to its results. For this they are severely criticised by the liberals. But will the liberals themselves submit if the vote is against them? Have they been submitting? Are they submitting now?[39]

Instead of voting, Radicals petitioned the General Conference of 1889 to make no changes in the Confession or Constitution and to enact a rule on secret societies that would maintain and render effective the article of constitutional law forbidding connection with secret combinations. The petition stated that to make changes on the basis of the commission work would "tend to perpetuate strife and alienation." Petition forms appeared in the *Conservator*, and readers were urged to clip and circulate them. Early in 1889 Radical leaders in the six strongly conservative annual conferences were appointed by the Constitutional Association to organize and superintend a general canvass with the petitions. A few ministers in other conferences were also appointed. There were districts of the church strongly Liberal where the petitions were not generally circulated. H. Floyd, who acted as field agent for the *Conservator* and Constitutional Association, visited ten of forty-seven annual conferences.[40] Liberal church officers and the *Religious Telescope* denounced the petitions as rebellious, and worked to prevent their circulation.

Floyd was refused an advisory seat by small majorities in Auglaize and Scioto Conferences in 1886. Though it was a common practice to give elders advisory seats when they visited other annual conferences, Floyd was refused because he was an officer of the Constitutional Association and Liberal majorities in these conferences wanted to avoid discussion of the commisssion and its work.[41] The characters of William Miller and William Dillon were arrested by their Auglaize Conference for their opposition to the commission act. An Auglaize quarterly conference action condemning Radicals as rebels was published in the *Religious Telescope,* August 11, 1886.

In North Michigan Conference, 1886, C. L. Wood's character was attacked for his opposition to the commission. At the same session Z. Warner, general missionary secretary, threatened to withhold $600 missionary appropriation unless the conference ceased opposing the commission plan. Effort was also made at that conference to keep William Dillon from preaching. But the Radicals held an edge, and when the itinerant list was revised, all sixteen Liberals asked for and were voted transfers.[42]

By 1887 it was clear that unless the course of events was halted or changed, a division of the church was likely to occur. Litigation was also recognized as unavoidable if division took place. Desiring to prevent these happenings, C. H. Kiracofe, president of Hartsville College, in the *Religious Telescope,* and D. K. Flickinger, foreign missionary bishop, in a letter to Bishop Castle, proposed a compromise: if the vote for the commission proposals be a two-thirds majority of the membership, let it be a request to the General Conference of 1889 to formulate a paper to send to the people for their vote. This would be an attempt to harmonize with the Constitution. Flickinger admitted that "some of the commission leaders will cry out against any compromise, and insist that it must go through as now." Flickinger offered to join with Bishops Castle, Dickson, and Wright in advocating a course that would not violate the Constitution. Bishop Castle replied:

Peace to the church, though it be secured at great personal cost, is a measure of great wisdom, but I see no way of securing it by any change of method that can acquire any considerable or sufficient advocacy to make it potential in that line; the danger is that of utter demoralization of methods so that there will be none to guide us.

In later years Flickinger wrote: "That was a time when good men were greatly perplexed, and there was a great conflict and struggle between their convictions of right, and what best to do to save the church from division and its consequent evils."[43]

Pamphlets on the commission, which were financed by the publishing house (as well as other commission expenses), advocated voting for the proposals. These publications subtly appealed for the voting of church members by such statements and phrases as "the people are supreme," "should the church so decree," "it gives each member an opportunity of affirming by his vote what he approves, and rejecting in a like manner what he disapproves," "to avoid all seeming unfairness," "surely the church does not wish to throw open its doors to combinations which it believes to be contrary to the Word of God," "in the ages to come higher degrees of light from the Divine Word may fall upon the church." The *1888 United Brethren Yearbook,* issued by the publishing house, included this partisan note:

An amended constitution, prepared by the above-mentioned commission, will be voted upon by the membership in November. It is much better adapted to the needs of the church than the present one, and should be adopted by a strong vote.

The position of the church on questions of moral reform, as is well known, has been decided.

For those who were seriously troubled about whether the commission plan and voting were lawful, the four bishops in their report about the commission in 1886 declared: "If . . . [the people] adopt a constitution which in any way conflicts with existing laws, such laws become void, because the decision of the people is above the will of the general conference."

During 1888 Bishop Weaver kept his pen busy writing articles for the *Religious Telescope* and letters to "those who were halting between two opinions."[44] He and other Liberals often remarked, "Wise men change, but fools never."

The ballot prepared by the general board of tellers—all commission members—was partisan, requiring a *no* vote to be *written in*. Neither the general conference nor the commission authorized any person to give notice of the time, place, and purpose of voting, and to do it at a reasonable time before the day fixed. This became another technicality of dispute, some Radicals claiming that on general principles the vote was not valid because proper notice was not given by duly authorized persons to all the voters.

The result of the vote was declared by the board of tellers on January 15, 1889, and their report was published in the *Religious Telescope* of January 23, 1889:

For the *confession*—	50,965	Majority for—	47,669
Against	3,296	Required to adopt—	36,174
For the *constitution*—	50,582	Majority for—	46,939
Against	3,643	Required to adopt—	36,150
For *lay delegation*—	48,722	Majority for—	43,104
Against	5,618	Required to adopt—	36,226
For *secrecy* section—	46,900	Majority for—	39,627
Against	7,273	Required to adopt—	36,114

Total votes cast for and against the four propositions—54,250. The results reported to the General Conference of 1889 were slightly higher, and 54,369 was given as the total votes cast. The membership of the

1888.

United Brethren in Christ

BALLOT

On Amendments to the Confession of Faith and Constitution.

Members wishing to vote NO on either proposition, must *erase* the word YES and insert NO.

Confession of Faith,	YES.
Amended Constitution,	YES.
Lay Delegation,	YES.
Section on Secret Combinations,	YES.

church as reported at the General Conference of 1889 was 207,800. For 1888 the number was 204,517. The highest affirmative vote on the commission proposals was less than one-fourth of the membership.

For several years prior to 1885 the Liberals had complained that a minority unfairly ruled the church because the representation plan for general conference was according to annual conference areas and not number of members. Now the Radicals cried that to allow less than one-fourth of the members to decide whether the church would have a new Confession and Constitution was an outrage.

Since delegates for general conference were also voted for at the same time as the commission proposals, and there were many who voted only for delegates, the total number of "voters" was larger than reported by the commission board of tellers. Wilbur Wright contended that "the 'vote at that election' is to be determined by taking the poll books, and by comparing them, find out how many different names they contain." He claimed that between 75,000 and 90,000 different persons participated in the elections.[45] If that were true, and his definition of "the vote" accepted, perhaps none of the commission proposals received a *two-thirds majority of those voting*. If the number of petitions to the general conference not to change the Constitution were added to the *no* votes on constitutional changes, that too would cast a different light on the election results.

In 1891 A. W. Drury stated "that the revision movement was not the movement of a few erratic thinkers, or of a few wayward and extreme leaders, but *of a whole people.*"[46] But in the General Conference of 1885 Bishop Dickson, in explaining why he was voting *no* on the commission plan, said that "no petition has come up from the people asking for such change."

The limited commission vote seemed to affirm what many Radicals had asserted—that the move for change in the Constitution was primarily the work of Liberal ministerial leaders, and that the scheme begun in 1885 and consummated in 1889 was pushed through by these men who were determined to have their way, even if it meant division.[47]

Division at the General Conference of 1889

At the General Conference of 1889, York, Pennsylvania, Liberals were in the majority. Some who stood with the Radicals in 1885 and as late as 1887 were now numbered among the Liberals—including Bishop Dickson. During the quadrennium some of these tried to pursue a moderate course, hoping that those at odds would come to a workable compromise. But Liberals had not shown a willingness to compromise in 1885 or since. Radicals had little hope for legislation on major issues that they could accept.

The bishops' address on the opening day of the conference reaffirmed the view that the general conference was above the Constitution, and therefore the acts of the General Conference of 1885 relating to the commission were legitimate, as well as the commission proposals and the vote on them. The address spoke of the proposals as a "full and careful expression," the commission report of November 1885 as "unanimously agreed upon," and the vote on the proposals as "the largest expression ever obtained in the denomination . . . being in excess of a two-thirds majority."

Five of the six bishops signed the address. Following its reading, Bishop Wright, whose name was not subscribed, fulfilled his "unwelcome and painful duty" of dissenting from part of the address. He said that while most of the address met his hearty concurrence and approval, the part on the church commission he could not in any way conscientiously endorse. He then presented his objections:

1. The address says that one of the views entertained is, "That we have a valid constitution, of absolute and unquestioned force, binding on all the members of the church, and also so bounding, restricting, and limiting the general conference itself, that it cannot legislate along certain lines or adopt certain measures, well defined in the limiting terms of the constitution, without being guilty of usurpation and revolution." I think this view, just cited, is, in principle, so completely in harmony with the established principles of constitutional law and jurisprudence that it ought to commend itself to the judgment of sound scholars in organic law, either political or ecclesiastical; yet this, which seems to me a wholesome view, is pronounced in the address to be one of the extremes which must be avoided.

2. The address further says: "It has been in a measure demonstrated that a feature of absolute immutability has been impressed on the constitution so that its amendment, according to its own terms, is an utter impossibility." And the address immediately adds this sentence: "This absolutism in our system, this inflexibility of provision of amendment is being regarded in the light of recent experience as exceedingly unfortunate."

I think these assumptions and some of the terms employed in these citations ought to be unsatisfactory to me in my official position, both as to correctness and as to due veneration for the organic law under which I hold office. I feel sure that the General Conference of 1873, in its action on lay delegation, neither expressed nor entertained such a view as to the absolute immutability of our constitution.

3. For similar reasons I could not assent to certain other declarations of the address, some of which may be stated substantially as follows: "That the church found itself" practically "beyond the possibility" of altering or modifying the constitution "when it came to meet a growing demand for more pliant and equitable measures arising from the exigencies of the times." . . .

Of course, my official position would forbid that I should say or do anything that, in the sight of our people, would dishonor, or weaken the force of the constitution under the provisions of which I was elected, and under which I am now acting. The obligation of a senator, governor, or bishop, to honor the constitution under which he is acting, is too well-known to need any apology. The obligation of a president or governor to honor and maintain the constitution of his commonwealth, could hardly be stronger than that of a bishop to reverence and uphold the constitution of his church. I could not do otherwise.

On the second morning of the conference the church commission reported. This was considered irregular by some, that a committee of a general conference reported to the conference that originated it. Also, the General Conference of 1885 took no action providing for this report. H. T. Barnaby and C. H. Kiracofe protested entertaining the report. But it was referred to a special committee which was to report to the conference not later than 10 a.m. the next day. This committee was to determine whether the commission had acted in compliance with the instructions of general conference, and whether the vote of the church had been orderly and regular. The committee was also to recommend to the conference such action as it deemed proper.

The third morning, at the beginning of business, H. Floyd and some others stated that they had petitions to present. These petitions from forty-one annual conference districts, aggregating 16,282 petitioners, requested that no changes be made in the Confession or the Constitution, and that a rule regarding secret societies in harmony with the 1841 Constitution be enacted. It soon became obvious that the plan of the Liberals was to defer any action on the petitions until after the report of the committee on the commission. J. W. Howe of Virginia said that it seemed to him these petitions ought to be brought before the conference before the committee on the commission was heard. Despite objections by several delegates, the petitions were referred to the committee on memorials and petitions.[48]

At 10 a.m. on that third day, as scheduled, the special committee on the work of the commission reported. The majority report recommended: 1) that the commission records, revised Confession, revised Constitution, methods of submission, and the voting be approved and confirmed; 2) that the revised documents become the fundamental belief and organic law of the church upon the proclamation of the bishops on May 13, 1889.

The chairman of the conference stated that "strictly speaking, there can be no minority report," but Milton Wright and J. M. Fowler rose to a point of order, and the minority report was presented by H. Floyd, who with ex-bishop Daniel Shuck composed the minority of the committee. They reported the work of the commission irregular: 1) some of the instructions of the General Conference of 1885 were not followed; 2) the commission calling an election was illegal; 3) the Religious Telescope was partisan; 4) the ballot was partisan; 5) the work of the commission came before the general conference as a petition, yet petitions against its work were ruled out in this consideration. This report asked the conference to consider not adopting the work of the commisssion, and that the conference determine amendments to the Constitution to be submitted to a vote of the members, and the vote be regarded as a petition for such proposed changes.

The debate that followed these crucial reports was only about half a day in length. At 3:40 p.m. on the third day of the conference a motion was passed to end the debate at 4 p.m. Barnaby entreated the conference not to rush through hastily, but rather to take some steps to harmonize the two factions. He stated that he had been promised by Bishop Weaver that steps would be taken to "bring about a state of things to which all parties could agree except those who would not agree to anything but their own particular selfish ideas."

W. H. Clay said ominously that acceptance of the commission work would mean division in annual conferences, in circuits, in classes, and even in homes. He requested that the commission work be withdrawn. Wright appealed and warned:

> . . . Would we break this church in two? Do you not know that you can take things from men when you do it in a method they acknowledge to be legal, and they will yield to it, while on the other hand, with disputed methods there is sure to be dissatisfaction, and almost sure to be disaster? Why are we not in the line of peace on this question and in this regard today? Is the church to be torn asunder to carry out a disputed method? Was it not proposed four years ago that a legal method would be acceded to? It has been said on this floor that there were those who rose and said they would never yield. They did not say that in that way, let me suggest. They did say that they would not yield until it was legally done.

Liberals persisted in their arguments that the acts of the General Conference of 1885 and the work of the commission were legal and would be so recognized by civil courts, and that since a principle of the church was that the majority rules, the Radicals would just have to take it on the chin. Liberals tried to minimize Radical objections by insisting that the new documents were better, the majority of the church wanted the new ones adopted, and that it was a mere technicality of method that was separating the two groups.

When the 4 p.m. deadline for ending the debate was almost reached, a Liberal delegate moved to postpone the vote on the commission work until Monday at 3 p.m. instead of that Saturday at four o'clock. He thought the Radical petitions ought to be considered first. The motion was defeated. Howe of Virginia spoke again regarding the petitions:

> I rise before the vote is taken simply to express my regret that the majority did not allow the petitions to have a fair showing. . . . it would have been far better for us all in the future to have granted the privilege of having those petitions properly considered.

The critical vote on the majority report was by roll call. Of the four delegates from Virginia Conference, which for many years had many ministers who supported Liberal positions, two voted *no,* stating that they objected to the "hot haste," the method, "the cool consideration given to a respectable minority," "the disposition to cramp the liberty of speech upon this subject on this floor, and the refusal to recognize the petitions." However, the final result was 111 for adoption and 20 against.

Immediately after that vote, J. W. Hott read a paper he had written in anticipation of a Liberal victory. It included this resolution:

> 1. We, the members of the General Conference of the United Brethren in Christ, assembled in York, Pa., hereby express our deep regret that any of our brethren should not be able to cheerfully acquiesce in the decision of the great majority of the votes of our people . . . and now approved by this General Conference.
>
> 2. We hereby express our appreciation of the honesty and sincerity of our brethren opposed to the action of the majority of the Church, and we honor them for their faithfulness to their beliefs.
>
> 3. We hereby tender anew to these brethren our sympathy and fellowship in the love of Christ our Savior, and in the charity of Otterbein and Boehm, the beloved founders of our church. We shall use our influence in the time to come to the end that these brethren shall be treated as if these differences had never existed; and we most sincerely welcome them anew to our fellowship in the work of the gospel, and we shall deeply regret it, if any of them should in any way diminish their interest in the work of the Church in which we have so long labored together, and which is alike dear to us all.

The Radical response to this olive branch was against its adoption. Barnaby and Floyd said that mere words of condolence were no substitute for action to bring about reconciliation. The paper could not heal the breach.

On Monday morning, May 13, the fourth day of the conference, the chairman, Bishop Kephart, read a proclamation signed by all the bishops except Milton Wright. It declared the Confession of Faith and Constitution recommended by the commission to be now in force.

That afternoon, Bishop Wright and fourteen of the twenty delegates who had voted against approval of the commission work met at the Park Opera House and continued the lawful session of the general conference. The fourteen delegates were: J. K. Alwood, W. H. Clay, C. H. Kiracofe (North Ohio Conference); H. T. Barnaby, W. S. Titus (Michigan); C. L. Wood, G. A. Bowles (North Michigan); C. Bender (Rock River); A. Bennett (Oregon); A. W. Geeslin (Missouri); H. Floyd, J. M. Kabrich, Z. McNew, I. M. Tharp (White River).

Added to the pain of division was the fact that "there were quite a number of Radicals elected as delegates, and a number of others voted for as supposed Radicals, who, when elected, acted with the Liberals."[49] However many Radicals stood firm, and some of these were on hand at York. From among them the following were seated as alternate delegates: William Miller, S. T. Mahan, S. L. Livingston, William Dillon (Auglaize); H. J. Becker (California); A. B. Powell (Central Illinois); B. A. Bonewell, J. Excell (East Ohio); N. R. Luce (Erie); J. K. Nelson (Maryland); J. A. Cummings (St. Joseph); J. French (Sandusky); B. W. Mason (Scioto); J. Kenoyer, J. C. Spoonemore (Walla Walla).

Encouragement came to them in a letter from their long-time mentor Lewis Davis:

Dayton, Ohio, May 14th, 1889

Bishop M. Wright, My Dear Brother:

This is to say I am entirely unable to be with you and the loyal delegates at York. Oh, I would if I could, but I cannot. Yes, I *am* with you in spirit and in the use of my means in the struggle for our rights in the United Brethren Church. So now let us go to work and do what we can to build up the church of our choice. The dear Master will help us. Yes, I am sure he will, if we trust him and do our duty. Be sure to give my love and hearty greetings to the loyal body over which you preside. Peace and love.

L. Davis[50]

The State of the Church report recognized some of the difficulties faced:

. . . WHEREAS, The outgoing party is in possession of the general running machinery of the church, and most of the church property, and also predominate in most of the annual conferences; therefore,

Resolved, 1. That we understandingly accept the situation and resolve to go forward, occupying such conferences, circuits and classes as we may be able to control, and meantime adopt such measures as may be deemed best to secure possession of the church property that rightfully belongs to us by constitutional guarantee. Resolved, further, that to command the respect of the Christian churches of this land, we deem it impossible to acquiesce in the illegal and revolutionary methods adopted by the liberal element now attempting to change the fundamental laws of the church.[51]

With the close of the General Conference of 1889 a great conflict in the church became history. But effects of the division would cause further conflicts between Radicals and Liberals for at least a decade to come.

FOOTNOTES

[1]Augustus Waldo Drury, *History of the Church of the United Brethren in Christ* (Dayton, OH: Otterbein Press, 1924), p. 724. White River Conference Minutes, 1869, 1870.

[2]United Brethren in Christ, *Proceedings of the First General Convention, 1878* (Dayton, OH: Publishing Committee of the Convention, [1878]), pp. 51-53.

[3]John H. Ness, Jr., *One Hundred Fifty Years, a History of Publishing in the Evangelical United Brethren Church* (Dayton, OH: Board of Publication of the Evangelical United Brethren Church, 1966), pp. 384, 385.

[4]*Religious Telescope,* March 15, 1876.

[5]Lewis Davis, *The Life of Rev. David Edwards* 3rd ed. (Dayton, OH: United Brethren Publishing House, 1883), pp. 288, 289, 306, 307. Page 309: "It has been supposed by some that a change took place in the mind of Bishop Edwards during the last few years of his life in respect to the restrictive rule of the Church on the subject of secret societies. For this there is no ground; but on the contrary, there is abundant evidence of his adherence to the principle of a prohibitory rule. This is seen in addresses delivered and letters written on the subject, after he went east, and but a short time before his death. We have, moreover, the unqualified testimony of Mrs. Edwards, who is still alive, to the same effect."

[6]United Brethren in Christ, *Proceedings of the Harrisburg Convention, 1877, and Proceedings of the Westerville, Ohio and Orbisonia, Pennsylvania Conventions* (Harrisburg, PA: Convention, 1877), pp. 6, 15.

[7]Ibid., p. 21.

[8]Ibid., p. 24.

[9]Ibid., pp. 9, 10, 13.

[10]Ibid., p. 12.

[11]United Brethren in Christ, *Proceedings of the Christian Convention, Salem Church near Chambersburg, Pennsylvania, 1877* (Harrisburg, PA: Convention, 1877), p. 1.

[12]Ibid., p. 8.

[13]In 1877, when the pastor and others in authority at the Chambersburg Church refused to enforce the secrecy law, and put out of office those standing loyal to the church laws, the presiding elder and bishop defended this course. Some of the members held meetings in private homes and in 1878 bought a church building at the corner of Second and King Streets. Not being recognized by the conference, and conference ministers being forbidden to preach at the King Street Church or give it their influence, it became an independent congregation, though its ministers and people considered themselves loyal to the United Brethren Church. *The Life of John Fetterhoff* written by himself, with an introduction by W. O. Tobey (Chambersburg, PA: United Brethren in Christ Print, 1883), pp. 253-268. Pennsylvania Conference Minutes, 1878, 1879.

[14]*Christian Conservator,* October 30, 1890.

[15]*Proceedings of the First General Convention, 1878,* pp. 28, 29.

[16]Ibid., p. 61.

[17]H. A. Thompson, *Biography of Jonathan Weaver* (Dayton, OH: United Brethren Publishing House, 1901), p. 223.

[18]Ibid., pp. 225-227.

[19]*Proceedings of the Eighteenth General Conference of the United Brethren in Christ* (Dayton, OH: United Brethren Publishing House, 1881), p. 173.

[20]Thompson, pp. 245, 246.

[21]*In the Supreme Court of Illinois, Northern Grand Division, March Term, 1893, Jacob Kuns, et al. vs. J. W. Robertson, et al., Abstract of Record* (Pontiac, IL: Lowry and Clark, printers, 1893), p. 361.

[22]Charles H. Keller, *A History of the Allegheny Conference of the Church of the United Brethren in Christ* (n.p., 1943), p. 190.

[23]*Christian Conservator,* March 23, 1898.

[24]*Proceedings of the Twentieth General Conference of the United Brethren in Christ* (Dayton, OH: United Brethren Publishing House, 1889), p. 149.

[25]*Supreme Court of Illinois,* p. 163.

[26]*Brief of William Lawrence in Behalf of the Original and True Church of the United Brethren in Christ, Argument for the Original and Only True Church Against the Claims of the Seceders and Their Adherents to the Property of the Church* (Cincinnati, OH: The Ohio Valley Co., Printers, 1890), p. 24.

[27]*Christian Conservator,* March 25, 1896.

[28]Wilbur Wright to Milton Wright, 3 August 1888, Wright Brothers Papers, Library of Congress, Washington, D.C.

[29]"The General Conference ordered and expected the work of the commission to be completed not later than January 1, 1886. It was also *implied,* and so understood, that soon after the completion of the work the questions involved would be submitted to the people for their approval or disapproval. This was not formally acted upon, but all parties spoke of it as necessary in order to put to rest exciting questions. . . . the fixing upon this time [Nov. 1888] for taking of their vote cannot hide from our people the real object in view, which seems to have been to legalize their proceedings and increase the number of votes for the commission." Lewis Davis, "The New Creed" (Dayton, OH: Christian Conservator Print, 1888), pp. 4, 5.

[30]*Supreme Court of Illinois,* p. 189.

[31]Ibid., p. 556.

[32]According to Philip Schaff, who was generally regarded as among the best if not the best living authority on creeds at that time, the tendency among Protestants was to diminish rather than increase the number of articles of faith, and to follow in any new formula the simplicity of the Apostles' Creed. (Davis, "The New Creed," p. 15.)

[33]*Supreme Court of Illinois,* p. 568.

[34]Ibid., p. 534.

[35]Daniel Berger, *History of the Church of the United Brethren in Christ* (Dayton, OH: United Brethren Publishing House, 1897), pp. 226, 138, 139.

[36]Augustus W. Drury, *The Life of Rev. Philip William Otterbein* (Dayton, OH: United Brethren Publishing House, 1884), p. 232.

[37]Davis, "The New Creed," p. 8 (Later quotes and thoughts in this chapter from Davis on the creed are all from "The New Creed.")

[38]*Religious Telescope,* January 29, 1890.

[39]Wilbur Wright, "Scenes in the Church Commission," (Dayton, OH: Wright Bros., Job Printers, 1888), p. 8.

[40]*Supreme Court of Illinois,* p. 188.

[41]Ibid., pp. 666, 175, 176.

[42]E. C. Clapp, compiler, *A Brief History of the North Michigan Conference of the Church of the United Brethren in Christ, 1878-1947* (n.p., n.d.), pp. 6, 7.

[43]Daniel Kumler Flickinger, *Fifty-five Years of Active Ministerial Life* (Dayton, OH: United Brethren Publishing House, 1907), pp. 190-192.

[44]Thompson, p. 320.

[45]*Christian Conservator,* January 9, 1890.

[46]*Christian Conservator,* September 19, 1891.

[47]Davis, "The New Creed," p. 4.

[48]The committee on petitions did not report until the sixth day of the conference, two days after the bishops proclaimed the new Confession and Constitution to be in force. In

spite of these proceedings, the committee appealed: ". . . we would earnestly pray such petitioners and their friends that they do not hastily form their conclusions touching the action of the general conference, on the work of the commission; also, that their interest in the church of their choice remain undisturbed."

[49]*Supreme Court of Illinois,* p. 40l.

[50]*Proceedings of the Twentieth General Conference of the United Brethren in Christ* (Dayton, OH: Milton Wright Publisher, 1889), p. 37.

[51]Ibid., p. 35.

Top: Philip William Otterbein
Bottom: The Old Otterbein Church, Baltimore, MD
        Erected 1785 *(from an early wood carving)*

Top: Martin Boehm
Bottom: Isaac Long's Barn, near Lancaster, PA

Top: George A. Geeting
Bottom: The Geeting Meeting House, Keedysville, MD

Otterbein (standing in center) assisting in the ordination of Bishop Francis Asbury, December 27, 1784

Christian Newcomer

Bonnet's School House, Mt. Pleasant, PA, where the first General Conference was held in 1815.

284

United Brethren Church,
Circleville, OH, in
basement of which the
Religious Telescope was
published from 1845-1853.

Home of Bishop William Hanby, Westerville, OH

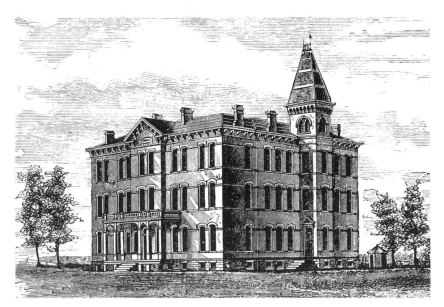

Union Biblical Seminary, Dayton, OH
Founded 1871

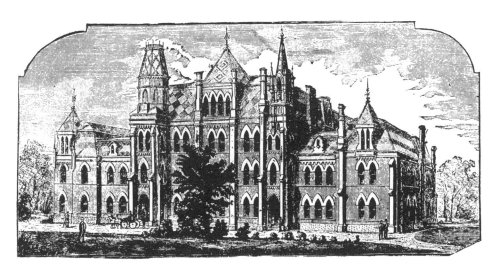

Otterbein University, Westerville, OH
Founded 1847

Hartsville College, Hartsville, IN (1850-1897)
Erected 1860-1865. Burned Jan. 30, 1898

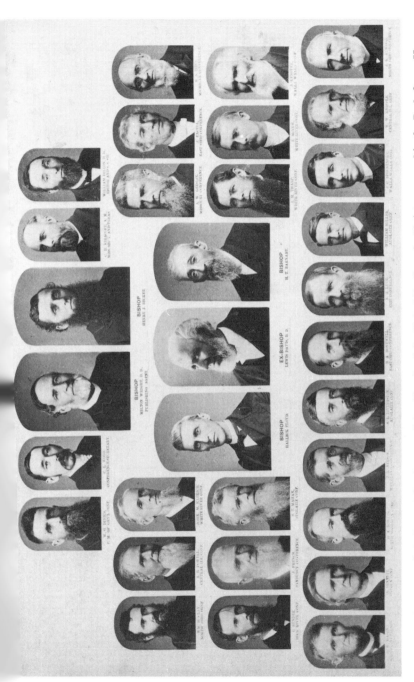

Members of the Twentieth General Conference of the Church of the United Brethren in Christ, convened in the Park Opera House, York, PA, May 9-19, 1889. Top row, left to right: W. O. Dinius, C. L. Wood, Bishop Milton Wright, Bishop Henry J. Becker, C. H. Kiracofe, William Dillon. Center: Bishop Halleck Floyd, Ex-Bishop Lewis Davis, Bishop H. T. Barnaby. 2nd row: W. H. Clay, A. B. Powell, John M. Kabrich, A. W. Geeslin, J. Excell, W. S. Titus. 3rd row: C. Bender, J. French, S. T. Mahan, I. M. Tharp, Z. McNew, J. Kenoyer. Bottom row: B. W. Mason, A. Bennett, G. A. Bowles, J. K. Nelson, S. L. Livingston. B. A. Bonewell, N. R. Luce, William Miller, J. C. Spoonemore, W. W. Knipple, J. K. Alwood.

BISHOPS, 1889-1981

Milton Wright
1889-1905

Horace Barnaby
1889-1905

Halleck Floyd
1889-1905

Henry J. Becker
1889-1893

William Dillon
1893-1897

Henry L. Barkley
1897-1913

Fermin L. Hoskins
1905-1933

Olin G. Alwood
1905-1921

Corydon L. Wood
1905-1920

BISHOPS, 1889-1981

Harold C. Mason
1921-1925

Clarence A. Mummart
1921-1925, 1937-1941

Walter E. Musgrave
1925-1949

Eli B. Griffin
1925-1929

Albert M. Johnson
1929-1951

Laurin B. Baldwin
1933-1937

Ezra M. Funk
1941-1957

Lloyd Eby
1949-1957

Clarence E. Carlson
1957-1965

BISHOPS, 1889-1981

Robert W. Rash
1957-1961, 1965-1969

Clyde W. Meadows
1961-1969

George E. Weaver
1969-1977

Duane A. Reahm
1969-1981

Raymond Waldfogel
1969-1981

C. Ray Miller
1973-

Wilber L. Sites, Jr.
1977-

Clarence A. Kopp, Jr.
1981-

Jerry F. Datema
1981-

Above: United Brethren Headquarters Building and Publishing Establishment, 1897-1916. Corner Front Street (now Riverside Drive) and South Jefferson Street, Huntington, IN.   Below: United Brethren Headquarters and Publishing Establishment, 1916-1976. Corner Franklin and Warren Streets, Huntington, IN.

CENTRAL COLLEGE
Dedicated September 21, 1897
(renamed Huntington College in 1917)

Huntington College, Aerial View, 1974

294

Wright Brothers' 1903 airplane, "Kitty Hawk," in first flight (12 seconds), December 17, 1903, Kitty Hawk, North Carolina. Orville Wright at controls, Wilbur standing at right. Photo courtesy Smithsonian Institution

Executive Secretaries of the WMA

1891-1906
Anvilla R. Kiracofe

1906-1930
Cora Loew

1930-1956
Effie M. Hodgeboom

Mary M. Titus
President of the
WMA Board of Managers,
1891-1931

1956-1965
Erma Carlson

1965-1977
Iona Wood

1978-
Hazel McCray

United Brethren Building, 1976-

Part Four

THE TRIALS AND TRIUMPHS

1889-1929

Dr. Harold R. Cherry

BIOGRAPHICAL DATA

Harold R. Cherry was born October 1, 1927, to Richard R. and Ruth L. (Snore) Cherry, Eaton County, Charlotte, Michigan. Harold was the second of four children—all sons: Maurice, Harold, Howard, and Herbert. The three younger are all ordained elders in the Church of the United Brethren in Christ and Maurice is an active member of the Charlotte United Brethren Church. The Cherry family was denominationally oriented and attended the Charlotte Church in Michigan Conference.

On July 8, 1948, Harold married Ruby M. Rawley a United Brethren student from Mt. Solon, Virginia. They are the parents of four children, all of whom have graduated from Huntington College: Paul Ross (1973), Constance Marie (1975), Richard Kevin (1976), and Ronald Kim (1984).

Harold received the quarterly conference license in 1943; joined the Michigan Annual Conference in 1945; and was ordained an elder by Bishop Ezra M. Funk in 1949.

In 1945 he received the Bachelor of Arts degree and in 1947 the Bachelor of Divinity degree from Huntington College and Huntington College Theological Seminary. He earned the Master of Theology from Calvin Theological Seminary (1953); the Master of Arts degree from Western Michigan (1960); the Doctor of Philosophy degree from Michigan State University (1970).

His pastoral ministry was in the Michigan Annual Conference exclusively; Dutton, Sunfield Circuit, Kalamazoo, Lansing, West Windsor, Grand Rapids, and Charlotte. It was while pastoring the Lansing congregation that he was instrumental in starting the West Windsor Church.

At the age of 27 he was elected for the first time to the General

Conference of 1953, probably the youngest delegate to ever be elected as a member to a General Conference—and he has been elected consecutively to every General Conference through 1981. Consistently he has served responsibly in the Michigan Annual Conference as its recording secretary for 35 years; as Conference treasurer 15 years; as District Superintendent for 5 years; the Conference Council for 30 years; and a member of the Board of Directors of Lane-Dulcenia Memorial Home Corporation for 20 years. He has served in various General Church Boards including Huntington College Board of Trustees, Board of Publications, Board of Missions, and the Ministerial Relations Board.

PERSPECTIVE

In writing the reconstruction and stabilization period of this United Brethren history, the author has sought to include some of its drama and tension, interwoven with many names and facts to give the account concrete detail. The writer believes that history is an orderly narration of events, presented in an objective manner, and from this belief he has included some happenings and statistics which are not necessarily flattering to the record.

Harold R. Cherry

24

A SURVEY OF CONDITIONS: UP FROM ASHES

The leaders of the Church of the United Brethren in Christ must have faced the quadrennium of 1889 to 1893 and beyond with mixed emotions. Surely within them was the feeling of satisfaction of being on the side where their consciences had led them and where they now bravely stood. One's reward for exercising such courage and commitment is the peace and comfort of knowing that he has obeyed the Lord and his own conscience. At the same time there were heavy hearts facing awesome burdens to be borne. W. E. Musgrave commented, "A survey of the conditions which our fathers were compelled to meet at the close of the General Conference of 1889 was sufficient to appall the stoutest heart."[1]

There was obviously much demoralization of spirit across the church, and confusion reigned as to which societies and conferences would survive and with which of the two churches the ministers would cast their lots. The bishops in their address to the General Conference of 1893 described conditions in this manner: "Many of our societies, torn by a revolutionary schism, were divided, and some left but the fragments of former organization. In some cases our members were isolated and as sheep without a shepherd."[2] In some communities congregtions retained their churches; in more cases they lost them. Because of the unsettled state of the church and of the yet unknown results of litigation, some members drifted to other churches and some gave up church participation altogether.

God blessed the church with able, dedicated leaders for this crucial period of reconstruction. Chosen by the General Conference of 1889, the four bishops were Milton Wright, Horace T. Barnaby, Halleck Floyd, and Henry J. Becker. It is important to note in some detail those men who were chosen to lead in this critical period of reconstruction.

Bishop Milton Wright

Bishop Milton Wright was born in Rush County, Indiana, November 17, 1828, the son of Dan and Catherine Reeder Wright, who were farmers in the primitive country of Indiana. His ancestors can be traced to Essex, England, with Samuel Wright coming to America and settling in New England in 1636. The Wright family lived in this region until Dan Wright moved to Ohio in 1814 and then on to Indiana in 1821.

Milton Wright received a meager public education in country schools and attended Hartsville College for a short time. The larger part of his education was the result of diligent and extensive private study.

He was converted in 1843 while working alone in his father's field. For four years he was unconnected with any church but was under the influences of the Presbyterian and Methodist churches. After having carefully studied the teachings and principles of the United Brethren Church, he chose to join it. After passing through the stages of exhorter and quarterly conference preacher, he became a member of the White River Conference in 1853. After brief pastorates in Indiana, he was chosen and sent as a missionary to Oregon, going by the Isthmus of Panama. During his brief stay in Oregon he was engaged in preaching as well as serving as principal of Sublimity College from 1857 to 1859. This was the first United Brethren school on the Pacific Coast. He returned to Indiana in 1859, and that fall he married Susan Catherine Koerner. To this marriage seven children were born, five of whom survived infancy. Their two sons, Wilbur and Orville, achieved worldwide fame because of their invention of the "flying machine."

Church historians covering Wright's era picture him as the crusader type, a man of strong persuasions and willing to take up the battle for what he believed to be right. "From first to last he was opposed to slavery, the rum traffic, and secret societies."[3] Daniel Berger reported, "His strong convictions on this subject [secret societies], and the active interest taken in opposing secret societies, led to his election as editor of the *Religious Telescope* by the General Conference of 1869, the first conference in which this question was made an issue in an election."[4] He served eight years as editor. This liberal[5] United Brethren historian revealed his bias when he observed, "During the eight years of his incumbency the columns of the *Religious Telescope* were intensely radical."[6]

Wright served two terms as bishop before the division, 1877-1881 and 1885-1889. He continued for four consecutive terms after the division, 1889-1905. Members of the Old Constitution[7] United Brethren Church believe that it was in the providence of God that Wright had served in the Bishop's office before the storm broke, and thus he was ready to help guide the "ship of state" through the troubled waters of reconstruction. Musgrave aptly made this comparison: "If Philip William Otterbein can be truthfully called the founder of the Church of the United Brethren in Christ, Milton Wright with equal truth can be called the preserver of that Church."[8]

As perceived by William Dillon, a radical United Brethren editor, Wright is described in the pages of *The Christian Conservator,* May 23, 1889: "Bishop Milton Wright stood like a hero. When all the other bishops faltered and fell prostrate before the commission compromise with the world, he stood 'faithful among the faithless,' and deserves great credit from every United Brethren."[9]

Bishop Horace T. Barnaby

Side by side with Bishop Wright stood Bishop H. T. Barnaby in the reconstruction of the church. Barnaby, slightly older than Wright, was born April 26, 1823, in Allegany County of western New York State. He was orphaned at an early age (some report it to be at twelve years) and then lived a few years with relatives. Thus being forced to make his own way early in life, he learned to be self-reliant at a young age.

Horace T. Barnaby moved to Michigan in 1842, settled in Hillsdale County, and cleared a farm. He went to California with a company of gold hunters in 1849, and returned a year later, still poor, but richer in experiences. In 1852 he was converted and joined the Methodist Protestant Church, from whom he received his first license to preach the gospel. In 1854 he moved to Gratiot County, where again he took up a new farm and cleared the ground. While there he held township and county offices and served in the Michigan legislature. In 1858 he joined the United Brethren Church, received his Annual Conference license from Michigan Conference in 1860, and was ordained three years later. According to his biography in the *United Brethren Year Book—1904,* "He was elected presiding elder in 1866 and continued in that office most of the time until elected bishop in 1889."[10] During this period he, like Abraham, migrated one more time, moving to the Gaines Circuit, Kent County, Michigan, in 1875, where he purchased an eighty-acre farm of virgin timber and again built a home and cleared the land.

His family life presents some unusual features. Barnaby was married

four times and still celebrated a golden wedding anniversary. Losing
wives by death in three early marriages, he fathered children from only
his first and fourth wives. Among his children were the Reverend Alvin
Barnaby, who began teaching at Hartsville College in 1893 and became
its president in 1896. Later he became a professor at Central College
(now Huntington College). Another son, Horace T. Barnaby, was an
attorney in Grand Rapids, Michigan, from which area he served in
turn both as a state representative and a state senator. The latter son
wrote a memorial tribute to his father, Bishop Barnaby: "He was stern
and positive, always, in his manner in the home; but kindly, indulgent,
patient, enduring and forgiving under all circumstances. He was an
excellent disciplinarian, but prided himself in governing by kindness
and respect."[11]

In his early ministerial years Barnaby preached in schoolhouses and
private homes. He held grove meetings when weather and circumstances permitted. As an itinerant preacher he went on foot long
distances, forded streams, and followed Indian trails. He carried a gun
for protection from bears and wolves which were often in evidence.

His preaching was characterized particularly by simplicity and
plainness. He was a master of illustration, usually choosing them from
the common scenes of life. At times he engaged in debate, and it is said
that as a debater, he never was defeated. His sermons were a rich mine
of biblical, theological, and inspirational truth.

Barnaby, like Wright, believed strongly in the constitutional principles of the historic United Brethren Church. He identified himself with
the radical wing of the church and went with this group when they
separated themselves from the New Constitution group at York, Pennsylvania in 1889. Barnaby was a close ally to Wright in the years of
litigation which followed the division. He concluded his bishopric at
eighty-two years of age and lived until nearly his ninety-fourth birthday. Michigan Conference honored him by naming their campgrounds
near Sunfield, "H. T. Barnaby Memorial Park."

Bishop Halleck Floyd

The state of Indiana and the White River Conference contributed a
second person to the board of bishops for the reconstruction period in
the person of Halleck Floyd. Floyd was born to pioneer parents on
April 7, 1839, in Shelby County. His parents moved to Indiana from
Virginia in 1826.

"The bishop's mother was a pious woman. She dedicated him to the
ministry when he was born. At the age of nine years he was converted

and joined the M. E. Church."[12] While attending Hartsville College in 1856, he was exposed to the United Brethren Church and was impressed with "the spirituality and simplicity of the church and the forms of worship, the brotherly love that seemed to prevail among United Brethren, and their principles in opposing slavery and Rome and secret societies."[13]

He was granted his quarterly conference license to preach in 1857, received his first pastorate in 1858 at the age of nineteen years, and joined the White River Conference in 1859. He held several short pastorates while attending Hartsville College from 1861-1863. In 1873 his conference elected him as presiding elder, and he served nine of the next ten years in that office.

In 1881 he was chosen to represent Wayne County, Indiana, in the state legislature, serving two terms there, part of it concurrently with his work as presiding elder. It is interesting that both Floyd and Barnaby served in their respective state legislatures, a practice sometimes frowned upon in recent years by some in conservative church circles, i.e., for clergy to sit in major legislative bodies.

Floyd was named associate editor of *The Christian Conservator* for the years 1885-1889. In 1889 he was chosen as a bishop by the Old Constitution branch at the York, Pennsylvania, General Conference. He served sixteen years as bishop and served well in this reconstruction period, seeking to restore the church that he loved. He felt he was where God wanted him at that time. Upon his election as a bishop he remarked, "I believe, in retrospecting the past history of the Church and my own relation to the Church, that the vote which placed this responsibility upon me today is the leading of Providence."[14] Another statement, made just after the division had taken place, indicates his devotion to the original position of the church. He said, "I believe the ground upon which we stand and upon which we all stand is solid ground. I believe it is Bible ground. And I am happy today that in the history of the church there has been no act of mine in violation of this cherished principle."[15]

Some of his peers describe him as being by inclination an evangelist. He held many blessed revivals, in one of which there were 180 reported conversions and 120 accessions to the church. He was a strong and trusted leader, strong in principle, yet pleasant in the social circle and a good conversationalist. In the providence of God Bishops Wright, Barnaby, and Floyd died in 1917.

Bishop Henry J. Becker

The fourth person chosen on the board of bishops at the time the church was fragmented in 1889 was Henry J. Becker, who was apparently a very gifted man, but who served only one term in the bishopric.

Born in Massillon, Ohio, in 1846, Becker went to the Pacific coast as a missionary pastor in 1877, and served several years as presiding elder in that area. Although he was not a delegate to the General Conference of 1889, he was seated by the radical United Brethren group as a delegate when the new body of delegates was formed at the Park Opera House. He was one of those who chose not to "pass from the old to the new."

"At the 1893 General Conference Bishop Milton Wright commended the services of Bishop Becker very highly. He was re-elected, but resigned; and then he was elected corresponding secretary of the Home, Frontier, and Foreign Missionary Society,"[16] where he served the quadrennium of 1893-1897. After being chosen editor of *The Christian Conservator* in 1901, he resigned a year later because of ill health.

An extensive traveler and very gifted speaker Becker was much in demand on the lecture platform. In 1888 he traveled through Europe and spent considerable time in the Middle East, particularly in the Holy Land. One of his most interesting lectures was on the subject, "Five Hundred Miles on Horseback Through the Holy Land." Becker was on the lecture talent list of the Island Park Assembly[17] in Indiana for five consecutive years and served four more years as its superintendent. In the later years of his ministry, Bishop Becker, transferred to the Presbyterian Church and pastored in that church before he retired.[18]

A Survey of Conditions

Prior to the division in the church quite a number of those of liberal persuasion had gained high posts in the church, both in offices and on boards. This state of affairs helped them to hold control of the various departments and funds of the church. Nearly all funds and property were lost by the Old Constitution church. The bishops reported in their quadrennial address of 1893: "Our missionary, church-erection, Sabbath-school, publication and educational funds and property were largely in the hands of those who had gone out from us, and these funds were turned against us. All our great connectional interests required readjustment, and some of them reconstruction."[17]

Of the six bishops serving in the 1885-1889 period, five went with the New Constitution branch, with Bishop Milton Wright being the only one of that board to remain loyal to the constitution and Confession of Faith of 1841. Evidently with the ministry as a whole, more ministers proportionately held to the so-called radical group. A. W. Drury, a liberal historian, observes, "On the radical side, the number of preachers enrolled was disproportionately large, because of the large number of older preachers and local preachers that held to that side . . . and a considerable number of earnest younger preachers cast their lot on the radical side."[18]

From the standpoint of membership no firm figures are available for the immediate period after the division. No statistics are reported in the General Conference proceedings of 1893. A. W. Drury estimates that "the loss in [liberal] church membership, due to the separation taking place in 1889, was about 15,000, this number perhaps, being increased to 20,000 by those that went to various churches or that gave up all church connection."[19]

Naturally the status of the conferences was highly confused. Shortly after the General Conference of 1889, Bishop Wright appointed a number of presiding elders to fill vacancies in conferences. The number of loyal ministers and loyal congregations had yet to be determined. Nevertheless a number of annual conference sessions were held in the summer and fall of 1889 as the conference work was reconstructed and administered. The bishops reported in 1893, "Some of the conferences, though somewhat depleted by the division of the church, remained strong and well organized [e.g., North Michigan, Michigan, North Ohio, and Rock River]. Others were weak and of limited organization. Sessions were held in thirty-four conferences."[20] In this period the church occupied much more territory than it has been able to retain and conserve for the Old Constitution church. Some conferences eventually vanished from the scene while others were merged together.

Missions

Prior to the division the United Brethren in Christ had foreign work in two locations: Sierra Leone, West Africa, and the fatherland of Germany. These fields were lost from the Old Constitution branch of the church, necessitating a new beginning. The story of this beginning is told in Chapter 26.

The Woman's Missionary Association had been organized and functioning a few years before the schism. The first branch organization was organized in the Miami Conference (Ohio) on May 9, 1872. A few years later the general organization of the W.M.A. was established, being effected at a Women's Missionary Convention in 1875. As local church societies were in a confused state after the storm had taken place in the church, so were the missionary societies disturbed, fragmented, and usually disorganized. There was no annual meeting of the Board of Managers in 1890. However a number of branch meetings were held that year. Musgrave in his history of the church stated:

> In the fall of 1890 many of these women, undismayed and undiscouraged, gathered together in branch meetings held in connection with the various [annual] conferences. At these meetings it was determined to hold a meeting of a Board of Managers, and delegates were elected to represent the Branches at such a meeting. By request of the branch officers and delegates elect, Bishop Wright issued the call for this meeting to be held at Elida, Ohio, May 14, 1891. In this the first convention after the division, a reorganization of the Woman's Missionary Association was effected.[21]

Publishing

In the field of publishing the church experienced a complete loss of facilities and publications and had to start over again. Persons of the liberal branch of the church were in possession of the publishing house at Dayton, Ohio. As will be described in Chapter 25, an attempt was made to gain possession, but all efforts were rebuffed. Milton Wright, who served in the dual role of bishop and publishing agent for the first quadrennium after the schism, together with his publishing board, rented a building in Dayton as a temporary measure to house the United Brethren Publishing Establishment. During the first four years all the printing was done by commercial printers, so no equipment was purchased. However, early in the next quadrennium equipment was purchased and printing begun.

In 1893 the bishops reported concerning the publishing interests, "Their financial success has been greater than the most sanguine could have hoped for under the circumstances."[22] They also reported that *The Christian Conservator* had a very large circulation and that the circulation of Sabbath school literature was rapidly increasing.

For some years the *Religious Telescope* had been the official paper of the denomination, and after the division it was retained and continued by the New Constitution church. Prior to the schism the publication known as *The Christian Conservator* had begun in 1885, initiated for the purpose of articulating the view of the conservative element in the church. With William Dillon editor, and Halleck Floyd as associate editor, *The Christian Conservator* was published by the Constitutional Association.

Bishop Wright reported to the General Conference of 1893:

"At the session of the Board of Trustees in June 1889, *The Christian Conservator* was adopted as the chief organ of the church, pending the recovery of our Printing Establishment."[23] This choice, though intended to be only temporary until recovery of the former printing and publishing business, resulted in a permanent, official periodical for the Old Constitution United Brethren.

Education

Prior to the division many small colleges and seminaries had been started across the denomination. Some had already passed out of existence while others survived. When the litigation process had cleared, only two college institutions were in the hands of the Old Constitution church, namely Hartsville College in southeastern Indiana, and Philomath in Oregon. Trustees of these institutions had pressed the cause of the radical branch of the church and had succeeded in holding these schools for the denomination. Both of these schools lasted a few years following the division. Hartsville College ceased operations in 1897 and its building was destroyed by fire in 1898. It was succeeded by Central College at Huntington, Indiana. Philomath College continued into the second decade of the twentieth century.

FOOTNOTES

[1]Walter E. Musgrave, *The Church of the United Brethren in Christ: Its Teachings and Progress* (Huntington, IN: Department of Christian Education, 1945), p. 75.

[2]*Proceedings of the Twenty-first General Conference of the United Brethren in Christ,* (Dayton, OH: United Brethren Publishing Establishment, 1893), p. 9.

[3]A. W. Drury, *History of the Church of the United Brethren in Christ* (Dayton, OH: The Otterbein Press, 1924), p. 475.

[4]Daniel Berger, *History of the Church of the United Brethren in Christ* (Dayton, OH: United Brethren Publishing House, 1897), p. 344.

[5]"Liberal" and "Radical" were terms popularly used before the division to connote those persons or groups which were for or against the rule pertaining to secret societies and/or favoring a change in the Confession of Faith. The *liberals* favored these changes while the *radicals* contended for the original position. After the division the terms were often attached, respectively, to that denomination which adhered to those views.

[6]Berger, p. 344.

[7]After the division, "Old Constitution" and "New Constitution" were designations used to distinguish between the two United Brethren churches since both continued to use

the same name.

[8]Musgrave, pp. 70, 71.

[9]William Dillon, [Editorial Tribute to Milton Wright], *The Christian Conservator,* May 23, 1889, p. 4.

[10]Bishop H. T. Barnaby, *United Brethren Calendar and Yearbook—1904* (Huntington, IN: U.B. Publishing Establishment, 1904), p. 15.

[11]Horace T. Barnaby, "A Filial Tribute," *The Christian Conservator,* April 11, 1917, p. 2.

[12]Bishop Halleck Floyd, *United Brethren Calendar and Yearbook—1904* (Huntington, IN: U. B. Publishing Establishment, 1904), p. 13.

[13]Musgrave, p. 73.

[14]Mary Lou Funk, "Under the Providence of God," *Contact,* Sept. 3, 1967, p. 9.

[15]Musgrave, p. 75.

[16]Mary Lou Funk, "Eminent as a Lecturer," *Contact,* Sept. 24, 1967, p. 9.

[17]The Island Park Assembly was located at Rome City, Indiana. It was called, earlier, The Rome City International Sunday School Congress and was modeled after the great Chautauqua Assembly of New York. It was a place where Sunday School teachers met annually and talked about the Sunday School work and Christian culture. They built a large tabernacle to hold 3,000 people. They built a building to cover a model of the land of Palestine. *History of Noble County,* 1882.

[18]H. J. Becker was a member of East Ohio Conference at the time he left the Church. We do not have East Ohio Annual Conference minutes for that year except for that which was printed in the *Christian Conservator.* Those minutes say that "H. J. Becker was granted a letter of dismissal." The Conference met September 28, 1905. His obituary says that he joined the Dayton Presbytery in 1905. Since other leaders left the denomination following the General Conference of 1905, it is most likely that he left for the same reason as the others.

[19]*Proceedings of the Twenty-first General Conference,* p. 9.

[20]Drury, p. 518.

[21]Ibid., pp. 518, 519.

[22]*Proceedings of the Twenty-first General Conference,* p. 10.

[23]Musgrave, p. 87.

[24]*Proceedings of the Twenty-first General Conference,* p. 10.

[25]Ibid., p. 29.

25

LITIGATION

Although United Brethren believe, that Christians should seek to settle their differences out of court, as taught in the Scriptures, the church also believes that there are occasions when resorting to the courts is necessary, as officially stated in the *Discipline,* ". . . when a member is in danger of suffering an unexpected loss of property."

Since there was controversy over which of the two factions was the true and legal Church of the United Brethren in Christ, there was naturally a contesting of property rights in cases of local church houses, parsonages, and general church property. Resorting to courts further seemed necessary, ". . . in order to inspire confidence and restore faith among our people . . . . The Bishops in their quadrennial address to the General Conference of 1893, made the following statement: 'If we should not maintain the trust confided to our care, by the pious living and sainted dead, we could not expect future benefactions to our church.' "[1]

After the time of division occurred, practically all of the general church property was in the hands of the liberal United Brethren Church. Through the years prior to the division those espousing a new Constitution had gained ascendancy in the church numerically and in leadership positions. This ascendancy is illustrated by the fact that five out of six of the incumbent bishops went with the New Constitution church. As a result of this dominancy in leadership posts and on general boards, nearly all of the general church property was in the hands and control of the New Constitution branch of the church.

Publishing House Suit

The first step in the long litigation process was taken on July 26,

1889, when Bishop Wright, who was also publishing agent, together with William Dillon and C. H. Kiracofe (General Secretary of Missions), appeared at the United Brethren Publishing House in Dayton, Ohio, and presented a written demand for possession of the printing establishment, with all its equipment, real estate, stocks, and accounts. The notice was presented to William J. Shuey, publishing agent for the New Constitution branch, who, of course, refused the demand.

The Board of Trustees of the liberal branch of the church immediately started proceedings to quiet title to the property by filing a petition in the Court of Common Pleas of Montgomery County, Ohio. After some intervening maneuvers, the case finally came up for a hearing on December 4, 1890, before Judge Henderson Elliott, of the Common Pleas Court. "The Judge, by mutual consent and at the request of counsel for the defendants, entered a decree *pro forma,* in favor of the plaintiffs, with the understanding that the case be carried to the Circuit Court of the said County of Montgomery."[2]

The trial before the Circuit Court began on June 17, 1891, before a panel of three judges. Berger described the leadership in the trial thus: "Counsel of high distinction for ability was retained on both sides, the attorneys for the Church [liberals] being Hon. Lewis B. Gunckel and Hon. John A. McMahon. Among the attorneys for the defendants was Judge William Lawrence, for whom special eminence as an ecclesiastical lawyer was claimed."[3]

Nine days were spent in trial, with many witnesses being called on both sides and a number of depositions from ecclesiastical notables being introduced. The radicals pressed their case on the contention that the New Constitution church through its adoption (illegally, the radicals believed) of an amended constitution and a revised Confession of Faith had ceased to be the Church of the United Brethren in Christ.

The result of the trial was a unanimous decision in favor of the plaintiffs (liberals). The defendants carried an appeal to the Supreme Court of Ohio. Four years passed before it reached the course of business before that tribunal. On June 13, 1895, a hearing was held for the case. After examining the reasonings and conclusions of the Circuit Court, the Supreme Court handed down its decision on June 27, 1895, affirming the findings and conclusions of the lower court, that the New Constitution branch was legal titleholder to the printing establishment.

Litigation continued in many places over a period of approximately ten years until property rights were settled. Bishop Milton Wright was chosen by the General Conference of 1893 as supervisor of litigation, and he was ably assisted by Bishop H. T. Barnaby in pursuing and protecting the interests of the church.

Court Cases in the States

Before the publishing house dispute was finally settled, suits were begun in different parts of the church for the possession of local property. According to historians Drury and Berger, of the New Constitution branch of the church, suits were instituted in seven states other than Ohio (where the publishing house suit was being processed and appealed), and in the Dominion of Canada. In each of the states the cases were carried through the lower courts to the Supreme Court. These states were Indiana, Pennsylvania, Oregon, Illinois, Michigan, Missouri, and California. In most states the verdict went in favor of the liberal branch, with one exception, namely, Michigan. In the latter state the New Constitution church was declared to be the seceder, and the original constitution group was given control of the property. "In Michigan, there had been early laws favorable to the control of property by majorities of local bodies."[4] While these laws had disappeared, there were still court decisions that continued to have an influence. However two of the academic institutions were retained in states where the decision went adversely, namely Hartsville College in Indiana, and Philomath College in Oregon, with the trustees of these schools carrying a successful battle for control. The boards of trustees of both schools were controlled by men of the radical persuasion.

Among the arguments used by the liberal pleaders were 1) that the Constitution of 1841 was not a valid instrument, having never been submitted to a vote of the members; 2) that the general conference can abolish the Confession of Faith and the constitution because they were made by a general conference, and that the general conference is the highest judiciary of the church; and 3) that the new constitution and new Confession of Faith were approved by a two-thirds vote of those voting in 1888.

The original constitution group pressed its claims along the following lines: 1) that the work of the Church Commission authorized by the General Conference of 1885 to revise the constitution and Confession of Faith was an illegal step, for the general conference had no power to initiate or propose such changes; 2) that "the question upon which the members of said church were asked to vote was not whether said proposed amended constitution and revised Confession of Faith should be submitted to a subsequent general conference for its action thereon, but whether they should go into effect merely upon a proclamation of the bishops of the church, without the action thereon by any general conference;"[5] 3) that the constitutional provision requiring any amendments to the constitution be passed by "two-thirds of the whole society" meant two-thirds of the total membership; and 4) that those who adhere to the original rules of organization and original Confession of Faith are the legal and rightful church and hence are entitled to the property.

One of the most weighty items used in the legal arguments and in those judges' decisions which were favorable to the liberals was the case of *Watson vs. Jones*. This case controlled the decision in two federal cases, one before Judge William H. Taft (later President of the United States), in a decision rendered May 24, 1897, and the other before the United States Court of Appeals with Judge Horace Lurton delivering the opinion of the court March 7, 1899. The latter said, "The case of *Watson vs. Jones* is of binding and conclusive authority on this court."[6]

In a nutshell, the appeals court decision said that the decision of the general conference, the highest judicial body of the church, was decisive in the case. They accepted the position that legal tribunals must accept decisions made by the highest church judicatories (such as the general conference in this case) in matters pertaining to their own rules, faith, customs, or laws.[7] As a little sidelight, W. J. Shuey, the publishing agent for the liberal denomination and leader in their litigation, was frequently heard to say through the long course of litigation, "And blessed be Watson vs. Jones."

Naturally legal costs ran high, and probably seemed heavy by monetary standards of the 1890s. According to A. W. Drury, the total cost of litigation for the New Constitution church, as borne by their publishing establishment in its defense, was $35,510.06. Considerable other money was raised locally in several states to pay for contests where local property was involved. Bishop Musgrave, who wrote in behalf of the Old Constitution United Brethren Church, stated, "The best evidence we can gather shows that the church, in defense of its sacred rights, had spent a total of approximately $10,000 in this litigation."[8]

Musgrave observed, "From the beginning of the period of litigation, all the advantage in the contest had been upon the side of the seceders for the following reasons,"[9] 1) that through a course of years persons of the liberal persuasion had infiltrated general offices and boards until at the time of the division they held actual possession of the general church property; and 2) the funds collected through regular sources of income "were now used to pay the expense of court procedure to deprive them [radicals] of the property their generosity of heart and their love for the church had created."[10]

As would seem natural, there was much rancor and bitterness expressed by both sides, as evidenced in articles in the *Religious*

Telescope and *The Christian Conservator,* the official publications of the two churches. Church histories written by those close to the time of action also record the conflict. Each side frequently called the other "the seceders." Berger spoke of the "sophistries employed" by the radicals in attempting to establish their claims. Since the division was very partisan and emotional, the writers and speakers frequently expressed themselves accordingly.

Both of the now distinct denominations continued to use the same official name. This practice caused some confusion in the public mind, and sometimes jealous feelings manifested themselves among those who adhered to one or the other of these denominations. On May 13, 1901, the Board of Bishops of the New Constitution United Brethren Church sent a communication to the general conference of the Old Constitution church, meeting at Chambersburg, Pennsylvania, requesting them to change their denominational name. The Board of Bishops of the so-called "radical" church responded on May 16: "We would respectfully say: 1. That we are not only satisfied with our respective name, but it is sacred to us by the symbols of faith which it represents . . . ."[11] Further they suggested to the liberal church that the Old Constitution church recognized the right of the New Constitution church to change their name if they desired to do so.

An Appeal for Reunion

Another event, which is not properly a part of the litigation process, is included here because it has a certain logical relationship in reverse. Twenty years after the division, in the year 1909, there was a serious appeal from the liberal United Brethren Church toward reuniting the two churches into one again. The liberal United Brethren Church was holding its general conference in Canton, Ohio, at approximately the same time as the Old Constitution branch was holding its corresponding quadrennial session at Huntington, Indiana. The former group sent fraternal delegates, Dr. C. I. B. Brane of Pennsylvania and Senator Matthew Edmonds of Kansas, to the Huntington General Conference of 1909 to invite serious negotiations toward reunion. They were graciously received at Huntington and invited to address that body. Each spoke eloquently and feelingly, soliciting the sympathies of the radical brethren toward a return. Brane read the official resolution which had been voted by the New Constitution group, a part of which read: "Therefore, Be it resolved: First, That we cordially and earnestly invite the return of our Radical Brethren to the church represented by this general conference."[12]

At the close of their presentations, Bishop F. L. Hoskins moved that the resolutions brought by these delegates, ". . . be referred to a special committee of five persons . . . in order that a suitable reply may be prepared and reported."[13] Appointed to that committee were W. H. Clay, William Dillon, A. J. Ware, C. A. Mummart, and C. W. Backus.

Some requested that Bishop Henry L. Barkley respond to the addresses of the fraternal delegates. Barkley was a very able speaker and rose to the occasion with a speech which was afterward printed in pamphlet form for circulation. Though courteous to the delegates, he made it clear that there was no interest in reunion on other principles than those for which this church had stood through the years. He declared, "What we want is a church not to federate but that develops regeneration in point of life and character. . . . I invite these brethren to advocate along these lines."[14]

When the special committee reported their response back to the plenary session, the substance of it is found in the following paragraph:

> With all due regard to the wishes of our Liberal brethren, and with no desire to contravene the spirit which prompted the communication so kindly presented, permit us in response to remind our brethren that, inasmuch, as our distinctive principles, as set forth in our book of Discipline, upon which we stood before and through the division of 1889, and which since, as before we have been steadfastly striving, under God, to maintain in the face of worldly opposition, we regard impracticable. From these principles we have never departed, but we would welcome the day in which a union between the two branches should be consummated, recognizing these principles in full force.[15]

Hence nothing had really changed in beliefs and principles since the time of the great schism, so the two separate groups went their independent ways to serve God in the manner that each saw fit.

<hr />

FOOTNOTES

[1]Walter E. Musgrave, *The Church of the United Brethren in Christ: Its Teachings and Progress* (Huntington, IN: Department of Christian Education, 1945), pp. 75, 76.

[2]Daniel Berger, *History of the Church of the United Brethren in Christ* (Dayton, OH: United Brethren Publishing House, 1897), p. 392.

[3]Ibid., p. 393.

[4]A. W. Drury, *History of the Church of the United Brethren in Christ* (Dayton, OH: The Otterbein Press, 1924), p. 515.

[5]Milton Wright, "Judge Taft's Decision," *The Christian Conservator* July 11, 1894, p. 4.

[6]Drury, p. 516.

[7]Drury gives us one section from the decision in the case of *Watson vs. Jones,* which is

as follows: "In this class of cases, we think the rule of action which should govern the civil courts, founded in the broad and sound view of the relations of church and state, under our system of laws, and supported by a preponderating weight of judicial authority, is, that whenever the questions of discipline, or of faith, or ecclesiastical rule, custom, or law have been decided by the highest of these church judicatories to which the matter has been carried, the legal tribunals must accept such decisions as final, and as binding on them, in their application to the case before them." p. 517.

[8]Musgrave, p. 76.

[9]Ibid.

[10]Ibid., p. 77.

[11]*Proceedings of the Twenty-third General Conference of the United Brethren in Christ* (Huntington, IN: United Brethren Publishing Estab., 1901), p. 198.

[12]*Proceedings of the Twenty-fifth General Conference of the United Brethren in Christ* (Huntington, IN: United Brethren Publishing Estab., 1909), p. 147.

[13]Ibid., p. 151.

[14]Ibid., p. 152.

[15]Ibid., p. 157.

26

FOREIGN MISSION WORK BEGINS AGAIN

In the nineteenth century, prior to the division, the United Brethren Church had only two sites of foreign mission work, that of Sierra Leone, West Africa, and Germany. The church had been at work in Sierra Leone since 1855 and in Germany, the fatherland of most United Brethren, since 1869. At the time of the division, the mission work suffered the same fate as did most of the homeland conference districts. The foreign mission work came completely under the control of the New Constitution branch of the church.

Prior to 1889 the dominant figure in the mission work was D. K. Flickinger, whom some have called the Father of United Brethren missions. He had served as General Secretary of Missions from 1857 to 1885. At the General Conference of 1885 he was chosen bishop of the foreign mission fields.[1] At the time of the schism of 1889, Flickinger went with the liberal United Brethren Church for a few years, but after an interval he cast his lot with the conservative branch of the church.

However, in 1897 upon the resignation of Henry J. Becker as Secretary of Missions and editor of the newly founded *Missionary Monthly,* Flickinger was chosen and accepted the position of editor and Secretary of Missions, serving until 1905. "In the General Conference of 1905 held at Gaines [Church near Caledonia], Michigan, Dr. Flickinger, who had reached the age of eighty-one years, handed over the responsibilities of his office to the newly elected secretary, Rev. Jacob Howe, a member of the Ontario Conference."[2]

As previously stated, the radical branch of the church was left without mission property of any kind after the division. When the properties of the Sherbro and Good Hope mission fields in Africa fell under the control of the liberal denomination, "The Church of the

United Brethren in Christ (Old Constitution) was now faced with the challenge of selecting and developing a new center of missionary activity in Sierra Leone. The attention of the church was directed to the area in the neighborhood of Gbangbaia."[3]

Starting Again

Figuring prominently in the re-establishing of mission work in Africa for the Old Constitution United Brethren Church was the role of a key man of African roots combined with a sequence of events which took place in Chambersburg, Pennsylvania. These two lines of developments were to interweave in a remarkable and providential way to contribute much to the rebuilding of mission work there.

The man, the Reverend Daniel F. Wilberforce, was the key personality for many years after the division in providing leadership to the mission work in Sierra Leone. A native African, his full name was Daniel Flickinger Wilberforce, having been named in an unusual manner after the General Secretary of Missions. According to a story passed along, an African family named Wilberforce was blessed with the arrival of a baby boy in February, 1857. At that time, Flickinger was in Africa and convalescing from an attack of malaria at a local pastor's home. A school lad brought a note to his pastor announcing the birth and asking him to send them a name for the baby boy. The sick missionary said, "Call him Daniel Flickinger Wilberforce," and so it was done. But the story by no means ends there.

Later when young Wilberforce was fifteen years of age, he was asked to accompany a sick missionary (not named) and his wife who were ill back to the States. He had served as nurse to the ailing missionary, who had become so debilitated by the African fever as to need help en route home. While Wilberforce waited in New York for return passage, Flickinger of Dayton, Ohio, came to New York with two out-going missionaries to aid them in completing arrangements. Seeing this young African, Flickinger inquired of him his name. "Daniel Flickinger Wilberforce," replied the young man. Flickinger was obviously greatly surprised and took Daniel into his care. Apprising the boy's parents of his plans, Flickinger had the lad return with him to Dayton for a proper education. Wilberforce stayed in the States for several years, was graduated, married, ordained, and then returned to the Shenge Mission. When he returned, he took with him his American-born wife, Elizabeth, who in a true sense became a missionary to Sierra Leone. They began their work at Shenge in 1878.

A second line of development in the restoration of mission work had its setting in the history of the King Street congregation, in Chambersburg, Pennsylvania. King Street was now an independent congregation, having withdrawn from the local United Brethren congregation in 1875. In 1878 this independent group purchased a church building on King Street, and three years later they voted to undertake a mission project through the Sunday School. The King Street Church corresponded with the Reverend Joseph Gomer and Wilberforce in Africa, offering to sponsor a new work at Gbangbaia. With the assistance of Wilberforce, who was still teaching at Shenge, a school was started at Gbangbaia about 1882, which was located in the Imperreh chiefdom. This constituted the first entrance into the Mende tribal area.

Closely related to the entrance into Gbangbaia is the origin of Danville, located across the river:

> The kinsfolk of Daniel Wilberforce—including the town chief of Gbangbaia— had given their son-of-the-soil a hundred-acre tract of land across the river as a homestead for the family, with the understanding that the town to be built on the land would be called, "The Village of Dan." As a matter-of-fact the village never materialized, for Dan wanted to use the land for a mission compound, and so the mission has been known as Danville to this day.[4]

With the continued support of the King Street congregation, the mission station at Danville was developed. By 1896 there was a two-story stone building, which served as a missionary dwelling, a chapel, and a school building housing a prosperous school. From Danville Boys' School came many church and national leaders.

This story has been told to show how in the providence of God events had developed to aid the United Brethren Church in re-establishing its mission work in Africa after all other of the work was lost. The circumstances that the property at Danville was privately owned by Wilberforce at this time and that the early years of mission work there were sponsored by the independent King Street congregation combine to show how God was providentially providing a footing there which was without any legal connections with the original United Brethren mission. In December, 1893, the interests of Danville Mission and the Women's Foreign Missionary Association of King Street congregation were deeded to the Domestic, Frontier, and Foreign Missionary Society of the United Brethren Church.[5]

Wilberforce served as the leader and stabilizing personality in the mission work there for about two decades after the schism in the church. He served as superintendent of the field from 1902 to 1905. At the urging of the District Commissioner and other officials, Wilberforce allowed himself to be made the Paramount Chief of Imperreh in 1899. In this capacity he made a distinct contribution in helping to bring calm and confidence to that troubled country at the close of the Hut Tax War (discussed later in this chapter).

Woman's Missionary Association

Quite naturally the women's missionary work was also lost to the liberal branch of the United Brethren Church, leaving neither a W.M.A. Board nor a "branch" work to the Old Constitution church. Dr. G. D. Fleming in his memoirs reported, "Nothing daunted, brave women sent out a rally call and in the fall of 1890 many of them gathered together in Branch meetings,"[6] held in connection with the annual conferences. "At these meetings officers were elected and it was determined to call a meeting of the Board of Managers, and delegates were elected to represent the Branches at such a meeting."[7]

Upon request, Bishop Milton Wright called a meeting of the Board of Managers and delegates to be held at Elida, Ohio, on May 14, 1891, for the purpose of re-organizing the Woman's Missionary Association. As a result the re-organizing of the association was effected. Miss M. M. Titus was chosen as president of the association that year and continued in that office until 1931, a period of forty years. The corresponding secretary was the officer who operated the W.M.A. office and was the chief executive of the organization. Mrs. Charles H. (Anvilla) Kiracofe (nee Rundles) of Dayton, Ohio, served in that capacity from 1891 until 1906, when Mrs. Fred A. (Cora) Loew of Huntington, Indiana, was chosen, who served until 1930.

In the decades after the division, the work of the Woman's Missionary Association seemed to focus on three functions: 1) promoting domestic and frontier missions in the United States and Canada; 2) co-sponsoring the mission work in Africa; and 3) supporting a Chinese Mission in Portland, Oregon.

The ladies' organization, along with the Parent Board of Missions, gave considerable attention to establishing Sunday Schools and churches in homeland areas where the church was weak or in new territory, raising money, and sending out home mission pastors.

In the early years of rebuilding mission work in Africa, the two boards proceeded somewhat independently in their work and yet in conjunction with each other. Missionaries in the 1890s and early 1900s were sent out by one board or the other. The two mission boards voted in 1911 to merge their activities in Africa in 1912, voting to share equally in support of the work.

Missionary work in Portland, Oregon, among the Chinese is an interesting story. Prior to the schism in the church the United Brethren Woman's Missionary Association had sponsored a school for Chinese in Portland, with the Reverend Moy Ling, a Chinese, in charge. This work passed to the liberal United Brethren Church in 1889, but in 1898 they gave up sponsoring the work there, and Ling appealed to the W.M.A. Board of Trustees for aid in supporting his school and church. As a result the Chinese school and church in Portland were turned over to the W.M.A. on March 5, 1899. For some years this day school, night school, and church operated in rented quarters and with frequent changes of site. In 1918 a permanent, three-story, brick building was purchased for the work of this mission. Ling died in 1926 after giving nearly fifty years of faithful service to the mission. During that time more than one thousand students had been enrolled in the school, and nearly two hundred conversions to Christ were reported.[8] Some of these converts returned to live in China.

The work in Portland was discontinued in 1931, but not until it had served as a bridge to the beginning of the work in China. A short time prior to 1925 a school had been opened on the island of Honan, opposite the city of Canton. It was at this time that the Reverend Yan Tze Chiu came into contact with the United Brethren work there and was made superintendent of the mission in China. Chiu was to be the leader of this mission endeavor in China for many years to come.

Missionary Monthly

Prior to the division the church was publishing two magazines of missionary interest, *The Missionary Visitor,* published by the general board of the church, and *The Woman's Evangel,* the official publication of the W.M.A. Both of these periodicals passed along to the New Constitution branch, and the Old Constitution group was left to start anew. In 1896 the two mission boards consulted together about launching a joint publication. As a result the first issue of the new publication appeared in January, 1897, a sixteen-page magazine with a subscription price of fifty cents per year, with the two boards sharing equally in any profit or loss. The secretaries of the two boards were named editors. "The selection of a name was left to them and from the two names proposed, *The Missionary Instructor,* and *The Missionary Monthly,* they chose the latter."[9] It is interesting that the fifty-cent subscription price was adequate to cover the costs for several years.

The Missionary Monthly continued as the regular missionary publication for several decades until it was merged with *The United Brethren* in 1954.

The Hut Tax War

The internal uprising in Sierra Leone in 1898, known as the "Hut Tax War," cast a gloomy shadow over United Brethren mission work and thwarted mission progress along with other kinds of progress in the land for several years. The British government had placed a small tax on each *hut* in the upcountry region. This tax in itself was not serious enough to cause a rebellion, but apparently it was the "last straw" in a list of grievances. "The Poro Society, a powerful tribal institution which largely controlled the civic life of the country people, decided to act."[10] In a called session of the society the decision was made and plans were formulated to drive these foreign intruders out of the country. Rumors spread of impending war and the intention to murder anyone connected with foreigners in any way, including English-speaking natives. A massacre ensued.

In this massacre seven missionaries of the New Constitution United Brethren Church were murdered. Only by miracle did the Old Constitution missionary, Miss Mary Mullen, and the Wilberforce family escape. However, Professor C. A. Clements, an African professor at the Danville school, was murdered, actually beheaded, along with eighteen others in a spot near Gbangbaia.

Mary Mullen, a minister of the Sandusky Conference, had gone to Sierra Leone in the fall of 1897 as the first white missionary to be sent under the re-organized mission board of the United Brethren Church. Miss Mullen ". . . was called upon to face those murderous natives with their bloody clubs, not knowing what moment they would take her life."[11] But in the merciful providence of God a government boat appeared at her wharf, and she was hurried to the boat, and she escaped. She was advised to return to America, which she did. The Wilberforce family also escaped by hiding in the bush for three days. The historian, A. W. Drury, reported that more than one thousand whites and blacks were killed during this massacre.

Medical Missions

A new type of missionary program was initiated in the early years of this century, known as "Medical Missions." According to W. E. Musgrave, "At the General Convention held at Hillsdale, Michigan, in 1911, Dr. W. H. Zeigler, of the White River Conference, proposed the plan for Medical Missions as a project."[12] The plan provided that Christian Endeavor societies across the denomination raise funds for the employment of a missionary (medical missionary preferred), to help in training such persons and to sponsor them on the field. This plan became quite successful, and many United Brethren Christian Endeavor societies supported medical missions for many years.

As a result the Reverend Vernon Kopp of the Kansas Conference, along with his wife, was chosen as the first part-time medical missionary. They were sent in September of 1913 to Livingstone Memorial College, London, England, to take a nine-month course in tropical medicine. They arrived in Sierra Leone around December, 1914, to begin their service there, serving two terms.

Progress During This Period

Progress in rebuildng the mission work was slow after the division, partly because the base in the home church was in a state of reconstruction and not in a position to mount much of a missionary thrust. Mary Mullen was the only missionary sent out during the last decade of the 1800's. In the first decade of the present century ten missionaries were sent to Africa, but few were able to stay for extended service. Some of these ten died in Africa, and a few others had to return to the States because of ill health. However conditions began to improve, and many churches and schools were eventually established during this period of history. Since 1910 missionary experience has improved and lengthened, with many missionaries being able to give extended service.

Among those missionaries giving two or more terms of service during this era are found the names of Mrs. Elizabeth Wilberforce, Miss Lena Winkel, the Reverend and Mrs. J. B. Woodard, the Reverend and Mrs August Stoltz, the Reverend Charles Linker, the Reverend and Mrs. George D. Fleming, the Reverend and Mrs. Vernon Kopp, and Miss Abbie Swales. Best known of this period is the name of G. D. Fleming, who later became General Secretary of Missions for a period of twenty-five years (1936-1961). He was preceded in this office by the Reverend Jacob Howe, who served thirty-one years (1905-1936), through many of the most critical years in the history of United Brethren missions.

FOOTNOTES

[1]It is interesting to observe that after several decades in the twentieth century without having a missionary bishop, *per se,* that the United Brethren in Christ turned to electing a Bishop of Overseas Conferences in 1973, a practice in vogue at the time of the division (1889).

[2]George D. Fleming, *Trail Blazers in Sierra Leone* (Huntington, IN: United Brethren Publishing Establishment, 1971), p. 123.

[3]Ibid., p. 59.

[4]Ibid., p. 61.

[5]Emmett D. Cox, *The Church of the United Brethren in Christ in Sierra Leone* (South Pasadena, CA: William Carey Library, 1970), p. 65.

[6]Fleming, p. 57.

[7]Ibid.

[8]Mary M. Titus, *History of the Woman's Missionary Association* (n.p., n.d.), p. 49.

[9]Ibid., p. 18.

[10]Fleming, p. 71.

[11]Walter E. Musgrave, *The Church of the United Brethren in Christ: Its Teachings and Progress* (Huntington, IN: Department of Christian Education, 1945), p. 90.

[12]Ibid., p. 94.

27

OUR PUBLISHING WORK:
TROUBLES AND TRIUMPHS

The work of printing and publishing Christian literature had long been an important arm of the work of the Church of the United Brethren in Christ, and so after the division it was one of the phases of reconstruction that needed immediate attention. After the division in 1889, ". . . the church found its adversary in possession of the Publishing House in Dayton, Ohio, and those for whom the plant was established and the church it was designed to serve were denied access to their own property."[1]

Milton Wright was not only elected bishop but also was chosen publishing agent for the new quadrennium. He, along with the publishing board, after being barred from possessing the existing printing plant, proceeded to rent a building in the city of Dayton, to serve as temporary quarters for the United Brethren Publishing Establishment. Within a very few years the first facilities were exchanged for a location on South Broadway in Dayton, where the publishing and printing department operated until November, 1897.

The General Conference of 1897 made provision for moving the publishing business from Dayton, Ohio, ". . . to a locality to be selected by the board, and that the board purchase a suitable building for operation of said plant."[2] The board decided to locate in Huntington, Indiana, and purchased a building on South Jefferson Street for $10,000. The machinery of White Printing plant of Dayton, Ohio, was purchased for $2200 and moved to Huntington to equip the new facility. On November 3, 1897, operation began in permanent quarters, and indebtedness on the new plant was soon liquidated. These facilities were to serve the church for the next nineteen years.

The Troubled Years

However all was not to be smooth progress in the new scene of operations. In the areas of business management and interpersonal relations some problems were to erupt which had rippling effects out across the church for several years.

Millard F. Keiter had been chosen as publishing agent at the General Conference of 1893 and again in 1897. A number of his business practices and actions were to come under strong questioning and accusations by at least part of the publishing board, particularly from Bishop Wright, the leader of those opposing Keiter. This controversy became quite popularly labeled as "the publishing house controversy."

Several of Keiter's business accounts, items purchased and charged to the publishing house, and other procedures were questioned by some of the members of his managing board. Further, two notes involving the publishing house—one a "bequest note" and the other a personal note—precipitated the bringing of Keiter into court.

Mary A. Bond, of Fairmount, Indiana, had in late December, 1898, or very early in 1899 given a bequest note to the publishing house for one thousand dollars. To this effect she testified in court. Soon after the giving of the note, so it was alleged, the $1000 figure on the note had been changed to $3000, which alteration came to light in 1901 during the transition of affairs from Keiter to the new publishing agent, W. H. Clay. According to some records, Wright had made arrangement with the state of Indiana for the arrest of Millard F. Keiter on the charge of forgery. He was brought to trial in the Huntington County Circuit Court on April 30, 1902, in a trial which lasted about one week. Actual innocence or guilt was not established, but Keiter was acquitted by the court on two technical points: 1) that a "bequest note" is not included in the laws against forgery; and 2) that the statute of limitations had run out, providing that prosecutions for forgery must be commenced within two years of the committing of the crime.[3]

A second note, given by Mrs. Elizabeth Bealor of Rohrersville, Maryland, in 1896 for one thousand dollars in favor of the publishing establishment, was evidently handled in such a way as to bring personal benefit to Keiter, which again caused Keiter and the publishing board to be involved in some litigation. The board minority, namely Milton Wright, William Miller, and Corydon L. Wood (later bishop), pressed the case, and Keiter was brought into court again.

Elizabeth Bealor's note was being held by the Local Endowment Board of the United Brethren Church of Rohrersville, Maryland, and when the new publishing agent, Clay, refused to pay the interest on the note as a valid debt, the aforementioned Endowment Board of Roh-rersville brought suit against the publishing establishment. As a result the majority of the board—namely Bishops Barnaby and Floyd with the Reverends Tharp and Montgomery—over the objections of the minority—namely, Wright, Miller, and Wood—voted to have attor-ney James M. Hatfield to appear in court for them and to accept judgment in this matter. Judgment was handed down July 2, 1902, in which Hatfield accepted in behalf of the publishing board the respon-sibility for paying the Bealor note with interest. The cleavage in the publishing board was obvious and feelings were strong.

During the quadrennium of 1897-1901 there were other develop-ments in the handling of the publishing establishment business which caused some of its board members to raise serious questions about apparent irregularities in the correctness of some of Keiter's accounts. As a result of these questions, the board engaged George D. Crane, an expert accountant of Fort Wayne, Indiana, to examine the books. He reported several discrepancies, resulting in an alleged shortage in the business accounts. The Prudential Committee of the publishing board proceeded to have a summons issued, which was filed in the clerk's office of the Circuit Court of Huntington County on April 27, 1901, praying that the court appoint a receiver to take charge of all monies, bank accounts, and assets of the publishing house until matters were clarified.[4] The court did not honor the petition, especially in the light of the soon approaching general conference, and it left the matter with that sponsoring body.

The question of the correctness of Keiter's accounts became a major issue in the General Conference of 1901, with Keiter on the stand giving his report in great detail and attempting to explain his accounts. The issue consumed much time in the conference, and feelings among some of the delegates were quite strong. A consensus could not be reached except that action was taken to refer it to a special committee of five to be appointed by the bishops to investigate the matter. Keiter was not re-elected to his post, and was succeeded by Clay.

The services of accountant Crane were continued, and he made a final, written report to the board on November 26, 1901. His report indicated a shortage of $1470.76. "A called session of the Board of Trustees of the United Brethren Publishing Establishment convened in Huntington, Indiana, February 11, 1902, and continued till the eve-ning of the 14th"[5] for the purpose of hearing the explanations of Keiter, now the former publishing agent, concerning alleged irregularities in his books and in the disbursement of funds. The board was highly polarized in these matters, divided down the middle, with bishops in both factions. At the close of the hearing, Bishop Halleck Floyd, a newcomer to the board, moved that a resolution be adopted declaring Keiter's books and accounts to be correct. Voting *yea* were bishops Barnaby and Floyd along with Montgomery and Tharp. Voting *nay* was Bishop Wright with Wood and Miller. The latter minority filed a written protest to the resolution, requesting that their protest be "spread upon the record."

These unpleasant details were of such a nature as to agitate the whole church. Because "the publishing house controversy" involved one of their own general officials and one of their own general boards, it was a matter of keen debate and strong feelings of delegates from across the denomination who were part of the General Conference of 1901. Further there were shock waves emanating from this controversy, which involved the senior bishop of the church, Milton Wright. As a member of the publishing board, Wright led in insisting on a fair and adequate examination of the accounts and felt compelled to tell his side of the story and that of the minority faction of the board. Therefore Wright wrote and published several pamphlets during 1902, among them being "The Publishing Board Controversy," "Partisan Control of *The Conservator,*" and "The Bealor Note Case." Because of things contained in these pamphlets and other related activities, Wright in turn found himself the recipient of charges of an ecclesiastical nature.

In May 1902, Keiter sent to Wright certain disciplinary charges, which the bishop ignored, believing that they were without a legal basis. Keiter then persuaded N. D. Wolford, a presiding elder in the White River Conference, to call a special quarterly conference of the Fairmount Circuit, where Wright held his membership. Keiter made his complaint at the July 5th quarterly conference. According to provisions of *Discipline,* a committee of investigation was appointed, who after investigation made three specific charges against Milton Wright: 1) libel; 2) insubordination; and 3) violation of *Discipline* in going to law with a brother contrary to *Discipline.*

As a result of the charges against Wright, a church trial was set for him at Huntington, Indiana, on August 7, 1902. When the date and hour came for trial, neither of those who had signed the charges (the Rev. M. V. Bartlett and Wolford) were present, and none of the prosecuting witnesses were present. Further the two committeemen, C. L. Wood and W. A. Oler, who were supposed to choose a third person, could not agree on such a person, so after several delays, the case was turned over to the impending White River Annual Conference.

At the 1902 White River Annual Conference, which convened on August 28, the Fairmount quarterly conference investigating committee reported their charges against Wright resulting from the July 5 special quarterly conference. The conference convened under the chairmanship of Bishops Barnaby and Floyd. The White River Conference was under the jurisdiction of Wright, but it convened at a time other than that appointed by him. This session proceeded to choose its own committee of investigation. This committee, after many hours of deliberation, without the defendant (Wright) being present to answer for himself, reported that they found Wright guilty of the three charges made by the quarterly conference. Part of their recommendation was that Wright, ". . . shall make full confession and satisfaction to the church, and to offended parties within sixty days, and if he fails to do this, at the end of the said sixty days, he shall be and is hereby suspended indefinitely."[6]

Evidently no early definite action was taken concerning the bishop, but his case came up at the next annual session, at Messick, Indiana, where on August 8, 1903, the White River Conference declared Milton Wright expelled. Bishop Wright ignored the action and went about his work as a general superintendent in the church.

In a speech on the General Conference floor of 1905 Wright stated, "I felt that the White River session of 1902 was illegal and so startingly [sic] out of conformity to all legality and justice that it was not to be regarded as an attempt to carry out law in the church and do justice, but to close the mouth and silence the tongue of a bishop in this church."[7]

Wright further stated in that same speech on the General Conference floor that he held all the annual sessions of his conferences that year (1902), and did the same in the years of 1903 and 1904, with one exception each year. That exception was the East Illinois Conference. The majority of the official members of the 1903 East Illinois Conference refused to allow Bishop Wright and Bishop Barkley (who accompanied Wright) to preside at the annual session, and instead they met at another location under the chairmanship of their presiding elder, W. B. McMunn. At this session a resolution was adopted ordering the removal of several ministers' names from the roll. The General Conference of 1905 took action to correct this deletion, ordering the East Illinois Conference to restore all names of members who were in good standing in that conference as of August 1, 1903.

Against this background the General Conference of 1905 promised to be a very engrossing one. Two major problems were gripping the top levels of the denomination, namely, the lingering publishing house controversy and the debate surrounding Bishop Wright. This quadrennial session convened at the Gaines United Brethren Church, south of Grand Rapids, Michigan. Probably because of questions about Wright's status as a minister and a bishop, he did not preside at any of the sessions of this meeting, although he was given the privilege of reading the bishops' address. It is interesting to note this bit of evidence in the minutes of the fifth day, that "Bishop Barkley again took the chair by *previous arrangement*," and an examination of the records shows that Bishop Barkley took Wright's place when his turn to preside came up again, as well as Barkley's own turn. The other presiding officers were Bishops Barnaby and Floyd.

Considering first the publishing house dispute, the issues which had split the publishing board in two had persisted unresolved throughout the quadrennium. The questions of four years earlier were around to occupy the attention of a second general conference. Barnaby spoke in that conference of the difficulty of getting together a report upon which all of the members of the publishing board could agree. Therefore two reports of the publishing board were presented to the General Conference: one known as the "majority report," and the other as the "minority report." The majority report, signed by four members, reported M. F. Keiter as cleared and released. The minority report protested the closing of the investigation and mentioned that several thousand dollars were in question. When these two reports were brought before the General Conference, a motion was made and prevailed that the minority report be substituted for the majority report. After much debate on the question of substitution, the minority report was adopted as the official one, by a 32 to 17 roll call vote. This vote not only indicated the sentiment of the personnel composing that General Conference as to the publishing house issue, but interestingly it was approximately the same ratio of votes which supported Bishop Wright when later votes were taken concerning his ministerial status.

Further, the General Conference adopted a set of resolutions instructing the incoming publishing board to submit the Crane (accountant's) report and the books and vouchers of Keiter as may be needed, to a competent and impartial accountant for an opinion as to the correctness of the books and accounts, and whether he (or they) found any errors of such a nature as to indicate that the condition of the business was not truly represented. In carrying out this order Cyrus M. Smith of Indianapolis and William Swaim of Huntington were chosen as expert accountants to make the investigation. These men made their report and it was published in *The Christian Conservator*, August 24, 1905.

They answered the questions posed to them in the following manner: 1) that the books and accounts were found by them *not* to be correct, and 2) that they found errors of such a nature and importance as to indicate that the books and accounts did not represent the true condition of the business. With the filing of this report the case was considered closed, and the aforementioned resolution provided that the subject be raised no more in the church paper.

The second of these major issues was considered on the third day of the General Conference of 1905. Four persons presented a resolution that the actions of the White River Conference in suspending Bishop Wright in 1902 and expelling him in 1903 were not legal actions, and further that he was justified in officiating as a bishop in the church.[8] This resolution provoked long parliamentary debate. The resolution was not adopted immediately, but it was referred to a special committee of investigation, composed of seven members. This committee's report was not decisive in that Wright indicated his willingness to use an appeal process which the church rules provided. As a result the Committee on Appeals (a standing committee) made its investigation, and reported ". . . that there was not sufficient evidence presented . . . to justify the action of the White River Conference against Bishop Milton Wright,"[9] and the report of the Committee on Appeals was adopted.

Milton Wright had had his supporters across the church, who defended and encouraged him through these trying experiences. Several of his annual conferences in their 1902 sessions voted resolutions of support and confidence. Also as a result of requests from many ministers and laymen across the denomination, a general convention was called and held November 25 and 26, 1902 at Huntington, Indiana, "to interpose in behalf of Bishop Milton Wright." Sixty-two ministers and laymen assembled for this convention. In summing up their actions, they voted to "express our entire confidence in Bishop Milton Wright's integrity and faithfulness as a servant of this church" and also adopted a committee recommendation that there be "a thorough examination of the books by competent bookkeepers," for the quadrennium ending 1901.[10]

The breach in the publishing board and the accompanying division in the general conference failed to become reconciled. The faction of Milton Wright and his supporters had triumphed, and the opinions of the group headed by Bishops Barnaby and Floyd had been rejected, along with the actions of White River Conference pertaining to Wright. Among some of Bishop Halleck Floyd's farewell remarks to the general conference were, "There is one thing however that makes me sad, and that is that we are divided today," and "there is one thing that I very much regret and that is that Bishop Barnaby, Dr. Flickinger and myself and others, are retired under a cloud."[11] Bishop Barnaby also expressed similar sentiments.

With the General Conference of 1905 an era came to a close. It was a period which had experienced reconstruction woes, the moving of the publishing business to Huntington, the launching of Central College, and now the retirement of several leaders of this period, such as Bishops Wright, Barnaby, and Floyd, along with Flickinger, Becker, and Kiracofe.

New Publishing House

Slowly and gradually these troubles were put behind, and the church took another step forward in the publishing field. In the providence of God an interested donor, in the person of John H. Null, wanted to see a new publishing plant built, a suggestion he made after examining the old one with a view to assisting in its repair. Null and his wife, Mary Shank Null, lived at Marion, Indiana, where she was a member of the United Brethren Church although her husband was not. After experiencing the death of his wife and suffering illness of his own, Null wrote a letter to Emmet Carlton Mason, the publishing agent, inquiring of the financial needs of the publishing house and of Central College. His first response was to send a draft for one thousand dollars for indebtedness on the publishing building on South Jefferson Street. He then received an annual report of the publishing business, in which he noted the need for a heating plant in the existing facility. Null came to Huntington to look over the building, but in turn suggested that they build a new one, with his aid. Because of this offer, the publishing board recommended to the General Conference of 1913 a proposal which was adopted—that a completely new building be constructed.

Lots were purchased in downtown Huntington on the corner of Franklin and Warren Streets on which a modern-fireproof, brick structure was built, four stories above the basement and forty by one hundred feet long. The building was constructed in 1915 and occupancy gained in 1916. The total cost of the new building, furnishings, and lots was $50,391.81.[12] Null, throughout his life and through his bequest gave a total of $24,417.46 toward the building. The former building was sold for $14,000, and the church at large contributed $13,000 to the building fund.

John Robinett, son of a United Brethren minister, was the contractor in charge, with Mason, the publishing agent, overseeing the project for the church. The building was dedicated May 2, 1917, by Bishop F. L. Hoskins. These new facilities housed all the offices for general officials, as well as the print shop, bookstore, and considerable office space for rental.

The Christian Conservator

Most denominations feel it is necessary and advantageous to publish some sort of official periodical to articulate the views of the church and to give publicity to its work. For many decades *The Christian Conservator* was that periodical for the Church of the United Brethren in Christ, Old Constitution, the *Religious Telescope* having been retained by the liberal branch of the church.

The Christian Conservator had its roots in the Constitutional Association, and it dated back to 1885, four years before the division. This periodical was brought into being to give expression to the views of the radical section of the church—views which were being given very little exposure in the *Religious Telescope*. The chosen name was significant in that the publication was designed to "conserve" the spiritual gains and historic position of the Church of the United Brethren in Christ.

A few weeks after the division *The Christian Conservator* was tentatively made the official church publication. The publishing agent reported to the General Conference of 1893: "At the session of the Board of Trustees in June 1889, *The Christian Conservator* was adopted as the chief organ of the church, pending the recovery of our Printing Establishment."[13] This action was hopefully viewed as a temporary measure until the publishing facilities and publications of the original church could be recovered. This was not to be, however, so that which was at first viewed as temporary, came to be permanent. Hence down through the years this periodical was "the defender, promoter, and champion of the original principles and faith of United Brethrenism."[14]

The *Conservator* was a weekly paper, with a subscription price in those days of one dollar per year. Just after the division the subscription list numbered about three thousand, and with some promotion it rose to 5800 on occasions, but for the most part it fluctuated below that number of subscriptions in succeeding years.

In the General Conference of 1901 there was some consideration given to renaming the publication, with a special committee studying the question. Three names were proposed, namely, *The United*

Brethren, The Otterbein Herald, and *The Christian Signal.* However when the report was made to the full conference body, none of these was chosen, and the name remained the same.

During the troubled years just after the turn of the century *The Christian Conservator* and its editor, Henry J. Becker, were involved in the publishing house controversy. Bishop Milton Wright had composed what he called a "Peace Proposition," designed to alleviate the tensions existing on the publishing board. Wright reportedly sent a copy of this proposition to Becker with the request that he publish it in the next issue of the paper, but the editor declined. The bishop lamented that the majority of the publishing board had opportunity to express their views in its pages, but the minority were not allowed to do so. This scenario gave rise to one of Wright's pamphlets, "Partisan Control of the *Conservator.*"

FOOTNOTES

[1]Walter E. Musgrave, *The Church of the United Brethren in Christ: Its Teachings and Progress* (Huntington, IN: Department of Christian Education, 1945), p. 77.

[2]Ibid.

[3]Milton Wright, "Partisan Control of the Conservator," (pamphlet, Dayton, OH: 1902), p. 7.

[4]*Proceedings of the Twenty-third General Conference of the United Brethren in Christ* (Huntington, IN: United Brethren Publishing Establishment, 1901), p. 72.

[5]Milton Wright, "The Publishing Board Controversy," (pamphlet, Dayton, OH: 1902), p. 1.

[6]C. B. Small et al, "The Facts and The Verdict," (pamphlet, Huntington, IN: 1902).

[7]*Proceedings of the Twenty-fourth General Conference of the United Brethren in Christ* (Huntington, IN: United Brethren Publishing Establishment, 1905), p. 82.

[8]Ibid., p. 62.

[9]Ibid., p. 164.

[10]*Proceedings of the General Convention of the United Brethren Church* (n.p., n.d.), p. 11.

[11]*Proceedings of the Twenty-fourth General Conference,* p. 145.

[12]*Proceedings of the Twenty-seventh General Conference of the Church of the United Brethren in Christ* (Huntington, IN: United Brethren Publishing Establishment, 1917), p. 67.

[13]*Proceedings of the Twenty-first General Conference of the United Brethren in Christ* (Dayton, OH: United Brethren Publishing Establishment, 1893), p. 29.

[14]Musgrave, p. 80.

28

EDUCATIONAL INSTITUTIONS

Throughout the 1800s many training institutions were started in various localities across the United Brethren Church, but the majority of these did not long survive. There were several institutions of higher learning operating at the time of the division, but only two were retained by the Old Constitution branch of the church, namely Hartsville College in Indiana and Philomath College in Oregon. Soon two more were to be launched, Central College at Huntington, Indiana, and Edwards College at Albion, Washington. Only the school at Huntington has survived to serve the denomination.

Hartsville College had been chartered in 1850 as Hartsville Academy, being situated in a picturesque portion of Indiana, southeast of Indianapolis. As a result of the division and litigation most all property in Indiana was lost to the control of the liberal branch. Through action taken by the trustees of Hartsville College, that school was held for the conservative branch of the church. The liberal historian, Daniel Berger revealed his bias when he wrote, "But a greater misfortune than even its financial or other limitations was destined to befall it, its trustees in the time of the radical defection succeeding in carrying it away with the secession."[1]

Records show that Hartsville continued operations until 1897 when the trustees "turned over all books, records of proceedings and students' grades to the General Board of Education . . . of Huntington (Central) College. . . . "[2] At least two of Hartsville's staff, Miss Mary Lena Barnes and the Reverend Alvin P. Barnaby, are listed on the faculty of Central College when it opened its doors in 1897. The Hartsville College building burned to the ground early on a Sunday morning, January 30, 1898.

West of the Rockies the church was served by Philomath College in the Willamette Valley about ninety miles south of Portland, Oregon, at the foot of the coastal range. Plans for the school were conceived in 1865, with the school opening in the fall of 1867. It continued operations into the post-division period, functioning under the auspices of the Oregon Conference. At the time of the division, possession of the school was contested by the two church branches. Berger reported that contest for possession of church property in Oregon was made to rest upon the case of Philomath College. After an appeal had been carried to the Supreme Court of that state, a decision was made in favor of the Old Constitution branch, but on a rehearing and a split decision, ". . . the decree of the lower court remained undisturbed, and the property was left in the possession of the Church,"[3] i.e., the New Constitution Church.

C. G. Springer in a thesis, "A History of Philomath College," presented more of the details. At the time of the division the liberals obtained possession of the building, but most of the trustees were of the "radical" persuasion and secured an injuction forbidding the "liberals" to use the building. As a result the building was unused by either group for three years. In 1890 the Old Constitution group built a three-room wooden building nearby and changed the name to "College of Philomath." This structure burned in 1893, and another building was built to take its place. This building also was lost by fire in 1905. And again a new building was erected.

Meanwhile in 1892 the liberal group secured dissolution of the injunction and gained possession of the original building. Hence both branches of the United Brethren Church continued to hold college operations in Philomath for several years. It appears from an examination of the Proceedings of the General Conferences of 1913 and 1917 that the College of Philomath functioned until 1913 when its services were terminated. The building stood unused for about a dozen years and was then sold to the other Philomath College.

Another college in the West was begun when Edwards College was founded in 1899 at Albion, Whitman County, Washington, with Laurin B. Baldwin as president. Baldwin was later to become a bishop in the church. The existence of Edwards College was of a tenuous nature, reportedly not operating during the years of 1903-1905, but continuing on until about 1914 when it ceased operation. So Edwards College and the College of Philomath, located in the sparsely populated West, lacked sufficient resources adequate to maintain them with finances and students.

The fourth and only surviving collegiate institution is Central College, renamed Huntington College in 1917. The denominational Board of Education in 1896 began to project plans for a new institution of learning, with the design to solicit from cities and towns any proposals they would make toward obtaining the school. Before such an appeal could be made, an unsolicited proposition was received from the Huntington Land Association of Huntington, Indiana. The Reverend Albert G. Johnson, a United Brethren minister and resident of Huntington, was the leader in forming this association. The plan of the association was to create a College Park Addition of 262 lots to be sold at an average price of $225.00, with sufficient acreage reserved for a college site, with a building to be erected thereon from the proceeds of the lot sales.

The plan succeeded and construction was begun in 1896, and the building was completed in the summer of 1897. The building was "three stories and basement, constructed of stone and brick with a slate roof. The 73 by 106 foot structure contained about 20 rooms including recitation rooms, offices, laboratories, library and auditorium with seating capacity of more than 600."[4] This building remains today as the Administration Building of Huntington College. What a boon this was to a small, struggling denomination to receive such a building virtually debt free!

The dedication of the administration building was celebrated on September 21, 1897, and the opening of school was the next day. The service was held on the third floor, which came to be known as Davis Hall, named after Dr. Lewis Davis, who is viewed as the father of higher education in the Church of the United Brethren in Christ. He had served as president of Otterbein University and of Union Biblical Seminary, as well as bishop.

Charles H. Kiracofe was chosen as the first president of Central College, serving from 1897 to 1902. Previously he had served as president of Hartsville College and had also served the denomination as Secretary of Missions. Other persons serving as presidents of Central and Huntington College through this period were: J. H. McMurray, 1902-1905; T. H. Gragg, 1905-1911; F. L. Hoskins, 1911-1912; C. A. Mummart, 1912-1915; Clare W. H. Bangs, 1915-1919; D. R. Ellabarger, 1919-1925; and C. A. Mummart, 1925-1932.

The name of Central College was originally chosen because of its central geographic location in relation to the United Brethren constituency. However since there were a number of other colleges in the country by that name, often it had to be identified with a city name. Hence the General Conference of 1917 adopted a recommendation to change its name to Huntington College. It was also thought that this renaming would encourage broader support from the Huntington community.

One of the acts of President C. W. H. Bangs was to recommend that steps be taken to receive accreditation from the state for teacher training. As a result the requirements were met and approval was given in 1917 for "Normal" teacher training.

Throughout the years of existence of Central and Huntington College a prominent emphasis has been given to ministerial training. In the early years in addition to other courses being offered at Central, "A three year Bible course was offered under the title of Preachers' Normal planned particularly for ministerial candidates."[5] In 1909 the bishops declared that through the enlarging of this field of study, the theological department was offering a course of study which was competitive with other schools of like training. Hebrew and Greek were taught along with homiletics, general church history, and other related subjects.

Two other buildings were added during this early period. A cement block building was built on the east side of the campus for an agricultural experiment station. Considerable interest was generated at this time in the subject of agriculture by Professor Fred A. Loew, professor of science and agriculture. Loew gave many years of faithful service to the college and was probably its best known professor in the first half of this century. The other building added was the first unit of Livingston Hall. This was a home built by Kiracofe and purchased from him by Dr. S. L. Livingston, professor of theology. When Livingston concluded his service in 1916 he donated the structure to the college. It was named Livingston Hall in his honor, and it became the first residence for women on campus.

Though the college started out without encumbrances, it had financial struggles through most of these years. Financial stress was especially critical during the mid-twenties when the school was considerably in arrears in paying its faculty. A suit was brought by some of the faculty in the spring of 1925, and the continued existence of the institution was threatened. Through some prompt action by the administration, the suit was not brought into court. Payment was arranged, permitting the college to continue to function.[6]

Throughout these years Huntington College was a great blessing to the United Brethren in Christ as well as others. Scores of ministers and dozens of missionaries have received training, as well as hundreds of teachers who have taught in the public schools. Reports of the bishops of this period acclaimed the belief that training of youth in their own denominational institution was necessary to the building and preserving of the Church of the United Brethren in Christ. In that belief many have labored and sacrificed to provide such a school.

FOOTNOTES

[1]Daniel Berger, *History of the Church of the United Brethren in Christ* (Dayton, OH: United Brethren Publishing House, 1897), p. 484.

[2]J. Ralph Pfister, *75 Years—Where Character and Culture Blend* (Huntington, IN: Huntington College, 1972), p. 15.

[3]Berger, p. 396.

[4]Pfister, p. 4.

[5]Ibid., p. 22.

[6]See speech by C. A. Mummart to the General Conference of 1925 in *General Conference Proceedings,* pp. 89-96.

29

THE RISE OF CHRISTIAN EDUCATION WORK

During the early part of the twentieth century Christian education activities and organizations developed in United Brethren work. Sabbath Schools, as they were then called, had existed for quite a few years, but in the late 1800s and early 1900s they began to receive new attention and promotion, and youth work began to emerge as a phenomenon of the early twentieth century.

Sabbath School Work

For many years the United Brethren Church had been publishing much of its own Sabbath School literature and maintaining a Sabbath School Board, but action was taken in 1901 to make the General Sabbath School Board a part of the work of the Board of Missions. This might seem today to be an unusual combination, but not so at that time. The name of the mission board during this period was "Domestic, Frontier, and Foreign Missionary Society." Its domestic and frontier work consisted of starting new Sunday Schools and churches in North America, hence Sabbath School work was an important aspect of the work of home missions. Pastors on the frontier were home missionaries and received mission support, and the new and "poor" Sabbath Schools received aid in paying for the Sabbath School literature. The work of the Sabbath School Board through this period before and after the turn of the century consisted chiefly in helping plant and maintain Sabbath Schools.

Around the turn of the century a shift in terminology occurred with the name "Sunday School" coming into use. During this period, missions were emphasized in the Sunday School, and the offering known as Sunday School for Missions was being practiced. Sunday Schools were urged to "hold missionary meetings and take missionary collections,"[1] to be sent to the general missionary treasury. Today one-half of these funds is usually retained in the respective conference areas to be used for church extension. Therefore gathering of a Sunday School for Missions offering today is but a continuation of the earlier practice of Sunday Schools taking offerings to help in starting new schools in needy areas.

In 1909 the church gave new recognition and status to Sunday School work when the General Conference created the office of General Sunday School Secretary. Sunday School work had been coordinated and promoted through a Sabbath School Association in the years prior to the division, but the radical branch did not provide for such a general department in the reconstruction years, until the step taken in 1909. The position initiated was a part-time office, to which. the Reverend J. W. Burton of the Scioto Conference was elected. His duty was to promote Sunday School work as he was able, along with his ministry. Burton reported in 1913 that there were 437 Sunday Schools with a total enrollment of 27,420 scholars. He also recorded that several of the conferences were holding their own Sunday School Conventions.

Young People's Work

A second thread in Christian education development was youth work. Organized work focusing particularly upon young people was newer than the emphasis upon Sunday Schools. However in the early years after the division, youth work achieved separate status among United Brethren before Sunday School did.

The General Conference of 1893 had commissioned Bishop Milton Wright to prepare a form of constitution for the organization of United Brethren Christian Endeavor societies, which was presented and adopted in 1897. The name given to it was "The Young People's Christian Association." In 1897 the bishops recommended that suitable arrangements be made for the organization of young people's societies in the church.

"Christian Endeavor" entered the stream of United Brethren activity a few years before the division. Christian Endeavor itself had been launched in 1881 in the Williston Congregational Church of Portland, Maine, by the Reverend Francis E. Clark. According to *The United*

Brethren Magnet, a publication of the church's Christian Education department, "In our own denomination the first society was organized in 1886 by the Reverend C. D. Jarvis, at Charlotte, Michigan."[2] A number of other local Christian Endeavor societies soon sprang up.

There was considerable cooperation with the United Society of Christian Endeavor, the official name of the inter-church organization at that time. The weekly topics of Christian Endeavor were frequently used as the basis for lessons in United Brethren societies, and weekly comments on these topics appeared regularly in *The Christian Conservator.* In 1901 the General Conference changed the name of the youth organization to "The United Brethren Christian Endeavor Society," and provided that quarterly offerings be received for the support of the work at large.

Recognition was further given to youth work when the General Conference of 1905 provided for the election of a General Secretary of Christian Endeavor, and the Reverend C. A. Mummart was chosen to fill that office. Christian Endeavor societies multiplied quite rapidly during the next few years, with Miss Mary Melissa Titus and the Reverend A. B. Bowman giving leadership as successors to Mummart.

General Conventions

Christian Endeavor began holding general conventions for young people of the denomination. "The first General U.B.C.E. Convention of the church was held June 27-29, 1911, at Hillsdale, Michigan, and was a decided success,"[3] so reported Miss Titus to the General Conference of 1913. These general C. E. conventions were held annually for several years, through 1918, with the interests of Christian Endeavor and Sunday School being merged into a single Christian Education Convention starting in 1919. Annual conventions of the combined interests of Christian Endeavor and Sunday School were held through most of the decade of the twenties, followed by quadrennial conventions in the 1930s.

A distinctive United Brethren institution grew out of the first general convention that was held. At the Christian Endeavor Convention at Hillsdale in 1911, the Reverend W. H. Zeigler "suggested that Christian Endeavor take up some special interest, preferably Medical Missions."[4] The suggestion was adopted and provided that Christian Endeavor societies raise money to constitute a fund for the employment of a missionary, preferably a medical missionary. The first fruit of of this plan was the sending out of the Reverend Vernon Kopp, who received some medical training in England, as the first United Brethren (Old Constitution) medical missionary to Africa.

Department of Religious Education

A notable forward step was taken when the General Conference of 1921 adopted a constitution for a new department in the church, the "General Department of Religious Education." This constitution provided for the merging of Sunday School and Christian Endeavor work into one department with a general secretary to oversee and promote the work, and also for an editor of Sunday School and Christian Endeavor literature. In 1937 the name of the department was changed to "Department of Christian Education." The Reverend Jesse E. Harwood of the North Michigan Conference was chosen to head the new Christian Education department. He proved to be a very excellent choice and headed the department for nearly sixteen years, until his death in early 1937.

Jesse E. Harwood was born into a devout Christian family on March 7, 1877, near Three Rivers, Michigan. Soon thereafter his family moved northward and settled near Hart, Michigan, where the family was active in the Methodist Episcopal Church. Four more sons were born into this home. One died at the age of seven years, and the other four became ministers of the Gospel: Frank, a pastor in the Michigan Conference; Harry, a pastor and presiding elder in the Scioto Conference; C. I., a pastor in the Church of the Nazarene in Michigan; and Jesse, a minister in the North Michigan Conference.

Converted at the age of seventeen years in a meeting held in a schoolhouse near his home, Harwood first joined the Methodist Episcopal Church, but within a few years he affiliated with the West Elbridge United Brethren Church in Oceana County, Michigan. He entered the active ministry in 1905 and pastored six years in North Michigan Conference, whereupon his conference in 1911 chose him as their presiding elder in which position he continued for ten years. The General Conference of 1921 elected him General Secretary of Religious Education, where he served faithfully and zealously until his death on January 24, 1937, at the age of fifty-nine years.

As the first General Secretary of Religious Education, he laid an excellent groundwork for Christian training in the denomination. He gave considerable time to constructing and writing leadership training classes and taught scores of such classes from coast to coast. It is reported that at his death he left twenty-five hundred young men and women who had had training in leadership training classes of the denomination. Instructing often in summer camps and Christian Endeavor, he was recognized as a gifted teacher and lover of youth. In honor and memory of this leader for a number of years an annual training class was held at Huntington College sponsored by the Department of Christian Education. These one-week training classes were known as Harwood Schools and were attended by lay people and ministers from across the church.

During the early years of the department of Religious Education, a variety of developments occurred. A new phenomenon in Christian Education work began to receive some attention, namely, Vacation Bible School. Harwood, in his quadrennial report of 1925, wrote, "The Vacation Bible School is a movement of quite recent origin. We are not fully organized as yet to carry on this line of work effectively."[5] Also for a time the Department of Christian Education had its own publication, known as *The United Brethren Magnet,* first appearing in 1924 as a sixteen-page monthly magazine. After a rather short existence, it was discontinued for lack of patronage. During the intervening years occasional numbers were published by mimeograph, with regular publication being resumed in October 1941. Throughout this period of the history of the church, remarkable progress had resulted in the important area of Christian Education. Very appropriately, increased attention was given to the training of children and youth, and a fully developed department of church work was created.

FOOTNOTES

[1]*Proceedings of the Twenty-sixth General Conference, United Brethren in Christ* (Huntington, IN: United Brethren Publishing Establishment, 1913), p. 48.
[2]"Christian Endeavor," *The United Brethren Magnet,* February, 1950, p. 4.
[3]*Proceedings of the Twenty-sixth General Conference,* p. 89.
[4]*The United Brethren Magnet,* p. 4.
[5]Record of the *Proceedings of the Twenty-ninth Quadrennial Session of the General Conference of the United Brethren in Christ* (n.p., 1925), p. 49.

30

THE OTTERBEIN FORWARD MOVEMENT

A crusade was launched in the denomination in 1920, intended to pump new life into a church which in many ways was in a state of decline. This movement was labeled the Otterbein Forward Movement, in memory of the revered founder, Philip William Otterbein. In that year the bishops "issued a call for each general board of the church to cooperate in a general forward movement by electing a representative to a council to be held in the city of Huntington, Indiana. All the boards formed the general council of the Otterbein Forward Movement."[1]

American Christendom in general was in a state of declension after World War I and in the early 1920s. Many Protestant denominations were losing members,[2] including the United Brethren in Christ. The *Guide Book* of the Otterbein Forward Movement described conditions in general in the following manner:

> Many conditions serious indeed are causing the true church of Christ grave solicitude. The pre-war boast that Christianity would advance by leaps and bounds with the coming of peace has proved to be the merest chimera. We are in the back-wash of the war . . . we are facing the mad onrush of the populace for pleasure, indifferent to the claims of religion and the church. Many of the returned soldiers are dullest to the ideals of life, with a feeling of indifference to their future.[3]

Denominationally, losses were reported in church membership, attendance in Sunday School, and in Christian Endeavor societies.

Observing this state in the church, the bishops launched in 1920 what was a "new crusade," which was a broad, comprehensive attempt to rejuvenate the denomination. The General Conference of 1921 approved a detailed plan of action for the Otterbein Forward Movement during the quadrennium and even authorized a special chapter in the *Discipline* covering the workings of the Otterbein Forward Movement. The breadth of the program is indicated by its goals: 1) A family altar in every home and the whole church attending the prayer meeting; 2) The achieving of 10,000 conversions during the coming five years; 3) An increase in church membership of 10,000 during the next five years; 4) An increase in attendance at Sunday School, United Brethren Christian Endeavor societies, and Women's Missonary Association of at least 15 percent each year over the next five years; 5) The enrolling of 5000 members in a tither's covenant; 6) An endeavor to enlist at least 300 young men and women for the ministry and missions; 7) An endeavor to educate the entire church with respect to the missionary, benevolent, and educational activities of the church at large; 8) The securing of not less than $750,000 over the five-year period for all phases of the church program, such as mission enlargement, church extension, improvement of colleges, Christian education, publishing interests, and evangelism, with a sizeable portion to go for an endowment fund for Huntington College.[4]

This Otterbein Forward Movement was perhaps the most ambitious program ever undertaken by the denomination. At the top of its structure was a General Council, comprised mostly of headquarters personnel, planning the overall strategy and overseeing the program. In every conference there was to be a conference organization for the movement, with the presiding elders as chairmen and a number of committee people promoting different facets of the program. At the local church level there was to be a committee of at least nine people, if possible, to promote the program. About one year prior to the General Conference of 1921, Bishop Olin G. Alwood was appointed Executive Secretary of the new movement. At the General Conference an aggressive minister, the Reverend Walter E. Musgrave of the Scioto Conference, was chosen to be the full-time Executive Secretary of the O.F.M. for the quadrennium of 1921-1925.

Musgrave and many co-workers evidently worked hard during the quadrennium, with only partial success. There were some modest gains in certain areas, but overall the movement fell short of its goals. The Executive Secretary reported to the General Conference of 1925 that during the four-year period the office had sent out 70,000 pieces of literature and 25,000 letters. Musgrave and several of his colleagues personally toured seventeen conferences seeking to accomplish the goals.

On the positive side the totals reported for the first three years of the quadrennium indicated 8947 conversions toward the 10,000 goal; and 5373 accessions to the church toward the 10,000 goal; and 1183 enlisted tithers, quite short of the 5000 goal.

Financially the gains were rather modest compared to the desired results. Of the $750,000 goal, $246,378 was reported in 1925 as having been raised in cash and pledges, both for distribution to the church departments and for the Endowment Fund. Some pledges were never received. Numerically the total of conversions showed the church to be a fairly fertile field for evangelism, but the problem was in conserving the results. Although 5373 were taken into church membership, nearly that many disappeared through losses during the same period.

Evidently the movement lacked sufficient support out in the field. Supporting organization was brought into being in some conferences and churches, but not in others. Musgrave reported, "One of the sad results growing out of these adverse conditions was our inability to get our local and general O.F.M. organizations to function in the various conferences."[5] He further stated, "This lack of preparation or set up work was the great obstacle in the way of accomplishing the largest results in the financial campaign. In many places the workers encountered the utter indifference of the conference administration and in some cases their positive hostility."[6]

Musgrave offered a helpful analysis of church conditions at the time, pointing out four factors which he believed contributed to church losses. These were: 1) a part-time ministry—many pastors of necessity were otherwise employed; 2) a lack of systematic effort in conserving gains; 3) the shift of some of the membership from the rural community to the city where they were lost from the church; and 4) young people attending schools other than those of the denomination where they were lost to the church.

Since the Otterbein Forward Movement was a five-year program, it was allowed to wind down in the years following 1925, except for the ingathering of standing pledges. No General Council was provided to operate the movement, and Musgrave was elected to the office of bishop. The General Conference of 1925 created a new position, Executive Secretary of the Board of Administration, and the Reverend W. C. South was elected to this office. One aspect of his work was to oversee the remaining aspects of the Otterbein Forward Movement. During the quadrennium of 1925-1929, $31,928 was received, almost entirely from existing pledges made during the previous quadrennium. Thus a noble endeavor ended, with only small gains, and without the satisfaction of seeing much of what its planners had envisioned.

FOOTNOTES

[1]*Proceedings of the Twenty-eighth General Conference of the Church of the United Brethren in Christ* (Huntington, IN: U. B. Publishing Establishment, 1921), p. 14.

[2]Ibid., p. 12.

[3]Ibid., pp. 4, 5.

[4]*Otterbein Forward Movement: A Guide Book* (Huntington, IN: General Council of the Otterbein Forward Movement, n.d.), pp. 6-8.

[5]*Record of the Proceedings of the Twenty-ninth Quadrennial Session of the General Conference of the United Brethren in Christ* (n.p., 1925), p. 77.

[6]Ibid.

31

AN OVERVIEW OF THE PERIOD, 1889-1929

In this chapter an overview of the period is presented from three perspectives: first, a description of the social, cultural, and religious climate of the period; second, a presentation of some of the church leaders of this era; and third, a summarization of the progress of the Church of the United Brethren in Christ during the period of reconstruction.

The Social, Cultural, and Religious Climate of the Period

The work of the United Brethren Church and of any church is closely related to the context of the times in which it lives. There are social forces, cultural influences, and political forces which determine to some extent the form which ecclesiastical activity takes and its degree of success. Therefore space is devoted to review some of the movements and forces of these decades and to relate them to the work of the church.

Through most of its history the church was highly rural, but that is not unusual because America was predominantly a rural society until the twentieth century. "In the year of 1860 only one out of every six Americans lived in towns of eight thousand or more; . . . and, as the century closed, one in every three."[1] People were in the countryside and in the small towns, and that is where United Brethren built their churches. The denomination had many more churches and preaching points during this period than are functioning today. Often churches were only two or three miles apart in some communities, where they could be easily reached by horse and buggy or afoot. In the early 1900s there was a great movement of people to the cities, necessitating the closing of many small rural churches or the consolidating of some with nearby ones. The denominational history reveals that the church was slow in taking her faith into the cities, but fortunately in the 1920s and 1930s she began to move more in this direction.

Simultaneous with the movement toward urbanization was the disappearance of the frontier. A part of the church's missionary work was home missionary work on the western frontier. Mission conferences existed in Oklahoma and Utah and in other places while these states were still territories, but time finally changed all territories into states as America spread "from sea to sea."

Railroads obviously played a significant role in the life of the church as well as in the life of the nation. Without them the westward movement in the nation would have been much slower. In the late 1800s and early 1900s travel by railroad was the chief mode of transportation beyond one's local community. Railroads had been extensively built in populated areas, linking town with town, and it was chiefly by this method that itinerating bishops and presiding elders made their rounds to their conferences and quarterly meeting appointments. Horace T. Barnaby, II, in writing a memorial tribute to his father, Bishop Barnaby, commented about his father's years as a presiding elder in the Michigan Conference:

> During this time it fell to my lot, probably more than any other one, to take him to the train on Friday and meet him on his return on Monday. I recall with pleasure our association on these many occasions and his gentle cautioning as he gave me instructions regarding the management of affairs at home in his absence.[2]

Some of the western railroads gave special rates to clergymen, and the bishops at times mention this in their reports, with appreciation.

The first few years after the division were difficult years economically in the nation, making the struggle to survive and to rebuild the denomination more difficult. History records the occurrence of "a financial panic early in 1893. By the close of that year, some five hundred banks had closed; major railroads were in receivership; industrial production fell off sharply,"[3] and in 1894 a depression swept the country. These were some of the years when congregations who had lost churches and parsonages because of the division were trying to rebuild.

Also in 1893 was that great event known as the Chicago World's Fair. The United Brethren Church has historically contended for a quiet, conservative observing of the Sabbath Day, and the General

Conference, which was meeting in its first quadrennial session after the division and near to the opening date of the World's Fair, voted to register its position that the event not be open on the Sabbath. The following communication was adopted and sent:

> To the Managers of the World's Fair,
>
> The General Conference of the Church of the United Brethren in Christ, assembled in Hudson, Indiana, representing upwards of fifty thousand communicants, most earnestly protest against opening the Fair grounds upon the Christian Sabbath; and believe that in respecting the Sabbath day you will promote the best interests of the institution which you represent, by bringing the best elements of this great Christian nation into closer sympathy with you. We will advise our people not to attend the Exposition, if the gates are open on the Sabbath day.[4]

The official sentiments of the church are further indicated in actions taken by the General Conferences of 1901 and 1905, when they adopted resolutions urging that no members of those bodies in departing to their homes travel on the Sabbath day.

Soon after the economic problems of 1893-1894, conditions began to improve. "The years from 1897 to 1920 were a golden period of American development. They were unusually prosperous years, marked by solid progress in living standards for all classes."[5] Great industrialization took place. Most prominent in the industrialization process was the advent of the automobile. Concerning the impact of the automobile, Arthur Link reported from two students of sociology who described its effect: "It is probable that no invention of such far-reaching importance was ever diffused with such rapidity or so quickly exerted influences that ramified through the national culture, transforming habits of thought and language."[6] The industry emerged as the largest single manufacturing industry in the United States, and it certainly became a major employer in a few areas of future United Brethren churches, such as those in the Detroit area. The coming of the automobile obviously had a sociological impact on church life along with all other aspects of society. It made people much more mobile, enabling them to move more easily and to cover greater distances; hence, there was no longer the need for churches to be so close at hand to the people.

Presiding elders who used to travel by train and pastors who used the horse and buggy soon switched to automobiles to make their rounds. How different from the old circuit-riding preacher astride his mount!

These were decades of great and rapid change. Almost simultaneous with the advent of the automobile was the invention of the airplane. The first successful motorized flying machine was created by Wilbur and Orville Wright, sons of Bishop Milton Wright. They performed their first successful flight on December 17, 1903 at Kitty Hawk, North Carolina. Four successful, brief flights were executed that day, with Orville first at the controls, and then Wilbur.[7] This invention too was to revolutionize travel around the world, but change came a little slower than that which attended the automobile. To relate secular history to church history at this point, in the quadrennium between 1901 and 1905, when the Wright brothers were working on gliders and airplanes, their father, Bishop Wright, was going through his trials with the general church and with White River Conference. His son Wilbur took a keen interest in the events involving his father and aided in defending his father in various ways.

A third invention, the radio, appeared during this period, which was destined to change the world. The radio came on the scene about 1920, and soon millions of sets were sold, changing the home life of Americans. United Brethren have never used the radio very widely as a mode of evangelism, but it certainly did become an influence in the homes of the people.

Reform movements were prominent in the life of the nation during the last third of the nineteenth century and the first two decades of the twentieth century. Prominent among these were the drives for prohibition and for women's suffrage. The Church of the United Brethren in Christ has long been on official record as opposed to the manufacture and use of alcoholic beverages, so its ardent sympathies were with the movement toward prohibition.

The most vigorous attack against liquor began in 1895, when the Anti-Saloon League was formed at Oberlin, Ohio.[8] This organization along with the National Temperance Society and the Women's Christian Temperance Union produced a ground swell of prohibition sentiment. "Dry" legislation began in 1907, and by 1918, thirty-three states had passed prohibition laws.[9] This wave of sentiment culminated in the passage of the Volstead Act, December 18, 1917, providing for national prohibition. It was adopted by a sufficient number of states by January 1919, so that it became law in January 1920.

Another manifestation of the reform movement was in the direction of women's rights and women's suffrage. By August 1920, the nineteenth amendment, granting nationwide suffrage to women, went into effect, having been ratified by three-fourths of the states. With the great accessibility of women to jobs there ". . . came a feeling of comparative economic independence. With the feeling of economic independence came a slackening of husbandly and parental authority."[10] One of the most conspicuous signs of what was taking place was the immense change in the dress and appearance of women. Skirt length rose from a low of six or seven inches above the ankle to knee length in the later 1920s. This change was noted in many a United Brethren sermon.

The religious scene in America was also experiencing great change and a few convulsions. In the latter half of the nineteenth century there arose a trend of thought in the churches which emphasized society rather than the individual. This social emphasis came to a flowering in the twentieth century and came to be popularly known as the Social Gospel, which stressed a reinterpretation of the social teachings of the Bible. Many of the mainline denominations switched to this new emphasis, but not the United Brethren in Christ. The United Brethren leaders and ministers felt that this shift was a dangerous deviation from the main task of evangelism, so the church was consequently opposed to this new social emphasis. United Brethren felt that their task was to save and sanctify the individual and to place as many regenerate people in the world as possible, rather than to seek to elevate an unregenerate society.

Also deeply rooted in this period of history is the modern ecumenical movement. It is the consensus of many present-day ecumenists that the modern movement definitely begins with the year of 1910, with the Edinburgh Missionary Conference, which gave rise to the International Missionary Council. This Council launched the worldwide ecumenical movement. Two years earlier (1908) on the American national scene a notable event took place with the formation of the Federal Council of the Churches of Christ in America. The Constitution of the Federal Council of Churches was written in 1905. It was ratified by thirty denominations, which composed its first membership. The Federal Council began operating in 1908.[11] The United Brethren Church, Old Constitution, was quite opposed to the FCCCA because of its liberal tone and its social gospel emphasis.

Perhaps the most convulsive development in the ecclesiastical arena was the crisis of the "Fundamentalist-Modernist Controversy." During the 1920s the struggle of fundamentalism with modernism became front page news in the secular press as well as with the religious news media. Fundamentalism was the view held by many that there were certain fundamental and irreducible articles of belief without which one could not be a Christian. This basic minimum of faith has been sometimes popularized as five points of fundamentalism: the inspiration and inerrancy of the Scriptures, the virgin birth of Christ, His atoning death for sin, His physical resurrection, and His second coming.[12] A deep cleavage took place in the Protestant Christian world, with those not concurring with fundamentalism becoming known as "Modernists." This issue split a number of denominations and seminaries. Probably the best known modernist representative of the period was Harry Emerson Fosdick, while J. Gresham Machen, a professor at Princeton Theological Seminary, emerged as perhaps the ablest exponent of the fundamentalist position. Machen withdrew from Princeton to help form the Westminster Theological Seminary. Fortunately this controversy did not cause much difficulty in the United Brethren Church. Although United Brethren may not particularly choose the label of "fundamentalist," they have been quite consistently committed to a conservative theological position.

Vignettes of Some Leaders

Institutions in a large measure are the reflections of those who have led them, and it is good to become acquainted with those stalwart men who have gone before. Earlier in this section the bishops who led in the reconstruction period were introduced, namely: Bishops Wright, Barnaby, Floyd, and Becker. Included now are some persons who have served in various general church positions for at least twenty years, whose names were well-known in their times and for years afterwards. These men, who served not only as bishops but in other general church capacities, are F. L. Hoskins, O. G. Alwood, and C. A. Mummart.

Bishop Fermin Lincoln Hoskins

One of the most outstanding bishops since the division has been Bishop Fermin L. Hoskins. The grandson of a well-known pioneer family, the Kenoyers, Hoskins was born a few weeks after the Civil War, June 8, 1865, near Scio, Oregon.

As a youth he was a great reader and student. It is reported of him that at times when he went out to plow, he put a book in his pocket, and when he would rest the horses, he would take it out to read and at times would become so absorbed as to forget to resume his work.

The Lord evidently endowed him well, physically, mentally, and spiritually. He is described as a tall, lanky westerner, with heavy black hair, heavy eyebrows, and mustache. His physique was impressive and housed an alert and keen mind. He dressed meticulously, but seldom wore a necktie, choosing shirts with turn-down collars. He is pictured as a rugged individualist, one who was his own man, yet was considerate of others.

Hoskins received his formal schooling at Washington Seminary Huntsville, Washington territory, a secondary school operated by the United Brethren Church, which he attended for six years. Following this he entered the College of Philomath. He received a Master of Arts degree from Central College (Huntington) in 1910, after becoming bishop. He taught in the elementary schools of Washington, Oregon, and Idaho for thirteen years, served as president of Edwards College, Albion, Washington, for one year, and also as president of Central College at Huntington the year of 1911-1912, while also being bishop. He was noted as a mathematician and was reported to be proficient at Latin, Greek, and several modern languages.

After his conversion at nineteen years of age, he joined the United Brethren Church at Huntsville, Washington territory. He entered the active ministry four years later in 1888, and went with the Old Constitution group at the time of schism. He traveled over several of the western states as a revivalist. After serving seven years as a presiding elder, he was elected bishop in 1905, reportedly at the instigation of Milton and Wilbur Wright.

His career as bishop was long and distinguished, serving longer than any bishop since the division—seven quadrenniums, from 1905 to 1933. Many written testimonials laud Hoskins as one of the ablest preachers in the history of the denomination. Several speak of his ability to hold an audience spellbound, even though his sermons were often of considerable length. As a preacher and as an administrator in the church he was firm and unwavering. He was considered an outstanding debater, especially in defending the doctrines and reform principles of the Church of the United Brethren in Christ. From his pen came a well-known pamphlet, "Our Position," setting forth a number of the reform positions of the church.

During his many years as bishop he continued to hold his residence in the West, and reportedly he made fifty trips East throughout those years as he served each of the bishop's districts of the church in the course of his career. His health was not good the last several years of his service, and he retired to his home in Myrtle, Idaho, without ever preaching again, passing away less than two years after his retirement.

Bishop Olin G. Alwood

Olin G. Alwood came by the United Brethren faith and ministry almost as naturally as one could come, being born into a United Brethren parsonage as the eighth child of the Reverend Josiah K. Alwood, a prominent minister in the North Ohio Conference. J. K. Alwood, after being a circuit rider for many years, became a presiding elder and was frequently chosen a delegate to General Conference. He authored the familiar hymn, "The Unclouded Day."

Within this home Olin received a cultured upbringing, from which he went on to Hartsville College for the two years, 1889-1891. It was during his first year at college that he became converted during a revival meeting held on campus. After teaching school in Nebraska for one year, he returned to Michigan where he took his first pastorate, the Sugar Grove Circuit near Camden, Michigan, in 1892. After several brief pastorates, he was chosen presiding elder in 1903 and elected bishop in 1905, being thirty-four years of age at the time and one of the youngest men ever chosen to that high office.[13] He served in that office for sixteen years, and during his fourth and last term he helped initiate the Otterbein Forward Movement. During the year 1920-1921 he was Executive Secretary of the movement. In 1921 he was elected editor of *The Christian Conservator,* where he served for four years. He finished out his years as a pastor in the New Constitution United Brethren Church.

One of his daughters described him as a broad-shouldered, heavyset man, and rather tall, being very distinguished looking and virile. He had a resonant voice, good for speaking and capable of "leading out" in singing. He appreciated many of the finer things of life. He loved music and played the piano with a firm touch. He and his wife made sacrifices in their parsonage so that their children might have music lessons and a good education. All of the children went on to college. He was extremely well read and was considered a student and a scholar.

"Culturally minded and scholarly, he encouraged the development of talents and was one of the strongest supporters of United Brethren higher education, and served on the Board of Education for 20 years. He held high standards of ministerial preparation."[14] Many young candidates to the ministry were encouraged to make the most of any educational opportunity available to them.

Bishop Clarence Allen Mummart

C. A. Mummart, who served the United Brethren Church in many ways, was born in Franklin County, Pennsylvania, July 14, 1874, to poor rural parents of German ancestry. At a very young age he was hired out to work on farms and attended school in the wintertime for a three or four month period each year. However by diligent application he developed himself and was able to obtain a contract to teach school by his twentieth birthday, a goal he had set for himself. This determination gives a clue to his nature, a bent to his life that manifested itself through all his years. He was a disciplined man, systematic in his ways, and was labeled by some of his peers as an incessant worker.

While living with some Lutheran people in Maryland in 1892, ". . . he felt directed toward the matter of becoming a Christian. There were no special meetings . . . but it was an entirely personal matter as God spoke to him."[15] He first joined the Evangelical Lutheran Church, but upon returning to Pennsylvania in 1896, he joined the United Brethren Church in which he had been reared. He received his quarterly conference license to preach later that same year. He began pastoring in 1897.

Mummart was a man with a thirst for education, and as a result he attended several different colleges and universities, often along with pastoring or holding administrative posts. He received the ". . . degrees of Bachelor of Arts from Huntington College, Bachelor of Divinity from Huntington College seminary, Master of Arts from Huntington, and Master of Sacred Theology from Garrett Divinity School of Northwestern University, Evanston, Illinois."[16]

"A long and varied record of leadership in the United Brethren Church distinguishes C. A. Mummart. With the exception of five years, from 1905 till 1941 he played leading roles in the Church."[17] Because he had much more formal education than most United Brethren ministers of his day, he was consequently elected to several positions of leadership over the years. In 1905 the denomination created the position of General Secretary of United Brethren Christian Endeavor and chose Mummart to fill that office. During the years of 1909-1911 and 1917-1920, he served as editor of *The Christian Conservator*. He also served two times as president of Huntington College, from 1912-1915 and 1925-1932. During those same years of his presidency plus a few additional years, he was head of the theological department of the college. Added to this were two terms as bishop: 1921-1925 and 1937-1941. During the latter term as bishop he also served as pastor of the United Brethren Church at Greencastle, Pennsylvania, where he continued to serve until 1954.

Being self-disciplined and methodical in his own life, he expected much of others, often making him a difficult person with whom to work. Some acquaintances describe him as stern and dogmatic, but at other times people found him sympathetic and understanding. Nevertheless by the assidious application of himself to education and to service, he made a great contribution to the Church of the United Brethren in Christ.

The Progress of the Church

After the trauma of the division, courageous men who were committed to the doctrine and principles of the historic position of the church began to build again in the face of very discouraging circumstances. Their faith and confidence that they were right gave them strength to rebuild from near ashes. The bishops commented in their quadrennial address of 1893: "The past four years has been a period of reconstruction. Many of our societies, torn by a revolutionary schism, were divided, and some left but fragments of former organization."[18] In 1897 the bishops reported that there were thirty-two organized conferences in seventeen states, the territory of Oklahoma, the province of Ontario, and the Imperreh territory in Africa.

It took a number of years for conditions to settle out and for people and ministers to find their places in the new circumstances. The church operated preaching appointments and mission conferences in many pioneer areas which did not prove successful. Some of the conferences listed in 1899 were Arkansas Valley, East Des Moines, West De Moines, Elkhorn, Nebraska, and Wisconsin, with the Women's Missionary Association sponsoring a Utah mission conference. After a few decades these conferences had faded into oblivion with scarcely a surviving church. A number of weaker conferences were consolidated with others until the list of conference organizations since that period has greatly decreased in number. As late as 1926 the General Secretary of Missions reported fifteen mission conferences being sponsored or aided by the mission board.

Some statistics are available, either from yearbooks or General Conference reports, which enable one to evaluate the state of the church and to observe trends. For the year 1898 it is reported that there were 839 organized churches, 597 Sunday Schools, 548 church buildings, and 27,515 members. It is noted that many of these churches did not yet have Sunday Schools, and some of them met in temporary buildings. Evidently Sunday Schools did not have the prominence and stature in the work of the church as they would in the next few years.

By 1912, 531 societies were reported, with 437 Sunday Schools, 450 church buildings, and 20,021 members, indicating a noticeable decrease in all categories. However, despite a decline in the statistics of that year, the bishops were very optimistic in their report to the General Conference of 1913. They stated that pastors reported 3090 conversions for the previous year and made these observations: "Since the sifting of the membership at the division we have never had more members than at present, never nearly so much church property nor have all the general interests of the church been in as good condition as now."[19] The statistics given for 1920 indicate that the above categories were at about the same level as in 1912. When reports were given for 1928, a regression is noted, with 358 societies reported on the chart, with 321 Sunday Schools, 351 church buildings, and 17,129 church members.

For whatever comfort it may be, the bishops in their quadrennial report of 1921 indicated that there was a marked slowdown in membership growth in the Protestant churches of America, starting in 1918. In 1919 many of the major denominations showed loss in total membership. Perhaps World War I had had an adverse effect, and it was observed by some that many of the returning soldiers had very little spiritual interest.

A number of good things did happen through this period of history. Headquarters offices and facilities were moved from temporary quarters in Dayton, Ohio, to permanent ones in Huntington, Indiana. Two denominational institutions were extraordinarily blessed in a material way: 1) when a college grounds and administration building were presented to the church virtually debt free, and 2) a splendid new publishing house was constructed through the incentive of one man's philanthropy. Missionary work, which had to start anew in Africa, struggled for about twenty years, but then growth and stability followed. Sunday School and Christian Endeavor moved decidedly forward during this period, resulting in the creating of the General Department of Religious Education.

A new feature of church work emerged during this period which deserves separate mention—the campmeeting movement. In the formative years of the church, United Brethren were often participants in the "great meetings," but the gathering of people into permanent campsights with annual encampments was a phenomenon of the late 1800s and early 1900s. The earliest campmeeting known is that of the Pennsylvania Conference, which started holding campmeeting at Rhodes Grove in 1898. Near the turn of the century, Michigan Conference held campmeetings at a Wesleyan Methodist campgrounds, but purchased its own site near Sunfield in 1906, with campmeetings starting there that same year. North Ohio held a campmeeting in conjunction with its annual conference in 1900, and after an interval it formed its Campmeeting Association in 1907 and began regular campmeeting, moving to the Rothfuss Assembly Park at Hillsdale, Michigan, in 1910.[20] The North Michigan Conference began holding campmeetings at different locations about 1909 before later locating near Carson City. The Auglaize Conference pitched a tent at a park in Decatur, Indiana, in 1921, and from that time they began holding regular encampments before settling near Rockford, Ohio, in 1936. Some of the other conferences as well joined in the campmeeting movement. Many who have shared in the experiences of these events will attest to the belief that the evangelism which took place at these campmeetings meant much to the life of these conferences.

The bishops in their 1929 report, at the end of this period of study, indicate they believed that there was some spiritual element lacking in the church of the 1920s. They wrote:

> We stand in need of a great spiritual awakening throughout the Church. A greater emphasis should be placed upon the actual presence of God in the person of the Holy Spirit in the lives of our people. A consciousness of the intervention of God in behalf of his church is the only antidote which will counteract the poison of materialistic teaching which is everywhere pouring in upon Christianity, killing the spirituality of the church and rendering the lives of thousands barren and unfruitful.[21]

No doubt many of their successors would declare their belief in the same, that the church stands in need of a new infusion of spiritual power.

FOOTNOTES

[1]Arthur M. Schlesinger, Sr., *The American Story,* ed. Earl Schenck Meirs (Great Neck, N.Y.: Channel Press, 1956), p. 255.

[2]Horace T. Barnaby, "A filial Tribute," *The Christian Conservator,* (Apr. 18, 1917), p. 2.

[3]Henry David, M. Miers, Earl Schenck, eds., *The American Story* (Great Neck, NY: Channel Press, 1956), p. 244.

[4]*Proceedings of the Twenty-first General Conference of the United Brethren in Christ* (Dayton, OH: United Brethren Publishing Establishment, 1893), p. 21.

[5]Arthur S. Link, *American Epoch: A History of the United States Since the 1890's* (New York: Alfred A. Knopf, 3rd Edition, 1963), p. 17.

[6]Ibid., p. 262.

[7]Library of Congress, *Photographs by the Wright Brothers,* (Washington, D.C.: Government Printing Office, 1978), p. 8.

[8]William H. Sweet, *The Story of Religion in America* (New York: Harper & Brothers, 1950), p. 411.

[9]Ibid.

[10]Frederick Lewis Allen, *Only Yesterday* (New York: Harper and Brothers, 1957), p. 98.

[11]Sweet, p. 389.

[12]Ibid., p. 407.

[13]Alwood was not the youngest bishop ever elected. That honor belongs to Harold C. Mason, who was elected to that office at the age of thirty-two.

[14]Mary Lou Funk, "Faithful and Wise Steward," *Contact,* Aug. 6, 1967, p. 9.

[15]"Clarence Allen Mummart," *The United Brethren,* Dec. 16, 1959, p. 14.

[16]Mrs. Russell Griffith, "Biography of Clarence Allen Mummart, 1874-1959," an unpublished paper.

[17]Mary Lou Funk, "A Long and Varied Record," *Contact,* July 2, 1967, p. 9.

[18]*Proceedings of the Twenty-first General Conference,* p. 9.

[19]*Proceedings of the Twenty-sixth General Conference of the United Brethren in Christ* (Huntington, IN: United Brethren Publishing Establishment, 1913), p. 16.

[20]*Yearbook and Calendar: United Brethren in Christ,* 1912 (Huntington, IN: United Brethren Publishing Establishment, 1912), p. 28.

[21]*Proceedings of the Thirtieth Quadrennial Session of the General Conference of the United Brethren in Christ* (n.p., 1929), p. 9.

Part Five

THE CHALLENGES

1929-1981

Dr. M. I. Burkholder

BIOGRAPHICAL DATA

Melvin Isaac Burkholder was born February 3, 1907, to Rankin Joseph and Emma Alice (Garman) Burkholder in Franklin County, Pennsylvania. He married Edith A. Holtry, October 1, 1931, and has four children—Juanita Alma, Marcus Skiles, Bernadine Joy, and DeEtta Jo.

His public school education was received in one room schools in Pennsylvania. He had earned a Bachelor of Arts degree (1939) and a Bachelor of Divinity degree (1940) from Huntington College, a Doctor of Theology degree from Northern Baptist Theological Seminary, Chicago, (1951), an emeritus rank (1972) and an honorary doctorate (1978) from Huntington College.

His professional pilgrimage began with his conversion as a youth, quarterly license to preach, 1924, an annual license, 1933, and ordination, 1937. He pastored churches in the Pennsylvania, Auglaize, and White River Conferences, served as district superintendent (White River), elected to several major denominational committees, and was elected as a delegate to the General Conferences of 1945, 1949, 1957, 1961, 1965, and 1969. His major function has been as dean of the Huntington College Theological Seminary (1942-1972); he also served as dean of Huntington College (1961-1962), and as President Pro Tem, (February-October 1965).

He is a member of such groups as *Tau Kappa* speech society, International Platform Association, International Society of Christian Endeavor, and the National Association of Evangelicals. He is listed in learned journals such as *Who's Who in American Education* and *Presidents and Deans of American Colleges and Universities*. Burkholder has been honored as Distinguished Alumnus (1972) by Huntington College Alumni Association, professor emeritus (1972) by the Huntington College Board of Trustees, and awarded an honorary Doctor of Divinity (1978). In 1983, the Mongul United Brethren Church—the congregation which first petitioned his local license—designated a multipurpose addition to its physical structure to be known as the Melvin I. Burkholder Building.

PERSPECTIVE

Melvin Isaac (better known in later years as 'M.I.') Burkholder's roots are in the Swiss-German heritage. He was born on the edge of the Pennsylvania Dutch culture. His parents and grandparents were evangelical and conservative in their theological orientation and manner of life. His home was denominationally oriented and usually included leadership roles on the parish level. He was perhaps in his mid-teen years before he was ever in a non-United Brethren house of worship.

His interdenominational and ecumenical exposures came through his seminary and post-graduate relationships. These exposures gave opportunity to meet and to become personally acquainted with some of the recognized Christian leaders of the past half century: Billy Sunday and Billy Graham as evangelists; Andrew Blackwood, Charles W. Koller, and Lloyd Perry as homiletics teachers; Clovis G. Chappell and Robert G. Lee as pulpit masters; Paul S. Rees and Harold J. Ockenga as expositors; Carl F. H. Henry, Wyeth W. Willard, and Donald Grey Barnhouse as writers and communicators; and E. Stanley Jones and Toyohito Kagawa as missionaries and social workers. These men and many more have influenced the Burkholder life and ministry.

M. I. expressed a feeling of indebtedness to the United Brethren Church and its personnel, a feeling that extends back to his earliest remembrance. The Church's divinely called pastors, its earnest evangelists, and its faithful Sunday School teachers have all left their deposits of truth in his mind and heart. To them he owes a heavy debt of gratitude. To his administrative leaders he owes a sense of responsive and responsible stewardship. In this relationship, Walter E. Musgrave, bishop, Jesse E. Harwood, Christian education teacher, Ezra M. Funk, pastor, presiding elder and bishop, and Harold C. Mason, Huntington College president have made more than ordinary contributions.

At the close of this period, labeled "change and challenge" it was possible for M. I. to say, "I have known either as a bishop, or denominational official, or fellow board member, or as a pastor, or as a student in seminary training practically every one whose role has been set forth individually in this monograph. The invitation to prepare this monograph was accepted as an opportunity to share a fantastic stewardship with a wider circle. The result is sent forth as an interest payment toward the debt I owe."

Melvin Isaac Burkholder

32

CONTEXT AND CULTURE

The period between 1930-1981 has been characterized in many ways as an era of change—sometimes rapid, sometimes radical. The American economy of this era began in a time of depression, passed through several recessions, and closed in a state of uncertainty. The effects of the 1929 disaster were not fully overcome for a decade. And the unemployment and inflation rates of 1980 reminded some people of the 1930-1936 years. While the economic factors changed from decade to decade, the United States became involved in several military conflicts—in World War II, in South Korea, and in South Viet Nam. There were also changes taking place in the societal or cultural aspects of American life. Some of the cities became victims of racial riotings, burnings, and threatening confrontations. The voices of "gay rightists," "abortionists," and "draft dodgers" came to the public attention. On the international scene "sky-jackings," terrorists "bombings," and political kidnappings also shared the headlines of the news media.

These years also witnessed unprecedented advances in technology affecting communications, travel, and health care. Just becoming acclimated to the radio in 1930, the average homeowner was soon to find competition for his attention from the shortwave, frequency modulation, and the television screen. Propeller-driven airplanes gave way to jet propulsion that led to space exploration. Changes in the health care field were no less spectacular. Miracle drugs, sulfa and penicillin; vaccines, polio and rubella; and organ transplants all appeared during these five decades.

The religious-ecclesiastical scene has also witnessed a number of developments. The fundamentalist-modernist controversy of the earlier years continued into this period. This controversy raised issues and confrontations in parishes and denominations; it involved college and seminary faculties; it affected interdenominational associations. Out of the clashes and confrontations came a number of Bible colleges and institutes, at least two new interdenominational associations of churches, and several new Sunday School lesson series. The theological controversy has continued under the terminology of conservative versus liberal. Leading the liberals, the National Council of Churches has taken the place of the Federal Council. As a conservative voice the National Association of Evangelicals and the International Council of Christian Churches, and the American Council of Christian Churches have developed service agencies in a number of fields such as missions and Sunday School curricula.

The latter part of this half century has witnessed two additional phenomena in the ecclesiastical realm. A number of mergers have resulted in the creation of new denominational bodies. The United Church of Christ is the result of a merger of the Evangelical and Reformed with the Congregational Christian churches. The United Methodist Church is the end result of several mergers culminating in 1968 with the merger of the Evangelical United Brethren and the Methodist Church. The Wesleyan Methodist and the Pilgrim Holiness bodies merged to form the Wesleyan Church. Discussions continued between branches or fellowships of Lutheran, Presbyterian, and Christian (Disciples of Christ) churches in terms of cooperation or pulpit fellowship. Rumors of larger dimension continued to be heard.

While these mergers of denominations were taking place, the American scene witnessed the spawning of a number of new parachurch organizations, independent churches, and occult groups. Youth for Christ International, Campus Crusade for Christ, and Inter-Varsity Christian Fellowship have captured the attention of church youth and challenged the high school, college, and post-college students but have remained outside the denominational structure. The Cathedral of Tomorrow along with an assortment of Gospel Temples and Calvary Ministries represent some of the new forms of independent churches of recent years. The Unification Church (commonly referred to as Moonies) and The Way International represent the unorthodox or occult expression.

The period under study closed with America witnessing the coalition of conservative (or rightist) religious and political groups into what was termed the Moral Majority. Concerned about developments in the family structure, humanistic encroachments in education, and liberal political tendencies, some evangelical pastors and some conservative congressmen took the initiative to join forces in the political arena.

Jerry Falwell rose to the place of leadership and was elected president of the Moral Majority. A general feeling seemed to prevail following the election of Ronald Reagan as president of the United States in 1980 that the Moral Majority could claim considerable credit for the presidential election.

Against this economic, cultural, and ecclesiastical background, the Church of the United Brethren in Christ is to be observed. Several questions may assess what has taken place in the United Brethren Church during these changing scenes and times of stress. Has it changed its position in response to external pressures? Has its evangelistic fervor been cooled? Has it lost its sense of mission or become caught up in a Laodicean spirit (Revelation 3:14-22)? Has it been ready to adopt strategies or adapt procedures to take advantage of the economic and social currents of the time? Has it had a role in influencing larger associations? Has it, or does it spend its time reviewing the past or envisioning the future? Has it seriously and aggressively sought to fulfill its God-given mandate?

It is difficult for one to evaluate or characterize the contemporary scene, 1930-1981. One faces the pitfalls of missing the beauty or the magnitude of the forest when he is so near a few sturdy trees or a clump of unusual ones. Since 1981 is the point from which the reflections over the past 50 years are to be made, these liabilities are accepted with the understanding that corrections may soon be necessary. The following data and conclusions are offered on these bases: official records of the Church of the United Brethren in Christ;[1] a small scale survey;[2] and personal observations and interviews.[3]

FOOTNOTES

[1]The published General Conference proceedings, 1929-1977; the quadrennially published *Disciplines,* 1929-1977; and minutes from the General Board of Administration. Church of the United Brethren in Christ.

[2]A written questionnaire was mailed to all the living ministerial delegates to the General Conferences of 1933 to 1977 for whom mailing addresses were available. The total number mailed was 102 from which responses were received from 36. Of the 63 mailed to active U. B. ministers, 22 were returned; from the 39 mailed to those no longer active in the U. B. ministry, 14 were received.

[3]The writer of this period has attended every general conference of the period since 1937. He was an official delegate to nine of these conferences. He was also a member of the Board of Missions for 12 years and the Board of Christian Education for 8 years.

33

THOUGHT AND THEOLOGY

It would perhaps be difficult to find a United Brethren member that is unaware that change has been constant and to a large degree increasingly so during the past few decades. Sociologists and psychologists have taken the forefront in introducing new terminology. As late as the sixties, talk centered about a person's habits, peculiarities, fashions, and tastes. In the seventies, such trappings became known as lifestyles. Years ago workers went on strike to demand a pay raise. Now they hold a job action to demand a salary boost or wage hike. During the first decade of this period, the United States experienced a "depression"; today economists say the nation has suffered from "stagflation." Premarital sex was labeled fornication or adultery, but now it may be described as a meaningful relationship. Some of these word replacements may be accepted as innocent attempts to update the language or vocabulary.

On the other hand, some changes in the ecclesiastical climate represent new concepts and meaningful change. In the 1980 survey responses, no one accused the United Brethren leadership of inviting revolutionary change in denominational positions. No one proposed that the church return to some ancient landmark. To compare the official Confession of Faith of the Church of the United Brethren in Christ in 1980 with that of 1929 is to find that there has been no change in terminology or phraseology. However, questions have arisen on occasion as to the interpretation of the Confession of Faith. In view of these questions, studies have been authorized, research has been made, and position papers have been adopted. Such studies and reports have been made on the subjects of "itineracy," "superintendency," "family life," "human rights," "baptism," "the gifts of the Spirit," "the Word of

God," and "the depravity of man."

Should the United Brethren Church have been actively pressing for change in some of these areas of thought and theology? By a large majority, the respondents in the 1980 survey thought the Church of the United Brethren in Christ was slow or hesitant in carrying out the Lord's mandate to the church.[1] It would be incorrect to conclude that the denominational leaders were unaware of the changes taking place or to say they refused to face the challenge of the new theological climate.

Moral reform issues were prominent in the General Conference of 1933 and since. National prohibition, secret combinations, and modernism were subjects of discussion, resolution, and action. The following position was reaffirmed in 1933:

> That in our preaching we point out the dangers of modernism when necessary; and fortify our people against such evils by means of an intelligent and constructive presentation of the truth on these doctrines as found in the Word of God.[2]

The same view was expressed in the report on education at the General Conference of 1933: "As far as is humanly possible no text books which teach modernism as either true or desirable, shall be used, and reference books shall be carefully selected and used to further orthodoxy."[3]

Two studies in the area of the gifts of the Spirit have been made in the last two decades. The first of these was authorized in 1963 and was undertaken by a committee of three (Bishop Clyde W. Meadows, J. Ralph Pfister, and M. I. Burkholder). The resulting report, *The Spirit-Filled Life and the Tongues Movement,* was adopted after amendment, by the General Conference of 1965. By such adoption it became "a valid doctrinal position of the Church of the United Brethren in Christ."[4]

A further study in this theological area was authorized by the General Conference of 1973 by the adoption of the following resolution:

> The document in the workbook on the Holy Spirit . . . shall be referred to a study committee to be appointed by the executive committee of the general board of administration. The general board shall have power to act.[5]

The general board responded by appointing a committee of seven ". . . chosen from a broad representation in the Church."[6] The report of this committee, *The Holy Spirit—An Approach to Understanding His Gifts,* was adopted by the general board of administration on May 24, 1974. It was set forth

. . . as a guide for all members of the Church of the United Brethren in Christ and is to be applied in their teaching, preaching and practice. It supercedes the publication *The Spirit-Filled Life and the Tongues Movement* together with the resolution adopted by the General Board of Administration, June 5, 1963.[7]

These reports were both warmly received and vigorously challenged. A few ministers, and in some cases a part of their parish membership, found more freedom of expression relative to 'the experience' in other denominations. In a few local situations, it was found expedient for the denomination to sell the property to the fractured congregation or to its withdrawing members.

Respondents to the 1980 questionnaire differed in their assessment of the position on the gifts of the Spirit taken by the denomination. Some agreed. Others disagreed. However, by a three to one ratio they indicated that the taking of this official position was one of the two most important actions taken in the past fifty years. The other action, given this distinction, was the amendment to the Church's Constitution whereby lay representation was permitted in general conference. Actually, from the respondents, these two items tied for first place in importance.

The positional paper on the Holy Spirit did not claim to be a new or different interpretation, but rather a fuller statement of the United Brethren position. The paper proceeded on two assumptions:

1) There is validity today for the expression of the biblical gifts of the Holy Spirit, 2) The reception of the gift of the Holy Spirit qualifies the believer for any of the gifts that the Holy Spirit may choose to give him.[8]

The conclusions set forth in the paper are four:

1) The Holy Spirit is a gift to the Church; 2) The Holy Spirit ministers to the believer; 3) The Holy Spirit ministers through His enabling gifts; 4) The Spirit superintends His gifts.[9]

"Biblical Revelation and Inspiration," a paper regarding the inerrancy of the Word of God was written and presented by the Reverend Paul R. Fetters. The study reaffirmed the church's evangelical position when it declared again "We believe that the Holy Bible, Old and New Testaments is the Word of God."[10]

The General Conference of 1969 adopted a revised heading and an enlarged statement for its Moral Reform paragraphs. Updated to reflect the church position on narcotics, gambling, pornography, human relations, and family life, parts of the section stated positions previously delineated while other parts introduced an official position for the first time. The *Discipline* heading was revised to read: Moral Standards and Social Concerns. The new statement reflected an awakened awareness of the church to the fact that family life and human freedom were being threatened at a number of points in the present culture.[11]

The General Conference of 1981 received "The United Brethren Understanding of the Depravity of Man," a position paper on depravity, written and presented by Dr. Fetters. The following summary statement, also given by Fetters, was adopted as the official doctrine of the Church:

> . . . that all men are born, because of the fall of the race in Adam, with an inherent tendency toward evil. This depravity has negatively [affected every faculty] and is operative in every faculty of one's being. Each person because of the inherited depravity, when confronted by the world, the flesh, and the devil, will follow his sinful nature, deliberately choosing to ratify sin and thus assumes the guilt and condemnation belonging to a sinner.[12]

FOOTNOTES

[1]50% of the respondents said "slow"; another 35% said "hesitant."

[2]*Proceedings of the Thirty-first General Conference of the Church of the United Brethren in Christ* (Huntington, IN: Board of Administration, 1933), mimeographed brief.

[3]Ibid., p. 15.

[4]*Proceedings of the Thirty-ninth General Conference of the Church of the United Brethren in Christ* (Huntington, IN: United Brethren Publishing Establishment, 1965), pp. 264, 359.

[5]*Proceedings of the Forty-first General Conference of the Church of the United Brethren in Christ* (Huntington, IN: United Brethren Publishing Establishment, 1973), p. 200.

[6]Inside front cover of the printed document. (Members of the committee were: Paul R. Fetters, Duane Reahm, Raymond Waldfogel, M. I. Burkholder, Kirby Keller, Kent Maxwell, and Marvin Price.)

[7]Ibid. (pages not numbered)

[8]Ibid.

[9]Ibid.

[10]Church of the United Brethren Confession of Faith, para. 5.

[11]*Proceedings of the Fortieth General Conference of the Church of the United Brethren in Christ* (Huntington, IN: United Brethren Publishing Establishment, 1969), pp. 42-45.

[12]*Proceedings of the Forty-third General Conference of the Church of the United Brethren in Christ* (Huntington, IN: United Brethren Publishing Establishment, 1981), p. 21.

34

POLICY AND PROCEDURE

Article IV

During the last half century, one of the most far-reaching actions in the area of policy change or policy making in the denomination has been the amending of the Constitution, Article IV. The division in 1889 had resulted in strong affirmations in defense of the Constitution of 1841[1] and some smugness in the idea that that original constitution should be preserved at all cost.

However, in the early 1940s, the question of lay representation in the general conference surfaced as an issue. The Constitution of 1841 limited the membership of the general conference to ". . . elders, elected by the members in every conference district throughout the society."[2] Article IV, of the Constitution, provided the means for the voiced change. However, the practicality of the procedure proposed in Article IV was questioned. The Bishops' Quadrennial Address to the General Conference of 1945 took note of the issue and recommended initial steps for bringing the dilemma before the church.[3]

During the 1945-1949 quadrennium ". . . the secretary of the (General) Board of Administration conferred with the church attorney, and petitions for lay representation were prepared, printed and circulated throughout the Church."[4] Considerable effort was made in the circulation of the petitions during the quadrennium. "However, the activity was not sufficient to bring to this (1949) General Conference any recommendation."[5] A total of 2572 signatures was reported. Thus the petition effort ended.

The Reverend Lloyd Eby, Detroit, refused to bury the call for lay representation. In the General Conference of 1949 he made the following proposal:

> In order to maintain the democracy of this church, and to show the workability of our constitution, we move that this conference authorize the General Board of Administration to conduct a referendum on the matter of lay representation to the General Conference, through the agency of the Conference Councils of Administration and by them through the local Councils.[6]

This proposal placed the responsibility of getting the petition to the people through the general and conference councils rather than through the pastors.

The Bishops' report to the General Conference of 1953 included these comments: "The vote on lay representation in General Conference reported to you today shows a wide divergence in interest and opinion from the vote given in the past . . . The average membership for the quadrennium was 18,554, and the percentage voted was 60.0%."[7] The bishops then added this recommendation:

> That this incoming General Board of Administration be authorized by this general conference to conduct a referendum throughout this coming quadrennium for the modifying of Article IV of our constitution.[8]

A change in procedure was offered in the General Conference of 1957. A referendum was proposed for amending Article IV. The proposed amendment was to change Article IV to read:

> There shall be no alteration in the foregoing Constitution unless by two-thirds vote of the General Conference, provided a request for such change has come from the majority of those who elected that general conference.[9]

The board of bishops reported to the General Conference of 1957 that the referendum conducted during the previous four years resulted (as of June 10, 1957, at 3 p.m.):

Adult membership	19,033
Affirmative votes	13,368
Negative votes	2,844
Total votes cast	16,212
Votes necessary to make the change	12,688.[10]

On June 14, 1957, the Board of Bishops affirmed that as of ". . . June 14, 1957, the Church of the United Brethren in Christ

passes from under the Constitution of 1841 (sic) and henceforth oper-
ates under the revised Constitution as presently declared.

(Signed) Ezra Funk

Lloyd Eby."[11]

Considerable significance has been credited to this particular action:
1) It answered a question that had haunted some members for years: Is
it going to be possible for the church to make any alteration to the
constitution? The answer given in the General Conference of 1957 was
a definite "Yes!" It was an already accomplished fact. Later receipts of
ballots showed that 84.7 per cent of the entire membership had voted
and that the affirmative vote for the change was 69.9 per cent. 2) This
action opened the door and encouraged the proposal of several other
referenda.

Terminology

The General Conference of 1957 adopted resolutions whereby four
separate items became objects for referenda during the ensuing quadrennium. These resolutions would provide, if approved, that 1) all
officials elected by General Conference become members ex officio of
that body; 2) provision be made for lay representation in General
Conference; 3) the term "quarterly" in the preamble of the Constitution be changed to "local"; and 4) the term "bishops" in Article I,
section 2 of the Constitution be changed to "bishop or bishops."[12]

One of the early actions of the General Conference of 1961 was to
consider the referenda results. By separate votes 1) to change the term
"quarterly" to "local" in the preamble of the Constitution was adopted
unanimously; 2) to grant lay representation in the general conference
was unanimously adopted; 3) making all officials elected by the general conference to become members ex officio was adopted by a 44-15
affirmative vote, and 4) making provision for "one or more" bishops
adopted by a 44-6 affirmative vote.[13] Thus the long-sought goal of lay
representation in general conference became a reality. Chairman Clarence E. Carlson announced the fact: "I declare the amendments to be in
effect . . . ."[14]

Further referenda were conducted. The General Conference of 1969
changed the term "class leader" to "lay leader." The General Conference of 1973 adopted provisions whereby ". . . church property may
be held by the local congregation" and for ". . . annual conferences to
provide nominees for the general conference."[15] It appears thus far that
the referendum completed in 1957 has made it possible to secure a

greater degree of flexibility in constitutional matters without endanger-
ing the basic structure.

The policy changes implied by the referenda have resulted in adapta-
tions in the field of administration. 1) Fewer visits are now made to
the local parish by the conference superintendents previously known as
presiding elders. 2) Lay persons have responded to the general conference delegate responsibilities in a commendable fashion. 3) There
are indications that the United Brethren Church is moving to more of a
congregational polity in relation to church property and to parish
assignments. The General Conference of 1981 took action to change
the *Discipline* so as to make it more difficult for local churches to
involve the total denomination in business or financial ventures.

Administrative Adjustments

The administrative structure of the Church of the United Brethren in
Christ, above the parish level, has undergone few changes during this
1930-1980 period. Some terminology has been changed and some
departmental rearrangements have taken place. During the period,
gradual departmental growth has become evident. However, the spot-
light of administration throughout this period has focused upon the
board of bishops. The office of bishop is filled first in the general
conference elections. Until 1969, it was a common practice to include
the bishops on practically all of the departmental boards.

The number of bishops elected to serve a quadrennium has fluctuated from two to four.[16] One new bishop was elected in 1929 to
function with two who were reelected to the overseer relationship.
From 1949 to 1969 the oversight was left to the responsibility of two
bishops. In 1969 a study committee recommended that five bishops be
elected. The General Conference of 1969 responded by electing four
and designating one of these to have an overseas jurisdiction. The same
conference replaced the General Secretary of Missions by the overseas
bishop.

At this same juncture (the General Conference of 1969), the pattern
of administration took a definite turn in the direction of a more
involved relationship with the pastors and the conference councils of
administration. The bishops' responsibilities were redescribed so as to
support the conference superintendent in some areas and to relieve him
of certain responsibilities in other areas. The purpose of the description
was to further personalize the bishop-parish relationship; and to
involve the bishop with the prospective minister in the early stages of

licensuring.

By virtue of a referendum, the General Conference of 1973 revised Article III of the Constitution so as to allow local churches to hold title to their property as ". . . provided for in the *Discipline.*"[17]

The net results of this referendum were cancelled eight years later:

> The General Conference of 1981 deleted from the *Discipline* the provisions whereby a local congregation can hold title to their property. The Board of Bishops, with legal counsel, has interpreted the deletion from the *Discipline* to mean that local churches cannot obtain title to their property since the provisions have been deleted from the *Discipline.*[18]

The constitutional provision remains, but no local church can receive title to its property unless and until a future general conference sees fit to include such provision through revision of *Discipline.*

The 1969-1973 quadrennium witnessed the introduction of briefing conferences, auditing days, and additional meetings with the conference councils. These were aimed at keeping the program from becoming static and to improve administrative procedures.

The overseas bishop was expected to personally preside at the annual conferences under his jurisdiction, the same as was the custom on the North American continent. The overseas conferences have responded well to this increased oversight. For the Hong Kong and Sierra Leone conferences this administrative change was a new recognition and seemed to reflect something of a new status for them also. Since this time, Jamaica and Honduras have received two visits per year from the overseas bishop.

Annual conferences seem to occupy a strategic place in relation to the total administrative effectiveness. It is in the annual conference that persons are licensed and ordained. It is in the annual conference that the denominational program and projects are largely interpreted for the local parish. And, through that local parish the goals are reached.

The observable trends are noticed in terms of the number of annual conferences during the past fifty years. 1) The first trend is in a continuing number of mergers among the annual conferences. Delegates from nineteen of the twenty annual conferences were gathered for the General Conference of 1929. Beginning with the General Conference of 1937 one or more annual conferences have been merged with another in most of the sessions held. Until 1981 the number of twenty conferences on the North American continent had been reduced to eleven. (See "Organized Conferences" graph in appendix.)

2) The second trend is in the growing number of new mission conferences established or upgraded from mission districts. The

Alberta (Canada) and the Imperreh (Sierra Leone) districts were the only ones recognized officially in 1929. The Alberta district was abandoned in 1949. Since 1940, the following mission districts have achieved conference status: 1941—Detroit, Africa; 1949—Honduras, Jamaica; 1965—Hong Kong; 1969 Florida; 1977—Africa was divided into the Provincial and the Western conferences. Geographically the United Brethren Church is ministering to increased areas but with fewer conferences than in 1929.

Administrative structure has been intertwined somewhat with statements of policy. The idea of having a general board of administration goes back to the General Conference of 1925. A budget basis for the finances of the denomination and the election of a general treasurer also date from that same conference.

At the General Conference of 1929 the General Board of Administration consisted of ". . . the bishops, ex officio, an executive secretary, and seven other members who shall be elected by the General Conferences."[19] The duties of the board were spelled out in some detail. In general it was charged with the initiation and the promotion of the plans of the church.

By 1933 ". . . the board of bishops together with the general secretaries of the several departments of the church" were to constitute the general board of administration ". . . by virtue of their office."[20] The publishing agent and the general treasurer were added in 1937.[21] And in 1949 the following additional members were added ex officio: the secretary of the Woman's Missionary Association, the editor of *The Christian Conservator,* and the superintendents of the various annual conferences.[22]

The office of executive secretary continued until 1965. At that time a limitation was placed on the number of conference superintendents that were to be included. The limitation affected only those conferences ". . . with multiple superintendents and less than 10000 members," in which cases only the senior superintendent was included.[23]

The conference superintendent representation at present is on the basis of church membership in the annual conference. Conferences with 1000 members, or less, have one representative on the general board; those with 1001 to 2500 members have two representatives; 2501 to 4000 members have three; and those 4001 or more members are entitled to four representatives.[24]

To provide for deeper study of issues and to facilitate operations, the general board has provided for such standing committees as an executive committee and an administrative committee. It frequently uses *ad hoc* committees for special studies or projects.

The area of organizational structure became an arena of renewed interest during the 1977-1981 quadrennium. Some were asking: Is the structure of multiple bishops and pastor-superintendents the most efficient one? Does the present departmental structure represent the most efficient use of persons and materials? Is some restructuring of administration essential to future growth?

In May 1978, authorization of a structure study was made by the General Board of Administration. Christian Service Fellowship[25] was selected to make such a study. In May 1980, the General Board went on record "to adopt the concepts and principles included in the Evaluation Study Report and recommend to the General Conference such measures as are needed to implement them."[26]

A task force consisting of one lay person and one minister from each bishop's district in North America was appointed. This task force reported to the executive committee of the Board of Administration in October 1980. The report was considered and after amendment was referred to the General Conference of 1981.

The recommended report to the General Conference of 1981 proposed a new emphasis on person-centered ministry and an administrative structure under the supervision of one bishop and four regional superintendents. (Such proposal would replace four bishops and more than twenty pastor-superintendents.) Departmental realignment was also projected in the report, with a goal of releasing some pastors from multicommittee responsibilities.

The members of the General Conference of 1981 agreed with the philosophy of ministry set forth. But after an hour or more of debate, the conference members voted 38 to 33 to have the study continued for another four years while the church continues to operate under the current structure for bishops.

In the departmental areas some changes were effected in harmony with the recommendations of the task force. Departments were reduced in number into commissions; commissions would be under the administrative direction of a board through a director. The board would establish philosophy, set policy, and evaluate results in the light of general conference action. The director would have the responsibility of carrying out the decisions of the board.

FOOTNOTES

[1]*Origin, Doctrine, Constitution and Discipline of the Church of the United Brethren in Christ 1941-1945* (Huntington, IN: United Brethren Publishing Establishment, 1941), Constitution, Article I, Section 1, p. 25.

[2]*Proceedings of the Thirty-fifth General Conference of the Church of the United*

Brethren in Christ (Huntington, IN: United Brethren Establishment, 1949), p. 266.

[3]The 4th recommendation read: "That the Annual Conference take the necessary steps looking forward to the necessary changes in the Constitution of the Church that will provide for lay representation in the General Conference," *Proceedings of the Thirty-fourth General Conference of the Church of the United Brethren in Christ* (Huntington, IN: United Brethren Publishing Establishment, 1945), p. 256.

[4]*Proceedings of the Thirty-fifth General Conference,* p. 266.

[5]Ibid.

[6]Ibid., p. 149.

[7]*Proceedings of the Thirty-sixth General Conference of the Church of the United Brethren in Christ* (Huntington, IN: United Brethren Publishing Establishment, 1953), p. 450.

[8]Ibid., p. 451.

[9]*Proceedings of the Thirty-seventh General Conference of the Church of the United Brethren in Christ* (Huntington, IN: United Brethren Publishing Establishment, 1957), p. 376.

[10]Ibid.

[11]Ibid., p. 377.

[12]Ibid., Part IV, p. 18.

[13]*Proceedings of the Thirty-eighth General Conference of the Church of the United Brethren in Christ* (Huntington, IN: United Brethren Publishing Establishment, 1961), Bishops' Quadrennial Address, Report 1-2 The Referendum.

[14]Ibid., p. 21.

[15]*Origin, Doctrine, Constitution and Discipline . . . . 1973-1977,* p. 5.

[16]See Appendix for names and years of administration.

[17]*Discipline: 1973-1977,* p. 9.

[18]Paul R. Fetters, "Are We By-passing *Our Constitution?" The United Brethren, May,* 1983, pp. 4-8.

[19]*Discipline: 1929-1933,* para. 108.

[20]*Discipline: 1933-1937,* para. 108, sec 1.

[21]*Discipline: 1937-1941,* para. 110, sec 1.

[22]*Discipline: 1949-1953,* para. 79, sec 1.

[23]*Discipline: 1965-1969,* p. 73.

[24]*Discipline: 1977-1981,* para. 224.2.

[25]Christian Service Fellowship, 6500 Xeres Avenue, South Minneapolis, Minnesota 55423.

[26]Minutes of the General Board of Administration, May 1980, Items 37-80.

35

OUTREACH AND ORGANIZATION

Denominational growth and outreach may be viewed from various perspectives: geographical spread, institutional development, membership gains, and ecumenical involvement. Geographically there was limited outreach between 1930 and 1981. It was noted earlier that there was a definite reduction in the number of annual conferences during this period, especially since 1945. But the geographical spread remained practically the same. The Alberta mission district in western Canada, disbanded in 1949, marked the sole loss geographically.[1] On the other hand the states of Florida, Arizona, and Colorado were entered by the Church of the United Brethren in Christ. Only in the state of Florida did this outreach develop into an annual conference.

Missions — Jamaica

The missionary spread of the United Brethren Church has been more noticeable. The African Conference was divided into two annual conferences; and three new mission fields were opened: Jamaica, Honduras, and Hong Kong. The United Brethren entrance into each of the three new mission fields was associated with a personal interest or contact which may be considered as unusual or providential. "Our denomination's work on the island (of Jamaica) began when God used a hurricane to answer prayer."[2] The beginnings of United Brethren work in Honduras date from a request ". . . to help in a struggling work which had been abandoned by another denomination."[3] The opening in Hong Kong resulted from the desire of the Woman's Missionary Association to have a work in China. A timely personal contact made by a Chinese teacher in Portland, Oregon, with a teacher in Lingnan University in Canton, China, eventually consummated this desire.

To appreciate what has transpired upon these mission fields between then and now, one needs a few additional insights. Space permits only a few selected highlights and in no way reflects the patient endurance exhibited by the pioneer workers nor the sacrificial efforts that have been contributed.

The mission boards[4] were sensing a call or obligation to explore opportunities in the western hemisphere when the first of these personal incidents occurred. An opportunity came in 1933 when the United Brethren Church was offered a work in Jamaica started by the Reverend Paul D. Ford and his wife. The Fords, faith workers from near York, Pennsylvania, had served in Jamaica prior to 1930. Mrs. Ford's illness temporarily terminated their missionary endeavor. Returning to York, the Fords came under the ministry of the Reverend Ezra M. Funk,[5] a United Brethren minister. As a result of this contact, Ford offered the station which he had established at Constant Spring, Jamaica, to the United Brethren denomination. That opportunity was lost because ". . . the Parent Board of Missions did not feel ready at the time."[6]

By 1944 another opportunity presented itself for missionary consideration in the Caribbean area. Ford had returned to missionary service in the Bahama Islands. In the meantime a young Jamaican, James B. O'Sullivan whom Ford had brought from Jamaica, had met the Funk family. Funk directed O'Sullivan to Huntington College from which O'Sullivan was graduated in 1942 with a baccalaureate degree. While at Huntington, O'Sullivan contacted the Parent Board of Missions. He was accepted as a missionary candidate and asked to make arrangements for going to the Bahamas to take up possible missionary work there. In 1944 the Parent Board also authorized a visit to the Bahamas by G. D. Fleming, the secretary of missions, and Clyde W. Meadows. After their visit, their recommendation was that missionary work be undertaken there. During the year 1944, O'Sullivan "was appointed by the Parent Board to open up mission work in the Bahama Islands."[7]

O'Sullivan left Tampa, Florida, October 10, 1944, expecting to pick up supplies in Jamaica to go on to the Bahamas. The ship *Kirkson,* on which he was traveling, was caught in a hurricane near the Grand Cayman Island. Unable to proceed, O'Sullivan found missionary opportunity in Jamaica. "In 1945, while waiting in Jamaica, where he stayed with his sister and brother-in-law at Kingston, he began holding services in a government community hall in a nearby settlement called

'Golden Spring'."[8] Thus what began as an attempt to open a mission in the Bahamas turned out to be a mission to Jamaica.

O'Sullivan saw the first United Brethren church building erected in Jamaica in 1946. Other congregations were established and by 1951 Bishop Funk organized the Jamaica Annual Conference with eleven organized churches. By 1957 the conference had grown to "17 churches and preaching points"[9] and over 800 members. In 1968 the conference leadership was turned over to the Jamaican nationals. The Reverends A. N. Braithwaite and Lloyd Spencer have served as conference superintendents respectively since that date.

In 1981 the United Brethren Church in Jamaica reported 1148 members, 19 churches, and nearly 1000 members in 13 Christian Endeavor societies. The potential for growth seemed to be present, and the outlook encouraging.[10]

Missions—Central America

The request to the United Brethren Church to enter Central America came as the result of the Wesleyan Church of England having abandoned its effort in Honduras. In accepting the invitation to enter Honduras, the United Brethren made a definite change. The Wesleyan work was limited to the English-speaking minority; the United Brethren decided to begin ministering to the Spanish-speaking majority. The first United Brethren Spanish church began in La Ceiba in 1953; by 1961 a conference was formed; in 1962 Tegucigalpa, the capital city, was entered; and by 1972 a conference venture into education was realized. The Reverend Archie Cameron, Ontario Annual Conference, has served as supervisor for most of the three decades during which the church has operated in Honduras.

The report for 1981 showed 30 organized churches with about 1100 members, a self-supporting bookstore, and an educational center with an enrollment of over 900.[11] A rapidly growing population, a stable government, and an aggressive evangelistic program all suggest good prospect for growth in Honduras.

United Brethren mission work in Nicaragua was begun in the capital of Managua in 1965. A national pastor, the Reverend Juan Campos, from Nicaragua had a great burden for his people and wanted to return from Honduras to his homeland to share the Gospel with them. Since then five churches have been planted. They were started by nationals with some direction from the staff in neighboring Honduras. Since the beginning, believers there have survived the upheavals of a devastating earthquake (1972) and a bloody revolution (1979). The Reverend Guillermo Martinez has directed the work since 1974 and the mission district is directly responsible to the Board of Missions.

Missions—Hong Kong

The United Brethren Church owes its beginnings in Hong Kong to the contacts and efforts of the Moy Ling and the Yan Tze Chiu families. Ling was serving as a teacher and the leader of a school for Chinese children in the city of Portland, Oregon, under the auspices of the Woman's Missionary Association. When that association expressed interest in opening a ministry in China, Mrs. Ling's cousin, Dr. Chiu, was teaching in Lingnan University, Canton, China. Ling's contact with the Chius resulted in the opening of a United Brethren school in Canton in 1932. An evangelistic outreach was begun through "Bible women" and contact was made with a number of villages.

The Communist takeover of mainland China, in 1949, hindered this evangelistic and missionary work. Mrs. Chiu and daughter Bessie were allowed to remain in Canton for a few years. By 1957 both mother and daughter had left the mainland by separate routes and were reunited in Hong Kong.

Y. T. Chiu had succeeded in starting United Brethren mission work in Hong Kong in 1950. However, he had come to the United States before his wife and daughter had arrived in Hong Kong. He became a member of the faculty of Huntington College in 1954. Dr. and Mrs. Chiu were united in America in 1958. He returned to Hong Kong in 1960 to reorganize the mission work. Bishop Clyde W. Meadows inaugurated the Hong Kong Annual Conference in 1962. Superintendent Chiu left Hong Kong in 1967, at which time C. C. AuYeung succeeded him. AuYeung was succeeded in 1980 by Peter K. K. Lee as superintendent.

The 1981 report showed five United Brethren churches with 449 members; a flourishing publishing house, free medical clinics, and a young peoples' drama society. A steady growth pattern since 1976, a conscious need for outreach, and a strong commitment to further mission work present a potential for growth in Hong Kong.

Missions—Sierra Leone

The division of the Sierra Leone Conference into the Provisional

Conference and the Western Area Conference [1973] reflected past growth as well as hopes for more efficient administration. The United Brethren missionary activities in Sierra Leone focus in evangelism, education, and health care.

Evangelism was a top priority from the beginning and continues to have the precedence as far as goals are concerned. Education and medical care are considered as means to an end—the salvation of the soul. Those responding to a call to teach in the mission schools or to share their God-given talents in the hospital are expected to do some gospel itinerating on weekends. Bible studies are conducted for the women; devotions are given for those coming to the hospital for medical help; evangelistic services are promoted. Thus, in a variety of ways the nationals have the Gospel presented to them by the mission workers. Doctors, nurses, teachers, business agents, and building contractors all are engaged in the evangelistic endeavor.

United Brethren educational efforts in Sierra Leone date back to 1913 when the Minnie Mull Primary School for Girls was opened August 4th at Bonthe.[12] A similar facility for boys was erected at Gbangbaia, better known as the Danville School for Boys. Other schools soon came into existence, until in 1981 "The United Brethren mission is also considered to be in a supervisory position over 30 elementary schools with over 4514 pupils."[13]

Plans were under way in 1950 for the opening of the Bumpe Bible Institute, a ministerial training school. It began as a faith venture and suffered some delay. However, on January 28, 1952, ". . . the Bible Institute was officially opened with twelve students."[14] The United Brethren Church was also involved in promoting a cooperative enterprise for the preparation of pastors and evangelists. The realization of this goal came in September 1964, when the first classes met at the Sierra Leone Bible College located in Freetown.[15]

Conceived in the mind of Lloyd Eby,[16] the idea of establishing secondary education in Sierra Leone was shared, providentially, with a U.S. Navy pilot, E. DeWitt Baker, whom Eby met while on his way to Sierra Leone. On their way for a second term to Sierra Leone, Lloyd and Eula Eby had been delayed in Brazil and detained for six weeks because of war conditions. Also Misses Erma Funk, Bernadine Hoffman, and Oneta Sewell were stopped there on their way to Sierra Leone.[17] In a letter from his wife, Baker learned of the whereabouts of these fellow Huntington College graduates and located them for fellowship and Bible study. During this six-week intermission, the idea of a secondary school was shared by Eby.

Months later Eby contacted Baker to inquire if he might feel led to establish a secondary school after his release from the military service. The reply came back that he had not felt called to be a missionary and that he was not a United Brethren, but, if the Lord should make such a call plain to him, he would certainly consider it. Following his demobilization from the military, Baker became principal of the Hanover-Horton Rural Agricultural School, in Michigan. He also began graduate studies at the University of Michigan and for a research topic chose, "The History of Education in Sierra Leone."

At about the same time, Baker and his wife, Evelyn, sensed the call to enter missionary service in Sierra Leone. They were appointed by the mission board and, with their two sons, Norman and Ronald, were on the mission field by 1949. During their five-term (sixteen years) missionary service, the Bakers served in a variety of roles, experienced the loss of their younger son Norman in an accident,[18] and established two secondary schools.[19] Baker's missionary service was concluded in 1965 when he accepted the office of president of Huntington College, Huntington, Indiana.

Another important educational feature for the missionaries in Sierra Leone is the Kabala Rupp Memorial School, a school established for missionary children. Started by the Missionary Church Association (now Missionary Church) in 1956, it is a cooperative venture offering studies in English for grades one through nine.

Few missionaries have invested as many years as the veteran Christian Education director Bernadine Hoffman, who has given thirty-seven years. In addition to the individuals already named, the following have given extensive years of service in the educational area: Russell and Nellie Birdsall, 3 terms; June Brown, 7 terms; Rita (Wild) Koroma, 3 terms; Bethel Mote, 6 terms; Nancy (Hull) 'Ngele, 3 terms; Ruby Parent, 4 terms; Jill VanDeusen, 3 terms; and Olive Weaver, 5 terms.[20]

The third area, health care, was the last of the three to be developed. It is, to a large degree, a development of the past half century. As early as 1913, plans were projected for the building of a dispensary facility. This construction plan coincided with the arrival of the Vernon Kopp family.[21] It reflected an awareness that a missionary that has had some medical training needed appropriate facilities in which to work. Kopp and his successors, Frank Prowell and Charles A. E. Saufley, each had a brief course in tropical medicine at Livingstone Medical College, London, England, before coming to the African field. "The year 1934 is entitled to be termed an epochal year in the history of our medical program, for it was in late September of that year that Doctor Leslie Huntley arrived to assume the responsibility as director of our Gbangbaia medical department."[22]

Leslie L. Huntley, M.D., was well received by the nationals and his presence proved to be a lift to the others on the medical staff. Additional help for Huntley, in the person of Emma Hyer, R.N., came in June 1936. The doctor and his nurse were busy from the time of Hyer's arrival. She wrote, ". . . my first morning in the dispensary was a new and strange experience . . . Few could converse with me . . . Sixty-five were registered for treatment for that day."[23] Huntley soon saw the need for larger quarters. By May 1939 he had written, "Our present accommodations are far too inadequate for the people who come for treatment . . . We have to refuse maternity cases and patients needing surgery almost every day."[24]

The outbreak of World War II placed a temporary delay on the fulfillment of the dream for a hospital. But with the close of hostilities in 1945, the mission board reaffirmed its desire to go forward with the hospital-building program. Within a short time the building project was approved and a director of construction was appointed. The Reverend Earl and Mrs. (Ruth) Ensminger were already preparing to return to Sierra Leone for their second term of service. Earl had been appointed to serve in the capacity as director of construction.

When the Huntleys returned to the States in November 1941, the hospital project in Gbangbaia was left without a doctor. Oneta Sewell, R.N., came to Mattru in June 1950. Juanita Smith, R. N., a new recruit in missionary service joined with Sewell shortly thereafter. By August 1950, the two nurses began a nursing class, the first in connection with the proposed hospital. More waiting was in prospect before another doctor became available or the hospital building became a reality.

In 1957, Alvin French, M.D., on transfer from another mission, came to Mattru for a two-year term of service. He was followed in 1959 by a young Sierra Leonian, Sylvester Pratt, M.D. Pratt had returned from the United States where he had received his medical training. A 15-bed hospital without electricity and modern plumbing may have shocked the young doctor. But it neither immobilized him nor clouded the dream that he had for a hospital in his area. "Dr. Pratt had not been in Mattru many months before the 15-bed hospital began bursting at the seams . . . . Seriously and critically ill children as well as adults had to be turned away for lack of beds."[25]

Appeals were made to the Sierra Leone government for funds in order to enlarge the hospital. At first the appeals received a cool reception. But suddenly a change of attitude on the part of the government took place and grants totaling $34,500 were received. A mining company in Mattru[26] gave a special INDEPENDENCE GIFT of

$7,000 to the hospital as a gesture to the country of Sierra Leone.[27] A gift from the mission board in America enabled the doctor to purchase a new operating table and sterilizer. A 34-bed medical-surgical building soon came into being with an operating room and the sterilizing equipment in place.

Pratt brought some aspects of the hospital "out of the bush." The missionaries had been inclined to accept circumstances as they were and try to make the best of the situation.

> Whereas he saw things as they were and set out to make them BETTER. He did not tolerate anything inferior whether it were drugs, techniques, or just lack of facilities. He had a captivating personality and that caused people to WANT to do the job and do it *right,* though it might be quite difficult . . . . Before he would minister to babies who were brought to the hospital laden down with charms around their necks, waists, wrists, and ankles, those charms must be removed. From the very first, he told the parents that there was one thing he wanted them to get straight—THAT GOD WAS THE DOCTOR AT THE HOSPITAL, and he was only God's instrument.[28]

Being a Sierra Leonian, Pratt not only had an advantage over missionaries from the United States in language, but also in climatic adaptation. From 1959 he continued until 1973 when he furloughed to the United States for treatment of a serious eye condition. Ultimately he established a medical practice in the city of Dayton, Ohio, where he had formerly completed his medical internship.

Ronald P. Baker, M.D., arrived in Sierra Leone as a doctor in September 1974. His knowledge of the Mende language[29] likewise gave him immediate access to many of the situations that a non-Mende speaking missionary had to learn. His knowledge as a physician and his skill as a surgeon have endeared him to the nationals.

Baker's goal is to add preventative health care to that of the remedial. By sending a health care nurse out into the villages, he hopes to instruct in preventive care. During his 1980-1981 furlough, Thomas Ritter, M.D., headed the health team at Mattru. Baker hopes that additional staff will be retained so that the preventive goal may be pursued.[30] The prospects for additional doctors of medicine for the Mattru hospital are very good, while the need for nurses is urgent.

The Mattru hospital which began as a dispensary, now consists of a 69-bed facility. It includes pediatrics, obstetrics, surgical, and outpatient units. Other buildings on the approximately 15-acre grounds include a pharmacy, a generating plant, as well as five residences for the doctor and nurses.

Fleming in *Trail Blazers* gave the roll call of registered nurses during the past 50 years revealing many names.[31] The following represent those who have served three or more terms in Sierra Leone: Martha Anna Bard,[32] Alice Blodgett, Eleanore Datema, Kathleen (Corcoran) Jones, Sharon Frank, Beverly Glover, Betty Ruedger, Oneta Sewell, and Juanita (Smith) Guenzler. Ruby Crum had returned to the field for a second term in January 1971 but died on the field in March 1971.

Scores of people have volunteered to go to Sierra Leone in other areas. Some have served in administration, in business responsibilities, in construction, as matrons, as field secretaries, or in a combination of these offices. The following names represent those with the longer careers: Bernadine Hoffman, Lloyd and Eula Eby, Clarence and Erma Carlson, Jerry and Eleanore Datema, Emmett and Shirley Cox, Earl and Ruth Ensminger, Ralph and Peggy Albrecht, Floy Mulkey, Cathy Jordan, Marion and Francis Burkett, and Floyd and Janet Lundy.

One further area of missionary change and challenge should be noted before concluding the Department of Missions overview. A home mission project was opened by the Woman's Missionary Association at Big Laurel, Kentucky. This project, like Jamaica and Honduras, grew out of a personal project and need. Miss Mabel Snyder, a registered nurse who had spent one term on the African field (1926-1928) and a short time with the American Inland Mission, felt challenged by the health care needs of the mountain people and gave herself to ministry among them. In July 1939 the Woman's Missionary Association took over the responsibility for the Laurel Misson which Snyder had established. Cedar Chapel, located near Big Laurel on Abner's Branch, was dedicated on November 26, 1939, by the Reverends Matthew Smith and Effie M. Hodgeboom.

The Kentucky mission was placed under the jurisdiction of the two mission boards in 1957. The Reverend and Mrs. Orion Fuller and the Reverend and Mrs. Raymond Gant supervised the work for over 15 years. During the years of their supervision, Sunday schools and Vacation Bible schools were started at Cedar Chapel and Galilee. Since 1977 the supervision of the Kentucky churches has been the responsibility of the Central Annual Conference, being established as a mission district with a district superintendent as chief administrative officer. Under this administrative arrangement, and in response to direct appeals, a number of local congregations from several adjoining annual conferences have sent teams to assist in building projects.

The outreach in these mission fields was made possible through a continuing appeal and promotion by the two mission boards—Parent Board of Missions and the Woman's Missionary Association. They worked side by side in a number of activities but maintained separate programs until they were united to form the Department of Missions in 1965.[33] They have shared equally in the financial appropriations to the fields since becoming united. But they have promoted their interests through special appeals such as the Lenten Self Denial, the annual Thankoffering, and Sunday School for Missions.

The women's work continues to be effected through *branches* and *local societies*.[34] The men respond through local and conference *brotherhoods* and conference *cabinets*. A portion from the general benevolences of the denomination is regularly dedicated to missionary outreach and church extension. Through the changing context of war, depression, and inflation the pulse of missionary giving in the Church of the United Brethren in Christ has been consistently rising, increasing almost 500% in the last 30 years.[35]

There is some inclination, at this point in time, to associate three casual factors with this outward or upward growth: 1) The viability of the Savior's commission for the 20th century. The urgency of obeying the Savior's mandate to preach, teach, and make disciples has never been relaxed. 2) The willingness to adapt methods and strategies to changing cultural conditions. 3) The stability in the mission office leadership and among the personnel of the mission boards has enabled the department to project long-range objectives and to follow-up the initiatives undertaken.

The Reverend Jacob Howe, who was in the mission office in 1929, was first elected to the office of secretary of missions in 1905. George D. Fleming, a five-term missionary to Sierra Leone, succeeded Howe in 1936 and served until 1961. His tenure of 25 years in the office and his knowledge and enthusiasm for missions made his title "Mr. Mission" justifiable. The Reverend Duane A. Reahm, a member of the Mission Board for several quadrennia, served as General Secretary from 1961 to 1969, when he was elected to the office of bishop and assigned the East District. Emmett D. Cox as general secretary of missions served from 1969 to 1973 at which time Reahm was elected as overseas bishop, an appointment which replaced the office of general secretary of missions. In this capacity Reahm served until his retirement in 1981. The Reverend Jerry F. Datema, missionary and field secretary in Sierra Leone, was elected to succeed Reahm in the office of overseas bishop by the General Conference of 1981.

In the women's work, the executive secretary of the Woman's Missionary Association served in a role comparable to that of the General Secretary of Missions. Leaders serving in the capacity of executive secretary of the W.M.A. were Miss Effie M. Hodgeboom, January 1930 to July 1956; Mrs. Erma Carlson, 1956 to 1965; Mrs.

Iona Wood, 1965 to 1977; Mrs. Carol Skinner, (interim) August 1, 1977 to March 1, 1978. Mrs. Hazel McCray accepted the office in 1978. The organization title, *Woman's* Missionary Association, was changed to Women's Missionary Association by action of the Board of Managers in 1965.

Higher Education

Higher education, as provided by the Church of the United Brethren in Christ during the past half century, has been reflected exclusively through Huntington College. And November 15, 1981, marked a significant occasion on the campus. That day, Eugene B. Habecker, J. D., Ph.D., was inaugurated as the eleventh president of Huntington College.[36]

The Merillat Physical Education Center provided the setting for this inaugural ceremony. There, in the presence of family and friends, faculty and students, trustees and guests, and nearly 50 official delegates from colleges, universities, learned societies, governmental organizations, and denominational executives, Habecker received the presidential medallion and official induction into the office of the president. The attendance at the inauguration was in the one thousand category; the occasion was termed "very significant." Habecker, in his inaugural address, accepted his role as analogous to that facing Queen Esther: "Who knows but that you have come . . . for such a time as this" (Esther 4:14 NIV).

The mood on campus was indeed a change, almost a contrast with the conditions and outlook of 1929 and 1930. At that time Huntington College was experiencing a low ebb in student enrollment, in financial support, and in faculty morale. Student enrollment reached a low of 50 in 1930. Operational income and contributed income for the same year were reported as $28,022.01; fixed assets amounted to $109,695; and liabilities totaled $41,242.[37] For most years, since Huntington College was founded, there has been something of a struggle to improve the cash flow. Despite the continual cash flow nemesis, student enrollment, curriculum improvements, and capital gains have moved ahead rather consistently. Faculty tenure, community support, academic accreditation, and administrative stability have been constructive factors in the progress of higher education in the United Brethren Church.

The trend of 1930 was reversed during the early years of Harold C. Mason's administration (1932-1939). Special appeals for funds, additional recruitment of students, and greater promotional efforts were productive. A new spirit on the campus became evident before the 40s. An enrollment of 201 students was reached during the 1934-35 academic year. State certification in education was received soon thereafter.

The resignation of Mason in 1939 left the administration of Huntington College in the hands of Oscar R. Stilson, academic dean, and the board of trustees until the General Conference of 1941 reelected the Reverend Elmer Becker as Secretary of Education. In the same year trustees elected Becker as president of Huntington College.

Becker served as Secretary of Education for the denomination and as president of Huntington College until 1965, at which time he was named chancellor. His development of an excellent "town and gown" relationship earned him the accolade "Mr. Huntington College" in the community. During his tenure as chief administrator, Huntington College moved on every front. Regional accreditation by the North Central Association of Colleges and Schools, a long sought goal of President Becker and Academic Dean, Wilford P. Musgrave, Ph.D., was received in 1961; a student body of 500 was reached during the academic year of 1964-65. The high mark in enrollment to date was in 1976-77 when it reached 709. Keen competition for students and inflationary pressures have kept the Huntington College enrollment figure in the 500 and 600 range since that date. The 1980-81 enrollment was reported as 617.

To accommodate the increased number of students enrolled, it became clear that additional classroom and housing space was needed. Livingston Hall was enlarged and remodeled for women's housing during Mason's administration (1938). Becker witnessed the building of Wright Hall for a men's residence (1948); the Loew-Alumni Library (1959); and the J. L. Brenn Hall of Science (1963). He also secured surplus buildings from the federal government following World War II that were used as classroom facilities and as married student's housing. Additional investments were made in private residences for faculty rental.

E. DeWitt Baker, Ph.D., was called from the Sierra Leone mission field, where he had established two high schools, to assume the presidency in October 1965. He came to the office at a time of physical plant construction. He witnessed in turn the groundbreaking and erection of Hardy Hall, residence for women (1966); the Huntington Union Building (HUB), student center (1968); the Orville and Ruth Merillat Physical Education Center (1974); the Student Venture Auditorium (1979); the president's new residence (1979); and the beginnings of the construction of a new residence hall for students. Begun in the spring of 1981, the construction of this building, named Baker Hall in his honor, marked the first step in a multi-million-dollar campus development plan.

President Baker, when asked concerning the realization of his goals for Huntington College during his 16-year administration, replied that he had set two from the beginning in 1965: 1) Continue and deepen the spiritual commitment of the student body, and 2) Maintain the financial integrity of the college. He saw the fact of increased numbers of students going into full-time Christian service, the formation of student prayer groups on campus, and the ratio that 49 out of the first 75 graduates of the Graduate School of Christian Ministries entered the parish ministry as evidence of spiritual commitment. Evidence in relation to the financial goal was based on the fact that "the bonded indebtedness (made necessary through the building operations of 1965 and 1968)[38] has been reduced on schedule over these 16 years."[39] The indebtedness of 1965 was $1,750,000 and as of July 17, 1980 it was $760,000. The net worth of the institution in 1981 is quoted as $5,976,042 as compared with $1,194,686 in 1967-68.[40]

The capital gains came, in a large measure, as the result of several substantial gifts. The Merillat Physical Education Center, valued at over one million dollars, was the gift of Orville and Ruth Merillat; the Huntington College Foundation contributed the J. L. Brenn Hall of Science and has helped underwrite other capital fund activities; the new home for the college president was a gift from the C. W. H. and Nellie Bangs family; the Student Venture Auditorium was the gift of over several years from the Huntington College student body.[41]

Increased library holdings reflect another aspect of the growth of Huntington College during the past fifty years. Five hundred volumes were reported in 1930; and 61,523 in 1981.[42]

Theological training has been among the offerings at Huntington College since before 1930. During the 30s the offerings shifted back and forth with diploma and degree courses outlined. In the early 40s the theological department at Huntington College was reorganized and restructured under M. I. Burkholder, Th.D., dean of the Huntington College Theological Seminary, 1942-1972. The Bachelor of Divinity degree was developed as a full three-year graduate course of study. The Bachelor of Theology continued as an offering as did a Bible diploma course for some years. Both undergraduate programs were later dropped as the students elected the graduate degree. The Bachelor of Divinity students came from all sections of the church, and in 1981 practically all of the annual conferences in North America were under the leadership of the students of the 1940-1970 years. The last six bishops elected by the denomination have had Huntington College Theological Seminary training.

Prior to Burkholder's retirement in 1972, a series of studies in theological education had taken place. As early as 1967, the Reverend Paul A. Graham was named to chair a seminary study committee.[43] In 1968, president Baker announced that the position of director of seminary development had been offered.[44] By 1970 a Theological Study Committee was named by the Board of Education.[45] By October 1970, the committee reported ". . . the basic decision to phase out the Huntington College Theological Seminary."[46] For ministerial training the committee recommended the Bachelor of Arts degree with a major in Bible and Religion or Christian Education at Huntington College. The general education requirements for the baccalaureate degree were required of the ministerial students and in addition they would be supplemented in four areas, namely, biblical, doctrinal, historical, and practical theology. Additional guidelines were presented as to course requirements for the fifth year of study. The committee recommended that a graduate School of Christian Ministries replace the Huntington College Theological Seminary under the academic administration of a director. The graduate program would culminate with the degree of Master of Christian Ministry (M.C.M.). The Reverend Paul R. Fetters was appointed by the executive committee of the Board of Trustees on January 14, 1972, to be the director of the School of Christian Ministries.[47] As director and assistant professor in practical theology, he began at once the task of developing the courses projected by the committee. The School of Christian Ministries opened with the fall semester 1972 and has witnessed substantial growth from year to year.

Huntington College was accredited in 1975 at the masters level and reaccredited in 1979. This was the first time that graduate instruction at Huntington College had been evaluated and accredited by the North Central Association of Colleges and Schools. In 1980, the title of director of School of Christian Ministries was changed to dean. The word "Graduate" was added to the name of the School of Christian Ministries by the Board of Trustees in 1982.[48] The name, Graduate School of Christian Ministries, more accurately reflects the level of instruction. The term also distinguishes it from the undergraduate and diploma programs offered by other institutions.

The outlook for higher education in the Church of the United Brethren in Christ has been materially changed since the 1929-1981 report was prepared. An incentive gift was offered to Huntington College in 1981 which attracted gifts for a new student housing hall.

The appeal was presented to the alumni, the church, and to friends. The response to the appeal was prompt and enouraging. Baker Hall, the end product, a 'new concept in student housing' was dedicated April 24, 1982. The total contributed gifts amounted to $1,020,000. It was occupied as early as September 1982.

At the Huntington College commencement in 1982, the chairman of the Board of Trustees, the Honorable J. Edward Roush, announced the receipt of a new challenge. This challenge was the offer to match 'dollar for dollar' new funds contributed to eliminate all accumulated indebtedness of Huntington College. The offer specified new or increased gifts and would be open for one year, beginning August 1, 1982. The offer specified matching funds for up to a total of $350,000. The Board of Trustees accepted the challenge and plans were soon put into operation for what became known as the "Huntington College American Dream." By July 31, 1983, the report was given that the 'dream' had been realized. The total response reported was $483,000 and the challenger agreed to match the total response. This challenge had also come from Orville and Ruth Merillat who had provided for the Merillat Physical Education center in 1974.

Publishing

The institution known as the United Brethren Publishing Establishment has played an important role in the life and outreach of the church throughout this period. The publications coming from its presses have reflected changing emphases and format but always as an undergirding support for the message and program of the denomination. Its publications have also found a marketplace beyond the church membership.

The following individuals have served as publishing agent and bookstore manager: W. C. South, 1928-1945; J. C. Peters, 1945-1955; Don B. Hammel (a layman), 1955-1967; Carlyle Seiple, 1967-1971; Eugene Riebe (a layman), 1972-1974; an interim team, 1974-1977. The publishing department was merged with the department of Christian Education in 1977 as a department of Church Ministries. Howard F. Anderson served as executive director from 1977-1981 with Paul E. Hirschy managing the print shop. In the reshuffling of the structure in 1981 the department of Church Ministries became a part of the division of Church Services under the directorship of Paul E. Hirschy.

Editors serving the Church over the past fifty years have been: W. H. Zeigler, 1925-1949; Ernest Gingerich, 1949-1957; George E. Weaver,

1957-1959; Stanley Peters, 1959-1981. An editor of Sunday School literature was employed for part of the period: George A. Shepherdson, 1925-1934; J. Ralph Pfister, 1934-1944; Mrs. Alice Griffin, 1944 (6 months); and J. L. Towne, 1944-1953. Since 1953 this responsibility has been delegated to an assistant to the general editor.

The *Christian Conservator* and the *Missionary Monthly* continued as weekly and monthly publications respectively. For a few years the department of Christian Education published the *United Brethren Magnet* on a quarterly basis. By action of the General Conference of 1953 these three publications were merged into one, *The United Brethren.* This magazine was updated in several respects: new format, added color, and a better quality of paper. The first issue was dated April 7, 1954. The publication was changed from a weekly to a bi-weekly beginning September 7, 1960, and to a monthly publication beginning Janaury 1974. In 1966 ". . . authorization was given to acquire an IBM compositor to replace the linotype, typesetting machine." The first issue printed by the offset method was June 18, 1969.[49]

In the Sunday School literature, *Gems of Cheer* and *Our Wee Ones* gave way to *Contact* as take-home papers. The lesson quarterlies were developed into *The Venture Series* which was a cooperative project of the Evangelical Congregational Church, the United Brethren Church, and the Primitive Methodist Church.

The building erected at Warren and Franklin streets in downtown Huntington continued to be the denominational headquarters and the base for the publishing activities. Additional buildings, adjacent to the United Brethren Building, were purchased in 1957. The bookstore was relocated in the newly purchased area. After extensive renovation was completed, additional rental space was offered to the public. Loading difficulties, parking limitations, and building overhead expenses became increasingly difficult experiences.

As early as 1972 questions were being raised as to the direction the publishing house should go. The executive committee of the Publishing Board recommended on April 6, 1972 that

> . . . an extensive study to determine the direction which Publishing House will go, either in spending up to $50,000 in the year for new equipment . . . or to discontinue in the printing operation and farm out our printing. (Minutes of the Executive Committee of the Board of Publications.)

This action was followed, on May 2, 1972, by the following motions:

> The Committee voted to plan to continue in the printing operations contingent

upon: . . . b. Relocation of the printing operation as a first step in a total project of relocation.

Bishop Weaver, Don Hammel, Eugene Riebe, and Ralph Pfister were selected as a committee to begin preliminary planning and study in implementing this policy. It was agreed that this committee investigate the purchase of suitable property. (Minutes)

The Federated Board of Christian Education and the Board of Publication, on April 15, 1975, recommended to the General Board of Administration that

. . . every possible effort be made to relocate to new facilities the offices of the denomination and the Publishing Establishment's print shop, by May 31, 1975. The Board instructed the Committee on Production and Marketing to conduct a thorough study of the costs involved in having other firms print our literature and other materials. (Minutes)

A new location, a 2.6 acre tract of land formerly part of the Mathias Wechsler orchard at the corner of Guilford and Lake Streets, was secured from Mr. and Mrs. Clifford Wechsler, Huntington, Indiana. On this site a one-story building 100 feet by 145 feet of modern design and function was completed. Occupancy of the new United Brethren Building took place in May 1976.

The General Conference of 1977 merged the departments of Christian Education and Publication into the Department of Church Ministries with an executive director. The Board of Church Ministries, in a meeting dated October 28, 29, 1980, recommended to the General Conference of 1981:

. . . that printing operations and the production of Sunday School literature be discontinued on or before December 31, 1981, and that *The United Brethren* magazine continue to be published. (Minutes)

The General Conference of 1981 adopted the recommendation of the Committee on Church Ministries:

. . . 4. That the present printing operation "United Brethren Publishers" and the production of the "Venture Series" Sunday School literature be discontinued on or before December 31, 1981, and that *The United Brethren* magazine continue to be published.[50]

Christian Education

The work of the Sunday Schools, the Christian Endeavor societies, the Vacation Bible Schools and the "leadership training" classes in the United Brethren Church has been the responsibility of the Department of Christian (religious) Education since the early 1900s. Religious instruction of the youth antedated the formal organization of the denomination. In the rules for the Baltimore Church, Otterbein included:

> The preacher shall make it one of his highest duties to watch over the rising youth, diligently instructing them in the principles of religion according to the Word of God. He shall catechise them once a week; and the more mature in years, who have obtained knowledge of the great truths of the gospel shall be impressed with the importance of striving through divine grace to become worthy recipients of the holy sacrament.[51]

The first United Brethren Sunday School in Baltimore was established in the old Otterbein Church in 1827.[52] Another Sunday School pioneer of the United Brethren Church was Dr. John George Pfrimmer. Christian Newcomer, in his *Journal* for May 21, 1800, made the following entry: "Today I came to Br. Fremmer's (Pfrimmer); about thirty children had assembled at his house, to whom he was giving religious instruction."[53]

Pfrimmer was trained in medicine, having for a time served as a physician and surgeon in the French navy, and began preaching in America soon after his conversion in 1790. He moved to Harrison County, Indiana, in 1808 and organized a United Brethren church near Corydon, Indiana, in 1812 known as Pfrimmer's Chapel. Grover L. Hartman, in his *History of the Sunday School Movement in Indiana,* believed that Pfrimmer started the first Sunday School in Indiana.[54]

The Sunday School has had good visibility in the United Brethren Church since 1849.[55] Periods of Recognition, 1849-1865; Development, 1865-1889; Reconstruction, 1889-1909; and Advancement, 1909-1921 were recognized by R. W. Rash[56] as forerunners to the period of Unification and Promotion, 1921-1964. A rather stable enrollment and average attendance prevailed from the mid 50s through the 60s (enrollment about 35,000 and average attendance of approximately 23,500). Christian education quadrennial reports for 1969 and since reflect a series of losses. The 1981 quadrennial report shows enrollment at 29,469 and an average attendance of 19,719.

The General Conference of 1921 provided for the combination of Sunday School and Christian Endeavor into the department of Religious Education. However, Christian Endeavor has its origin in the United Brethren Church about 35 years earlier in what was known as "The Young People's Christian Association." The young peoples' work was recognized by the General Conference of 1897 which adopted a constitution for the "Y.P.C.A." The name was later changed from Young Peoples' Christian Association to the United Brethren Christian Endeavor. In the General Conference of 1905, C. A. Mummart was elected as the first general secretary of Christian Endeavor in the United Brethren Church and served from 1905-1909. Miss M. M. Titus served from 1909-1917. A. B. Bowman served in this capacity from 1917 until 1921 when the Christian Endeavor department was merged into a department of Religious Education.

The Christian Endeavor statistics reflect much the same picture as the Sunday School. Prior to 1957 "societies" and "membership" were both reported in terms of "total." Beginning in 1957 the categories were reported as "North America totals." In 1957 the total number reported in North America was 300 with a membership of 6225. By the General Conference of 1969, the total number of societies reported had increased to 320. However, the membership of these societies had dropped to 4414. The 1981 quadrennial report showed 4496 enrolled in Youth in Action.

In spite of the United Brethren involvement in the Christian Endeavor movement and organization, the Christian Endeavor picture on the parish level has faded considerably over the past two decades. Even though United Brethren personnel were directly involved in Christian Endeavor 'decision-making' and in leadership roles on the international and state levels, the number of local societies decreased and the individual participation suffered losses. The United Brethren picture is not unique in this respect.

In some instances an aging leadership in Christian Endeavor may have been a contributing factor to the decline, but other factors appear to have been more decisive. A desire to experiment with new materials, changed emphases, and new forms of activity may all have contributed to the changed situation. Some of the new forms of youth activity in the United Brethren Church are seen in "Youth in Action," Bible quizzing, Bible clubs, or youth study groups. Some para-church clubs, such as Campus Life have looked largely to church youth for leadership and consequently for their time and talent.

The third programming area of the department was that of the Vacation Bible School. Mummart, chairman of the General Sabbath School Board, was chosen as a delegate in 1923 to represent this department in the Vacation Bible School Conference held in Chicago. Vacation Bible Schools were held as early as 1925,[57] but official recognition did not come until 1937 when R. W. Rash was appointed as the first director along with his ministerial duties. No official data has been available for the Vacation Bible School prior to 1937. The grand total enrollment (denominational and community schools combined) reached its highest point in the year 1961. The enrollment reported for 1961 was 14,593 and compares with 2336 reported in 1945.[58]

The year 1925 marked the opening phase of organized Training Course development and promotion by the United Brethren Church. "Immediately following the General Conference of 1925 the department began reorganizing the entire training program."[59] Summer training schools were introduced into nearly all of the eastern conferences by the end of the quadrennium. Training courses written by United Brethren authors began to make their appearance. "3rd series" courses were provided beginning in 1940. This series, when offered in schools, was named "The Harwood School of Leadership Education" in honor of J. E. Harwood, the founder of the advanced level of leadership training in the church.

The Harwood School was held at Huntington College on an annual basis from 1941-1946 and intermittently into the 1950s. "These schools were to consist of 18 hours of class work and a similar amount of out-of-class study and activity and the student doing satisfactory work would be eligible for college credit on work done."[60] The registrations for this type of training reached their zenith in 1945 when total credits given were 72. Three classes were offered under the instructorship of Bishops Musgrave, Johnson, and Funk.

The two mission boards cooperated with the Department of Christian Education on five or six occasions by offering a missions study. This was known as a School of Missions and the students received third level credits through the Christian Education department.

The 'schools' were authorized on an extension basis by the General Conference of 1941. And extension schools were provided in the following annual conferences: California, Idaho, Kansas, Ontario, and Oregon.

Growth continued in the 'schools' until conditions of increased student enrollment on the Huntington College campus following W W II forced postponement due to lack of space for housing and classes. These efforts at training were directed into other channels and the 'schools' were never restored.

Three observations come to the surface as this brief review of the Department of Christian Education is concluded. 1) The role of the department has never been in doubt. Its goal has been consistent: to teach and to disciple the Christian believer. It has always assumed the necessity of regeneration or a 'new birth' experience as the starting point of the Christian life. It has accepted the command of Jesus "to teach" and "to make disciples"[59] (Matthew 28: 19, 20). It has kept the goal of the growing and maturing Christian in focus. 2) Its strategy has been to update its methods and its media of instruction so as to keep it educationally alert. Changes have come, in emphasis, under the different general secretaries. Leadership Training was the strong emphasis under J. E. Harwood's leadership 1921-1937. During Elmer Becker's term in the office, 1937-1941, evangelism received a strong emphasis. R. W. Rash, 1941-1957, put many of the courses or study guides into a more permanent and revised form as well as producing much new material. Walter M. Burkholder, 1957-1973, set out to strengthen conference and local church programs of Christian education. "Camping was also developed as a strong part of all the conferences."[61] 3) The personnel elected to the secretary's office of this department were men of action. They made themselves available for extensive field service. They set up and/or addressed Sunday School conventions and Christian Endeavor events; they organized schools for leadership training; they constructed course outlines; and they taught many, many classes in local church or community contexts. Two men stand out as "plantings of the Lord" in this field: Jesse E. Harwood and Robert W. Rash.

In 1977 the Department of Christian Education was merged with that of Publications to form a Department of Church Ministries with Howard F. Anderson as executive secretary. In the General Conference of 1981 the Department of Church Ministries became a part of the Department of Church Services with Paul E. Hirschy, director. Other services placed in this department were stewardship, the archives, and Pension Trust. Thus within the span of the past 50 years the Department of Christian Education has come into being, has consistently maintained its role, and has lost its public identity. But the task of teaching and making disciples has not been lost sight of nor discarded.

Stewardship

Stewardship has been in the vocabulary of the United Brethren preacher and the denominational press for much of this century. In many instances it was applied primarily to the Christian's use of money. It was highly visible in the Otterbein Forward Movement of the 20s, in the preachers' aid program, in the promotion of Huntington College, and in the Missions Department.

Stewardship has reached a new status during the past two decades. In June 1973, the stewardship commission recommended to the general board of administration:

> That the General Board recommend to the General Conference [of 1973] that a department of stewardship be established with a limited budget . . . and the administering of it be assigned to one of the administrative personnel.[62]

This action culminated in the assignment being given to Bishop Raymond Waldfogel of the West District.

The General Conference of 1977 advanced the stewardship program when it elected the Reverend Carlson Becker as the denomination's first full-time Executive Director of Stewardship. Since 1977 the stewardship concept has been enlarged in its application to include time and talent as well as treasure. In the realignment of the departments made by the General Conference of 1981, stewardship services were placed under the Department of Church Services with Becker continuing as director.

Archives

Interest in the preservation and care of historical information and artifacts of the church has surfaced from time to time. The United Brethren Publishing Establishment had been charged with some such responsibility for years, especially with reference to annual conference minutes and department materials. The General Board of Administration raised the issue again in the late 40s and appointed W. E. Musgrave, Elmer Becker, and J. Clair Peters as a committee to explore the possibility of establishing a historical society in the United Brethren Church. The Board of Administration, in its report to the Genereal Conference of 1949, said that by-laws and regulations for such a society had been prepared but the sad feature was "to date the manuscript of such provision cannot be found."[63]

In 1962 the executive committee of the General Board of Administration approved the following motion: "That Miss E. Faye Connor, Huntington College librarian, be appointed a committee of one, with authority to enlist additional voluntary help, to gather materials of historic value to the Church of the United Brethren in Christ for the Archives of the Church."[64] From 1962 to 1968 Connor did collect and catalogue work along with her librarian duties at Huntington College. The first recorded minutes of the Archives Committee (January 1968) listed the members: J. Ralph Pfister, chairman, G. D. Fleming, E. Faye Connor, and Mary Lou Funk. Connor reported that the archives began operating as separate unit from the college library in August 1969. Upon her retirement as Huntington College librarian in 1969, Connor began working as an archivist on a part-time basis.

The plans for the new headquarters building included space for the archives with a fire-proof vault. The records were transferred to the new building in 1976. The response to appeals for archives materials has been generous to date. And, with the phasing out of the print shop in the headquarters building, the floor space for the archives was doubled.

Mrs. Jane Mason was secured as archivist in October 1977 and has continued to the present time. She has attended national and state association meetings of archivists which have been means for updating methodology and organization of materials.

Hymnal

As a possible means of further unifying the congregations of the Church of the United Brethren in Christ and enlarging her borders, a new United Brethren hymnal was proposed. Dr. Clyde W. Meadows, pastor of the King Street congregation, Chambersburg, Pennsylvania, was one of the early promoters and consistently a member of the hymnal committee. In 1933 the following were appointed as the hymnal committee: Clyde W. Meadows, chairman, J. E. Harwood, W. H. Kindell, Lewis A. Regnier, and Mrs. Lydia (Burton) Gingerich.

After much individual work, much of it from the office of the chairman, a report was made to the General Conference of 1937. Since Harwood had passed away during the previous quadrennium, the names of J. Ralph Pfister and Elmer Becker were added to the committee. The publication of the hymnal became a reality in 1938. It was well received—even surpassing expectations. The General Conference of 1945 updated the committee by renaming Meadows, Becker, Pfister, and Gingerich and added the names of R. W. Rash and Mrs. Pauline Roush with J. Clair Peters, advisory. *The United Brethren Hymnal— Revised* was published in 1952 and went through several editions.

A new study, in anticipation of an enlarged hymnal with additional worship aids, was made between 1965-1969. The committee for this study was Meadows, Rash, Pfister, Roush plus Mrs. Carol Skinner and Mrs. Madge Musgrave Witmer. The new volume, *United Brethren Hymnal* was published in 1973. Meadows thus continued being involved throughout these several publications. He is said to consider the hymnal to be one of his major contributions to the church.

By-Lines and Themes

From the beginning of this period to 1962 the denominational magazine or journal—the *Christian Conservator* and the *United Brethren*—carried a Scriptural challenge or admonition on its masthead. Prior to 1930 two admonitions were used from time to time: "Remove not the ancient landmark which thy fathers have set," or "Speak unto the children of Israel that they go forward." From March 5, 1930, through August 31, 1949, they were paired. From September 7, 1949, through March 31, 1954, "Conserving the faith which was once delivered unto the saints," was used. Beginning with the first issue of *The United Brethren,* April 7, 1954, through April 4, 1962, "The foundation of God standeth sure." Since that latter date no such admonition has appeared on the cover page.

Beginning with the General Conference of 1945, a quadrennial projection through a theme has been made. The same plan has been followed each quadrennium through the General Conference of 1981. The themes, with year of adoption, have been as follows: 1945 - "A New Crusade with Christ"; 1949 - "Victory with Christ"; 1953 - "Further with Christ"; 1957 - "Loyalty to Christ"; 1961 - "United in Christ"; 1965 - "Christ Calls . . . Advance"; 1969 - "Forward-. . . Together with Christ"; 1973 - "Venturing with Christ"; 1977 - "United in Venture"; and 1981 - "Great Commitment."

Two observations seem apparent from the themes when viewed as a group. First, the focus has been consistently "Christ-oriented." Second, the emphasis had a forward thrust. In general the themes remind United Brethren that, whatever activities are programmed for ministry, they are to present a witness for Christ and only to be attempted under His authority and leadership. The thrust is forward! The attempted "crusade," "the advance," and "the venture" call for and are dependent upon "loyalty," a "united" effort, and logically a call for "great commitment."

During the 60s and 70s "goal orientation" began to take place on all levels of church structure. Management principles from non-ecclesiastical organizations came into the study picture for church executives. Achievement ratings on these projections, which were adopted and promoted, have not been widely publicized. It would seem apparent that through their continued use they have been deemed to have value.

The "Great Commitment" has been approached with considerable study and planned promotion. The preliminary work included the preparation of workbooks, transparencies, briefings on the local level, and brochures. The commitment set forth is a "Commitment to growth," with goals reaching 12 years into the future. The overall goals were expressed as "doubling our membership" and "establishing 100 new churches."

The thrust of the Great Commitment starts with a statement of purpose for the denomination:

> The mission of the Church of the United Brethren in Christ is to effectively communicate the Gospel of Christ by word and deed toward the end that all men and women shall be saved and become faithful disciples of Christ and responsible members of His Church.[65]

It proceeds with these objectives: 1) to worship God; 2) to edify believers; 3) to evangelize the lost; and 4) to demonstrate social concern.[66]

In launching the program, care was taken to remind the church that success was not going to be realized in anything short of a personal and churchwide incarnation of great commitment. It must surpass words, charts, and plans; it must become a matter of flesh and heart.

Membership

Church membership is generally viewed or charted when a denomination's outreach is being considered. Total church membership of the Church of the United Brethren in Christ appears at times to have been difficult to ascertain precisely.[67] Statistics on church membership seemed to take second place to the number of conversions reported. Increased calls from denominational bodies and government agencies have demanded more precision in record-keeping. The book *U.S. Census of Religious Bodies* for 1926 [issued September 28, 1928] indicated ". . . the United Brethren Church (Old Constitution) reported 372 churches and a membership of 17,872."

The report of 1980 indicates that United Brethren Churches in North America number 271 with a total membership of 28,023.[68] New churches have been built throughout this period. Some of them represent relocations; a few represent consolidations or mergers. But there is no escape from the fact that this size reduction in the number of churches has played a part in the minimal growth of the membership. Prior to 1930 and for a number of years since that date, the United

Brethren Church was overwhelmingly a rural church. The country church has been subject to the same movements as the country school and the country store. The conservatism of the theology of the church may have been reflected in its methodology. At least the church did not pioneer any general movement toward the city and its relocated members found other places of work and worship. The past four decades have witnessed a new awareness of the changed cultural situation in America. Church extension, on the general and on the annual conference levels, has been approached with the city in mind.

In a 1980 report on "The 40 Largest Churches" in the United Brethren fellowship, approximately one-half represent new congregations since the late 40s. Four of the top ten would be basically within the last 30 years.[69] It appears evident that the city is open to the United Brethren Church and its message. New converts reported for the 1977-1981 quadrennium were 9152; baptisms reported were 4652. The disparity comes when the conversions reported are compared with the members received. Of the 9152 conversions reported, only 4840 were received as members on profession of faith—3853 adults and 987 youth. It appears that "discipleship" and "discipleship training" are proper first steps in the "Great Commitment" thrust.

Affiliate Local Churches

In the mid-1960s, officials of the Church of the United Brethren in Christ were approached by a few Evangelical United Brethren congregations concerning affiliation with the United Brethren fellowship. The questions came during the time of merger of the Evangelical United Brethren and the Methodist Churches into the United Methodist Church.

When these inquiries came, the Church of the United Brethren in Christ had no stated provision for such a relationship. The inquiries appeared to be serious[70] and the theological stance appropriate to make it a subject for serious consideration. The Board of Bishops presented the matter to the General Board of Administration and a general policy statement was produced.[71]

The General Conference of 1969 accepted and adopted the report of the Committee on Administration and Supervision whereby a provision for an Affiliate Local Church was identified and recognized by the Church of the United Brethren in Christ. An affiliate local church was defined:

. . . an organized local church which has not accepted the Constitution but which adopts the Confession of Faith and is pastored by a minister of the Church of the United Brethren in Christ.[72]

The General Conference of 1973, through revision of *Discipline,* provided a category for individual associate members. This was accomplished by a redefinition of the term *connection.* This provision allowed any local church that desired to do so to receive into associate membership individuals who were members of secret combinations. The provision also contained several limitations in respect to such membership, e.g. associate members were not eligible for the office of lay leader nor to serve as a delegate to annual or general conferences; nor to vote for delegates to those conferences or in referenda pertaining to the Constitution. This provision was presented as not being in violation of the Constitution.

A minority, opposed to the above change, entered a protest to the definition of *connection* being used. The protest continued until the General Conference of 1977 and resulted in the 'associate membership' provision being stricken from the *Discipline.* However, individual members having been received as associate members between 1973 and 1977 were allowed to remain in that status.

Ecumenical Involvement

The Church of the United Brethren in Christ has manifested a cooperative rather than a separatist spirit throughout its existence. An ecumenical spirit was quite apparent in the days of its formation as a denomination. Attempts were made to fellowship with other groups prior to the mid-1800s. New attention has been given during the past four decades to interdenominational cooperation. The bishops' quadrennial report to the General Conference of 1949 reflected increased cooperative activity.

Association with other denominations and inter-denominational bodies has called for delegates to various meetings and participation in planning. All this calls for much committee work and extensive study. The office work in connection with the new features of today's activities has increased. It does seem that the work along these lines has more than doubled during the past four years.[73]

The United Brethren Church has been allied with the Christian Endeavor movement throughout the past fifty years. It has used the Christian Endeavor materials for its youth program for most of those years. In several situations it has provided leadership personnel for Christian Endeavor Unions on the state or provincial level. Elmer Becker served as president of the Ontario (Canada) Union and Clarence A. Kopp, Jr. served the Ohio Union as president. Robert W. Rash, Walter M. Burkholder, and David G. Jackson from the Department of Christian Education served the International Society of Christian Endeavor in important committee leadership roles. Clyde W. Meadows had a prominent role in Christian Endeavor leadership during the 1960s and 1970s. He was elected president of the International Society of Christian Endeavor in 1959 and served in that capacity for four years. In 1962, in Sydney, Australia, he was elected president of the World Christian Endeavor Union. As president he had the opportunity to witness before and work with hundreds of thousands of youth around the world. When he retired from that position in 1974, he was elected honorary president for life.

The United Brethren Church has also been involved with the National Association of Evangelicals since the earliest days of that organization. Bishop Ezra M. Funk was a member of one of its earliest committees. The Reverend J. Clair Peters was an officer in its Sunday School outreach (the National Sunday School Association) for more than ten years. During the past 10 or 15 years, United Brethren bishops and other executive officers have been commission and board members of the National Association of Evangelicals. Throughout the history of the church, individuals have served responsible offices in cooperative organizations such as The Lord's Day Alliance and State Sabbath School Associations.

While the United Brethren Church has not sought constitutional union with other denominations, it has welcomed the opportunities for cooperative or federated relationships with other churches. For several years Evangelical Congregational, Primitive Methodist, and the United Brethren churches have been involved in joint publications, such as The Venture Series of Sunday School materials and in missionary outreach.

The General Conference of 1981 moved a step further in the direction of merger. It approved the recommendation from the Board of Bishops "That we continue cooperation in the Federation with five persons being appointed as our representatives by the General Board of Administration."[74] The general conference also voted "that this general conference go on record as being in favor of aggressively pursuing a merger with the Evangelical Congregational Church and/or the Primitive Methodist Church."[75] Follow-up action was taken during 1981 to explore possibilities for organic union. Reports of progress were to be reported by the United Brethren bishops at their 1982 annual conferences.

The General Board of Administration followed up the authorization of the General Conference of 1981 by appointing Bishop C. Ray Miller, administration; Bishop Jerry F. Datema, missions; Dr. Paul R. Fetters, theology; Dr. Eugene B. Habecker, education; and the Reverend Paul E. Hirschy, church services as the official representatives of the United Brethren Church to a merger steering committee. By October 1982 it was decided that each of the three denominations should consider the question, "What are the benefits of merger that could not be achieved through federation?" This was done and the steering committee on merger met in Huntington, Indiana, on January 14, 1983. The committee reviewed the possible advantages and disadvantages of merger and the adjustments and problems likely to be encountered if merger were approved. The January 14 meeting ended on this note: continue federation, but stop the efforts to merge. For the United Brethren the final word had to come from the general board and not the merger committee. Bishop Miller presented a four-part recommendation to the general board in May 1983: 1) that the exploration of merger be discontined, 2) that the merger committee be disbanded, 3) that this matter be reported to the General Conference at 1985, and 4) that the federation be strengthened. All four parts of the recommendation were passed by the general board. "These decisions are to be placed before the official meetings of the denominations for final disposition."[76]

FOOTNOTES

[1]*Proceedings of the Thirty-fifth General Conference of the Church of the United Brethren in Christ* (Huntington, IN: United Brethren Publishing Establishment, 1949), pp. 353, 354.

[2]*Mission to Sierra Leone, Honduras, Jamaica, Hong Kong,* Department of Missions, Church of the United Brethren in Christ. n.d., p. 16.

[3]*United Brethren Missions in Honduras.* (One of four brochures prepared by the Board of Missions, 302 Lake Street, Huntington, Indiana. n.d. (assumed to be in 1981). Others were *U.B. Missions in Jamaica; . . . in Hong Kong; . . . in Sierra Leone.*

[4]The Parent Board of Missions and the Women's Missionary Association, hereafter referred to as "the two mission boards."

[5]A future bishop in the United Brethren Church, Funk lived in Strinestown, Pa., while serving as a presiding elder in the Pennsylvania Conference.

[6]*Our Mission in Jamaica.* (2-page typewritten paper: n.d.).

[7]*Mission to . . . Jamaica.,* p. 16.

[8]*Our Mission in Jamaica,* Ibid.

[9]*United Brethren Missions in Jamaica.* (brochure)

[10]Ibid.

[11]*United Brethren Missions in Honduras.* (brochure)

[12]George D. Fleming, *Trail Blazers in Sierra Leone,* 2 volumes (Huntington, IN: Hill Crest Lithographing, 1973), 1:166.

[13]*United Brethren Missions in Capsule Form* (Huntington. IN: Board of Missions, n.d. (1981), n.p.

[14]Fleming, 2:170.

[15]The Sierra Leone Bible College is sponsored jointly by the Missionary Church, the Wesleyan Church, the United Brethren Church, and the German Baptist Church, but controlled by its own Board of Governors.

[16]The Ebys served as missionaries in Sierra Leone: 1923-1925; 1944-1947; 1958-1962. He was later elected bishop in the United Brethren Church.

[17]Misses Funk, Hoffman and Sewell, R.N., were on their maiden voyage as missionaries. Sewell went on to serve three terms: 1944-1947; 1949-1952; 1965-1966. Funk served three terms also: 1944-1947; 1948-1951; 1952-1955. Hoffman's service (1944-1983) entered upon the twelfth term in August 1980.

[18]The older son, Ronald, after completing his medical degree in the United States, returned to the hospital in Mattru as physician and surgeon.

[19](1) The Centennial Secondary School, the first coeducational, boarding, secondary school in Sierra Leone, was dedicated January 7, 1955. The name Centennial was given in recognition of 100 years of United Brethren missionary service in Sierra Leone. The enrollment for the first term was 90. (Fleming: *Trail Blazers,* 2:184) (2) A second high school was founded by DeWitt Baker in Bumpe, in 1963. Baker also served as its first principal.

[20]Fleming, 2:402-409.

[21]Fleming, 1:165.

[22]Fleming, 2:72.

[23]Ibid.

[24]Ibid., p. 89.

[25]Ibid., p. 238.

[26]An American British, Australian company with Sierra Leone headquarters in Mattru.

[27]Fleming, 2:240.

[28]Ibid.

[29]Ronald Baker was a lad of three when he first set foot on Sierra Leone. His knowledge and use of the Mende language came from that young age. His fluent use of the Mende gave him access to observe a witch doctor's performance with her permission.

[30]Rotary International, at the suggestion of the Huntington Club, of which Ronald Baker's father, E. DeWitt Baker is a member, has undertaken a $300,000 project to provide polio and measles immunization for children in Sierra Leone, ages birth to 4 years.

[31]Fleming, 2:403-409.

[32]Nurse Bard began her service in Sierra Leone in 1931 and has spent most of the time until the 70s in Africa. (A few years were spent in the employ of the Pittsburgh Plate Glass Company.)

[33]Proceedings of the Thirty-ninth General Conference of the Church of the United Brethren in Christ (Huntington, IN: United Brethren Publishing Establishment, 1965), pp. 192-193; reports pp. 14, 49, 50.

[34]Branches are, for the most part, organizations conforming to annual conference boundaries. Local societies are parish identities, sometimes there are multiple societies within a local parish.

[35]The following statistics, from the reports of the missionary secretaries from decade to decade, reflect the missionary giving through the denominational channels:

for year ending	Parent Board totals	W.M.A. totals	combined totals
1930	$ 13,908	$ 23,390	$ 37,298
1940	10,823	17,071	27,894
1950	62,157	69,517	131,674
1960	125,386	134,424	259,810
1970	167,238	168,905	336,143*
1980	287,088	365,416	652,504

*The figure for this and following years represents the Department of Missions.

[36]This was the 12th inaugural occasion for Huntington College, but Dr. C. A. Mummart had served on two separate occasions in the teens and twenties.

[37]From a charted report sent to the United Brethren pastors in 1939, presumably prepared by President Mason.

[38]Bond issues were used in connection with the building of Hardy Hall (1966) and the Huntington Union Building (1968).

[39]From a personal interview between the writer and Dr. E. DeWitt Baker, before the 1981 college report was completed.

[40]President Baker's report to the 1981 General Conference.

[41]The Merillats are of Merillat Industries, Adrian, Michigan. They are lay leaders of the Trenton Hills Church of the United Brethren in Christ, North Ohio Conference. J. L. Brenn founder of Huntington Laboratories Incorporated, served as president of H. C. foundation. C. W. H. Bangs, former Huntington College president also served as mayor and attorney for the city of Huntington. He and his wife were members of the College Park Church of the United Brethren in Christ.

[42]Data from the quadrennial reports show the following for Huntington College:

year ending	enrollment	library holdings	net worth
1937	169	11,369	$ 95,019.54
1941	133		124,075.99
1945	158		158,887.58
1949	339	15,982	146,722.56
1953	222	17,093	158,003.28
1957	319	22,523	163,066.24
1961	478	27,490	725,085.89
1965	627	32,230	1,531,954.63
1969	660	38,000	1,288,765.00
1973	599	47,500	3,329,614.00
1977	789	49,300*	4,170,338.00
1980	645		5,976,042.00
1981	617	61,523	

* Library holdings reported 2200 Government Documents and 1547 microfilms.

[43]Huntington College Board of Trustees, Executive Committee Minutes, September 12, 1967.

[44]Ibid., January 9, 1968 and July 2, 1968.

[45]Ibid., January 12, 1970.

[46]Ibid., October, 1970.

[47]The Reverend Paul R. Fetters came to the campus from his pastorate at the Kettering Church of the United Brethren in Christ, Dayton, Ohio. He had been graduated with his A.B. from Huntington College; a B.D. from the Huntington College Theological Seminary; an M.Div. from Eastern Baptist Theological Seminary and additional work at Wright State University. Since coming to the Graduate School of Christian Ministries, he has completed a Masters of Science in Education at St. Francis College, Ft. Wayne, Indiana, and the Doctor of Ministry from Fuller Theological Seminary, Pasadena, California.

[48]Minutes of the Board of Trustees of Huntington College, February 5, 1982, p. 5.

[49]J. Ralph Pfister, *A History of the United Brethren Publishing Establishment,* 1970 (Earl Peters, 1979). A paper read before the Huntington County Historical Society, March 1970. (unpublished) pp. 13, 4, 14.

[50]*Proceedings of the Forty-third General Conference . . . 1981,* pp. 13, 87.

[51]R. W. Rash, (revised by Walter M. Burkholder), *Christian Education* (Huntington, IN: Department of Christian Education, The Church of the United Brethren in Christ, Revised edition: August, 1964), p. 65.

[52]Ibid.

[53]Christian Newcomer, transcribed, corrected, and translated by John Hildt, *The Life and Journal of the Rev'd Christian Newcomer* (Hagerstown, MD: F. G. W. Kapp, 1834), p. 67.

[54]Grover L. Hartman, *A School for God's People: A History of the Sunday School Movement in Indiana* (Indianapolis, IN: Central Publishing Co. Inc., 1980), n.p.

[55]Rash, p. 27.

[56]Ibid., p. 27f.

[57]Ibid., p. 54.

[58]Ibid., p. 55.

[59]Ibid., p. 59.

[60]Ibid., p. 60.

[61]Rash, Ibid., p. 70.

[62]Board of Administration *Minutes,* Item 54, 1973.

[63]*Proceedings of the Thirty-fifth General Conference . . . 1949 . . . Reports,* p. 270.

[64]Minutes General Board of Administration 1962.

[65]From a brochure prepared for the annual conferences and presented at the General Conference of 1981. n.d.

[66]Ibid., A personal resolution is included in the brochure with a personal commitment and an individual's signature form.

[67]Denominational statistics then, as well as now, were based on compilations from annual conferences. But there was no uniform date for compiling the annual data, since annual conferences presented the data of their conference year. That year might begin in June or it might begin in October.

[68]*Proceedings of the Forty-third General Conference . . . 1981.* Bishops' Quadrennial Address.

[69]*The United Brethren,* January 1981, p. 4.

[70]"51 E U B Churches Protest Merger," from World News reported in *The United Brethren,* July 17, 1968, p. 13.

[71]*The United Brethren,* September 27, 1967.

[72]*Proceedings of the Fortieth General Conference . . . 1969,* pp. 12, 152. For further guidelines see Discipline, 1969-1973, para. 209.

[73]*Proceedings of the Thirty-fifth General Conference . . . 1949,* Bishops' Quadrennial Address, p. 260f.

[74]*Proceedings of the Forty-third General Conference . . . 1981,* p. 29.

[75]Ibid., p. 21.

[76]As reported in "Never the Twain Shall Merge" and "Joint Merger Statement" appearing in the *United Brethren,* July 1983, pp. 6-8. (Last quote over the signatures of C. Ray Miller (UB), John Moyer (EC), and Mel Lewis (PM).

36

MINISTRY AND MINISTERS

The 1930-1981 period of the denominational history witnessed three developments in relation to ministry and ministers that have already showed results or appear as good omens for the future. The first development was the upgrading of the licensuring requirements for the prospective minister. In the General Conference of 1925, the church set the entrance of high school as the minimum requirement for an educational level at which one might be recommended for annual conference licensuring. This educational level was raised to the tenth grade in 1929 and to the completion of four years in high school in 1945. In 1965 the requirement was advanced to ". . . one year of work in residence at Huntington College" or ". . . one year of the minister's training program by correspondence under the direction of the Seminary of Huntington College."[1] The General Conference of 1977 again raised the level to the completion of ". . . two years of academic training either at Huntington College (or at such other schools or colleges as may be academically approved by the board of education.) or through ". . . the minister's training program by correspondence, under the direction of Huntington College School of Christian Ministries."[2]

The second development came in the upgrading of the requirements for ordination. Pre-ordination studies have been updated throughout the past 45 years. While maintaining a core area of studies (such as theology, Bible, preaching, and church history) as the minimum requirement for ordination, the standard set before the annual conference licentiate has continued to rise. In the years between 1929 and 1937 a prescribed four-year course was the only one listed in the church *Discipline* for annual conference preachers. The examinations on this reading course were administered by an annual conference board of examiners using questions prepared by the book committee of the denomination. "A certificate of graduation from a regular three years' theological course given by any institution of learning under the control of this church may be accepted in place of an examination on the course of study."[3]

For ordination the General Conference of 1937 continued to recognize the four-year reading course but also authorized an alternate *correspondence course* with examinations to be given through the Huntington College Theological Seminary. Furthermore, in 1941, graduation from the four-year *English Theological Course,* the five-year *Bachelor of Theology* degree, or the seven-year *Bachelor of Divinity* degree was encouraged as an ordination requirement.[4] The four-year reading course was discontinued in 1949. In that same year, the seminary was charged with the responsibility of arranging a "three year course of training" which ". . . shall include the usual studies for the preparation of the ministry."[5]

Since about the middle of this century, increased emphasis has been placed on the graduate program for ministerial preparation. The Bachelor of Divinity offerings were expanded into a full three-year program including some field work experience. This was followed, in turn, with further refinements, and the degree was adjusted to that of Master of Divinity.

A major restructuring took place in the early 1970s following a two-year study initiated by the Board of Education. The end result of the study was the introduction of the Master of Christian Ministry degree in a restructured Graduate School of Christian Ministries. This offering is set forth as ". . . a practice-oriented graduate course of study . . . . It consists of one year of advanced study requiring a Baccalaureate degree with a directed major in Bible and Religion or Christian Education."[6] The Graduate School of Christian Ministries is regionally accredited by the North Central Association of Colleges and Schools. The Master of Christian Ministry program, somewhat of an innovation when introduced at Huntington, has gained recognition by other graduate schools and seminaries, and similar graduate degrees are now being offered by several other schools.

Standardized testing for use in career guidance has come to a new emphasis during the past four years. In addition, the Graduate School of Christian Ministries and/or annual conferences have provided, for the past decade, opportunities for continuing education for pastors and/or their spouses. These provisions have taken the form of short courses, seminars, and retreats.

The third development in the area of ministry has been that for new roles for lay persons. A provision for "lay ministers" was set forth in 1977 whereby "the Church recognizes that some of its laity possess gifts which qualify them for acts of ministry which are not generally performed in the more general ministry of the laity."[7] Licensuring for lay ministers is the responsibility of the local congregation, the pastor, and the conference superintendent. Individual parishes have gone beyond the above provision to establish a lay pastoral care commission for a more extensive or comprehensive lay ministry. The office and duties of the deacon and deaconess have also been updated and clarified.

During these decades of change, the Church of the United Brethren in Christ has not tempered its position on having a God-called ministry. The ministerial candidate is called upon to witness to the Divine call at several junctures prior to ordination. The classification of ministers as "itinerants" and "local ministers" has continued. In the General Conference of 1977, the term "itinerant" was redefined and the ministers were reclassified. Itinerants are now described as ". . . all annual conference licentiates and ordained elders . . . who, . . . have given themselves without reserve for service in the Church of the United Brethren in Christ."[8] Hence the denomination has raised continually its standard of preparation and enlarged its vision as to opportunity for ministry.

Along with this updating of requirements, the church and/or the annual conferences have greatly undergirded the provisions for the material support of the parish minister. Annual conferences have shown their support for pastors through the establishment of minimum salaries, housing allowance if the pastor opts to purchase his own residence, utilities and mileage reimbursements, medical/hospital plans, social security support, paid vacations, seminar expenses, and professional aids.

At the opening of this period very little, if any, general provision was made for the preacher's retirement years. In 1933 a Preachers' Aid Board of three members was established and an annuity plan was proposed.[9] By 1937 a proposal was initiated whereby the pastor was to pay one per cent of the cash salary received into the Preachers' Aid Fund. Benefits from this fund were limited to "superannuates in good standing, recommended by their respective annual conferences as beneficiaries."[10] Profits from the United Brethren Publishing Establishment were also dedicated to the Preachers' Aid Fund. Limited profits from this source and an annual allocation from the general benevolence funds constituted the major denominational provision for retirement until the 1960s. On October 6, 1966, a Pension Trust was initiated ". . . as authorized by the general conference on June 11, 1965 . . . (This Pension Trust Plan) provided not only retirement benefits, but also death benefits should death occur prior to retirement."[11] Amid the changes of the past 50 years, the minister's financial status in 1981 is more easily contrasted than compared with that of 1931.

Individual Ministers

From a casual reading of the biblical record, one might readily conclude that God works through men rather than movements. Some interpret history to be the lengthened shadows of men. God chose Noah, Abraham, Moses, Joseph, Gideon, David, Isaiah, Peter, Paul, and a host of others as individuals rather than the temple priests, a political party, or organized governments for the fulfillment of His purpose.

From its beginning as a denomination, God has used individuals to highlight the Church of the United Brethren in Christ. For the past 50 years the divine approval has rested upon those called to leadership positions in the denomination. They appear to have been worthy of the prophet's appellation, "God has planted them like strong and graceful oaks for his own glory" (Isaiah 61:3 *Living Bible*). This review of the past half-century would be incomplete without pausing to reflect upon a few of them.

To make a selection from among the "graceful oaks" is bound to be somewhat subjective and arbitrarily limiting. The writer has had personal and/or official contacts with all the general officials of the United Brethren Church since 1932, except Bishop L. B. Baldwin.[12] His contacts with Bishop Fermin L. Hoskins were limited to that of a listener at the General Conference of 1929. The one sermon which he heard Hoskins preach was based on Mark 6:48: "And the wind was contrary." Hoskins is reported to have been an excellent parliamentarian—rigid in enforcing the "rules" but gracious in dealing with the offender personally. He was also an engaging platform man. A non-United Brethren told the writer in the late 30s of a personal experience which had happened about 25 or 30 years earlier. This man had gone to listen to Hoskins give a public lecture in the community. He reported that after Hoskins had spoken for some time, he (Hoskins) paused, looked at his watch, and speedily concluded the lecture. The auditor then, out of curiosity, looked at his watch and discovered that Hoskins had been speaking for about two hours. He commented that it seemed but a short time.

For the most part, United Brethren ministers still living and serving have been purposely omitted from this observation. The exceptions are limited to those whose service has been more extensive than the average, or whose area of contribution is already generally recognized or completed. However, before detailed attention is given to particular personalities, let a few generalities be noted.

Laurin B. Baldwin and Clarence A. Mummart brought to the office of bishop collegiate experience as administrator and classroom teacher. Mummart excelled as a master of detail. He could tell not only the total amount of an offering for which he had the responsibility but also the exact number of checks, paper currency, and coins which were contributed. Walter E. Musgrave and Albert M. Johnson came from a context of the role of presiding elder and earlier pastoral experience. Musgrave had also had a term in the office of executive secretary of the Otterbein Forward Movement. Ezra M. Funk brought the disciplines of the public schoolteacher and the insights of a psychologist. Lloyd Eby and Clarence E. Carlson came to the bishopric fresh from experience on the foreign mission field. Robert W. Rash had served 16 years in the department of Christian Education just prior to his election as a bishop. Clyde W. Meadows came to the office of bishop from the largest parish in the denomination and a role in international youth activities.

George E. Weaver brought military disciplines and journalistic skills which have left their marks on the denominational structure. Duane A. Reahm came to the bishopric with an evangelistic fervor and a missionary outlook which remain as challenges following his retirement. The quiet influence of Raymond Waldfogel in the area of church extension span both the West and Central districts of the Church. C. Ray Miller will be remembered by many for his evangelistic visitation training and materials as well as his background in Christian education. Wilber L. Sites, Jr., brings experience from the pastorate and conference with special background in denominational budgeting. To join Miller and Sites in administrative responsibility and spiritual oversight, in 1981, Jerry F. Datema and Clarence A. Kopp, Jr., come from active ministry on the mission field and the city pastorate. The following personal reflections of the writer are shared with a personal sense of gratitude for the privilege of being co-laborers together.

Walter Emmet Musgrave

Walter Emmet Musgrave, a dynamo in the pulpit or on the platform, was a determined man in the administrative role. In his examination of pastors' reports at annual conference time, he overlooked no detail. He was inclined to pursue the question until the detail was fully clarified.

A public schoolteacher's characterization of his platform presentation was, "You don't just listen to him, you cannot help but listen." This conclusion may well have been shared by many. His pulpit mannerisms may have appeared unusual to a polished orator, but they underscored the point being made. His habit of closing one eye and pointing with the index finger of the right hand gave emphasis and direction. He defended his bold style by reminding his hearers, on occasion, ". . . that he attended the school of 'hard knocks,' where the colors were 'black and blue,' and the yell was 'ouch'."

Musgrave had an alert mind, did extensive reading, and preached new sermons. He allowed that if he ever used old sermons it was an indication that he was growing old. On the other hand, however, he had several lectures which he presented again and again. The lecture: "Modernism—the Child of Freemasonry" was initially presented during the General Conference of 1929 in Chambersburg, Pennsylvania. But it was frequently given during the 1930s and published in booklet form. Another lecture presented frequently, following the repeal of the 18th amendment, gave John Barleycorn the title "Public Enemy No. 1."

The impression gained by young United Brethren preachers of Musgrave as a bishop was that he was a dynamic fighter for righteousness and an exponent of the Church of the United Brethren in Christ with all its departments. The Scioto Annual Conference felt the extension of his personality for another generation. A later bishop of the district was heard to comment, "We have a lot of little Musgraves in Scioto."

It was not in keeping with Musgrave's nature to sit along the sidelines while others were playing the game. But the time arrived when the physical would no longer support the emotional or rational drive. He was able to accept the role of the retired. The writer recalls that during his final pastoral call on the bishop in his home that he remarked, "I don't know what the Lord has for me on this earth, but whatever it is, He has all of me." He answered the heavenly summons on May 6, 1950.

Albert Meric Johnson

Albert Meric Johnson, of the Auglaize Annual Conference, served as a minister in the Church of the United Brethren in Christ for 50 years, 23 of which were as a bishop. He joined the Zion Church, Mercer County, Ohio, membership in 1892 and reported that he had "never been transferred or dropped (sic) from the roll from the date in which I joined."[13]

As a pastor he was a successful evangelist. On two occasions he reported conversions on the field near the 100 mark.

> On my first pastorate the Berne Mission I built the Winchester church. In a revival meeting held at the Otterbein church we had over one hundred conversions in a single revival meeting, and at Fairview on the Pleasant Grove Church [circuit] we had near one hundred conversions in a single revival meeting. On my first pastorate at the Winchester Church during a revival I was unable to get into the house by way of the door because of the emense crowds (sic) I was helped into the church through a window, this happened on three different occasions.[14]

Johnson served all three bishop districts in North America. He ". . . presented his resignation to the General Board of Administration that met during the month of May, 1951, in Shippensburg, Pennsylvania. The resignation was accepted and Bishop Johnson was elected Bishop Emeritus of the Church."[15] His death occurred on November 18, 1954.

In a memorial tribute to bishop Johnson, his colleague on the mission board, George D. Fleming, characterized the bishop as

> a friend to mankind, he was known and loved throughout the denomination. Known for sympathetic understanding of the problems which faced the ministers and conference officials who served the church under his leadership; known for his sense of humor, a characteristic trait which helped make smooth the times of tension and the pressure of long hours of strain at conference business sessions; he was loved for his kindly mannerisms, his impartial decisions, his commonness among the people.[16]

Ezra M. Funk, a colleague in the bishopric and close associate of Johnson, said of him:

> He enjoyed fellowship with his fellowmen. He was an interesting associate and a genial companion. He was of a poetic nature and enjoyed good literature. He appreciated the beauties of nature and reveled in the handiwork of God as manifest in earth, sea, and sky. He enjoyed preaching the 'unsearchable riches of Christ.'[17]

Ezra Myers Funk

Ezra Myers Funk will be remembered by many United Brethren

ministers as the individual whom God used to challenge them to become ministers of the gospel. To many more, including the writer, the name of Ezra M. Funk brings memories of that moment when they passed from death unto life. Funk, whether as pastor, teacher, friend, presiding elder, or bishop, was on constant guard to sense a soul under conviction for sin or in need of spiritual help. The time might be during a public service, a personal conversation, a pastoral visit in the home, but it seems that he seldom lost opportunity to present Christ as the Savior. He was used of God for 52 years to lead many persons to Christ and to guide them into the deeper Christian life.

His heritage of being born into the home of Pennsylvania "plain people," his avid reading habits, and his experiences as a teacher in the elementary schoolroom all contributed to his effectiveness in the pulpit, in Christian education role, and in the oversight of the bishop's jurisdiction.

Though he was small of stature,[18] he learned to develop his speech and his mind. Throughout his life he was a person of keen intellect. The greater strength of his life was in the spiritual realm. "As God touched his life and he yielded to His will—God made him a spiritual giant."[19] His life and ministry were reflections of his dedication to God. His singleness of purpose was exhibited again and again in his ministry. "He was a man of deep convictions and stood faithfully for Christian principles regardless of how he or anyone else were affected by the truth."[20]

Funk was an avid reader. He read prose and poetry, he read psychology, most of all he read the Bible. He was a rapid reader and he had disciplined himself to carry a book with him and use short intervals of time as opportunities for reading. It is told that on one occasion when he was to speak at a conference or convention near Niagara Falls, that, during some unscheduled time, while others went to see the natural wonder, Funk stayed behind. He said:

> When I knew I was to bring the message this evening on the Holy Spirit, I decided it best to refresh my mind and heart in the book of Acts, and since I awoke this morning I have read the book three times. Since I started to keep count this brings the total to 111 times.[21]

On another occasion, while supplying the pulpit for a son-in-law, he took the occasion to read through the Bible—Old and New Testaments—for the purpose of looking at the larger dimensions of the Bible. This self-assigned task was completed in one week.

Scripture memorization and expository preaching were important features of his ministerial career. He memorized the Scriptures by the chapter rather than by the verse. His sermon preparation often included some physical exercise. If he were confined to a room, he might be seen walking back and forth; if he were free to take a walk in the outdoors, that might be included. His sermon outline might be a word-outline noted on the margin of the Bible page. His saturation with the Scripture, his cultivated memory work, and his thorough analysis of the passage gave the Holy Spirit an opportunity to speak through him when he preached.

He retired from the office of a bishop at the General Conference held in Huntington, Indiana, June 11-17, 1957. He was granted an emeritus relationship at the same conference. He served briefly as a conference superintendent in Pennsylvania Annual Conference during his retirement. He went to be with the Lord, June 1, 1958.

Lloyd Eby

Lloyd Eby, of German Mennonite ancestry, after a conversion experience in the Salvation Army, began serving in the United Brethren Church while still a teenager. Born in Kitchener, Ontario, (originally known as Eby's Settlement),[22] he united with his parents as a member of the Evangelical Church because there was no Mennonite church in the community.[23] His active ministry in the United Brethren Church began when he responded to an invitation to go to Toronto to open a United Brethren mission Sunday School. His activities in the Sunday School developed into areas of pastoral care since there was no pastor present. Soon he was licensed as a quarterly conference preacher, and began a ministry that ultimately touched many parts of the world.

His years in Toronto (1916-1921) witnessed the opening of three Sunday Schools, of which two developed into parish churches. He combined a year of studies at Huntington College with the pastoral ministry of Etna Avenue congregation, Huntington, Indiana. In 1923 Lloyd Eby and his wife, Eula, began the first of three terms of missionary service in Sierra Leone, West Africa (1923-1925; 1944-1947; 1958-1959). The Eby's served in Detroit, Michigan, from 1926-1944. During those years they were instrumental in opening seven United Brethren missions, five of which were developed into separate parishes. From 1947 to 1949 Eby served as conference superintendent of the Detroit and the Ontario Annual Conferences of the United Brethren Church.

The members of the General Conference of 1949 elected Lloyd Eby to the office of a bishop. He was assigned to the West district, which at the time included all of the United Brethren annual conferences west of the Mississippi River and the Honduras Mission District. In this relationship he continued for the next two quadrennia. In 1957 he was voted Bishop Emeritus.[24] He was elected by the Auglaize Annual Conference as conference superintendent. In 1958 the Ebys were asked by the United Brethren Board of Missions to accept a short term of service in Sierra Leone.

Bishop Lloyd Eby never retired in the sense of laying aside the role of an active and interested partner in the proclamation of the Good News in Christ. From his Fort Wayne, Indiana, home he continued his correspondence and intercession. His regular newsletter went to more than 500 at times. He shared his prayer support with pastors, evangelists, teachers, physicians, Bible translators, and others on the cutting edge of Christian witness. His prayer partnership was interracial in its depth, international in its dimensions, and interdenominational in its direction. Thus the spiritual journey of Lloyd Eby which began in a Salvation Army revival was concluded in partnership with those of many different fellowships around the world. The conclusion for Bishop Emeritus Eby came on Thanksgiving Day, November 27, 1969.

Clarence Edward Carlson

"Could I fit in?" He was considered a proper candidate and in a few weeks was on his way to the mission field in Sierra Leone, West Africa. Thus began what was to become a field service of five terms for Clarence Edward Carlson. Carlson had recently arrived at the Huntington College campus, when the Reverend Jacob Howe shared with him the urgent need on the African field. Carlson's question represented his personal approach to the denomination's needs on several occasions. Following his retirement from the active ministry, he wrote:

> From the beginning of my Christian ministry I have followed a rule that few men accept: Let the voice of the Church be the voice of God to me. I have never asked the church for any particular favors or for the privilege of serving in any particular field or area of activity . . . . If my memory serves me correctly, the only request that I have made was when I asked the General Conference of 1965 to grant me a retired relationship with the church.[25]

Carlson served in Sierre Leone: 1925-1928; 1931-1934; 1936-1938; 1940-1942; and 1947-1949. He served as superintendent of the African Mission for 15 years. During his second term he married Erma Burton, a first-term missionary, whom he had met earlier at Huntington.

Between the periods of time spent on the African continent, Carlson served as pastor for several United Brethren churches in the United States: College Park, Huntington, Indiana; Burbank, California; and Philomath, Oregon. On at least two occasions he served as a conference superintendent; California (1945-1946) and Oregon (1946-1947) Annual Conferences.

He served as bishop from 1957 to 1965, at which time he was honored with the title of bishop emeritus. He continues to serve, as of 1981, as the local leader of his church, the Third Street Church of the United Brethren in Christ, Fort Wayne, Indiana.

Carlson's effectiveness in the pulpit will be remembered by his quiet manner of speaking—never bombastic; never a 'pulpit pounder.' With his Bible open in his hand, he seemed to be saying, "Let's hear what God is saying to us." Of his own ministry he wrote on one occasion:

> The outstanding characteristic of my ministry has been the persistent effort to develop the spiritual life of the church. Most of my sermons have dealt with the Spirit-filled life and prayer. I have used the Bible as the Sword of the Spirit.[26]

Robert William Rash

Robert William Rash was born March 16, 1904, in Auglaize County, Ohio. From the farm, Rash heard and acknowledged the call to the Christian ministry. He completed his high school education after receiving his first pastoral assignment. He combined pastoral responsibilities with collegiate study and graduated from Huntington College with the Bachelor of Theology (Th.B.) degree in 1936. His pastoral assignments were exclusively within the Auglaize Conference except for three years at the College Park Church in Huntington, Indiana.[27] The Auglaize Conference elected him as superintendent in 1940.

From 1941-1957 Rash served his denomination as Secretary of Christian Education. During those years he authored or co-authored at least 15 books or booklets for use in leadership training and youth work. Rash was elected to the office of a bishop during the General Conference of 1957. His interest in Christian education never subsided. To it he added the administrative and oversight duties of the West Bishop's district. Church extension took on a new dimension as he traveled the district. New churches owe their beginning to his years of administration. He was not re-elected in 1961, but in 1965 the Church called him again to the office of a bishop.

He suffered a critical heart attack on August 13, 1968, while engaged in conference work in Kansas. This attack resulted in a time of inactivity and rest. It finally resulted in his resignation "because of health reasons," effective as of March 16, 1969—his 65th birthday.

Rash spent about three and a half of his remaining years as chaplain at the Huntington Memorial Hospital, where he enjoyed a rewarding ministry. On January 18, 1975, after spending hours of service at the hospital, he answered, from his home, the summons of his Savior and Shepherd, "It is enough, come up higher."

Elmer Becker

"Elmer Becker, pastor, church leader, educator, counselor of youth, friend of man, servant of Jesus Christ," thus opens the citation presented to the tenth president of Huntington College upon his moving from the office of president to the office of chancellor.[28]

The person thus recognized was born in Waterloo County, Ontario, Canada. As a youth he came to the United States to attend the college of his church at Huntington, Indiana. It was there that he met the young woman who was to share the trials and frustrations, the joys and the victories of a college president—Miss Inez Schad. Debate experience and book sales during their college days were part of the preparation they received for his future leadership role. After receiving their baccalaureate degrees, the Beckers returned to Canada where he served United Brethren churches in Stevensville and Kitchener, Ontario.

His contacts with Christian Endeavor, which began prior to his college experience, began to widen and intensify. He became involved, on the Ontario Union level, with those of other than United Brethren background. These interdenominational contacts undoubtedly provided excellent background for his later personal contacts with college students with differing denominational heritage.

The General Conference of 1937 called Becker from the local parish to broader responsibilities. For four years he served his denomination as Secretary of Christian Education. In 1941 he was elected to the office of Secretary of Education, and the Huntington College Board of Trustees promptly elected him as the president of the college. He held those positions for nearly a quarter of a century.

The new president was not long in learning what problems presented themselves. The United States was soon engaged in the World War II conflict, and its manpower requirements meant a sudden decrease in male applicants for college. With the conflict ended, an opposite situation came upon the college campus. The returning veterans pushed the Huntington College enrollment to record numbers. Through careful planning President Becker tackled both problems with adjustments in curriculum and physical property.

The building program began in 1943 with the second addition to Livingston Hall, a residence hall for women. Wright Hall, a residence for men, and Loew Alumni library building soon followed. The program continued throughout his administration with the completion of the J. L. Brenn Hall of Science and the ground-breaking for Hardy Hall for women. "Finances have always been the biggest single problem for the college head. Dr. Becker has not found his administration to be an exception."[29]

To enhance the 'Town and Gown' relationship, Becker established a monthly breakfast meeting where faculty members, business personnel and professional leaders of the city and county came into closer contact with each other thus developing a better understanding of the college role and its needs.[30] The Huntington College Foundation has supported the college in its building projects and initiated several capital fund drives.

President Becker maintained active contacts with the annual conference secretaries of education and with the pastors throughout the denomination. He maintained an active file on the birthdays of the high school students of the church. On that occasion the student would receive a congratulatory note from the president. He was known and well received throughout the United Brethren Church. In the Huntington community he was frequently termed "Mr. Huntington College."

Becker's basic goals for Huntington College included North Central Association accreditation. This goal was attained in 1961 after years of self-study and preparation. The institutional goals never limited his interest and concern for the individual student. He could, almost without exception call any student by name, because he made it a policy to have a private conference with each one in the registration line.

President Becker enjoyed a few years of further service to Huntington College after being named president emeritus and chancellor. The role enabled him to have a more relaxed life and yet provide a service of support to the institution which meant so much to him. His departure from earthly service was sudden and unexpected. It came in the evening of August 28, 1969.[31]

The citation with which this reflection began concluded as follows:

> . . . a leadership which has brought Huntington College to a point of national recognition as a liberal arts college; a leadership that has developed a

new consciousness of Christian education throughout the supporting denomination; a leadership that has established a community relationship with the city and county of Huntington that is unique among church-related institutions; a leadership that was matched by a personal dedication which placed the opportunity to serve above considerations for personal welfare . . . .[32]

George Daniel Fleming

A casual reflection is scarcely sufficient for the name of George Daniel Fleming whose missionary service on foreign soil was nearly completed in 1930. George Fleming and his wife Daisy returned from their fifth term of missionary service in Sierra Leone in April 1932. Plans to return were interrupted by illness. At the urging of Bishop Johnson they accepted an interim pastoral assignment to the New Dundee-Roseville circuit in Ontario, Canada. The assignment lasted for three and one-half years.

May 1936 marked the beginning of a new role in missionary service for the Flemings. At a missionary convention at the Fairview United Brethren Church, near Hartford City, Indiana, George D. Fleming was appointed to the office of Secretary of Missions, a role he filled with dedication and enthusiasm for 25 years.

Fleming was more than an eight to five secretary. His time was divided between the office and the field—the field being the Church of the United Brethren in Christ; its congregations and its pastors. In the office were records to be kept, reports to be made, articles for the *Missionary Monthly* to be written, and correspondence to be answered. In the field he was responding to invitations for missionary sermons and addresses, weekend evangelistic meetings, and convention resources. When the field activities became heavy, the office hours became lengthened.

His correspondence seemed to increase as the years accumulated. Missionaries on the field or on furlough, as well as pastors throughout the Church, could expect a prompt reply to their inquiries. Mission conferences, mission board meetings, and annual conference sessions were year by year priorities. Missionary travel arrangements, deputations schedules, visas, and passports were always a part of his concern. The School of Missions in the 1940s was somewhat of a special assignment. The opening of the new mission fields in Jamaica and Honduras required considerable time and special attention.

From 1961, when he retired from the office of missionary secretary, to the time of this writing G. D. Fleming was not idle. As a succeeding secretary of missions observed:

To some people, retirement means just that—cessation of their former normal work activity—but in the life of Dr. Fleming we see one who continues to spend his life and energy in the cause of Christ in missions—evangelism at home and abroad.[33]

For a few years Fleming assisted Duane A. Reahm, his successor in the office. In the early 1970s he authored two volumes of the Sierra Leone missionary enterprise.[34] At the age of 88, he made a return visit to Sierra Leone in 1978. He continued to make frequent visits to churches in the mid-west in the interest of missions. God gave Fleming the opportunity of more than a half-century of ministry; and Fleming gave a faithful stewardship to the Gospel entrusted to him.

After the close of the General Conference of 1981 George D. Fleming added a significant note or two to his missionary endeavors. At the time of the 1982 Annual Conference sessions in Jamaica (February) the conference brethren there extended an invitation to Fleming to make a return visit to the Island.

In response to that invitation and encouragment by the Bishop Jerry Datema, Fleming went to Jamaica in 1983, to spend about two weeks there. In spite of his advanced age he visited a majority of the local United Brethren parishes. His partner for the trip, Harry Herzog, reported[35] that Fleming preached 13 sermons in those two weeks (February 26 to March 14, 1983). Such an itinerary would appear to be something of a record for one in his 94th year.

Fleming's personal letter-writing and prayer commitment to missionaries and pastors continued until his hospitalization on October 21, 1983. He exchanged life here for the life beyond on October 29, 1983, passing away at the St. Joseph Hospital in Fort Wayne, Indiana.

Clyde Williamson Meadows

A leader in his parish, in his community, in his conference, in his denomination, and in interdenominational projects—by which United Brethren leader could all of these distinctions be claimed? Only one United Brethren preacher in the past 50 years seems to fit the role. That person is Clyde Williamson Meadows.

From a rural county in Virginia to a White House commission indicates something of the versatile life he has lived; from a series of smaller parishes in the middle west to the denomination's largest parish represents the strength of his leadership; from a parish role to the office of bishop indicates the esteem of his brethren; and from a secretary's position in a local Christian Endeavor society to that of president of the

World Christian Endeavor Union reflects his continuing rapport with youth.

Meadows was born in Appomatox County, Virginia, and was converted at the age of 9 in a Baptist revival. He dedicated himself to the gospel ministry while a student at Huntington College. His educational pursuit resulted in the Bachelor of Arts degree from Huntington College, the Bachelor of Divinity, and the Master of Sacred Theology degrees from the Lutheran Seminary, Gettysburg, Pennsylvania. He was awarded the Doctor of Divinity degree from Huntington College in 1940.

His pastoral ministries were performed in the North Ohio, White River, Ontario, and Pennsylvania Annual Conferences. His pastorate at the King Street United Brethren Church, Chambersburg, Pennsylvania, was from 1928 to 1961. During the years at King Street he also served as a presiding elder or conference superintendent for 27 years. Meadows has been an official member of every United Brethren General Conference since 1937.[36]

From 1940 to 1946 Meadows served as chairman of the Franklin County local draft board. The Chambersburg Rotary Club also had his leadership as president. Other contributions and involvements in the community included instruction in singing schools and in district Sunday School promotion.

He served as president of the Pennsylvania Sabbath School Association from 1945-1958, and has continued to be a member of the state staff. The International Society of Christian Endeavor elected Meadows as its president in July 1959; and the World Christian Endeavor Union made him its president in August 1962. He holds the title of honorary president in the World Christian Endeavor Union.

The United Brethren Church elected Meadows as one of its two bishops in 1961. He was re-elected in 1965, and was given the bishop emeritus honor in 1969 when he retired. At the time of his retirement he had compiled a record of 49 years of service with the following data: sermons and addresses—14,998; commitments to Christ witnessed—7,106; members received into church membership—2,343; baptisms—1,860; and marriages performed—429.

Since 1969, Meadows has accepted invitations to preach, to conduct weekend evangelistic services, and to address Sunday School and Christian Endeavor conventions. His schedule usually reaches about two years into the future. His speaking engagements still average over 200 per year.

Preaching, as can be concluded from the above record, is a key factor of his continuing ministry. His graduate studies in hymnody and his world-encompassing travel as a Christian Endeavor executive have given him a fertile field for illustration. His illustrations are mostly of the person-related type and thus come with the personal touch and emphasize the personal application. His literary illustrations come from many of the familiar hymns. His artistry as a musician enables him to recreate the details and setting of the quotation so as to make them vivid in the imagination of the hearer.

His experience in the World Christian Endeavor connections enabled him to sense the universal need of youth and to proclaim the sufficiency of Christ wherever he ministers. "The torch is in your hand," he told the graduating seniors at the 1981 Huntington College commencement. In this constructive pattern Clyde W. Meadows continues during his retirement years.

Melvin Isaac Burkholder

Melvin Isaac Burkholder,[37] the expositor and teacher of preachers, is a man paying a debt of trust. Fulfilling his indebtedness to a denomination that has given him "good pastors, good churches, good leaders, and good education." Burkholder was the first United Brethren ordained elder to earn a doctoral degree. He was a student under the great expository preacher Charles W. Koller, Northern Baptist Theological Seminary, and was awarded the Doctor of Theology (Th.D.) in 1951.

Burkholder, the eldest of three sons, was born in 1907 to Rankin J. and Emma (Garman) Burkholder. He grew up on the five point Orrstown-Rocky Springs circuit in rural Pennsylvania near Shippensburg. His pastor, the Reverend Ezra M. Funk, led him to conversion in the summer of 1917 during a pastoral visit. He grew up on a farm with his mother and brothers. A sister, Pearl DeEtta, died in infancy and his father died in 1915 when Melvin was 8 years of age.

Most of his adult life has been lived in Huntington and invested in the college and graduate ministerial education. He entered Huntington College in 1935 as a student and graduated with a Bachelor of Arts degree in 1939 and with a Bachelor of Divinity degree in 1940. In 1942 he returned to Huntington as the Dean of the Huntington College Theological Seminary, a position he held for 30 years (1942-1972). Along with administrative title he held faculty rank as professor of Theology (1942-1951), professor of practical Theology (1951-1972), and professor emeritus since 1972. In 1965, Burkholder served as interim president of the college after Dr. Elmer Becker retired and until the time Dr. E. DeWitt Baker assumed the post.

During his tenure, prerequisites for admission to the seminary were upgraded. The Bachelor of Divinity degree was fully developed into a three-year classical seminary program with studies in the four traditional areas of theological education. In 1969 the degree was renamed Master of Divinity. A three-year Bible diploma course and the ministerial training correspondence program authorized by the denomination were developed. The Bachelor of Theology degree was also offered by the seminary.

During his years at the college and seminary he served for a limited time as District Superintendent of White River Annual Conference. He pastored an independent congregation, Union Church, east of Huntington, 1944-1946; the College Park United Brethren congregation 1946-1951; the Etna Avenue (New Hope) United Brethren congregation 1951-1958. Burkholder served during this period of time as a liaison with the denomination as a member of nearly every committee, commission, and board at the general level. The college and denomination honored him in 1978 with the honorary Doctor of Divinity degree.

Individuals to whom he specifically feels indebted for his role in ministry are Bishop Ezra M. Funk, who led him to conversion; O. A. Kern, pastor, who affirmed his call to the ministry; J. C. Coulson, district superintendent, who issued his quarterly conference license; Bishop A. M. Johnson who granted his annual conference license in 1933; and Bishop C. A. Mummart who administered the ordination rites in 1937.

M. I. Burkholder married Edith A. Holtry in 1931 and they are the parents of four children. Since his retirement in 1972, he has served as chaplain of the Huntington Memorial Hospital and actively remains a member of the Exchange Club, a civic organization to which he has given much energy since 1947.

Current bishops, denominational leaders, and a majority of the active pastors owe a debt to M. I. Burkholder, expository teacher and preacher. They reflect his style of preaching and have received theological education designed and directed by the one who has spent his life paying a debt of trust to a denomination that has given him unlimited avenues of service for Christ.

FOOTNOTES

[1]*Origin, Doctrine, Constitution, and Discipline of the Church of the United Brethren in Christ 1965-1969* (Huntington, IN: United Brethren Publishing Establishment, 1965), Para. 34, Section 1.

[2]*Discipline . . . . 1977-1981*, Para. 159, Section I.

[3]*Discipline . . . . 1929-1933*, p. 78.

[4]*Discipline . . . . 1941-1945*, Para. 83, Section 3.

[5]*Discipline . . . . 1945-1949*, Para. 56, Section I.

[6]*Huntington College Bulletin*, 1978-1980, p. 54.

[7]*Discipline . . . . 1977-1981*, Para. 154, Section I.

[8]Ibid., Para. 162, Section 3.

[9]*Proceedings of the Thirty-first General Conference of the Church of the United Brethren in Christ* (Huntington, IN: Board of Administration, 1933) mimeographed brief, pp. 11, 17.

[10]*Discipline . . . . 1937-1941*, Para. 149.

[11]*Proceedings of the Fortieth General Conference . . . . 1969*, pp. 121f.

[12]Of those elected prior to 1969, the writer's role was one of listener, pastor, conference superintendent, or committee partner; from 1969 to 1981 those elected by General Conference to leadership roles, except George Weaver, have been students under the writer's direction.

[13]Autobiographical data filed in the United Brethren Archives.

[14]Ibid.

[15]*Proceedings of the Thirty-sixth General Conference . . . . 1953*, Bishops' Quadrennial Address, p. 446.

[16]"In Memoriam," *The United Brethren*, December 22, 1954, p. 6.

[17]*The United Brethren*, December 15, 1954, p. 3.

[18]He seemed to feel that tall men had a built-in advantage over the one of lesser stature. After listening to a shorter man speaking at a teachers' institute, he was heard to say, "I guess a little man can have something to say too."

[19]*The United Brethren*, July 30, 1958, p. 4.

[20]Ibid.

[21]*Contact* (a Sunday School take home paper), June 11, 1967, p. 9.

[22]Named from the fact that his forefathers had settled there.

[23]Lloyd joined the Evangelical Church with his parents, but changed his membership to the Alma Street United Brethren Church because he did not feel at home in the large church.

[24]*Proceedings of the Thirty-seventh General Conference of the Church of the United Brethren in Christ* (Huntington, IN: Board of Administration, 1957), p. 39.

[25]From a letter written by Carlson to Miss Mary Lou Funk, associate editor of United Brethren Publications, dated December 10, 1966, and filed in the United Brethren Archives.

[26]Ibid.

[27]College Park United Brethren Church was at that time within the boundary of the White River Annual Conference. In 1972 the Auglaize-Scioto and White River Conferences merged and have become known as Central Conference.

[28]*Huntington College Alumni Newsletter*, October, 1965.

[29]*Contact*, April 26, 1964, p. 1f.

[30]The breakfast was inaugurated in 1955, according to the obituary notice of Dr. Becker, in the *Herald Press*, Huntington, Indiana, August 29, 1969.

[31]*The United Brethren*, October 22, 1969, p. 7.

[32]*Huntington College Alumni News Letters*, October, 1965, p. 8.

[33]G. D. Fleming, *Trail Blazers in Sierra Leone* (Huntington, IN: Hillcrest Lithographing, 1973) 2: viii.

[34]Ibid.

[35]"Jamaica Revisited," *The United Brethren*, June 1983, p. 16f.

[36]He gave the official welcome to the General Conference of 1929 which met at the King Street Church. The appointment of a hymnal committee at that conference was at Meadows' suggestion to a delegate.

[37]Data included by the general editor through an interview with Melvin Isaac Burkholder.

37

CONCLUDING COMMENTS

This survey of the past half-century of the life and activities of the denomination leaves the writer with a number of unanswered questions and without powers of predicting the future. Has the Church remained silent in some of the public forums when its message and distinctives needed broadcasting? Has the church been guilty of treating symptoms rather than dealing with causes? Will the adoption and application of better business methods and management translate into growth realities? Can a denomination accommodate both the congregational and the episcopal polities?

In the presence of these and possibly other questions, there are a few affirmations that need to be made relative to the Church of the United Brethren in Christ as it moves into the 1980s and 1990s. The Church has been blessed in that it has had a responsible, conscientious leadership. When one surveys the list of 17 bishops elected since 1930, he will soon discover that there has been diversity in their background and experience.[1] Some were college presidents, some were conference superintendents (or presiding elders), some had departmental experience on the denominational level, others were missionary executives, and very few came into that office with nothing beyond the local parish experience. Geographically they came from all areas of the church. They were selected at the time of mature years—neither at the 'young Turk' stage nor at the brink of mental senility. They brought denominational loyalty. Some reflected the rugged individualism of the West while others shared their experiences with the inter-denominational contacts and the international context. No two of them were alike, yet each of them shared a shepherd's concern for those under their oversight.

In the midst of change the church has maintained its evangelistic thrust with an evangelical message. Administrative refinements have aimed toward efficiency of operation. The increased role of the laity in ministry and administration has enlarged the role of the lay person. This enlarged role has been accepted in a responsible manner. The introduction of the "Great Commitment" has made it clear that slogans and themes need "flesh and blood" before the goals perceived become victories achieved.

The mood of the General Conference of 1981 demonstrated a definite unity of spirit, but some diversity on details. Will 1993 witness a doubling of the church's present membership? Where will the 100 new churches be erected? Only time has the answer. The Church of the United Brethren in Christ, is, hopefully, more aware of its mandate than it has been for years. The answer, in part, is at the point of the individual's motivation and decision. "Here am I, send me!"

FOOTNOTES

[1]Selected Data relative to the U. B. Bishops, elected since 1930

Name	Age when elected	Conference membership	Previous administrative experience	
Hoskins, Fermin Lincoln	39	Walla Walla	College president	3 yrs.
Musgrave, Walter Emmet	45	Scioto	Exec. Secy of OFM Presiding elder	4 yrs. 5 yrs.
Johnson, Albert Meric	47	Auglaize	Presiding elder	5 yrs.
Baldwin, Laurin Burton	63	Oregon	College president Presiding elder	2 yrs. 1 yr.
Mummart, Clarence Allen	47	Pennsylvania	College president Presiding elder	10 yrs. 5 yrs.
Funk, Ezra Myers	55	Pennsylvania	Presiding elder	7 yrs.
Eby, Lloyd	58	Detroit	Missionary; Conf. Supt.	2 yrs.
Carlson, Clarence Edward	60	No. Michigan	Denom. treas. Missionary; Conf. Supt.	4 yrs.
Rash, Robert William	53	Auglaize	Sec'y Chr. Ed. dept. Conference Supt.	16 yrs. 1 yr.
Meadows, Clyde Williamson	60	Pennsylvania	Pastor/Supt. World C. E. Union pres.	27 yrs. 12 yrs.
Weaver, George Edward	42	Pennsylvania	Pastor/Supt. U. B. editor	8 yrs. 2 yrs.
Waldfogel, Raymond	43	North Ohio	Conference Supt.	5 yrs.
Reahm, Duane Andrew	52	Michigan	Sec'y of Missions	8 yrs.
Miller, Charles Ray	45	Pennsylvania	Pastor/Supt.	10 yrs.

Sites, Wilber Lawrence, Jr.	43	Pennsylvania	Pastor/Supt.	12 yrs.
Datema, Jerry Frederick	52	Michigan	Miss. Field Sec'y	9 yrs.
Kopp, Clarence Adam, Jr.	54	Central	Pastor/Supt.	4 yrs.

Notes: Of the 17 persons elected to the office of a bishop since 1930:

8 were in their 40s; 6 in their 50s; and 3 were in the 60s when first elected.
14 had served as a presiding elder or a conference superintendent.
5 had experience in denominational departments.
3 had college presidency experience.
And, they have been selected from 8 of the annual conferences.

Appendix

OUR CONFESSION OF FAITH

God, the Father

IN the name of God we declare and confess before all men that we believe in the only true God, the Father, the Son, and the Holy Ghost; that these three are one—the Father in the Son, the Son in the Father, and the Holy Ghost equal in essence or being with both; that this triune God created the heavens and the earth, and all that in them is, visible as well as invisible, and furthermore, sustains, governs, protects, and supports the same.

Jesus Christ, the Son

WE believe in Jesus Christ; that He is very God and man; that He became incarnate by the power of the Holy Ghost in the Virgin Mary, and was born of her; that He is the Savior and Mediator of the whole human race, if they with full faith in Him accept the grace proffered in Jesus; that this Jesus suffered and died on the cross for us, was buried, rose again on the third day, ascended into heaven, and sitteth on the right hand of God, to intercede for us; and that He shall come again at the last day to judge the quick and the dead.

The Holy Spirit, The Comforter

WE believe in the Holy Ghost; that He is equal in being with the Father and the Son, and that He comforts the faithful, and guides them into all truth.

438

The Christian Church

WE believe in a holy Christian church, the communion of saints, the resurrection of the body, and life everlasting.

The Holy Bible

WE believe that the Holy Bible, Old and New Testaments, is the Word of God; that it contains the only true way to our salvation; that every true Christian is bound to acknowledge and receive it with the influence of the Spirit of God, as the only rule and guide; and that without faith in Jesus Christ, true repentance, forgiveness of sins and following after Christ, no one can be a true Christian.

Salvation

WE also believe that what is contained in the Holy Scriptures, to wit: the fall in Adam and redemption through Jesus Christ, shall be preached throughout the world.

Christian Ordinances

WE believe that the ordinances, viz.: baptism and the remembrance of the sufferings and death of our Lord Jesus Christ, are to be in use and practiced by all Christian societies; and that it is incumbent on all the children of God particularly to practice them; but the manner in which, ought always to be left to the judgment and understanding of every individual. Also the example of washing feet is left to the judgment of every one to practice or not; but it is not becoming of any of our preachers or members to traduce any of their brethren whose judgment and understanding in these respects is different from their own, either in public or in private. Whosoever shall make himself guilty in this respect, shall be considered a traducer of his brethren, and shall be answerable for the same.

GENERAL CONFERENCES

1815 - June 6-10, John Bonnet's School House, Mt. Pleasant, West-moreland Co., PA

1817 - June 2-4, Mt. Pleasant, Westmoreland Co., PA

1821 - May 15-17, Dewalt Mechlin's, Fairfield Co., OH

1825 -*June 7-10, John Jacob Shaup's, Crooked Run, Tuscarawas Co., OH

1829 - May 15-19, Dewalt Mechlin's, Fairfield Co., OH

1833 - May 14-   , George Dresbach's, Pickaway Co., OH (minutes say Ross Co., OH)

1837 - May 9-   , United Brethren Church, Germantown, Mont-gomery Co., OH

1841 - May 10-20, Dresbach's Church, Pickaway Co., OH

1845 - May 12-22, Circleville, Pickaway Co., OH

1849 - May 14-26, United Brethren Church, Germantown, Mont-gomery Co., OH

1853 - May 9-21, Miltonville, Butler Co., OH

1857 - May 12-25, First Church of the United Brethren in Christ, Cincinnati, OH

1861 - May 14-24, Chapel, Otterbein College, Westerville, OH

1865 - May 11-20, Chapel, Western College, Western, Linn Co., IA

1869 - May 20-June 1, Salem Church, Lebanon, PA

1873 - May 15-28, St. Paul's Universalist Church, Dayton, OH

1877 - May 10-23, Chapel, Westfield Colege, Westfield, IL

1881 - May 12-26, First United Brethren Church, Lisbon, IA

1885 - May 14-27, Academy Chapel, Fostoria, OH

1889 - May 9-13, York Opera House, May 13-19, Park Opera House, York, PA

1893 - May 18-27, United Brethren Church, Hudson, IN

1897 - May 27-June 6, United Brethren Church, Dublin, IN

*The minutes give the date of this General Conference as May 7, but Christian New-comer in his journal says the General Conference convened on June 7. S. S. Hough in his 1941 edition, *Christian Newcomer His Life Journal and Achievements,* says "the fact that the Eastern conference was held in Adams County, Pennsylvania, May 10, and the Muskingum at Mount Pleasant, Pennsylvania, May 23, that same year, as reported by Newcomer and by the minutes of these conferences, there is good reason to believe that Newcomer was correct in reporting June 7th, 1825, as the date of this General Confer-ence, and that a mistake was made when the minutes were copied and put into final form."

1901 - May 9-18, King Street United Brethren Church, Chambersburg, PA

1905 - May 11-20, Gaines United Brethren Church, nw of Caledonia, MI

1909 - May 13-22, Davis Memorial Hall, Central College, Huntington, IN

1913 - May 8-17, United Brethren Church, Blissfield, MI

1917 - May 10-17, Alma Street United Brethren Church, Kitchener, Ontario, Canada

1921 - May 12-18, United Brethren Church, Messick, IN

1925 - May 14-22, United Brethren Church, Adrian, MI

1929 - May 9-17, King Street United Brethren Church, Chambersburg, PA

1933 - July 20-27, Rothfuss Assembly Park, Hillsdale, MI

1937 - July 8-15, Barnaby Memorial Park, Sunfield, MI

1941 - June 19-25, Rhodes Grove Camp Ground, south of Chambersburg, PA

1945 - June 7-13, Rothfuss Assembly Park, Hillsdale, MI

1949 - June 7-13, Huntington College, Huntington, IN

1953 - June 9-15, Huntington College, Huntington, IN

1957 - June 11-17, College Park United Brethren Church, Huntington, IN

1961 - June 6-16, College Park United Brethren Church, Huntington, IN

1965 - June 7-13, College Park United Brethren Church, Huntington, IN

1969 - June 10-14, Huntington Union Building, Huntington College, Huntington, IN

1973 - June 26-July 1, Huntington Union Building, Huntington College, Huntington, IN

1977 - June 21-26, Huntington Union Building, Huntington College, Huntington, IN

1981 - June 22-26, College Park United Brethren Church, Huntington, IN

BISHOPS OF THE CHURCH OF
THE UNITED BRETHREN IN CHRIST

Name	Served	Conference Membership When Elected	Age When Elected
Philip William Otterbein (1726-1813)	1800-1813	Original	74
Martin Boehm (1725-1812)	1800-1812	Original	74
Christian Newcomer (1749-1830)	1813-1830	Original	64
Andrew Zeller (1755-1839)	1817-1821	Miami	62
Joseph Hoffman (1780-1856)	1821-1825	Miami	41
Henry Kumler, Sr. (1775-1854)	1825-1845	Miami	50
Samuel Hiestand (1781-1838)	1833-1838	Scioto	52
William Brown (1796-1868)	1833-1837	Pennsylvania	37
Jacob Erb (1804-1883)	1837-1845, 1849-1853	Pennsylvania	33
Henry Kumler, Jr. (1801-1882)	1841-1845, 1861-1865	Miami	44
John Coons (1797-1869)	1841-1845	Scioto	44
John Russel (1799-1870)	1845-1849, 1857-1861	Pennsylvania	46
Jacob John Glossbrenner (1812-1887)	1845-1885, Emeritus	Virginia	32
William Hanby (1808-1880)	1845-1849	Scioto	36
David Edwards (1816-1876)	1849-1876	Scioto	33
Lewis Davis (1814-1890)	1853-1861	Scioto	39
Jacob Markwood (1815-1873)	1861-1869	Virginia	45
Daniel Shuck (1827-1900)	1861-1869	Indiana	34
Jonathan Weaver (1824-1901)	1865-1889	Muskingum	41
John Dickson (1820-1907)	1869-1889	Pennsylvania	49
Nicholas Castle (1837-1922)	1877-1889	St. Joseph	39
Milton Wright (1828-1917)	1877-1881, 1885-1905	White River	48
Ezekiel Boring Kephart (1834-1906)	1881-1889	Iowa	46
Daniel Kumler Flickinger (1824-1911)	1885-1889	Miami	61
Horace Thomas Barnaby (1823-1917)	1889-1905	Michigan	66

Halleck Floyd (1839-1917)	1889-1905	White River	50
Henry Jacob Becker (1846-1934)	1889-1893	California	42
William Dillon (1841-1919)	1893-1897	Auglaize	51
Henry Levi Barkley (1858-1915)	1897-1913	Oregon	39
Fermin Lincoln Hoskins (1865-1935)	1905-1933, Emeritus	Walla Walla	39
Olin Good Alwood (1870-1945)	1905-1921	North Ohio	34
Corydon L. Wood (1852-1925)	1905-1920	North Michigan	52
Harold Carlton Mason (1888-1964)	1921-1925	North Ohio	32
Clarence Allen Mummart (1874-1959)	1921-1925, 1937-1941	Pennsylvania	46
Walter Emmet Musgrave (1880-1950)	1925-1949, Emeritus	Scioto	44
Eli B. Griffin (1867-1950)	1925-1929	Michigan	57
Albert Meric Johnson (1882-1954)	1929-1951, Emeritus	Auglaize	46
Laurin Burton Baldwin (1869-1947)	1933-1937	Oregon	64
Ezra Myers Funk (1886-1958)	1941-1957, Emeritus	Pennsylvania	54
Lloyd Eby (1891-1969)	1949-1957, Emeritus	Detroit	58
Clarence Edward Carlson (1897-)	1957-1965, Emeritus	North Michigan	59
Robert William Rash (1904-1975)	1957-1961, 1965-1969, Emeritus	Auglaize	53
Clyde Williamson Meadows (1901-)	1961-1969, Emeritus	Pennsylvania	60
George Edward Weaver (1927-)	1969-1977, Emeritus	Pennyslvania	42
Duane Andrew Reahm (1917-)	1969-1981, Emeritus	Michigan	51
Raymond Waldfogel (1926-)	1969-1981, Emeritus	North Ohio	43
Charles Ray Miller (1928-)	1973-	Pennsylvania	45

Wilber Lawrence Sites, Jr.			
(1926-)	1977-	Pennsylvania	50
Clarence Adam Kopp, Jr.			
(1927-)	1981-	Central	54
Jerry Frederick Datema			
(1929-)	1981-	Michigan	51

George Adam Geeting (1741-1812) is included in H. A. Thompson's book, *OUR BISHOPS,* as the third Bishop of the Church of the United Brethren in Christ. At the end of chapter 4 he has this note—"We find no record of the election of Mr. Geeting to the office of bishop, but as he did the work associated with the office he was practically a bishop and we have so classified him." It is a matter of family history and tradition that Geeting was elected bishop in 1812. He did preside at the conference of 1812.

Colleges	Founded
1. Otterbein University, Westerville, Ohio	1847
2. Mt. Pleasant College, Mt. Pleasant, Pennsylvania	1847
3. Hartsville College, Hartsville, Indiana	1850
4. Evergreen Seminary, Seven Mile, Ohio	1851
5. Blandinsville Seminary, Blandinsville, Illinois	1855
6. Western College, Western, Iowa	1856
7. Leander Clark College, Toledo, Iowa	1857
8. Sublimity College, Sublimity, Oregon	1858
9. Michigan Collegiate Institute, Leoni, Michigan	1859
10. Bourbon Seminary, Bourbon, Indiana	1861
11. Westfield College, Westfield, Illinois	1865
12. Lane University, Lecompton, Kansas	1865
13. Philomath College, Philomath, Oregon	1865
14. Smithville High School, Smithville, Ohio	1865
15. Lebanon Valley College, Annville, Pennsylvania	1867
16. Cottage Hill College (Female Seminary), York, Pennsylvania	1868
17. Green Hill Seminary, Green Hill, Indiana	1869
18. Roanoke Classical Seminary, Roanoke, Indiana	1869
19. Ontario Academy, Freeport, Canada	1871
20. Union Biblical Seminary, Dayton, Ohio	1871
21. Avalon College, Avalon, Missouri (moved to Trenton)	1872
22. Elroy Seminary, Elroy, Wisconsin	1876
23. Shenandoah Institute, Dayton, Virginia	1877
24. Edwards Academy, White Pine, Tennessee	1877
25. San Joaquin Valley College, Woodbridge, California	1878
26. Fostoria Academy, Fostoria, Ohio	1879
27. Washington Seminary, Huntsville, Washington	1880
28. Gould College, Harlan, Kansas	1881
29. Ontario College, Port Elgin, Canada	1881
30. Dover Academy, Dover, Illinois	1882
31. Campbell College, Holton, Kansas	1882
32. West Virginia Normal and Classical Academy, Buckhannon, West Virginia	1883
33. Erie Conference Seminary, Sugar Grove, Pennsylvania	1884
34. Gibbon Collegiate Institute, Gibbon, Nebraska	1886
35. College of Philomath, Philomath, Oregon	1889
36. Huntington College, Huntington, Indiana	1897
37. Edwards College, Albion, Washington	1899

COLLEGE PRESIDENTS

PRESIDENTS OF PHILOMATH COLLEGE
Philomath, Oregon
Incorporated Nov. 22, 1865—Opened for classes October 1867

Joseph Hannon, acting president	1867-1868
E. P. Henderson	1868-1869
James Chambers	1869-1870
J. A. Biddle	1870-1872
J. R. N. Selwood	1872-1873
R. E. Williams	1873-1876
Wayne S. Walker	1876-1884
G. M. Miller	1884-1886
Thomas C. Bell	1886-1887
James C. Keezel	1887-1889

PRESIDENTS OF THE COLLEGE OF PHILOMATH
Philomath, Oregon

James C. Keezel	1889-1890
Sarah L. Keezel	1890-1894
Henry L. Barkley	1894-1896
William Dillon	1896-1897
William H. Davis	1897-1899
William T. Wyatt	1899-1903
Laurin B. Baldwin	1903-1905
Stanley O. Watkins	1905-1906

The College Building burned on October 30, 1905. The college was closed for the next 3 years until a new building was finished.

Roy S. Kindel	1909-1913

PRESIDENTS OF EDWARDS COLLEGE
Albion, Washington

Laurin B. Baldwin	1899-1903

The college was closed for the next two years.

Fermin L. Hoskins	1905-1906

The college was again closed for 2 years.

William H. Davis 1908-1912
Asa M. Calvert 1912-1913

PRESIDENTS OF HARTSVILLE COLLEGE, 1850-1897

James M. Miller 1850-1852
David Shuck 1852-1865
John W. Scribner 1865-1873
David Shuck 1873-1874
William J. Pruner 1874-1879
Charles H. Kiracofe 1879-1889
Edwin G. Paine 1889-1891
Louis J. Freese 1891-1892
William H. Davis 1892-1895
Halleck Floyd 1895-1896
Orrin W. Pentzer, acting president 1895-1896
Alvin P. Barnaby (winter term) 1896-1897
Laurin B. Baldwin (spring term) 1896-1897

PRESIDENTS OF HUNTINGTON COLLEGE
The college was called Central College until 1917

Charles H. Kiracofe 1897-1902
James H. McMurray 1902-1905
Thomas H. Gragg 1905-1911
Fermin L. Hoskins 1911-1912
Clarence A. Mummart 1912-1915
Clare W. H. Bangs 1915-1919
Daniel R. Ellabarger 1919-1925
Clarence A. Mummart 1925-1932
Harold C. Mason 1932-1939
Elmer Becker 1941-1965
E. DeWitt Baker 1965-1981
Eugene B. Habecker 1981-

EDITORS
THE RELIGIOUS TELESCOPE - 1st issue December 31, 1834

William R. Rhinehart 1834-1839

William Hanby	1839-1845
David Edwards	1845-1849
William Hanby	1849-1852
John Lawrence, Assistant Editor	1850-1852
John Lawrence	1852-1863
Daniel Berger	1863-1869
Milton Wright	1869-1877
Daniel Berger, Assistant Editor	1869-1873
W. O. Tobey, Assistant Editor	1873-1877
J. W. Hott	1877-1889
W. O. Tobey, Assistant Editor	1877-1881
M. R. Drury, Assistant Editor	1881-1889

THE CHRISTIAN CONSERVATOR - 1st issue July 15, 1885

(Published by the Constitutional Association until 1889 when it was transferred to the Church of the United Brethren in Christ, old constitution.)

William Dillon	1885-1893
Halleck Floyd, Associate Editor	1885-1889
Charles H. Kiracofe	1893-1897
William Dillon	1897-1901
Henry J. Becker	1901-1902
Charles H. Kiracofe	1902-1905
William H. Clay	1905-1909
Clarence A. Mummart	1909-1911
William Dillon	1911-1916
Clarence Young, Editor Ad Interim	1916-1917
Clarence A. Mummart	1917-1920
Albert B. Bowman	1920-1921
Olin G. Alwood	1921-1925
William H. Zeigler	1925-1949
Editor Emeritus, 1949-1979	
Ernest Gingerich	1949-1954
Harold Snyder, Associate Editor	1953-1954

THE UNITED BRETHREN - 1st issue April 7, 1954

THE CHRISTIAN CONSERVATOR, *THE MISSIONARY MONTHLY and *THE UNITED BRETHREN MAGNET were combined into one publication which was named THE UNITED BRETHREN.

Ernest Gingerich	1954-1957
Harold Snyder, Associate Editor	1954-1955
George Weaver	1957-1959
Mary Lou Funk, Associate Editor	1957-1959
Stanley Peters	1959-1981
Mary Lou Funk, Associate Editor	1959-1968
Lois Breiner, Assistant Editor	1971-1974
Elsa Houtz, Assistant Editor	1975-1976
Dennis Miller, Assistant Editor	1976-1978
Steve Dennie, Assistant Editor	1978-1981
Steve Dennie	1982-

*Editors of THE MISSIONARY MONTHLY were the General Secretary of the Department of Missions and the Executive Secretary of the Woman's Missionary Association.

THE UNITED BRETHREN MAGNET was the publication of the Department of Christian Education and edited by the General Secretary of the Department.

SABBATH SCHOOL PERIODICALS (English)

David Edwards	1854-1857
Alexander Owen	1857-1859
Solomon Vonnieda	1859-1869
Daniel Berger	1869-1889
J. P. Landis, Assistant Editor	1881-1885

EDITORS OF SUNDAY SCHOOL LITERATURE

From 1889 until 1917, the editor of the CHRISTIAN CONSERVA-TOR was also the editor of Sunday School Literature.

William H. Clay	1917-1921
Albert B. Bowman	1921-1925
George A. Shepherdson	1925-1934

J. Ralph Pfister	1934-1944
Alice A. Griffin	March 1-September 1, 1944
Jerry L. Towne	1944-1953

The General Conference of 1953 again gave the responsibility for editing Sunday School literature to the editor of the CHRISTIAN CONSERVATOR.

GERMAN PERIODICALS

John Russel (privately owned)	1840-1841
Jacob Erb	1841-1842
Nehemiah Altman	1846-1847
David Strickler	1847-1851
Henry Staub	1851-1855
Julius Degmeier	1855-1858
Solomon Vonnieda	1858-1866
Ezekiel Light	1866-1869
William Mittendorf	1869-1885
Ezekiel Light	1885-1889

UNITY MAGAZINE

| David Edwards | 1853-1857 |
| Alexander Owen | 1857-1859 |

WOMAN'S EVANGEL

| Mrs. L. R. Keister | 1882-1889 |
| Mrs. L. K. Miller, Associate Editor | 1888-1889 |

PUBLISHING AGENTS

The trustees, John Russel, Jonathan Dresbach, George Dresbach, and Editor, W. R. Rhinehart	1834-1837
William Hanby	1837-1845
Samuel Bright (3 months)	1845
Nehemiah Altman	1845-1852
William Hanby	1852-1853

Solomon Vonnieda	1853-1861
Henry Kumler, Jr., assistant (10 months)	1854
Thomas N. Sowers, assistant	1857-1861
Thomas N. Sowers	1861-1865
J. B. King, assistant	1861-1863
William J. Shuey, assistant	1863-1865
William J. Shuey	1865-1889
William McKee, assistant	1865
Milton Wright	1889-1893
Millard F. Keiter	1893-1901
William H. Clay	1901-1905
Hiram C. Foote	1905-1909

Dr. Foote was re-elected by the General Conference
of 1909 but died August 13, 1909

Emmet C. Mason	1909-1921
James W. Burton	1921-1928
Walter C. South	1928-1945
J. Clair Peters	1945-1953

The General Conference of 1953 created a Department of Publication and changed the title of Publishing Agent to General Secretary of Publication.

GENERAL SECRETARIES OF PUBLICATION

J. Clair Peters	1953-1955
Don B. Hammel	1955-1967
Carlyle Seiple	1967-1973
Don B. Hammel, Interim Manager	1971-1972
Eugene Riebe, Manager of Publishing Estab.	1972-1974
C. Stanley Peters	1973-1977

The General Conference of 1977 combined the Departments of Christian Education and Publication forming the Department of Church Ministries.

The General Conference of 1981 adopted a recommendation that closed the Publishing Establishment December, 1981.

The General Conferences of 1925 brought into existence the General Board of Administration and created the office of Executive Secretary of the Board of Administration. The General Conference of 1925 also provided for a General Treasurer who should handle all general funds and become the treasurer of all the General Boards.

EXECUTIVE SECRETARIES OF THE BOARD OF ADMINISTRATION

Walter C. South	1925-1929
L. M. Davis	1929-1930
John G. Connor	1930-1932
Margaret M. Cook	1932-1933

The General Conference of 1933 added the duties of the Executive Secretary to those of the General Secretary of Preachers' Aid.

GENERAL CHURCH TREASURERS

Emmet C. Mason (Resigned in September 1925 because the illness of his wife made it impractical to move to Huntington. One of the requirements was that the General Treasurer live in Huntington)	1925
John W. Brubaker, elected by BD. 9-22-25	1925-1945
Orion Fuller	1945-1953

The General Conference of 1953 combined the office of Executive Secretary with the office of General Treasurer.

Clarence E. Carlson	1953-1957
Lawrence D. Dellinger	1957-1961
Wanna Mae Sell	1961-1966
Anne E. Bruner	1966-1973
David G. Jackson	1974-1979
Title is now General Treasurer/Administrative Assistant	
Marda J. Hoffman	1979-

EXECUTIVE SECRETARIES OF THE WOMEN'S MISSIONARY ASSOCIATION

Mrs. L. R. Harford	1875-1876

Mrs. B. F. Marot	1876-1881
Mrs. L. R. Harford	1881-1889

After the division in 1889, the WMA reorganized in 1891

Anvilla Rundles Kiracofe (Mrs. Charles Kiracofe)	1891-1906
Cora Sebright Loew (Mrs. Fred A. Loew)	1906-1930
Effie M. Hodgeboom	1930-1956
Erma Burton Carlson (Mrs. Clarence Carlson)	1956-1965
Iona Lemmon Wood (Mrs. William Wood)	1965-1977
Carol Gardner Skinner (Mrs. Leland Skinner), Interim Secretary	1977-1978
Hazel Schuneman McCray (Mrs. Robert McCray)	1978-

PRESIDENTS OF THE BOARD OF MANAGERS OF THE WOMEN'S MISSIONARY ASSOCIATION

Mrs. T. N. Sowers	1875-1879
Mrs. Sylvia Haywood	1879-1887
Mrs. L. K. Miller	1887-1889
Mary Melissa Titus	1891-1931
Clara Rose Harwood (Mrs. Harry Harwood)	1931-1960
Margie Kuhn Herr (Mrs. Charles Herr)	1960-1964
Marjorie Alwood Johnson (Mrs. Harold Johnson)	1964-1965
Hazel Schuneman McCray (Mrs. Robert McCray)	1965-1978
Mossie Baker Sites (Mrs. Wilber Sites)	1978-

GENERAL SECRETARIES OF THE BOARD OF MISSIONS
or
General Secretaries of Missions

J. C. Bright	1853-1857
D. K. Flickinger	1857-1885
(J. C. Bright acted as Secretary for a number of months during 1857 and 1858, but was compelled by declining health to leave the work.)	
Wm. McKee, Acting Secretary	1887-1888
B. F. Booth	1888-1889
Charles H. Kiracofe	1889-1893
Henry J. Becker	1893-1897
Daniel K. Flickinger	1897-1905

Jacob Howe	1905-1936
George D. Fleming	1936-1961
Duane A. Reahm	1961-1969
Emmett D. Cox	1969-1973

In 1973 the position of General Secretary of Missions was eliminated. A fourth Bishop was elected to serve as Overseas Bishop.

OVERSEAS BISHOPS

Duane A. Reahm	1973-1981
Jerry F. Datema	1981-

ASSOCIATE DIRECTORS OF DEPARTMENT OF MISSIONS

The General Conference of 1965 merged the Parent Board of Missions and the Women's Missionary Association, forming the Department of Missions. The Executive Secretary of the WMA was given the title of Associate Director of Missions. This General Conference also authorized the hiring of an additional Associate Director.

Harold Wust	1970-

GENERAL SECRETARIES OF PREACHERS' AID

Henry L. Barkley	1913-1915
William A. Oler	1915-1920
John L. Buckwalter	1920-1929
James W. Burton	1929-1931
John G. Connor	1931-1937

The General Conference of 1937 placed the Preachers' Aid Society under the management of the Board of Bishops and six trustees elected by the General Conference.

EXECUTIVE SECRETARIES OF
THE OTTERBEIN FORWARD MOVEMENT

Olin G. Alwood	1920-1921
Walter E. Musgrave	1921-1925

GENERAL SECRETARIES OF
THE SABBATH SCHOOL ASSOCIATION

Isaac Crouse	1865-1877
Robert Cowden	1877-1889

SECRETARIES OF
THE GENERAL SABBATH SCHOOL BOARD

William Dillon	1889-1893
William H. Clay	1893-1901

The work of the Sabbath School Board was placed under the Board of Missions at the General Conference of 1901.

GENERAL SECRETARY OF THE SUNDAY SCHOOL

James W. Burton	1909-1921

GENERAL SECRETARIES OF
THE UNITED BRETHREN CHRISTIAN ENDEAVOR SOCIETY

Clarence A. Mummart	1905-1909
Mary Melissa Titus	1909-1917
Albert B. Bowman	1917-1921

GENERAL SECRETARIES OF RELIGIOUS EDUCATION

The General Conference of 1921 combined the Departments of Sunday School and United Brethren Christian Endeavor forming the Department of Religious Education.

Jesse E. Harwood	1921-1937
Sara Trull Harwood, Acting Secretary, following the death of her husband until the end of the quadrennium.	1937

The General Conference of 1937 changed the name to the Department of Christian Education.

Elmer Becker	1937-1941
Robert W. Rash	1941-1957
Walter M. Burkholder	1957-1973
Howard F. Anderson	1973-1977

The General Conference of 1977 combined the Departments of Publication and Christian Education forming the Department of Church Ministries.

DIRECTORS OF CHURCH MINISTRIES

The General Conference of 1981 created the Department of Church Services, combining under that title, The Departments of Stewardship and Church Ministries. The Department was given oversight of the work of Pension Trust, Ministerial Aid, insurance programs, The Archives and the management of the United Brethren Building.

DIRECTORS OF CHURCH SERVICES

DIRECTOR OF DEPARTMENT OF STEWARDSHIP

The General Conference of 1977 elected a Director of Stewardship.

GEOGRAPHIC EXTENSION OF THE UNITED BRETHREN CHURCH BY 1841, 1861, AND 1889

ORGANIZED CONFERENCES
and
MISSION DISTRICTS
(1929-1981)

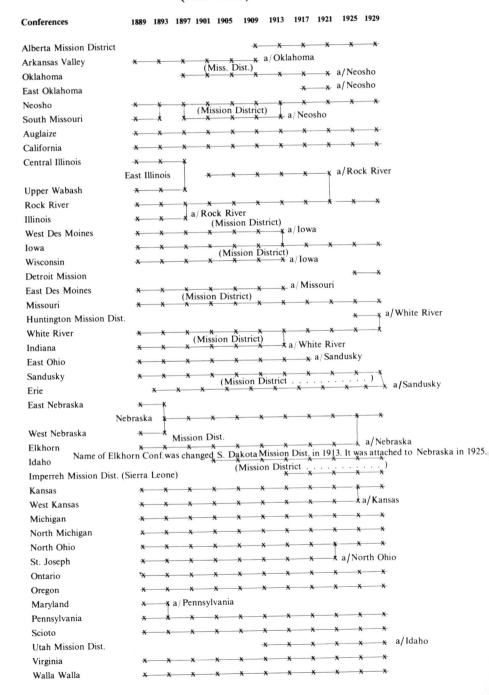

Conferences	1889	1893	1897	1901	1905	1909	1913	1917	1921	1925	1929
Alberta Mission District						x—x—x—x—x—x					
Arkansas Valley	x—x—x—x—x a/Oklahoma										
Oklahoma	(Miss. Dist.) x—x—x—x—x a/Neosho										
East Oklahoma	x—x a/Neosho										
Neosho	x—x—x—x—x—x—x—x—x										
South Missouri	x—x (Mission District) x—x a/Neosho										
Auglaize	x—x—x—x—x—x—x—x—x—x										
California	x—x—x—x—x—x—x—x—x—x										
Central Illinois	x—x—x										
East Illinois	x—x—x—x—x a/Rock River										
Upper Wabash	x—x—x										
Rock River	x—x—x—x—x—x—x—x										
Illinois	x—x a/Rock River (Mission District)										
West Des Moines	x—x—x—x—x—x a/Iowa										
Iowa	x—x—x—x—x—x—x—x—x—x										
Wisconsin	(Mission District) x—x—x a/Iowa										
Detroit Mission	x—x										
East Des Moines	x—x—x—x—x a/Missouri										
Missouri	(Mission District) x—x—x—x—x—x—x										
Huntington Mission Dist.	x—x a/White River										
White River	x—x—x—x—x—x—x										
Indiana	(Mission District) x a/White River										
East Ohio	x—x—x—x—x—x—x a/Sandusky										
Sandusky	x—x—x—x—x—x—x—x										
Erie	(Mission District . . . .) x a/Sandusky										
East Nebraska	x—x										
Nebraska	x—x—x—x—x—x—x—x										
West Nebraska	x—x Mission Dist.										
Elkhorn	x—x—x—x—x—x a/Nebraska										
	Name of Elkhorn Conf. was changed S. Dakota Mission Dist. in 1913. It was attached to Nebraska in 1925.										
Idaho	(Mission District . . . .)										
Imperreh Mission Dist. (Sierra Leone)	x—x—x—x—x										
Kansas	x—x—x—x—x—x—x—x										
West Kansas	x—x—x—x—x—x—x—x a/Kansas										
Michigan	x—x—x—x—x—x—x—x—x										
North Michigan	x—x—x—x—x—x—x—x—x										
North Ohio	x—x—x—x—x—x—x—x—x										
St. Joseph	x—x—x—x—x—x—x a/North Ohio										
Ontario	x—x—x—x—x—x—x—x										
Oregon	x—x—x—x—x—x—x—x										
Maryland	x—x a/Pennsylvania										
Pennsylvania	x—x—x—x—x—x—x—x										
Scioto	x—x—x—x—x—x—x—x										
Utah Mission Dist.	x—x—x—x—x a/Idaho										
Virginia	x—x—x—x—x—x—x—x										
Walla Walla	x—x—x—x—x—x—x—x										

ORGANIZED CONFERENCES
and
MISSION DISTRICTS
(1929-1981)

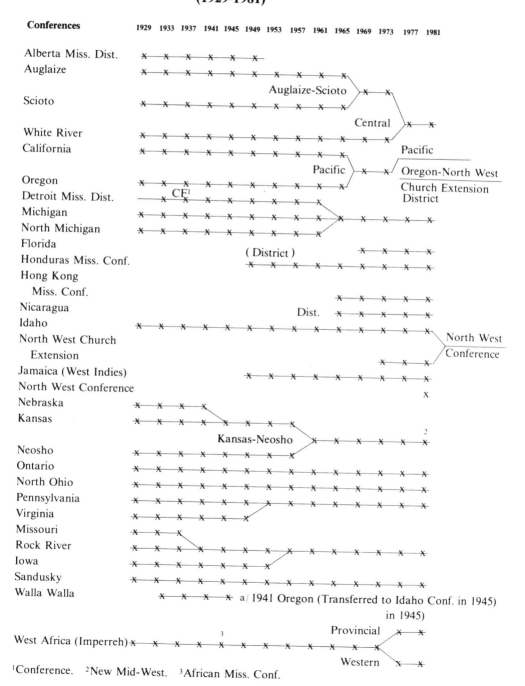

Conferences

1929 1933 1937 1941 1945 1949 1953 1957 1961 1965 1969 1973 1977 1981

Alberta Miss. Dist.
Auglaize

Auglaize-Scioto

Scioto

Central

White River
California

Pacific

Oregon
Detroit Miss. Dist.
Michigan
North Michigan
Florida
Honduras Miss. Conf.
Hong Kong
    Miss. Conf.
Nicaragua
Idaho
North West Church
    Extension
Jamaica (West Indies)
North West Conference
Nebraska
Kansas

Kansas-Neosho

Neosho
Ontario
North Ohio
Pennsylvania
Virginia
Missouri
Rock River
Iowa
Sandusky
Walla Walla

Pacific

Oregon-North West
Church Extension
District

(District)

Dist.

North West
Conference

North West
Conference

X

Kansas-Neosho

a/1941 Oregon (Transferred to Idaho Conf. in 1945)
    in 1945)

West Africa (Imperreh)

Provincial

Western

[1]Conference. [2]New Mid-West. [3]African Miss. Conf.

Index of Subjects

(not exhaustive)

Index of Persons

(not exhaustive)

Index of Conferences

(not exhaustive)